PROBLEMS OF VISION

PROBLEMS
OF VISION

Rethinking the
Causal Theory
of Perception

GERALD VISION

New York   Oxford
Oxford University Press
1997

Oxford University Press

Oxford   New York
Athens   Auckland   Bangkok   Bogota   Bombay   Buenos Aires
Calcutta   Cape Town   Dar es Salaam   Delhi   Florence   Hong Kong
Istanbul   Karachi   Kuala Lumpur   Madras   Madrid   Melbourne
Mexico City   Nairobi   Paris   Singapore   Taipei   Tokyo   Toronto

and associated companies in
Berlin   Ibadan

Library of Congress Cataloging-in-Publication Data

Vision, Gerald.
Problems of vision : rethinking the causal theory of
perception / Gerald Vision.
p.   cm.
Includes bibliographical references and index.
ISBN 0-19-510498-6
1. Perception.   2. Sense (Philosophy)   3. Visual perception.
4. Senses and sensation.   I. Title.
BD214.V57   1996
131'.3—dc20   96-23100

1 3 5 7 9 8 6 4 2

Printed in the United States of America
on acid-free paper

PREFACE

By the time I originally set out to tie up loose ends in the causal theory of perception (in a tidy monograph!), the view already suffered from a badly split personality. From its seventeenth century renewal till well into this century, the causal theory has been a codicil to sense-datum philosophy, citing causes in the physical environment to explain how the purely subjective contents of our experience could be regarded by us as providing information about that environment. In that role it has been an embattled view, coming under a barrage of epistemological and semantic objections. The causes that it cites remain forever beyond the compass of any humanly possible experience. Later, shortly after midcentury, just as sense-datum philosophy was undergoing a steady and seemingly permanent decline, causalism was defended on grounds independent of its former function. Thus, paradoxically, causalism was enjoying something of a minirevival while the philosophy of perception to which its fate had been heretofore linked was becoming a quaint historical relic. (Of course, a few devoted, talented sense-datum theorists are still around. Philosophy seldom totally obliterates old and unfashionable views. But the merits of the case aside, this accurately summarizes recent trends in philosophy.)

This state of affairs has fostered some confusion, and in my naive enthusiasm for the subject I had failed to realize what labrythine paths it would take me down. More than a few philosophers are bewildered about where a causal theory fits: "If it is not an emergency exit from sense-datum philosophy and that view's dreadful consequences, of what use is it?" The somewhat cryptic answer, which I develop further later, is that it explains how sensory evidence is a product *of* what it is evidence *for*. Meanwhile, certain critics, unable to detach causalism from its classical associations, are astounded that recent thinkers continue to rely on it. "Hasn't this new breed of causalists heard about the devastating objections both to subjective contents and to appealing to a forever-beyond-our-grasp reality to rescue our chestnuts from the fire?" Up to the time of this writing, objections to the causal theory from some usually reliable quarters begin with a familiar warning that normal perceptual experience doesn't involve purely subjective contents.

One reason for reopening this issue is to set the record straight on this score. In that respect, this book is a hopeful monster; the sort of mutation that selectionists give some better than usual, but still slight, chance for taking root in the evolutionary soil. I cannot claim it is a reason I had for undertaking the project in the first place. For, as I mentioned, until I intensified my search for sources, both pro and con, I failed to realize just how deeply entrenched was the confusion between the two versions. Before that I had assumed that the philosophical community at large was aware that defending a causal theory no longer meant one was throwing in her lot with classical empiricist theories of the objects of perception. When this eventually dawned on me, I sought to separate sharply the different grounds believed to sanction causal theories. All this was in the service of showing that causalism's defense *can* shed the idealist, sense-datum, and subjectivist baggage that so many still see it as dragging along. (This is as true of the so-called continental tradition as it is of the English-speaking, equally so-called, analytic one.) In the present context this is not so much a matter of rejecting an older conception as avoiding unnecessarily giving hostages to fate. If anyone prefers her causal theory garnished with subjectivism, she's welcome to it for the price of a defense. But it is worth notifying critics that current causalists cannot be assumed to be card-carrying sense-datum philosophers. Such a disengagement has been close to the surface in a number of causalist treatments in the past thirty-five years, but here I want to make the point unmistakably explicit. Critics of causalism cannot satisfy themselves by dusting off objections to its seventeenth- and eighteenth-century forerunners.

At about the time of this change in the fortunes of sense-datum philosophy, things also began to brighten for employments of causation. For a lengthy stretch before that philosophers seemed embarrassed by natural causation. Mere mention of such figures as Descartes, Leibniz, and Hume should bring to mind the horrors awaiting anyone who attempted to understand causal connections between independently existing individuals (or substances). This induced a certain level of nomophobia (perhaps etiophobia), which carried over to the employment of causation elsewhere in philosophy. Perhaps causation's fortunes hit bottom with Bertrand Russell's quip that though the concept does no good, it is "a relic of a bygone age, surviving, like the monarchy, only because it is erroneously supposed to do no harm." Some still shy away from accounts with a causal component. However, the revival of the causal theory of perception shortly after midcentury coincided with, and contributed to, a rise in the estimate of causation's role in elucidating such central ideas in the philosophies of cognition and action as knowledge, intentional action, memory, reference, and semantic content. The old difficulties about causation didn't magically disappear. Some were reconceived; others remain. But thinkers don't appear as reluctant either to scrap the concept of *causation,* or to forbear from employing it in accounts of something else, only because it is still a subject of competing analyses and ongoing controversy (as are, indeed, most interesting philosophically charged notions).

However, the kind of serious examination causation deserves would permanently derail me from my main business. I have sought to keep my focus firmly fixed on perception, and brief remarks later on the analysis or status of causation are no more than casual asides. Therefore, allow me to state dogmatically that I take causation to be a nonintentional, real ingredient of events in the world. (That there are instances of causation and a world is part of the background of this claim; but, strange as it may seem at first, it is unnecessary to the stated commitment.) Not everyone accepts this. However, in order to get anything accomplished on our main subject, the temptation of trying too much must be resisted. Thus,

I'll take this view of causation as a given for the duration of the work. This is certainly realism with regard to causation; but my view takes on a much more profoundly realist caste in maintaining that anyone who has mastered the concept of visual perception presupposes in her judgments about what things are seen a connection very much like that one. (At least it is difficult to see how anyone's willingness to regard something as an instance of perception could survive intact if causation goes by the boards.)

Whether or not this is glad tidings for visual perception falls outside the scope of the present study. But, unofficially, I welcome it. Causalism has seemed to present an opportunity to remove some further obstacles to metaphysical realism. This is a bedrock motivation for this undertaking. Suppose we ask what we are to make of our encounters with the external world, much of which is populated by particulars whose ontological standing is blissfully indifferent to the capacity of various species of creatures to apprehend or cognize them. This will be easily recognized as one of philosophy's perennial problems, straddling basic issues in both metaphysics and epistemology. Metaphysical realism, which I (along with a host of other philosophers) accept on independent grounds, is the view that a cognition independent reality exists. One is mildly abashed to put forth such a triviality. However, a host of thinkers either deny it outright, imply its denial, or claim that it's just the sort of thing it is illegitimate to state in a philosophical voice. But even if we take for granted the existence of this world, were our practice of gathering sensory evidence wholly disconnected from the subject-matter about which it is supposed to deliver information, our views about it would be a colossal delusion—no more reliable than astrology or divination.

In such an environment the causal connection implicit in perception seems to offer the best hope of explaining how it is even conceivable that our perceptual states put us in cognitive contact with a mind-independent world. But we must be careful not to read too much into this idea. Some current impressions notwithstanding, it does not even address the most popular varieties of epistemic skepticism. That misguided expectation has led to unfounded criticisms of causalism.

The issue properly raised by a causal connection is whether the common practice of justifying belief via perception is autonomous, or whether it is anchored in the aspect of reality it is taken to report on. Although the skeptic may use the autonomy ploy against causalism as premise for her own conclusion, the causalist's most natural adversary is not skepticism but constructive epistemologies that appear to rule out such direct relationships to the world. Radical forms of coherentism and holism maintain that beliefs, and hence justifications, form closed systems. Despite claims that this is merely an analysis of current practice, it is difficult to see why we should continue it. What point is there in placing confidence in such an insulated method of belief fixing? On the other hand, attempts to link the causal aspect of perception to the world are sometimes rejected, say, on grounds of misfit: causation is the wrong kind of concept to enter normative treatments of belief; it hasn't the proper sort of hooks to anchor justification, and, thereby, belief. Where causalism can be made plausible it goes a long way toward refuting conceptions of this sort. But as far as typical varieties of mind-world skepticism are concerned, causalism goes off in an entirely different direction.

Nothing in a causal connection guarantees that the content thereby attained is good enough or clear enough to be of any use. Its conceptual contribution to perception falls short of showing either that we are not brains in vats of nutrient fluid or that we aren't deluded by a deceiving demon. That may be why John Locke, in defending causally generated perceptual knowledge against the skeptic (*An Essay concerning Human Understanding,* bk. IV, chap. 2, §14), settled for a *bon mot* rather than a serious reply. However, if we may set aside external world skepticism in order to address other concerns (and, some might say, equally pressing ones), causation *does* supply a link to perception's subject-matter. In that way it makes palpable why gaining justification is worth the effort. For, *pace* the holisms just parodied, it shows how the source of its news can be the sort of world that we ordinarily take to supply the objects of our perceptions. And this, I take it, is some modest progress on a troubled front.

Again, to avert misunderstanding, we should not say that the foregoing issue fails to engage classical skepticism at every level. Should the skeptic insist on the autonomy of justification, causalism is a response. But even with that issue settled to the causalist's satisfaction, there is much room for disagreement about justification between the skeptic and nonskeptic. Thus, it would be a mistake to dismiss causalism on the grounds that in and of itself it doesn't secure the sort of justification the skeptic challenges us to achieve.

But even certain of those who accept the requisite causal connection and acknowledge its conceptual import express doubts about causal *theories.* The doubts cover quite a bit of ground, but they all concern difficulties in completing the view beyond noting a causal element. Some are worried about weeding out the wrong sorts of causal chains, others about an inability to distinguish the contribution of the object from different causal factors in perceiving, yet others believe the causalist is burdened with the enormous task of framing strictly causal necessary and sufficient conditions for perceiving, and to this we may add a perplexity over various noncausal conditions that already seem firmly embedded in any notion of perception. In sum, a host of puzzles seems to stand between the simple causal condition and a completed causal theory. A further reason for embarking on this project is to discover whether those puzzles can be solved for one sensory modality in particular: vision. My conclusion, argued in Part III, is that they can; therefore a causal theory of perception is within reach. While it may not meet everyone's prior expectations or aspirations, it is hard to see how the result could be taken for anything less than a causal theory.

I am grateful to the following publications for permission to use parts of earlier writings: *Metaphilosophy* for material from a 1989 paper, "Sight and Cognition," used in chapter 4; and *The Philosophical Quarterly* for material from a 1993 paper, "Animadversions on the Causal Theory of Perception," used in chapter 2. Also, my thanks to Fred Dretske for permission to reproduce (in altered form) a diagram from p. 162 of his *Knowledge and the Flow of Information* (MIT Press, 1981). I thank Temple University for support that provided several months of free time for writing. A number of (I assume) well-intentioned critics have helped me greatly by discussing these issues or reading parts or all of this work in progress.

No doubt I have forgotten some of them, but those I can recall, and whose help I gratefully acknowledge, include Jerrold Aronson, Thomas Blackson, Roberto Casati, William Child, John Heil, Hugues LeBlanc, Brian McLaughlin, Peter Roeper, Michael Tye, Eileen Way, David Welker, and Abraham Witonsky.

Parts of this work, in various drafts, have been used in my classes and presented in talks at The University of East Anglia, SUNY at Binghamton, Le Centre de Recherche en Epistemologie Applique (CREA), Swarthmore College, and Temple University. Those discussions were invariably helpful to me, and I thank the respective audiences for them. Unfortunately, this book was in production before the appearance of William Child's *Causality, Interpretation and the Mind* (Oxford University Press), whose chapter 5 has a number of points that make close contact with the present work. Child and I do not agree about everything by a long shot; but I was most struck by our substantial agreement on some basics, and the convergence of our different considerations tend, in my opinion, to reinforce those views.

I owe thanks to Todd Vision for keeping me honest in my use of biological information and for supplying reliable details and morals of examples. Finally, I have the good fortune to have a reference librarian, Sue Vision, as a mate. She has cheerfully, and lavishly, responded to my many requests for esoteric research materials. To my family who suffered through my monomania, I'm afraid my only excuse, lame as it is, is summed up in a few lines that Hilaire Belloc facetiously penned for his epitaph:

When I am dead,
May it be said:
His sins were scarlet,
But his books were read.

CONTENTS

PART I

The Basic Causal Requirement

1

Introduction

Only from the senses comes all credibility, all clear conscience, all self-evidence of truth.

FRIEDRICH NIETZSCHE, *Beyond Good and Evil*

JENNET. My father broke on the wheel of a dream; he was lost
In a search. And, so, for me, the actual!
What I touch, what I see, what I know, the essential fact
THOMAS. In other words, the bare untruth.

CHRISTOPHER FRY, *The Lady's Not for Burning*

I

The topic of perception has never drifted far from philosophical consciousness, but it turned obsessive with the seventeenth- eighteenth-century ascendancy, first, of epistemology and then, more particularly, of idea empiricism. It is difficult to find a prominent philosopher of that period who did not have much to say about the nature of perception or its objects. Even Spinoza, who held sensory information in lower esteem than virtually all his contemporaries did, shows inordinate concern for explaining the senses. In one, perhaps attenuated, sense this book has its roots in the preoccupations of that philosophical era. It was then that the causal theory of perception (CTP) became a heated topic of controversy. A central aim here is to defend, elaborate, and clarify (though not necessarily in that order) that theory for visual perception. But it is as important to distinguish the present approach from work in the aforementioned tradition as it is to trace its origins within it.

Thus, I commence with two caveats. First, contemporary rationales for CTP are seldom close to earlier ones. Seventeenth- and eighteenth-century thinkers, as well as most of their early twentieth-century successors, were principally interested in securing a foundation for empirical knowledge, one impervious to the assaults of skepticism. Although the subject of perceptual knowledge, as such, is scarcely mentioned in these pages, I will be concerned (in chapters 4–6) with how belief gets fixed by perception. But there my primary interest is only the proper understanding of perception's exact role in generating belief, not the latter's justification or truth. Even when I consider the connection implicit in CTP between perception and the world, I will not take up questions of universal epistemic skepticism. My main concern in this area is the nature of the connections rather than establishing that they exist.

Second, much of my defense of CTP will consist not in engaging in polemics with its critics, old or new, but in clarifying the view and seeing the extent to which the causal elements can form a well-rounded theory of vision. Some critics have abandoned causal theories not because of a principled antipathy to them, but because they have concluded that technical obstacles to fleshing out the view are insuperable. In the later chapters of this book, I explore the extent to which such pessimism can be overcome.

Before turning to the major problems of this book, it will be helpful to get our bearings back in early modern philosophy. As will become apparent, 'the causal theory' is a label originally applied only in retrospect to the views of several philosophers. Among the great Homeric shades whom historians label causal theorists, the actual nexus between object and experience was a secondary theme, and probably distant enough from their main concern (i.e., skepticism about the senses) for them not to have contemplated emphasizing this aspect. (For example, Descartes and Locke, perhaps the two most prominent early causalists, never supposed it worth doubting whether the true objects of our perception were caused. The only question for them was whether they were caused by anything like a material world.) Let's briefly consider the larger scene in which these solutions arose.

The view that we see such things as sparrows, trees, cathedrals, stars, snowflakes, daggers, bottles, and mountains; their states; and events in which they figure—that is, the objects of everyday reporting and perceptual belief—and not just by way of having other experiential objects, scarcely seems worthy of the title of a philosophical theory; it's the merest platitude. But because it is attacked by various philosophers with specialist theories, and is the default position when alternatives fail, it has been called *direct realism*. (The more common title is *naive realism*, but since a number of *truly naive* tenets are by now associated with that name, I prefer *direct realism*.) Descartes initiated a long-standing tradition against it. He took it to be self-evident that perception "in the precise sense" excises any commitment to an external world. Because whatever we see might have been seen, "properly speaking," even if we had been hallucinating, seeing's most direct (immediate) objects are other than the material (or physical or corporeal) things and scenes of unphilosophical perceptual belief. The true objects of perceptual experience, of which we could be certain even if no corporeal world existed, were then usually called *ideas*. To say that they are immediate or direct objects is to say that objects of ordinary reporting are dependent on them: all seeing of corporeal things is *by way of* seeing, experiencing, sensing, or having ideas, whereas the latter is never accomplished by way of the former. Thus, there might be (indeed, are) seeings, experiencings, or sensings of ideas where there is no correlative seeing of a corporeal object, but no seeing of a corporeal object where there is no correlative sensing, and so on, of an idea.

In this century, philosophers have devised a number of terms for what Descartes, Locke, and their immediate successors called *ideas* (or impressions or perceptions). They have been known, inter alia, as *sensibilia, sensa,* and *qualia.* The term for these items that has taken root is *sense-data*. (This despite the fact that it was introduced as a neutral term to designate whatever the objects of our perceptual experience might turn out to be.) For our purposes, we can ignore nuances between the newer idiom and that of ideas. The central point is that sense-data are mind-dependent, private, and thus contrasted with the mind-independent, public phenomena of the physical world.[1] We may then say, without significant distortion, that most philosophers of the tradition in question were sense-datum theorists rather than direct realists.

The most obvious question for any sense-datum theory is how to connect the objects of direct acquaintance, sense-data, with those of prereflective perceptual reporting. In fact, this embraces two inquiries. The first concerns whether we in fact have any indirect contact with that apparently familiar world. The second is about how, if at all, we may show that we can have knowledge, justified belief, or even intelligible cognition of it. Sense-data are conceived as iconographic in the most straightforward way: that is, by common agreement, *resemblance* is the only way they are thought to *represent* mind-independent reality. *A fortiori*, while the question "Do sense-data yield knowledge (or justified belief or sensible belief) about the world?" includes (or is exhausted by) the question "Do sense-data (ever, usually, normally) represent the material world?" the latter becomes a question about whether the strictly internal characteristics of sense-data mimic those of the world.

If the objects of the corporeal world *cause* our sense-data, the first disquiet is resolved. Descartes and Locke supported this causal solution. Their realism is labeled *indirect*. To guarantee knowledge, Descartes settled for nothing less than an appeal to the nondeceitful nature of God. Locke, on the other hand, appealed to a measure of certainty that our ideas resembled, to a limited extent, the features of their causes. But not all their early commentators accepted a causal connection. Berkeley rejected mind-independent matter and placed conditions on causation that made it impossible ("a manifest repugnancy") for matter or its properties to cause ideas. Malebranche and Leibniz, while not denying the existence of matter, held that it couldn't cause ideas, and again invoked God (in different ways) to establish the reliability of our ideas for knowledge of matter. Fundamental principles of Hume's theory of the origin of ideas prevented him from accepting any intelligible connection between an unexperienced (and unexperienceable) material object and what he called our impressions (bk. 1, pt. 4, ch. 2); subsequent theorists, coming to Hume's conclusion for their own reasons, substituted for a causal relation the material world's reduction to classes of actual and possible sense-data. (Rephrased as a semantic thesis, these theorists replaced the causal relation with the material-object language's analysis into a sense-datum language.) And so the debate has gone.

In that atmosphere, CTP could be nothing more than an afterthought, subordinate to the effort to secure a foundation for knowledge. That is one difference between its historic treatment and the present one. But a more important difference, and one from which the above difference flows, is its location on the map of positions.

Historically, consideration of CTP has arisen only after direct realism was abandoned. It has been a handy way for some accounts to explain how the sense-data of immediate experience are related to material things. This role has become so well entrenched that it is still often assumed that a causalist must be an *indirect* realist, committed to sense-data as the primary objects of perceptual experience. Despite several attempts to revive the fortunes of sense-data (e.g., Jackson 1977; Ayer 1956; Mackie 1976; Anscombe 1963), its philosophical partisans are now in a decided minority. Without fanfare or a dramatic staking of claims, most writers on perception appear to accept some form of direct realism. Disputes still rage over such matters as distinctively subjective qualia. But given the way such notions are elucidated, differences amount to internecine quarrels between direct realists rather than attempts to reinvigorate past sense-datum doctrines.

In light of this chronology of events, it is ony natural to assume that the fortunes of CTP will have ebbed with those of sense-data. After all, as presented here, CTP historically was no more than one of serveral options for a sense-datum philosopher—a way to explain the relationship of a sense-datum to a mind-independent world. However, more recently H. P. Grice (1961) has defended a version of CTP strictly on the strength of its causal elements. (See also Martin 1959.) Although Grice himself held that this also required a sense-datum theory, a matter discussed further in chapter 2, the potency of his arguments for the causal theory were quite clearly independent of questions that fueled debate between direct realism and sense-datum philosophy. (I examine those arguments at length in chapter 3.) This opened the prospect of isolating the question of whether an object's causation is essential to its perception from the seemingly independent issue of the intrinsic character of perceptual objects. In an age of near consensus direct realism, this is perhaps the most significant impetus we have been given to study in greater detail the philosophical principles underlying the concept of perception.

It is this recent version of CTP that forms the main topic of subsequent chapters. Although the exposition assumes direct realism throughout, the advantage of the newer version is that it is compatible with direct *and* indirect realism. Nothing is lost by not first settling the issue of whether the most direct objects of perceptual experience are elements of the physical world rather than sense-data. That issue has been thoroughly examined and debated elsewhere, and readers should be spared one more rehashing of those arguments. Nevertheless, when the opportunity arises, I will not shy away from pointing out how principles under discussion bear on the plausibility or clarity of this traditional opposition. But these are restricted forays, not pieces of a focal topic. Equally important, one should not suppose that in defending CTP we are committed to sense-data by the causal relation itself. In chapter 2, I explore but reject arguments for the view that a causal theory requires sense-data. However, throughout most of this work, that issue is orthogonal to matters I want to discuss. I have belabored the difference only because it may be difficult for some, familiar with the events briefly chronicled here, to disentangle the sense-datum and epistemic elements of CTP's history from the conceptual investigation I am about to undertake.

II

Without entering too deeply into details, what is the initial attraction of the causal theory? Undoubtedly, our interest in perception stems from our interest in knowledge about our environment. Lucretius has called the senses "the straightest highway to belief," and Montaigne has said that the senses form "the beginning and end of human knowledge." It is a plausible speculation that unless the senses reliably yielded information about our immediate environment these faculties would have atrophied long before our ancestors climbed ashore. But for them to achieve this, their distinctive ways of gathering data must provide justification that things are as sense presents them; the senses must, as it were, attest to the information's reliability. How is this possible? For starters, we would expect that if a justification of beliefs about the external world is genuine, what it delivers is, in general, anchored in that world. Epistemic justification is not something that can be autonomous or self-contained. Were things otherwise, it would be a mystery why such justification should be of value to anyone. If we discovered (as some have argued) that it were autonomous—inherently isolated even from speculation about real connections with the world, deliverances about which seem to form its main subject matter—the only reasonable course would be to forsake, if possible, such a tenacious delusion. Justification would be a ritual rather than a solid advantage. But how can perception be anchored in the world? The most natural suggestion seems to be that, under normal conditions, what we sense (perceive) is a *cause* of our perceptual state. Because different 'whats' cause systematically different qualitative states, we can normally rely on the sort of causation in question to be an integral part of justifications for placing our confidence in sensory input.

This isn't the whole of CTP, but it embodies the insight at its core. As I mentioned earlier, I will for the most part confine myself to one sense: vision. Thus limited, this insight may be captured in the following condition:

> (C). For all perceivers S and objects or visual arrays *o, S* sees *o* only if *o* is a cause of S's seeing.

Although, as I will explain shortly (and in chapter 3), some thinkers reject (C) and similar conditions for the other sense modalities, while a broad spectrum of others accept it. In fact, more philosophers accept (C) than accept CTP, which— if we discount the hypothesis that this is simply widespread, flagrant inconsistency—leads us to conclude that CTP is committed to more than (C). What more?

Some maintain that to be truly *causal* a theory must supply a sufficient condition (in causal terms) for perceiving an object. (C) yields only a necessary condition. Various critics accept (C), but hold that this further condition is not met. Even for those who disagree, it must be conceded that unearthing causally sufficient conditions would be a gargantuan labor, one whose successful outcome is far from assured. For one thing, it seems that such conditions shouldn't include noncausal clauses. Thus, it must be shown that no proposals for noncausal conditions are necessary or even part of a disjointly necessary condition. Furthermore, it would be highly problematic if there were, in addition, alternative noncausal, but equally substantive, sufficient conditions for seeing. To avoid this, the causalist must show that the causal sufficient conditions also contain enough in the way of causal clauses that are necessary conditions to rule out that option. This conception of CTP imposes a rather daunting standard for success. And that is not all. Although, strictly speaking, a sufficient condition for S seeing o needn't select the causally distinctive contribution of o, those who insist on sufficiency normally require of CTP that it provide just this sort of information. The motivation for this is that many of the causal factors in an instance of seeing (e.g., the lighting source, the perceivers' eyes) are not the thing seen, the visual object. Accordingly, it is demanded for an analysis of what is sometimes called *transitive* seeing (that is, S's seeing *of o* rather than the intransitive S's seeing, period) that the object's contribution be distinctive, and distinctively causal.

Against this tide, I recommend a more relaxed attitude toward whatever beyond (C) may be required for a causal theory. Although the foregoing would suffice, we needn't view it as essential to CTP. Differentiating o from other causes in causally related terms may not yield a sufficient condition for seeing o. For example, it may yield a condition sufficient for o being the visual object *if anything is,* but it may not guarantee that the experience is a perception, and thus not guarantee that o is perceived. If we can discover just such a distinguishing mark, and thus describe more satisfactorily the kind of causation relevant to perception, that may be enough to consider the resulting theory causal. Even in the absence of the stronger conditions, the causal role of an object remains so crucial to the account that it would be unreasonable to withhold the title of causal theory from it. Put otherwise, essentially the same sorts of inclinations that persuaded some that (C) is too anemic to be the whole of CTP incline us to the view that the prospective account just mentioned is too meaty a part of a whole account of sight, even if noncausal elements are also present, to refrain from considering it a causal theory. In chapter 8, I will try to make out a view along these lines, but massive foundation building remains before I can return to this task.

A word of warning. I have insisted on the name 'CTP' largely because my own interest in the issues stems from the question of the causal grounding of this source of knowledge. Moreover, its adoption seems reasonable and more in accord with the less ambitious projects traditional causal theorists have set for themselves. But since I do not claim to supply a sufficient condition for seeing in exclusively causal terms, whether anyone else accepts that title for the final product is ultimately a question of terminological preference. The view I propose to defend will have substantial causal clauses. It is crucial to my overall view that they all pan out. It is of little moment what someone calls the completed account. Nevertheless, I wanted to explain to readers why we are entitled to regard this view as a, if not the, causal theory of (visual) perception.

III

Although not the whole of CTP, (C) is its most important single component. The greater share of disputes between causalists and their critics revolve about the truth and status of (C) rather than any of the further items in a completed theory. Moreover, the sort of thing being maintained with (C) is a good clue to the overall nature of the theory. Dwelling on it a bit longer will help us to avoid getting sidetracked by inessential squabbles. In conformity with (C), I concentrate on visual perception throughout this book save where the discussion of another's work requires examples that use other senses. Purely for ease of exposition, the qualifications 'visual' and 'perceptual' are used interchangeably where their difference isn't crucial. This is not meant to imply that whatever is true in my account of vision is true, mutatis mutandis, of the faculties of hearing, touch, taste, and smell. But, as a matter of fact, in general outline much in their treatments will be parallel, and it is not unreasonable to expect that if sight yields a causal account, some form of this view will work for the other senses.

In an idiom no longer fashionable, (C) is a conceptual thesis. What it asserts pertains to the 'concept' of sight. At this stage, it is unimportant to probe further into this use of 'conceptual'. It is primarily a foil to exclude certain contrasting classifications. The details of disputes surrounding the notion of a conceptual thesis can be left to one side for all that (C) conveys. There is perhaps one exception. A certain brand of holism maintains that each of a subject's or community's beliefs is (equally?) relevant to the determination of each of its concepts, and vice versa. In claiming that (C) is a necessary condition for sight, I am certainly suggesting that some links are more strongly privileged than others in determining what counts as seeing. Globalizing the issue, I'm suggesting that there is at least one instance of conceptual implication, though little more is claimed about the character of such implications. In the lexicon of currently raging disputes, even this relatively innocuous-sounding claim is in jeopardy. I will say no more about that here. In chapter 3, arguments will be given for (C). *If they are successful,* we will have grounds for accepting this one implication, which, I maintain, would render futile any top-down arguments in the literature that purport to prohibit all implications of this type.[2]

The tag 'conceptual' helps us to see more clearly that (C) and its complementary CTP theses aren't in the business of resolving certain pressing epistemological and ontological issues about sight. First, even if we assume for the sake of argument that in fact we perceive things, CTP as an account of perception does not guarantee that perception yields knowledge. The causation of perceptions by their objects is compatible with knowledge-defeating confusion about those objects (say, through unsystematic distortion of the signal). The fact that what we perceive is a cause of that perception doesn't rule out such possibilities.

Perhaps it will be replied that if continuous distortion prevented us from gathering visual information, there would be no sight. The very notion of sight depends on the general absence of this sort of circumstance. Underlying the objection is an assumption about the inherent *function* of sight. It seems to me to be infected with serious problems. Any view about vision must leave room for *some* knowledge-defeating distortion, for it is generally agreed that seeing is sometimes distorted. How much is permissible? Is the function preserved if seeing is *always* distorted for some subjects as long as other members of their species can thus gather knowledge? Or must each perceptual subject be in a position *usually* or *normally* to gather perceptual knowledge? Perhaps it is sufficient that the species (or individual) once could gather such knowledge via perception, though it may no longer be able to do so. (And if a former capacity of an actual species is sufficient, why not the capacity of a merely possible species?) It should strike us as problematic that if the considerations on behalf of this functionalist assumption about perception provide any evidence, they provide equally, but no more, compelling evidence for several of these mutually exclusive options. This should be a grave concern for its partisans.

However, I need not challenge the objection or the assumption underlying it. (The latter reappears in chapter 7.) It suffices to notice that even if I accept the objection, the ability to acquire perceptual knowledge would follow not from the causal component, but from perception's alleged function. (C) does not impart a knowledge guarantee into the concept of perception. If perception implies such a guarantee, it is owing to something else (say, the functional considerations). (C) doesn't even supply evidence for the functional view. The most that could be said of their relation is that (C) provides a mechanism by means of which the function ascribed to perception can be performed. This does not make (C) indispensable to the functional view, and in fact it is not favored by some functionalists. The same may be said of any other causal clauses CTP incorporates.

On the other hand, as we will see presently, one shouldn't conclude from this that (C) has no role whatsoever to play in the potential for perceptual knowledge. I will return to this point after first dealing with the aforementioned ontological irrelevancy of (C).

Next, (C) is of little help in determining whether particular visual episodes are instances of perception. No doubt interest in perception is driven by an assumption that it is a commonplace occurrence. But in practice it is seldom easier to discover whether *o* is a cause of one's visual episode than that one is seeing *o*. (C) doesn't even guarantee that perceptions ever occur. This is not simply because (C) is put forth only as a necessary condition for seeing. Possessing a set of sufficient conditions never guarantees as such that anything satisfies it. If sight were to have turned out to be as illusory as caloric or phlogiston, our conditions wouldn't be affected. The distinction is not without application in disputes over CTP. Certain accounts of perception in the history of philosophy preclude (C) in a radical way. For example (a brief caricature for the sake of comparison), an older view known as occasionalism—motivated by what seemed to its author to be insuperable difficulties for mental-physical interaction—states that God is the common source of both the placement of material things in our environment and of perceptual contents in our minds. On this view, there is no causal link running from the object to our experience. With so strong a supernatural assurance, this would seem to be a more reliable source of information about the world than the merely natural one afforded by CTP. I freely grant it. Nevertheless, given (C) occasionalism is not a scheme of visual perception. If we may, for illustration, assume *both* occasionalism's causal claims (minus its contention that it is an account of perception) *and* (C)'s validity, no perception takes place in its natural world. But that doesn't invalidate the *concept* of perception.

These qualifications are offered in the hope that they further clarify what I have been calling the conceptual nature of the thesis. Delineating more precisely the causalist's doctrines may be of some use in nipping in the bud irrelevant objections and exaggerated inferences. In the other direction, we must not over-state the differences. (C), in particular, is certainly relevant to our interest in justification and knowledge in a different way. Given that our belief in the ordi-nary occurrence of genuiune perception is not a colossal delusion, (C) explains how the justification of belief that we derive from that source is grounded in the world about which we take it to yield information. This issue will present itself again shortly (§V). For the nonce, readers should bear in mind that disengaging (C) from various epistemic and metaphysical tenets does not mean that it is alto-gether without implications for those concerns.

IV

Critics have also been concerned that (C) imposes an expert concept of perception on its many lay possessors. Few of those who know what seeing is are aware of the scientific details, and indeed many who have held scientific theses about per-ception have gotten it wrong. That might even include us. In addition, beyond the sophistication of the information, (C) reads into the ordinary conception of vision tenets of our strictly modern outlook. It thereby imposes recent scientific concep-tions on throngs of the concept's possessors who lived before the inception of this outlook.

The criticism must be careful not to overshoot its mark. Certainly some mas-ters of the concept *perception* amply display that they do not accept (C): namely, philosophical antagonists of this view (e.g., occasionalists such as Malebranche, preestablished harmonists such as Leibniz, and the critics discussed in chapter 3). But unlike masters of the concept to whom the objection appeals, each of these possesses a sophisticated, if flawed, notion of causation; and their conclusions have been supported by highly abstract reasoning that involves causation. If it were a desideratum that for something to be an component of a conceptual under-standing of X, *everyone* had to accept that it was component, the mere presence of a dispute about it would be enough to defeat claims on X's behalf. This absur-dity is enough to discard that desideratum. Thus, we cannot use philosophical dissent, its merits aside, to show that (C) is false. Rather, our concern is with the allegation that there are many who lack the learning or scientific wherewithal to embed object causation in their concept *vision*.

As to the first part of the charge—that causation imports a level of scientific understanding into vision absent in many masters of the concept—we will see (in chapter 3) that elucidating vision with our causal clause mandates much less detail than critics appear to assume. For example, it is neutral with respect to the likely sorts of differences that arise over the nature of causal mechanisms, and it does not favor any among, say, various popular regularity or counterfactual analyses of causation that have appeared in the literature. The level of understanding required is no more esoteric than requiring that the concept of killing, also widely pos-sessed by nonexperts, include in its elucidation that of *causing* to die. This does not require that mention of causation be displayed in actual elucidations. Minimally, in addition to requiring that the possessor of the concept of killing have a disposition to display behaviorally a grasp of some sort of causation, it demands that if she grasps the phrase 'causing to die' (or its translation in another language), she neither sincerely reject, nor be baffled by, the latter's relevance. Certainly that much is available to lay possessors of the concept of killing. It is difficult to see how those same individuals could form the requisite concept of killing without this much of an assumption about causation. (C) demands no more by way of understanding causation than a similarly ordinary grasp of killing does.

It may be worth mentioning that it is not atypical for philosophers to ascribe to ordinary users much less causal sophistication in their notions than controlled empirical study reveals. A good analogy for our case is the development of natural- and functional-kind concepts. Here certain philosophers and psychologists, in part to avoid lumbering ordinary language users with the theories of specialists, attribute to lay users classifications based on nothing more than congeries of immediately accessible perceptual features. However, recent studies (e.g., Armstrong, Gleitman, and Gleitman 1983; Keil 1989) clearly indicate that these sorts of classifications of kinds better fit the concepts of younger children (say, at the kindergarten level), but are rapidly replaced by less superficial notions involving underlying causal mechanisms or functions in children of about eight or nine years of age. And the accessible-feature views disappear virtually completely as children mature. Moreover, evidence of this shift from surface characterizations to those in terms of underlying mechanisms seems to survive in dramatically divergent cultures (see Keil 1989, p. 145), further indicating that these results are not peculiarities of our own scientifically saturated outlook. If this is so for classificatory notions generally, I do not see why we should be reluctant to extend it to the very modest suggestions about perceptual causation contained in (C) and elaborated in the preceding paragraph.

As for the charge that this is an anachronism—foisting notions proper to a scientific age on older or very different conceptions—it is more difficult to know exactly what its proponents take to be the basis for deciding that issue. The challenge obviously relies on a particular reading of the historical evidence. But once we abandon our unsupported preconceptions, where are we to look for data? Our best source would appear to be the written records of different ages and distant civilizations. But doesn't this once again raise the problem of using only highly educated possessors of a concept to fathom the understanding of the hoi polloi? That is risky, but I can't imagine an alternative to the method of consulting the written records where they are available. It may be imperfect evidence for the competence of the multitudes, but it is certainly as reliable a clue as we are likely to obtain. And, when we do consult the texts, we find abundant evidence that a causal requirement is not nearly so parochial as the criticism suggests, that critics have rather relied on stock misconceptions about the march of progress in understanding. Here as elsewhere, "received wisdom" has resulted in complacency that is easily embarrassed by even a brief perusal of the historical texts. This is not to say that a term (in the writer's language) for *cause* is always used. However, in each case the imposition of what can only be considered a causal requirement is clear.

Not only do we have the detailed causal view Plato attributes to Empedocles in the *Meno* (76c–d) but Aristotle makes it clear in *De Anima* that the question is not whether perceptions are caused by their objects, but how this is achieved (417b18, 419a17), comparing it at one point to the way a ring makes an impression in wax (424a17). The evidence is not only from the ancients. To cite some representative passages:

> Sense is a receptive faculty, and is naturally transformable by the external sensible. Hence, the external cause of such transformability is what is *per se* perceived by the sense. (Thomas Aquinas (1265–72), I, qu.78, art. 3).

> [W]e have a cognition proper to one singular thing, not on account of a greater likeness to one than to another, but because this intuitive cognition [= a form of perceptual experience] is naturally caused only by the one and not by the other, and cannot be caused by the other. (William of Ockham (1957), I, qu. 13, p. 30).

> We see no object, unless rays of light come from it to the eye. (Thomas Reid (1814–15), essay 2, chap. 1, p. 80).

Similar examples are legion. It may not be easy to unearth just what the aforementioned critics intended, but if this isn't relevant counterevidence, I have failed in the most rudimentary way to understand the objection.

If we turn our attention yet farther afield, we have evidence from disputes in the classical Indian tradition in epistemology, dating roughly from the second to fourteenth centuries A.D., that a causal condition, such as (C), was a commonplace assumption in theories of perception. Of course, this was not universal, for a healthy strain of Buddhist phenomenalism was a party to the controversy, and phenomenalists as such reject any causal relations to mind-independent reality. But the school commentators call Nyāya realism quite explicitly imposed (C) on sight. (See Mohanty 1988, pp. 254–55; Matilal 1986, p. 135.) There is nothing especially recondite about their appeal to causation, either as the generator of the perception itself or as a *pramāna*, a combination consisting of the cause of the perception and the knowledge it (once again) causally generates. This is but another indication of the ease with which a causal component in a conception can be separated from the occasionally not generally accessible details of how such causes operate.

Let me reiterate. Certainly, no one has claimed that everyone with the concept of perception accepts (C): a number of philosophers discussed herein explicitly reject it. But the question confronting us is whether the information contained in (C), and more particularly in the concept of causation it employs, is somehow outside the ken of certain historical peoples who nevertheless have mastered perceptual concepts. If it can be shown even that the question of perceptual causation is raised in a given language community, the critic is robbed of her best evidence. For this is sufficient to show that the concept is accessible to members of that community, and that undermines the basis for the complaint. Indeed, if we separate historical from recent opposition to causal theories, formerly, when (C) was rejected, the main concern never seemed to be the esoteric nature of causation, but its plausibility as applied to the sight of God or distinct soul substances. (See, for example, the epigraph on p. 56.) Thus, the charge that the condition imposes on the past a contemporary preoccupation is in desperate need of some empirical support, and I haven't a clue about where it is to be found.[3]

V

A further, well-publicized challenge to CTP is the claim that causation is altogether out of place for elucidating concepts, such as perception, which are regulated by epistemic norms. One version of this charge is developed by Richard Rorty (1979, esp. chap. 3). Beginning from the view that knowledge, belief, and the entire panoply of information-gathering concepts occur at the level of reason, justification, and other evidential notions, he holds that when we give an account of such concepts, among which we must count perception, "we are," in Wilfrid Sellars's terms, "placing it in the logical space of reasons."[4] John McDowell (1990) aptly modifies the Sellarsian phrase to "the space of concepts."[5] But for either space the point is that treatments operating within it can relate target propositions (what is known, perceived, etc.) *only* to the sorts of things that support or weaken them. Examples of broadly relevant relations are *following from* and *being evidence for*. As such, they are appropriate for a conceptual contribution to perception, not, say, for the Given or for what a Kantian might call a sensible manifold. Consequently, the effort to ground empirical knowledge in causation falls outside the boundaries of sensibleness. A causal 'foundation' provides no reasons, justifications, or so on, that belong to the space of concepts. Call this objection that of 'distinct logical spaces'. In Rorty's version, the critique is fortified by a brief history, tracing CTP's flaw to confusions in Locke and the Lockean tradition.

The objection might be directed at either of two supposed perceptual relations. The first is that enshrined in (C): the relation of object to episode. The second is the fixation (causation) of a perceptual belief by a perceptual episode. (A visual episode is an effect in the first relation, a cause in the second.) Of course, for those who hold that a perceptual episode is already a species of belief, these relations collapse into one. In chapters 4–6, I argue against that and related views, and thus against the grounds for collapsing these relations. Although 'distinct logical spaces' advocates aren't inclined to argue explicitly that perceptual episodes *are* beliefs, their assumption of the view is not incidental to the initial plausibility of their challenge. Thus, to the extent that this objection is advanced by the view that a perceptual episode is a belief, the extended refutation in chapters 4–6 can be taken as another answer to it. There I claim that the objection rests on a confusion of perceiving and believing. But for initial clarity it is best to approach the present objection by separating the two causal relations. Chapter 6 deals with the charge as it might apply to the second relation: that of belief fixation via perception. In that context, it raises the question whether there can be justificational relations between anything other than belief contents or propositions. Here I will concentrate on the distinct-logical-spaces objection as if it were directed at the first relation: that of an object/to its episode(s).

An answer to part of this objection was anticipated earlier. If perception is a source of information, this is so only on the condition that what is perceived belongs, or is epistemically related, to the world about which it is information. To know that it fits into a network of justificatory notions tells us nothing if it does not presuppose that this network is connected in the right way to the subject about which we generally suppose our perceptions are deliverances.

No doubt, some are inclined to respond that the domain of justification is self-contained; it would only be contaminated by the inclusion of alien causal elements. The philosophical literature is replete with doctrines of the autonomy of various conceptual networks (or language fragments). And current strains of antirealism and quietism seem to concur for justificatory notions. But the autonomy doctrine is not sufficiently self-evident to let stand without additional support. For that reason alone it would be difficult to use it as a basis for ruling out such theses as (C). To illustrate, a promising argument for the autonomy of justification might be the misfit of the causal with the justificational idiom. However, this would effectively bar one, on pain of circularity, from employing the autonomy thesis to establish the impossibility of a causal grounding. The circularity problem aside, it is not compelling to use the autonomy thesis as evidence for the misfit of the idioms. The autonomy thesis is, if anything, *less* evident than the claim that the causal grounding of justification makes no sense.

Thus, we are left with the original appearance: the vocabulary of justification—along with the luster that its possession is supposed to impart to the justified—does not appear to attach independently of a connection to the world. It is because being a justified X heightens the chances that X is true or that X contains information about something beyond our representative medium that we think justification worth the bother. That we regularly assume such a connection in ordinary conversation seems undeniable given the ease with which we are able intelligibly to raise such points without special explanation. Indeed, I venture that the assumption that this sort of connection obtains—whether or not it turns out to be well founded—seems crucial for an ascription of justification to have its customary force. The critic may reply that talk of causal connection seldom if ever enters familiar chat about whether a (perceptual) belief is justified. True enough, but not telling. Only if *some, but not all,* justified perceptual beliefs presuppose causal connections would it be purposeful to cite it for particular cases. Rather, the assumption of a causal relation must underlie and underwrite all such discourse. That is what must be maintained by someone who holds that causation grounds our jusitificational practices. And this explanation of why such a connection is seldom or never mentioned when instances are in question is certainly preferable to the only alternative apparently on offer from the critics: namely, that the connection has absolutely no bearing on the ordinary use of justificatory notions. It may be the case that even if a connection to the world is secured, this does not go very far toward warranting perceptual input in a way that foundational epistemologies aspire to, but it would be the sheerest folly to believe that our justificatory notions might get us anywhere without such a connection.

For all that has been said, the need for justification to be grounded does not show that the grounding must be achieved via causation.[6] But the fact that justification doesn't seem to be autonomous shows just why an interest in the manner in which we may apprehend a cognitively independent world forcibly intrudes itself. It is that concern that leads to proposals like (C). A causal connection subsisting between the world and our perceptual contents could be a factor in a possible solution to this quandary. That is all we need to fend off the objection—a demonstration that causation *could be* relevant to the inquiry. Whatever goals or particular metaphors directed Locke's deliberations, and however guilty he may have been of other confusions between epistemological and genetic questions, this query is an altogether legitimate part of the general approach to knowledge bearing the eponym 'Lockean'.

To characterize this rejoinder in yet another way, the objection does not threaten just the causalist solution. Rather, as Rorty is quick to point out, it attacks as spurious the whole enterprise of seeking ways in which our evidential practices link up to the world. But nothing I discern in the objection's outlook, focusing on, but not restricted to, causalist approaches, shows why such inquiries shouldn't complement the evidential ones. Although various projects have been undertaken to show that our justificatory practices are autonomous, here I can only say that none of those I am acquainted with have been convincing.[7] But even if one doesn't share my impressions of the current state of the art, what has been argued suffices for my immediate purpose. Recall that I sought to show only how a causal query *might* be made to fit together with certain normative (viz., justificational) concerns. There may be yet unexamined grounds of a different order for rejecting any causal clause. But they don't relieve the foregoing objection.

We are not yet home free. Although I have shown that a causal connection is needed, it will be claimed that I have not shown that it is possible for it to operate as required. To explain, consider a broadly Kantian distinction between what have come to be called 'scheme' and 'content'. On this distinction, the space of concepts is confined to the scheme, whereas the content would provide the causal connection to the unconceptualized external world. Put crudely, concepts can be viewed as imposing form on the amorphous mass delivered to our external faculties. (Kant: "Thoughts without content are empty; intuitions without concepts are blind.") However, importing causation into the account of a concept with epistemological affiliations creates a patent misfit. The causal work applies only to the so-called "manifold of intuition," and has no role in the conceptual side of the topic—the only thing at issue in a conceptual account.

The objection rests on the notion that perception consists of two different, if not separably articulable, elements: one corresponding to matter, the other to form. The way out is to reject the dichotomy, at least as stated. But that is not enough. In one sense, it is done even by those who offer the distinct-logical-spaces objection. For example, Sellars and Rorty may be viewed as rejecting the dichotomy by accepting one of its terms while discarding the other. They discard the contribution from the untapped external world, called perhaps the Given or the content. They retain the conceptual element, contributed not by the world but by the subject. For them, keeping both parts would involve the categorization of that content into divisions determined by or determining the structure of our understanding. But they find it hard to see how the categorizing part can intelligibly connect to the part caused by external reality until the latter has already undergone the conceptualization that the subject brings to it. Since information is conceptual, it seems futile to attempt to ground a concept in a relation between the perceiver and an item in uncategorized reality. Indeed, because causation itself forms a category of understanding for Kant, we are doubly stymied in our effort to go outside our cognition in order to connect it, via an uncategorized casual relation, to precategorial reality.

That is a price theorists of this stripe seem willing to pay, but the cost is that we have made it impossible for our body of 'beliefs' to be controlled by the way the world is. And it is no consolation to be told, as such theorists tend to tell us, that we can retain a connection of our thought to the world if we just stick to ordinary explanations; trouble only ensues when we ratchet the talk up one level into a metaphysical thesis. The audience for which this solace is intended will merely be baffled by this ill-defined notion of different levels at which seemingly indistinguishable things are and are not sayable. Moreover, someone who originally supposed that the external world must exercise some control over our conceptualization will have believed all along that there was really nothing more to her view than a systematic way of stating just what the theorist says she is entitled to say at an ordinary level; the philosophical thesis was supposed to be continuous with the commonsense sayings, not a radical departure from this mode of cognition. She resents being sublimed into a metaphysician for the minor peculation of systematization.

We may readily elude this predicament, however, by declining the initial gambit. Nothing in the argument thus far demands that the conceptual elements that have been noncommittally described are contributed solely by the subject. Some holders of a scheme/content distinction may attribute everything on the classificatory or descriptive side of perceptual reporting to the conceptual, and then attribute everything belonging on the conceptual side to the subject. But a realist can and should maintain that what we perceive is not only the inchoate *thisness* of things, but a world of thickly describable objects. Crowns and cabbages are perceived, not merely the formless stuff onto which our understanding projects crowns and cabbages. If we see the objects themselves *with their features,* then the relevant causal relation need not reside in a different space, inaccessible to that of concepts. Indeed, it already belongs to the space of concepts, and thus to that of justification. Or, if this is not so, at least one can't rely solely on the scheme/content distinction to show that it is not. In short, all we need is the addendum that our empirical classifications, when accurate and not wholly groundless, are discovered in the perceptual world rather than projected onto it. This is sufficient to allow the causation involved in perception into the same conceptual space as justification and evidence. That does not imply that there couldn't be legitimate doubts about the extent to which the causal connection supports justification. In fact, I expressed a strong doubt earlier (pp. 11–13) about some exaggerated claims that others have taken to follow from (C). But such doubts arise in the context of specific concerns. The failure of the objection undermines what might have been thought to be a transcendental warrant for holding that *no* intelligible links in a single analysis can exist between causal relations and epistemic norms.

It may be replied that young children and nonhumans with perceptual faculties do not have the refined classifications of mature humans. What sort of information do they receive? On one level, they receive information, say, about crowns and cabbages—precisely the same information as mature humans. But they are in no position to make use of it. For the length of the objection, let us confine ourselves to what they can make use of (roughly, but only roughly, what they may be said to *notice*). Whatever they see in this sense, it is not a totally indistinct agglomerate; the world is not for them, *pace* B. L. Whorf (1956, p. 213), "a kaleidoscopic flux of impressions which has to be organized by our mind," and which we "organize into concepts, and significances as we do, largely because we are parties to an agreement to organize it in this way . . . that holds throughout our speech community." Although our mature concepts may divide the world in ways that cross-classify other possible divisions, there is good reason to suppose that *what* is perceived already arrives separated into some of the same bundles that our later divisions make use of. In coming to enlarge our appreciation of the world, we may change even the conditions for reidentifying and principles of individuating these bundles. Such changes are indeed fundamental. But it would require a deeply rooted prior commitment to antirealism to maintain that all distinguishability in what is perceived emanates from our classifications and is not previously taken in from the world during our earliest perceptual interactions with it. We may conceive our maturing perceptual selves as becoming primarily not world makers but progressively refined instruments for detecting more precisely features that await discovery. Thus, however deeply we probe, it seems that even the most passive level of perception that can be characterized is already firmly entrenched in just the sorts of divisions of the world that qualify a content for the so-called space of concepts.[8] And, mistakes aside, the content part of this may be wholly due to the way the world, untainted by our mental contribution, comes to us. What makes this possible and just what the further details of our receptive capacities may be are questions that go well beyond the scope of this study. But in attempting merely to describe what actually transpires, why is it less plausible (indeed, why isn't it a good deal *more* plausible) to hold that this takes place rather than it is to read into the process a scheme/content distinction that segregates those aspects into operations at two distinct stages of the perceptual process?

VI

My limited focus forces me to slight some legitimate concerns. I have already mentioned the short shrift I am giving to the sense-datum issue, and I must add to the list of issues that are largely ignored those of perceptual qualia, the digital versus analog character of perception, and the (putative) demonstrative character of perceptual content. But some issues regarding visual content command greater attention. For example, the question of the structure, what might also be called the 'logical form', of visual content cannot be avoided. I broach the issue, with some simplification, by noticing that two prominent styles of reporting what we see seem to reflect deeper differences in the nature of our contents. I will briefly elaborate here, but fuller discussion awaits chapter 4.

Forms of the verb 'to see' may be followed by various types of clauses, for example, prepositional clauses, as in 'see in,' and conditional clauses, as in 'see whether.' But perhaps the most common objects of the verb are noun phrases, the sorts of semantic elements dedicated to referring to what we may, in some intuitive sense, regard as things. Thus, such phrases as 'the green bracelet', or even such heavily decorated phrases as 'the green bracelet behind the books on the far table', may follow the verb. This is not to say that every qualification marks something visible (now) or even visual. J. L. Austin's famous example, "I saw a man born in Jersaulem" (said of viewing someone in Oxford) illustrates the point. On the other hand, forms of the verb 'to see' are often followed by a special kind of noun clause called 'propositional': characteristically, these are "that" clauses, as in 'She sees that the boat is taking on water,' although occasionally the connective 'that' is elided. Styles of reporting in conversation are certainly not decisive, but they do provide a way of posing what seems to be a legitimate difference between thinglike and propositionlike visual contents. The question of whether the contents of what we see are more like the former or more like the latter appears to make sense. Using these styles of conversational reporting as our touchstone, there are very different implications in choosing the one rather than the other. This makes it very unlikely that 'what we see' is willy-nilly of either form. At a minimum, it would appear that if we see things of both types, one of these asymmetrically depends on the other. I entitle the view that all seeing is ultimately propositional *cognitivism.*

There are a number reasons for taking up this issue, but a few stand out. For one, the notion is abroad that perception is a form of belief or is belieflike in various ways. Refinements aside, a straightforward way to represent this view is to say that the content of what is perceived is, as such, a belief content. But belief contents cannot be of just any old form. Although there exist behavioral and other analyses of belief that do not indicate any apparent need for a propositional form, one clear point is that whatever is believed *can be* cast into propositional form (without change of content), even if it is not originally so represented. Let's call the view that perceiving is believing (or an inclination to believe or can only be understood via potential belief, etc.) *doxasticism.* Doxasticism appears to favor cognitivism. And just as there are views about the structure of perceptual and belief contents, there are views about the permissible structures of causal relata. These, too, must be taken account of in any consideration of a causal theory.

Chapters 4–6 are devoted to a discussion of the pros and cons of cognitivism and doxasticism. My results lean heavily toward the cons.

There is another question about visual content we should address: the question, as it has come to be known in the philosophies of mind and language, of individualism versus nonindividualism (or externalism).

An older popular view concerning, say, propositional belief holds that it is at least possible that one could have all the same beliefs one has in the ordinary world in a totally delusional one. The nonexistence of everything outside my consciousness, if I were unaware of it, wouldn't automatically require a change in my mistaken beliefs about that nonexistent world. A materialist way of putting this is that the proposition believed supervenes on the physical (customarily, neurological) states of the believer. Thus, I might believe that there is a tiger approaching even if I have been, for the duration of my conscious existence, a brain in a vat of nutrient fluid (say, fed impulses by the chief technician, my thought contents having little to do with my actual environment) or victimized by Descartes's evil deceiver. But a few celebrated thought experiments, supplied mainly by Hilary Putnam (1975) and Tyler Burge (1979), challenge this view. On Putnam's Twin Earth example, my molecule-for-molecule duplicate on twin earth may be experiencing something indistinguishable, so far as I can tell, from what I would be experiencing when I'm inclined to believe that a tiger is approaching. Can my twin arrive at a belief that a tiger is approaching? Biologists have several tests for two specimens belonging to the same species, among them the potentiality of interbreeding and common evolutionary descent. It is customarily taken as decisive that two specimens belong to different species if there is no realistic possibility of their stock interbreeding. Geographical isolation has been generally regarded as ruling out such a possibility. Certainly the ferocious, four-legged, striped carnivores on Twin Earth can't interbreed with our tigers, and consequently may be supposed to belong to a distinct clade. They couldn't be tigers, no matter how superficially, or even morphologically, similar to tigers—or so it's plausible to conclude on some widely shared assumptions in biology. Thus, twin GV doesn't believe that a tiger is approaching.

My discussion of the perceptual fixation of belief doesn't commit me to any position on externalism (= anti-indidivualism) *about beliefs,* but direct realism does commit one to externalism about seeing. That is, if I am a direct realist, the tiger seen is a factor in the analysis of my state of seeing a tiger. The object and content of my perception, often distinguished in classical theories, are one. (That is not quite accurate, for the direct realist doesn't require that every feature of the scene *as perceived* be identical with what I see. Some of it might be quale, some of it perceptual noise. Again, I oversimplify for the sake of exposition.) Theorists occasionally try to avoid this by speaking of the visual (perceptual) experience, or episode, in place of seeing, as if they were thereby isolating a separable stage of a proceess (whose final product is normally seeing) with its own nonpublic quasi object. But the commitment to direct realism carries with it the commitment to the view that when in fact this is a case of seeing, the visual experience is nothing distinct from the seeing. Talking about a visual experience is just that—a style of talking. It is a way of mentioning an episode without committing oneself to the implication that something is seen. But such noncommittal talk is not the discovery or isolation of a distinct type of episode: it is just an instance of seeing in the ordinary case, and as such has no objects or quasi objects that are not members of the publicly accessible visual world.

But it is also important to emphasize a direct realist's additional reasons for externalism. Even the indirect realist may be committed to externalism if she accepts a certain principle widely adopted by perception theorists. Let's inspect the difference.

A frequently espoused necessary condition for the truth of (alternatively, an implication of) "S sees *o,*" where *o* is a nonpropositional object, is that *o* exist.

Let's call this implication N. Thus, seeing requires the existence of the thing seen. There is nothing comparable to N for sentences like "S worships *o*" or even "S fears *o*." Even belief, which in a different way (indicated by our thought experiment) is ripe for externalist treatments, does not require that "S believes that the so-and-so is such and such" imply that the so-and-so exists. Of course, even with regard to seeing, not everyone accepts N (e.g., Anscombe 1963). Some argue that seeing spots before one's eyes and similar phenomena are counterexamples to it. But the condition has been thought plausible enough by some to try to neutralize such putative counterexamples. Few would be tempted nowadays to undertake defending anything parallel for worshiping, fearing, or believing. The present point is not to show that N succeeds where parallel conditions for the others fail, but only to indicate why N has been held by a host of theorists across a wide sprectrum of perceptual theories. When accepted by an indirect realist, it is sufficient to commit her to externalism. More specifically, states of seeing could not supervene on internal states of an organism, for they wouldn't be states of seeing without the existence of *o,* which we may suppose is external to the organism. She can preserve her indirect realism by claiming that within states of seeing (and in some nonseeings) there are episodes we may call visual experiences of ϕ, and ϕs needn't exist (save as sense-data) in order to have that visual experience. Now, depending on how the ϕs get described, the indirect realist may also be subject to Putnam-type thought experiments for adopting externalism about them. But that matter, perhaps affecting the plausibility of sense-datum philosophies, is not something we need pursue here. The point here is only that the reason under discussion for embracing externalism—namely, N—needn't cover the quasi objects of visual experience. Nevertheless, *any* causal theorist who accepts N is committed to externalism for cases of seeing. (Moreover I am not assuming that S has the concept under which we would be inclined to describe *o*. This affords us the luxury, not present in the case of belief, of remaining neutral at this stage about the applicability of the Putnam–Burge thought experiments to non-self-ascriptions of seeing.)

   Direct realism is, however, committed to the existence of *o* in yet another way. Of course, the direct realist can (but needn't) also accept N. More important, when what S does see is an existing public thing, feature, or scene, that object is a constituent of S's state of seeing on that occasion. There is no strictly organic state of S with a distinct ϕ that may serve as a substitute for the thing seen in an analysis of that seeing. I am not suggesting that we need, or are in a position to give, a complete analysis of propositions of the form "S sees *o*" (where it is assumed that *o* is in public space). But *any* analysis one attempts cannot avoid including *o* in its analysans. Not only is this different from the justification for externalism implicit in N, but the direct realist can accept it while rejecting N. The direct realist *needn't* deny that, when we see spots before our eyes, (a) the spots don't exist, and (b) this is a case of seeing. She need affirm only that when someone, say, sees Nelson's Column, the column, and not a mental substitute for it, is a constituent of the seeing episode that has taken place. This leads to two related topics, *representationalism* and *match*.

Is sight representational? This feature, when ascribed to mental contents, is sometimes used interchangeably with, or as a corollary of, intentionality. Occasionally, to say that a content is representational is to say that its mental episode is *of* or *about* something, or that the content may be judged on an accurate/inaccurate scale. As befits this ambiguity in its characterization, representationality is involved in at least two importantly different kinds of contrasts. On the one hand, there is the contrast between what has one or another of the above features and what is unsuited by nature for any of the above. For example, a self-contained mental occurrence, such as an itch or a toothache, which may be totally intrinsically specified while containing reference to nothing beyond its psychic tone, is nonrepresentational on this contrast. On the other hand, there is the distinction between what is standing for something else and the something else for which it stands. Given that I assume throughout much of this study that the objects of sight, and thus the objects of visual episodes when we see, are things and events in our external environment, I also assume that sight is *presentational* not representational. That is, on the second contrast, I do not take sight, and perception generally, to be representational. In this respect, perceptual content contrasts sharply with the content, say, of belief. When this is the load 'intentionality' is meant to carry, talk of the representational nature of perception brings a theorist to the precipice of some version of sense-datum theory. However, it seems to me that more frequently when the representational character of perceptual content is mentioned, the contrast is with features, such as *qualia,* which are defined by their exponents not to have the office of falling under any accurate/inaccurate test. In this sense, the sense of the first contrast, I cannot foresee any harm in speaking of perceptual content as representational. I will continue to do so throughout this work. But we must bear in mind the proviso that, strictly, and at the personal rather than the subpersonal level, seeing *presents* something to us rather than *represents* something for us.

What then of *match?* We will encounter more than once a problem about vision that some theorists will attempt to solve through an appeal to a match between visual content and the scene perceived. Here, too, there appears to be no absurdity in something matching itself, thus no requirement that match be irreflexive. But the only natural way I can conceive of these solutions working is to posit two things that are then compared in either qualitative or quantitative terms. It seems to me that all such appeals must fail on two grounds. First, for direct realism, there aren't two things to compare. The relevant parts of the content in question just are the object. So match amounts to no more than that the object enters the comparison, which is an oblique way of saying that the object is seen. Such match depends on seeing rather than vice versa. (I realize that I am, by and large, assuming rather than formally defending direct realism here.Thus the argument at this stage rests on the assumption that this view is correct. But, curiously, those cited later as offering solutions of this nature also in effect, if not explicitly, seem to count themselves among direct realists. Thus, it is difficult to imagine how they can suppose two distinct items involved, although their solutions seem to demand it.) Second, even if we ignore the first problem, it doesn't appear that there is any lower limit on acceptable qualitative or quantitative similarity that must be met for seeing to take place. Details are provided where 'match' solutions to concrete problems are offered.

VII

Briefly, here is how the rest of the discussion proceeds. Chapter 2 is devoted to a further clarification of issues concerning visual content. I have already broached the issues of sense-data and the competing, direct and indirect, versions of CTP. They will be discussed in greater detail in chapter 2. Moreover, some influential writers have described competing theories of perception in terms that restrict the available options and create misleading expectations in readers. If my account fails to fit a certain category on a preexisting list, it is not always because it can be found in a different pigeonhole. Occasionally, I want to reject the set of options altogether. Chapter 2 also attempts to clear up loose ends of this sort: not by mentioning all the concrete proposals offered in the recent literature, and commenting on them seriatim, but by better clarifying what I take to be the phenomena to be further explained.

Chapter 3 runs through arguments that, I believe, conclusively establish (C) as a condition of visual perception. (Up through chapter 2, it will have been clarified, but not directly defended.) I also consider, and answer, the arguments of those who reject (C) or seek to replace it with a noncausal alternative.

The next three chapters (4–6) form a continuous discussion, taking up the matters of cognitivism and an intimately related view, doxasticism. The fixation of perceptual belief is treated in chapter 6, at least to the extent of rejecting certain positions. But I wish to leave that subject largely open to a number of competing proposals, only blocking what I consider to be one unpromising approach to the topic.

Chapters 7 and 8 resume the task of fleshing out a robust version of a causal theory. A problem that has beset causal theories generally (e.g., of knowledge, intentional action, memory) is the threat of deviant causal chains. It is not enough to have the subject's state caused by the object; there are limits to the way it can be caused by the object if the state is to count as seeing (or knowing, remembering, or doing such and such). Chapter 7 confronts this issue as it concerns vision. A certain sort of counterfactual solution is offered, and other solutions—both of a counterfactual and a noncounterfactual variety—are examined and rejected.

In chapter 8, I address the need for CTP to account for not only why we are seeing but why we are seeing some particular thing. Call this the problem of object determination. Some theorists demand that anything worthy of the title 'causal theory' should give, in causal terms, a set of conditions that is at least sufficient for the seeing of o. I explain why I believe this is too strong a requirement for CTP and attempt to supply in its stead a standard by means of which the theory I am offering can select the perceptual object on a causally related basis.

A brief chapter 9 ties up some loose ends. In rejecting doxasticism, my own view, it would seem, must locate perceptual content somewhere in the vast expanse marked off as 'phenomenal'. But in declining the sense-datum gambit that doxasticists offer their opponents, the nature of this content may bewilder some (particularly those accustomed to the usual austere menu). Here I briefly explain what this commitment to phenomenal content does and doesn't imply. Playing it off against qualia and nonconceptual content—two other notions sometimes imported to elaborate the phenomenal—enables me to clarify the extent of the commitment to phenomenal content.

2

Objects, Sense-Data, and Visual Episodes

"When I came home to you in the evenings you would be sitting with your hands held out to the fire: you would say, 'But these little bits and pieces you are dealing with in these experiments—atoms, nuclei, particles, whatever—you do not in fact know what it is that exists.' "

"Exactly."

"What you see, hear, touch, are little clicks that come out of an amplifier; lines and bumps on a screen—"

"Right."

"But because, according to science, you have to ask what causes these bumps and clicks, and because you have to give names to what you say are causing them, you make up atoms, nuclei, particles, neutrons—"

"I said, 'But what else do we do anyway with our sense-impressions?' "

NICHOLAS MOSLEY, *Hopeful Monsters*

I

(C) foreshortened reads, "S sees *o* only if *o* is a cause of S's seeing." It contributes significantly to our understanding of sight. Although its full-dress defense must await chapter 3, it remains the focus of our interest. But even if it and the rest of the CTP clauses had been established, we would be left with a host of unresolved issues about the nature of the emerging view. For example, we cannot ignore what occurs to the subject whenever seeing takes place (and occasionally when it doesn't)—what I will usually call 'visual (/perceptual) episodes' and sometimes call 'visual (/perceptual) experiences'. What are they, and what are their ingredients? Recent discussion has been shaped by the following widely shared suppositions. Perceptual episodes may be characterized either phenomenally or, taking note of the effortless transition from perception to belief, as a distinctive species of believing, coming to believe, or inclining toward belief—varieties of a view earlier christened *doxasticism*. Even if we abandon doxasticism, as I will recommend, it is hard to deny that perception and belief are intimately connected. Thus, those who argue for characterizing perception phenomenally will no doubt still want phenomenal episodes of a type that easily positions them for the fixation of belief. On one not uncommon outlook, phenomenal accounts lead ineluctably to sense-datum philosophy. As mentioned earlier, the tide of philosophical opinion

27

runs strongly against sense-data. Thus, to continue this line of reasoning, direct realism leaves doxasticism as the sole survivor. Plausibility by default!

I opt for a view that rejects certain assumptions of this dichotomy. At just what point it rejects them depends on how one unpacks 'phenomenal'. Broadly interpreted, I defend a phenomenal account that is direct realist (viz., is *not* a sense-datum theory), and in which visual episodes and the seeings of which they are normally constituents aren't incipient beliefs. Thus construed, I reject the supposition that sense-datum philosophy is a desideratum of a plausible phenomenal account. On the other hand, if *phenomenal* is interpreted so as to preclude a mind-independent object of a perception from belonging to a phenomenally character-ized target, my claim is that there are plausible, yet-to-be-explored, nonphenome-nal alternatives to doxasticism.

Before we get to that, we must sort out some further matters. Let us suppose we are discussing the issues from within a causalist perspective. Various reasons are offered to show that we are forced toward a sense-datum version of that view, whatever our predispositions. Thus, as a first step, I will set aside the phenomenal/doxastic dispute to see what the respective merits of indirect and direct realist versions of CTP might be. This chapter is devoted to showing that indirect realism is not only uncompelling, but inferior in some respects to its direct competitor. This raises the prospect of a phenomenal view without sense-data. Of course, on the preceding division of issues, it may appear to drive us directly into the arms of doxasticism. That matter will have to await chapters 4–6, where I argue that our perceptual states cannot be species of (incipient) belief. However, if there is to be a form of CTP that is both non-sense-datum and nondoxastic, I must first show that it is possible (indeed desirable) for it to be non-sense-datum. That is the task of the present chapter.

The remainder of this chapter proceeds as follows. I begin (§§II–III) with a comparison between two- and three-termed conceptions (not analyses) of vision, that is, with a comparison of direct and indirect realism. Then (§IV) I expose an advantage attaching to the two-termed conception: it isn't beset by the problem of what it is for a sense-datum to be *of* one thing rather than another. The difficulty is called the "content problem"; although I formulate a potential condition for satisfying it that embraces both sorts of causal theory, it remains unresolved for indirect versions. Next, I examine some familiar *alleged* failings of direct causal theories, failings that would drive those still attached to CTP to countenance sense-data. The first of these (§VI) concerns whether a direct version has enough terms for causation; the second (§VII), whether the terms it can conjure are suffi-ciently distinct to bear a causal relation to each other. A third objection in this direction (§VIII) considers the role of perceptual *looks* in supporting an indirect causal view. In each instance, I argue that the indirect causalist has not made out a case against a direct-realist version and, in some instances, may have inadvertently provided reasons against her own view. Totaling up the results, direct realism is not vulnerable to a problem that besets sense-datum versions of CTP, while a survey of the various reasons for requiring sense-data for a causal theory reveals flaws in each of them.

The oblique way in which the sense-datum issue enters our considerations may foster confusion. There are other, more serious, objections to *any* sense-datum view; but since that theory is not a focal topic here, I do not discuss them. As mentioned in the last chapter, they have been thoroughly vetted elsewhere and their retelling here would only distract us. But neither can we diplomatically retreat altogether from that vexed issue. It is worthwhile, and even unavoidable for a comprehensive study of CTP, to review ways in which its sense-datum articles interact with its strictly causal requirements—all the more so because, on some common assumptions, causal theories must be sense-datum views. Thus, it goes to the heart of my topic to show that, contrary to certain expectations, in some respects there is a strain between the sense-datum and causal elements of indirect causal theories. It is for such reasons that sense-datum philosophy gets an airing here.

In locating my work within this set of options, I emphasize the nondoxasticist rather than the phenomenal character of perception. Although I agree that vision has a distinctive character—so that not just any way of gathering information about publicly described features counts as *seeing* the featured thing—I do not explore systematically or in detail the phenomenal character of visual perception. Some philosophers may feel cheated when a proposal fails to address everything already on their plates. But undertaking too many distinct tasks in the course of outlining a theory hinders progress on one's chosen focus. History indicates that perception is no exception to this rule. Thus, it should be our first concern to distinguish sharply what is vital to CTP from offshoot issues with which it has been confused. The psychological character of perception does intrude itself into my exposition at various points. But the questions I need to raise are tangential to many of the (otherwise legitimate) concerns of those concerned with it. Nevertheless, as in politics, common decency demands respect for the opinions of mankind. Thus, to satisfy readers that this generic talk of visual episodes that are neither beliefs nor sense-data is not just so much empty rhetoric, I do attempt in chapters 5 and 9 to say something, albeit a brief something, about what I take to be right and wrong about treatments of the phenomenal aspects of visual episodes.

II

As recounted earlier, originally CTP entered the consciousness of early modern philosophy as an adjunct to sense-data. The sense-data themselves were to have possessed various features, usually based on our knowledge of them. For example, whenever something perceptually *seems* F, there is a sense-datum that *is* F,[1] knowledge of a sense-datum never has to be secured by inference from any other experienced object, and its sensible qualities are transparent to our experience of it. Arguments for this view fell into roughly two kinds: first, those based on the possibility of perceptual error or misrepresentation (such as the so-called 'argument from illusion') and, second, those based on the chain of psychophysical processes involved in perception. Under those assumptions, the causalist's first question was "What, if anything, puts us in a position to have the sort of firsthand knowledge about the physical world that we take for granted?" The stock answer was that, because under normal circumstances sense-data are caused by material things, we can infer to the latter from the former by reasoning backward, from sense-data to their causes. Perception of *o* is inferential, though the inference might be so routine and habitual as to go unnoticed in ordinary reflection. Using 'sensa' rather 'sense-data', C. D. Broad concisely describes the view as follows:

> Under certain conditions I have states of mind called sensations.These sensations have objects, which are always concrete particular existents, like coloured or hot patches, noises, smells, etc. Such objects are called sensa. Sensa have properties, such as shape, size, hardness, coldness, and so on. The existence of such sensa, and their presence to our minds in sensation, lead us to judge that a physical object exists and is present to our senses. To this physical object we ascribe various properties. . . . [A]ll the properties that we do ascribe to physical objects are based upon and correlated with the properties that actually characterise our sensa. (1923, p. 243)

A natural comparison for this inference is the sort of scientific reasoning that results in theoretical constructs (a point driven home by the colloquy in this chapter's epigraph). In addition to being causal, the view just sketched is the commonest form of indirect realism.[2] It will be known here as 'indirect CTP'.

This crude overview cries out for elaboration. But it will serve as our starting point. It lends itself to a three-termed account of our perception of physical reality: a state of the subject, a physical thing (or scene), and sense-data of that thing. Direct realism (hence, direct CTP) omits the last of these, settling for a two-termed account.

III

Let's look first at the two salient constituents on which both accounts agree. First, the psychological aspect. This is the fact that seeing *happens to* or *is enjoyed by* something conceived as the subject: the visual episode. (Context often allows us to drop 'visual'.) It conforms to the 'what' in the phrase 'what is caused'. We are committed to this absolute minimum by allowing, say, that a state of *seeing* a certain tree at a given time is distinguishable from the state of that tree at that time. Its being seen is, intuitively, among the tree's so called 'Cambridge relations', just as its being ten miles south of an auto accident at 5:00 PM, or its being discussed at a conference, or its not shading Kublai Khan. None of these count, without special circumstances, as relevant to the present state of the tree itself. But the visual episode is straightforwardly a state of the perceiver, albeit a relational one when the episode is also a seeing. It needs no special pleading or asterisk when awarded this status.

Countenancing visual episodes leaves virtually every detail of interest about them unsettled. Nothing of philosophical weight is conveyed by calling them 'psychological'. Nothing is implied about their irreducibility or about a subject's consciousness of them. For all I have said, they needn't be detectable by introspection or contain felt tones, though, again, they may. (Shortly, I will explain why they might not be first-person detectable in the manner, say, of dread.) Nevertheless, 'psychological' seems an appropriate epithet, because they are episodes in the history of a subject qua sentient creature.

Second, there is *the thing seen*—what we might naturally call 'the object', or, where this overworked term threatens confusion, 'the ontological object'. All seeing is seeing something. A philosophical favorite for illustrating the point is a nonsense exchange between Alice and the White King in Lewis Carroll's *Through the Looking Glass*. The king asks Alice to tell him if she can see the messengers coming. Alice: "I see nobody on the road." King: "I only wish I had such eyes. . . . Why, it's as much as I can do to see real people, by this light!" Until shown otherwise, we are entitled to suppose the class of objects to consist in the mind-independent, public things we normally take ourselves to see.[3] Subsequent discussion proceeds on this assumption.

To this combination certain theorists wish to add sense-data. The arguments for sense-data are commandeered as reasons why acquaintance with ontological objects cannot be unmediated. Perception of the latter is obtained only via another object, although sometimes sense-data are not counted as objects *of seeing* but of experiences nested within the total visual occurrence. Thus, it is not uncommon to read or hear that we never see sense-data, but instead sense, have, or experience them.

For indirect realists, sense-data are *merely* representational, ontological objects represented.[4] Of course, even for direct realists, a subject may see one thing by means of seeing another. But for direct realists, neither experiential object in this process is a sense-datum. Thus, it might be allowed that we can see the bacon's frying *by* seeing it sizzling on the grill; in this case, one ontological object, the bacon's frying, is mediated by another, its sizzling. Nothing in such cases—or in those of seeing in mirrors or on television—requires that, because a certain object is seen indirectly, a sense-datum is involved. (Direct realism is a familiar view in a broader spectrum of issues involving perception, but for the limited aims of this study it is considered only as it would be embodied in CTP.)

As mentioned in the previous chapter, some apparent direct realists have recently provided new employment for the notion of 'sense contents' or 'qualia'. Qualia are *the way things seem to one*; consequently, different subjects seeing the same token things have different instances of qualia.[5] I bypass closer examination of them, because they aren't promising candidates for sense-data. On standard accounts, qualia are universals rather than instances. This is not meant to disparage the study of qualia. Their status will be a centerpiece for those inquiring into the nature of consciousness or involved in the polemics over functionalist theories of mind. But because they aren't intended as representational, or as 'objects' experienced in lieu of ontological ones, but rather are ways in which we are supposed to enjoy those objects themselves, their status isn't relevant to the current issue. On the other hand, whether or not they are properly dubbed, the motives behind the defense of qualia are similar to those for claiming, as I shall show (see chap. 9), that not just any old way of acquiring typically visual information counts as seeing.

For the sake of exposition, it is convenient to have a neutral way to discuss the substance of our most direct acquaintance without having to decide whether it is mind-independent and public or is a sense-datum. Let us call it a 'content' and hope that previous uses of this term (as, for example, by Moore 1922, pp. 21–29) do not erect insuperable obstacles to its present understanding. For all I have said, the content of a visual episode *could be* identical, in whole or part, with its ontological object. Nor have I ruled out that it *merely* represents that object in the manner of a sense-datum.

IV

With the differences between two- and three-termed accounts now in sharper relief, let's assess our options. I commence with a consideration of two not inconsiderable advantages that direct realism has over its indirect counterpart (although I dwell only on the second of them). The points may be minor, perhaps negligible, to the larger defense of CTP. Moreover, since I cannot pursue the inquiry to the very end, they are more strategic or procedural advantages than strictly substantive ones. They provide reasons for preferring a direct-realist over an indirect-realist research program, but yield no evidence for the truth of the first and precious little for the falsity of the second. However, since it is more common to notice incongruities between causal theories and direct realism, it is worth remarking that in some respects the latter view is a more comfortable fit for causal theories than its widely chosen historical antecedent.

The first advantage has already been touched on: direct realism clearly partitions the task of explaining perception from the ancillary one, with which it is conflated in classical treatments, of supplying a foundationalist account of perceptual *knowledge*. I needn't expand on this now, but more than once the exposition comes across ways in which difficulties can be averted if we do not try to achieve these separate goals at one fell swoop. Moreover, the reasons enlisted in the next chapter on behalf of CTP are quite different from those discussed by foundationalists. This case for CTP is untouched by the success or failure of epistemological foundationalism. (Some thinkers still suppose that their objections to what they regard as classical epistemology—primarily, foundational theories of knowledge—also doom causal theories. I cannot imagine what basis they suppose themselves to have for this unless they have failed to distinguish the epistemological issue from the metaphysics of perception.)

Second, whereras the direct realist needn't be troubled with the problem of explaining why we are entitled to say we see ordinary perceptual objects, the sense-datum causalist owes us an explanation which there is no assurance she can supply. For the indirect causalist has yet to show us why her sense-datum should be considered a sense-datum *of* one ontological object rather than any other. Sense-data are supposedly representational. Naturally enough, they represent what they are *of*. The earliest causal theorists did not seem bothered by the need to show how something that is not an artifact (unlike a name), and thus not produced by a creature with intentions, is entitled to this discriminating relationship. When it soon became recognized as a problem, it was immediately set aside. My hunch is that it was relegated to the "future projects" box for two reasons. First, it may have been supposed that since no other views were on the horizon, we had no choice but to live with it, and, second, it was thought that a solution was at hand with a bit of ingenuity. But the presence of an alternative (direct realism) brings the problem back onto center stage, and it has proved thornier than many (H. H. Price being a rare exception) had anticipated.

The rest of this section is devoted to a discussion of this particular *of* relation.

CTP is forced to place upon any experience that plays the vital role in its account what we may call a 'content restriction'. Suppose we ask ourselves what relation a content must bear to an ontological object for it to figure in a perception. The function of the content restriction is to lay out those that are compatible with having perceived the object. Whatever problems direct realism may encounter elsewhere, it is unproblematic here, because where the content *just is* the thing seen no question can arise about why *that thing,* rather than something else or nothing at all, is seen. The thing seen is a constituent of the complex <subject + (intentional) occurrence + content>. The onus is on those who would support something else to show that their alternative fills this slot. The early prognosis is that although direct realism is unproblematic here, whether any other view is depends entirely on its further account of the relation of content to object. This may sound peculiar when stated abstractly. Let's see how the problem emerges when we approach our perceptual situation as a typical indirect caualist.

We must begin with an episode that strikes the subject visually. Since not all visionlike episodes are seeings, what further conditions take one from the episode to an actual case of vision? Certain obvious suggestions will be immediately seen to fail. For example, it is not enough that the content be produced by something material and visible. The general run of hallucinations, which aren't cases of vision, are caused by material, visible conditions. But neither is it sufficient that there be something in the vicinity *resembling* in its features and situation the episode's content. (C) is a necessary condition even for sense-datum versions of CTP, and the resemblance might obtain where (C) doesn't. In sum, neither impeccable bloodlines nor resemblance satisfies the content restriction.

A natural suggestion is that the combination of the proposals might work where they separately fail. Isn't the objection to resemblance overcome by supplementing it with a causal connection to the original? The suggestion is foiled by instances of what has been called 'veridical hallucination'. P. F. Strawson (1974, p. 77) discusses the following specimen. S's febrile brain causes S to hallucinate, and coincidentally what S hallucinates could be described as similar to, even indistinguishable from, what S might have seen were she looking at her own brain. S's brain is a cause of this experience, and the experience matches or resembles S's brain. (C) is met if we take S's brain as *o*. Nevertheless, the content restriction remains unsatisfied, though this may not be the only reason why the episode isn't a case of sight.

Compare this with a somewhat similar puzzle that may arise for information theory. A signal carrying information—say, that *s* is F—contrasts with vision because the former is an abstract (not to say, abstracted) quantity. Nevertheless, students of information theory may also wonder how we are to distinguish what we might call the transmission of something (viz., information, an ontological object) from its mere duplication. Fred Dretske (1981) notes the problem and demands that for the signal to carry the relevant information "The quantity of information the signal carries about s is (or includes) that quantity generated by s's being F (and not, say, by s's being G)." But, commenting on what this achieves, he remarks that the formulation has yet to tell us "what it could mean to say that one quantity (amount of information the signal carries) is (or includes) another quantity (amount of information generated) *when this is meant to imply something more than a numerical comparison*"(p. 64, my emphasis). Although Dretske squarely faces the issue, I find no suggestion of a solution. This may be because there is no solution for information theory. By its very nature, a study whose subject matter is the abstracted character of its tokens will find it virtually impossible to distinguish between a discontinuous signal being the same token or merely a reproduction of a former one. On what could it pin such a distinction? The inability to make this distinction may make the problem itself seem chimerical. On the other hand, each form of perception is a modally specific medium whose objects are concrete; many would say demonstrative. Whether or not one accepts the foregoing view of the objects of information theory, it is certainly not the situation for perception. Here the distinction not only is real, but the problem is pressing. Failure to resolve it fuels perplexity over what it is about a sense-datum that makes it *of* a certain state of affairs in the world. Let us chart what progress we might make.

Consider a corollary Christopher Peacocke (1979, ch. 2) attaches to a theory he calls 'Differential Explanation'. The whole theory, intended to cover both perception and action, is not our chief business here, since it is designed to solve a very different sort of problem (although one that plagues all causal theories, and is discussed further in Chapter 7). Rather, we are concerned with the view that he calls 'Stepwise Recoverability'. Stepwise recoverability is a condition Peacocke places on a differentially explanatory chain, say, for sight, leading from an object through various transformations into photons, the bleaching of photoreceptors, charges transmitted through bipolar and ganglion cells of the retina, mapping in the lateral geniculate nucleus, and so on. (I am supposing the chain is the psychophysical one just illustrated. This is not altogether clear from Peacocke's exposition, but we don't do his view a disservice by making this assumption.) Crudely put, stepwise, as distinct from 'jump', recoverability requires that at each stage we be able to recover—in a yet unexplained sense—the explanandum of the previous stage from a combination of the explanandum at the present stage, the initial conditions governing it (save for the explanandum of the previous stage), and its covering law. As far as perception is concerned, Peacocke concludes that this ensures that its content has not only the right set of intrinsic characteristics, but also the right ancestry. He evidently thinks that this is enough to meet our (still intuitive) content restriction. The proposal certainly addresses our problem. Does it work?

Although the details of Peacocke's account aren't as clear as we might hope, on the basis of the foregoing outline it doesn't seem to supply what is needed. The problem lies in the sorts of beasts we have in explanans, explananda, and recoveries. This can be brought out by considering more closely the term 'recovery', an expression whose range of uses may hold larger lessons for the general problem of content preservation. On one use, what is recovered *is strictly identical with* that which has been, say, lost or misplaced. Thus, if I recover my umbrella, I don't obtain another one just like the original, but the very thing itself. On this interpretation, stepwise recoverability must enable one to summon at each step precisely what was at the last stage; its Dopplegänger won't do. But we also speak of recovering a lost skill, or one's composure or reputation. Such abstracta haven't well-marked identity conditions that permit us to decide whether what has been gained is strictly the same as what has been lost. Moreover, numerical identity may not make sense even for the recovery of certain relatively concrete things, as when we recover our gambling losses. Thus, Peacocke's term obscures the intended force of his proposal. On all but the first interpretation of 'recovery', it is uncertain that the problems I examined earlier with some failed attempts don't reappear. Let us look, for example, at how the dispute would proceed with Peacocke's proposal.

At first blush, stepwise recoverability reintroduces previous steps in a chain, but it is a chain *of explanation.* The most we seem able to achieve, with the aid of initial conditions, is a formula (/explanandum) like the one obtainable at that earlier stage. Describing our acquisition as anything more than this appears to be gratuitous. Thus, we are generating a new and distinct token of the same type as one we had or could have had earlier by other means. Stepwise recoverability, so it seems, is satisfied with an entity matching a preceding one, and we have already seen why matching is insufficient to satisfy a content restriction. But, perhaps we have been too hasty . . .

At second blush, because explanations by their nature abstract away from concrete situations in which they occur, such a verdict may be inapplicable. We should not even begin by looking for the same token. Perhaps, this line continues, what has been recovered is not a new token, but the old type. (I am not suggesting that Peacocke would accept this, since in various of his writings he seems to agree with much that I say in the next paragraph. But I am pursuing what seems to me the only remotely promising method for making do with what stepwise recoverability can offer.)

Unfortunately, the response is inadequate. One point of the earlier contrast with information theory is that for perception we cannot settle for an abstract (typal) object. Whatever we see is particular, singular, and concrete. There is simply no provision in stepwise recovery for the preservation of *that,* even as a transduced quantity of something. The importance of the senses for information gathering and transmitting can at times overwhelm us into supposing that nothing else about perception is vital. Thus, the vehicle of the information may be relegated to the status of an inconsequential accompaniment. Although undoubtedly there are some features that are inconsequential, I do not see how such a wholesale dismissal of everything beside belief contents yielded is viable. Suppose the particular seen is an orange. Suppose also that it conveys the information that an orange is present and that this information is useful. The useful part of the information is wholly general in one important sense: it doesn't matter which particular orange it is. Any of its distinguishing informational marks, however specific, will be equally nonparticular. Nevertheless, what we see is a particular orange, even if its hæcceity adds nothing to the informational transaction. How can stepwise recoverability, with its scheme of explanations, capture that?

Frank Jackson (1977) provides the indirect realist with a sufficient condition for a sense-datum S to 'belong to' a material object M: S belongs to M if S has a *functional spatial dependence* on M (p. 170). In other words, the spatial properties of S vary because those of M do. But it is doubtful that this notion of belonging to can capture what we want in the relation of S being *of* M. For example, suppose I have a contraption with a number of dials tracking the spatial positions of material objects. In this case suppose it is tracking a rubber ball. It can operate on any number of principles: it can be attached to a camera or run by a demiurge. The crucial point is that the dials register macrovariations in the spatial properties of the ball. I see the contraption and the changes in its dials despite the fact, let us suppose, that I cannot see the ball. Thus, presumably my sense-datum belongs to the contraption and/or dials. On Jackson's view the sense-datum also *belongs to* the ball. However, even overlooking the many other problems with sense-data, it is certainly not the case that the sense-datum captures what is intended when it is claimed that it is a sense-datum *of* the ball. Thus, whatever the other employments Jackson accords 'belonging to', it does not overcome the indirect realist's current problem.

This discussion is only meant to indicate a sort of difficulty; it is not intended as a knockdown refutation of all indirect realism. Even if that view has no way to distinguish a transformed original from a mere copy, it might avail itself of a naturalized representationalism to explain the troubled *of* relation. The general idea—say, along lines suggested by Dretske above (see also Stampe 1979; Stalnaker 1987, esp. pp. 12–13)—is that given customary initial conditions and causation, our visual state will be a certain way if and only if physical reality is. This combines the resources of causation with those of information or indication. This may be more promising than approaches recently pilloried, but it is not wholly unproblematic. For example, for some of the same reasons that *natural functions* (discussed in chap. 5, §VI) look to many like impositions onto brute reality, so, too, information inherent in brute nature may also seem to be a subtle form of reading into noncognitive reality our own cognitive opportunities (see Searle 1995). Also, informational relations seem to fare better when the object is predicative than, as I argue for perception in chapter 4, when it is referential or objectual. But it is not my purpose to critically examine the notion at this place. I note only that it is unfinished business, and thus that indirect realism raises a controversy that has no hold for its direct competitor.

In light of these difficulties, suppose we decide not to settle for anything less than the content of the visual experience being *identical with* the object. It is clear that it won't do simply to put it straightaway as I just have. Complications rush to mind, such as a case in which a content has additional features not found in the object. Thus, if we decide that this is the most reasonable view, a first stab at formulating the content restriction might go as follows:

(R1) S directly sees o only if, for any visual episode (/sensation /experience) that is a constituent of the seeing, there is an ingredient i of the episode's content such that $i = o$.

Though *i* could be the whole of the content, we want to provide for situations in which some of what S saw is an addition to *o*. Nor does the formula require that perceptual overlays—such as afterimages, floating optical particles, or even intervening panes of cloudy glass—be part of what is seen. Nevertheless, (R1) effectively encapsulates the direct realist's chief tenet: in the standard case, seeing does not involve representational intermediaries. Despite this, the qualification 'directly' is needed for cases in which S sees things on television, in a mirror, and so on. Here there may be intermediaries, but they are other public things, such as video screens and glassy surfaces. What is seen indirectly is seen by virtue of seeing other public things directly, and the relation between a direct and an indirect seeing is not that of a constituent sensing to a distal sentient episode. (R1) doesn't definitively foreclose on a role for sense-data, but it deprives its supporters of a leading motive for the view. It need hardly be said that on sense-datum theories there can be no indirect seeing without there being some direct seeing, and if the latter is elucidated by (R1), it appears to rule out any indirect form of CTP. Thus, we may regard (R1) as disparaging an expected employment of sense-data. Finally, it should not be supposed that (R1) implies that one can infallibly infer from a given content what, or even that, one is seeing. Enjoying a visual episode is no guarantee that one is seeing anything.

It has not been my purpose to rule decisively against indirect realism, but merely to highlight one of its disadvantages when compared to a direct causal theory. Thus, for subsequent discussion we may want a formulation of the content restriction that embraces both forms of CTP. The best available formula seems to be something along the following lines:

> (R2) S sees *o only if*, for all constituent havings (/experiencings/sensings) of a seeing episode—including that episode itself—there is an ingredient *i* of its content that has a certain detailed character just because *o*'s character gives rise to that kind of character in *i* in those circumstances.

(R2) subsumes the case in which *i* = *o*; thus it includes as special cases those covered by (R1). Moreover, anyone who accepts (R1) will have to count (R2) as true: for direct realists, (R2) is vacuously true for sense-data sensed, and it is simply true when seeing something. Moreover, if we overlook the fact that Peacocke is discussing explanatory chains, not causal ones, such a broadened formula seems closer to the spirit of his proposal.

I am not recommending (R2) as a cure for the indirect causalist's troubles. Indeed, it still appears to finesse the distinction between a transduction of the object and the production of something that bears relations only of resemblance and causal ancestry to it. Moreover, it is satisfied by Strawson's case of veridical hallucination (as it is by an imaginary case in which a would-be perceptual object emits a vapor whose inhalation causes one to hallucinate an object just like it). What (R2) adds to our earlier, clearly unsatisfactory answers is a hint (in the prhase 'just because') of a detailed counterfactual dependence of the features of the content on those of the object. We might make this perfectly explicit by adding to (R2) the words: 'and *i*'s having that character is part of a suitable pattern of counterfactual dependence'. Call the altered condition (R2a). Its source is David

Lewis (1986a), who suggests that "if the scene before the eyes caused matching visual experience as part of a suitable pattern of counterfactual dependence, then the subject sees" (p. 281). (Lewis later qualifies this, but his refinements don't bear on the present issue.) (R2a) seems to avoid the Strawson and hallucinatory-vapor cases. I explore Lewis's view in greater detail in chapter 7, §V.

To protect against a potential misunderstanding, notice that the counterfactual dependence of (R2)/(R2a) goes beyond anything implicit in the causal requirement of (C). It is generally agreed that causation is counterfactual supporting. Consider, for example, the causation of *e* by *c* (where *c* and *e* are event-, fact-, or processlike). Ignoring for present purposes cases of overdetermination, this may be said to support the counterfactual 'if *c* had not obtained, *e* would not have obtained.' Similarly, for (C) we might say 'if the object's state hadn't obtained, S's particular experience of that object wouldn't have obtained.' But the truth or acceptability of that is compatible with the falsity of 'if *c* didn't have such and such a character, *e* wouldn't have had such-and-such a character.' Thus, whatever the involvement of counterfactuality in causation, it does not support the counterfactuality in (R2a). The latter is a more specific dependence of features of the visual state on those of the objectual state. A warrant for (R2a) must be sought elsewhere.

V

The completed view toward which I am working embraces both direct and indirect forms of CTP. It is not part of my overall purpose to rule out (R2)/(R2a) as an acceptable formulation of the content restriction. Rather, since it seems that many writers have been persuaded that the objections to sense-datum philosophy are lethal, it is probably more urgent to show that direct realism is not incompatible with CTP, despite historical associations and some considerations I will presently review. It has been my limited goal to show that (R1), the formula for direct CTP, is trouble-free just where indirect CTP has a problem that, at a minimum, it is unclear it can handle. Since it is open to an indirect causalist to claim that (R2a) provides just the answer we were looking for, let's ponder further whether (R2a) is indeed a solution to the content problem.

For starters, (R2a) certainly seems to allay fears of falling short of sufficiency. But complications arise. As Lewis explains this counterfactual dependence, it relies on a crucial use of 'matching experience'.[6] I noted earlier (chapter 1, §VI) and will elaborate on it later (chapter 7, §V), that match is a problematic notion to use in this connection. For one thing, it depends for its elucidation on some rather dicey notions that are most at home with indirect realism. Despite my earlier assessment, there may be no way to discover what a matching experience is on the assumption of direct realism. For another, a match with perceptual *belief* seems to introduce the wrong item (a matter whose full airing must await chapter 4). Even if these difficulties are overcome, others arise; I will later examine what may be insuperable problems in settling on any reasonable standards for what is to count as a match. Lewis's proposal, like Peacocke's differential explanation, is directed toward solving a problem I take up in detail in chapter 7: deviant causal chains. There I maintain that it is the wrong sort of counterfactual solution, because it relies on the wrong sorts of covariants. The basis for rejecting the Lewis–Peacocke view is not unconnected with the difficulties for match, but a full investigation of that issue will need to await the more systematic treatment of causal deviance. There is no way to descibe a similar set of problems for (R1). Thus, we can at least claim that (R2a) must steer clear of shoals effortlessly circumnavigated by (R1).

To sum up, (R1) solves the content problem but presupposes direct realism. (R2a) is compatible with both direct and indirect realism (subject to the qualification of the preceding paragraph), but doubts about it linger. Nevertheless, the latter has not been refuted here, so in what follows I won't assume it has failed. This is not a major concession; whereas (C) will continue to play a central role, that of the content restriction is minor. However, the latter and what I have said about it do bear on the question of the form the most plausible version of CTP would take. It tells us that direct realism suits CTP nicely in an area in which indirect versions face a serious challenge. That by itself isn't likely to move those otherwise committed. Part of the reason may be that there is still the problem, pressed by classical versions, that direct realism has insufficient complexity for CTP. Let us flesh out that objection.

VI

I mentioned that earlier incarnations of CTP were nearly always indirect and until recently have remained so.[7] Their main concerns were certainty and unshakeable knowledge in perception, for which direct CTP is of little help. But advocates of indirect CTP may have other grounds for being dissatisfied with its direct counterpart, grounds having to do more with causation and the phenomenology of perception than with knowledge. Let us devote the rest of this chapter to those. The first such indirect-causalist objection I consider may be stated as follows:

> The dyadic, irreflexive nature of causation requires more elements for the perceptual nexus than direct CTP supplies.

A cause and its effect are, as Hume put it, "independent existences." One existence, the cause, is the (state of the) ontological object. What is the second existence, or effect? Indirect causalists maintain that it is a sense-datum or idea (or, perhaps, the having of such). But, as (R1) indicates, for the content of direct realism, $i = o$. Thus, the would-be effect, S seeing o, contains (part of) its cause as constituent. Consequently, S seeing o is not a (totally) distinct existence from o and is ineligible to be an effect of o. But it doesn't appear as if the direct realist has anything better to offer as effect. The outcome is that she fails to satisfy this desideratum, and on her principles the notion of a cause has no purchase. Perhaps this is what led Grice to remark that unless perceiving a material object involves the having or sensing of a sense-datum "the special features of CTP become otiose" (1961, p. 123).

Let's grasp the nettle. Despite the objection, for direct realists *the episode of seeing o* will serve as the effect, and second term, in instances of visual causation. (Seeing how this is possible will take some explaining. This and the next section are devoted to it.) As claimed earlier, all defenders of CTP, and not just direct realists, must distinguish, say, between a tree in the forest and the seeing of it. A phenomenalist or Berkeleyan idealist could reject such a distinction, but those views exclude *any* version of CTP. Thus, given a distinct *o* or its state, all holders of CTP will admit that whenever *o* is seen, there is a visual episode distinct from what is seen. The special character of the causal relation is not violated by this account, and no representational intermediaries need be introduced to complete it.

This will continue to strike some as unsatisfactory. Part of the reason no doubt is that incorporating *o* into the effect's description still seems to violate the Humean insight. I will put off addressing that concern until §VII. Now I want to discuss another source of misgiving, which may be crystallized in the questions, 'Doesn't giving the visual episode this role oblige us to say more about its empirical nature?' and, if it does, 'Won't this lead us back to sense-data and their sensing?' Whatever is caused in this interaction needs a psychological realization. But, as G. E. Moore succinctly described our predicament, "[w]hen we try to introspect the sensation [/seeing] of blue, all we can see is the blue: the other element is as if it were diaphanous" (1922, p. 25).[8] The episode's phenomenological transparency is an obstacle to conceding it the empirical reality it needs to be an effect.

Of course, the conundrum itself incorporates a controversial assumption about visual experience, namely, that it should be unproblematically introspectible. For present purposes, we needn't take a stand on the ultimate analysis of visual episodes. But should the psychological supervene on the physical here, a token episode's realization, and even identity, might consist in nothing more than neurological events whose presence the perceiver might not be able to confirm introspectively. This is not the only way to get around the need for introspective verification of psychological occurrences. A functionalist analysis of perception, emphasizing its occupancy of a certain role in our total psychological economy, would serve as well.

These sorts of ploys are useful reminders about the complexity of the sorts of things we consider mental. But we needn't rely on them alone. It is enough to notice that there is a perfectly acceptable explanation for the so-called diaphanous character of a visual episode, one compatible with its having even an irreducibly mental realization: it is simply the nature of seeing, or even apparent seeing, that it cannot be reflected on without reflecting, *eo ipso,* on what is seen. This may strike readers more as a restatement of the problem than as its solution. But if we reflect on the fact that the feature is commonplace among intentional states (e.g., beliefs, expectations), and then examine *other* differences with those states that incline us to overlook or misread this crucial similarity, the aura of puzzlement surrounding this fact should dissipate. We will have reclassified the phenomenon from the puzzling to the familiar.

Not just any old intentional states but other sensory modalities in particular share this feature: attempts to focus on them result in reflection on their objects. But the point can be lost, because not all sensory modalities are alike in this regard. For example, a tactile sensation accompanies the touching of something.

This may lead us to expect to discover a similar sensation for sight, but nothing comparable shows up in household cases. Accordingly, we may be driven to the other extreme and compare sight to belief. With belief also, a distinctive visceral state (e.g., a feeling of certitude) seems absent for a central ranges of cases. Thus, thinkers on occasion have offered behavioral, dispositional, or functionalist accounts of belief. We needn't accept any of these accounts, but it is important to note what inspires and nurtures them. The only remaining role left for belief once we give up on a characteristic introspectible reaction seems to be its management of putative information. Such accounts seem well suited to this remaining role. Wouldn't it be promising to take a similar approach to sight? Indeed, this sort of consideration, which would count everything except sight's information-processing function as inessential, may be a significant inducement to embrace doxasticism. But just as with the sense of touch, there is a central disanalogy between, say, belief and sight: sight involves a specific medium (though not one detachable from its object); belief lacks one. Thus the problem of qualia!

I will not attempt to resolve the larger issues here. Rather, for the remainder of the immediate discussion, let's assume that perception has a phenomenal character. In that setting, my limited point is only that the diaphanous character of sight is a commonplace situation, and thus no more incompatible with sight's psychological realization than it would be for a host of intentional states. More-over, the impressive dissimilarities with the other states with which sight has been compared should not induce us to overlook the crucial similarity regarding the feature in question.

Compare the phrase 'the grey cat sitting on the front table at Great Expectations' with a visual experience of that cat.[9] The former can be either used or mentioned. As normally used, it will refer to a specimen of *Felix domesticus*. But the ever-present phrase, rather than being used to draw attention to something else, can also become the focus of attention. Excluding general ruminations in the philosophy of mind, no such division of attention is available for seeing, or for mental episodes *as a class*. The class of conscious states—e.g., pains, itches—provide opportunities for felt tones, whereas many intentional states do not. But unlike natural language, in which there is a clear reference/vehicle distinction, psychological states in general (embracing both conscious and intentional states) do not afford an opportunity for such shifts of attention. An older assumption has been that it is self-evident to anyone that we will (always) be able to find something directly introspectible in contentful mental states *other than* the content. But one needn't have a methodological antipathy to claims on behalf of introspection to question this widely shared belief: it just seems false to common experience. I cannot apprehend or consider my seeing without at the same time considering *what* I am seeing. If I attempt to capture the seeing introspectively, I am led inexorably away from it to its object. There is no isolable mental goings-on for me to detach for further contemplation. We are occasionally asked to perform the following thought experiment: put yourself in the position of a painter who concentrates not on what is out there, but on the visual quality that descends on you when you see something. Even a successful performance of the experiment doesn't seem to bring us closer to our target of focusing on the sensation rather than its object. Sense-datum theorists have recommended this experiment as a way to get audiences empirically to confirm their claims. But even if we assume it successful, it merely replaces one sort of visual object with a different, perhaps more subjective, one. As for the experience of what it feels like to see, that again seems to elude our grasp in favor of this new object of a visual quality.

It is this translucence that makes seeing appear to be such a flimsy psychological occurrence and that frustrates those who seek substantial introspective accounts of it. In fact, it merely marks a difference between a host of mental episodes and linguistic ones. However, the linguistic model of separable medium and designation continues to mesmerize. In our effort to understand sight, it seems preferable to root out expectations grounded in this languagelike model than to abandon the notion of visual episode altogether. The distinction between such episodes and what is seen is apparent for the nonintrospective reasons given earlier: the state of an object must be distinguished from the state of seeing the object in that state.

This disanalogy between seeing and, say, singular description is also useful in exposing a fallacy underlying a significant sense-datum gambit: as Frank Jackson has put it, "I can be in exactly the state I am in when the orange looks red to me without there being any appropriate material object looking red to me" (1977, p. 98). *Exactly the same state!* In the present context, this could mean either a state that is numerically the same (whether or not I am actually seeing) or one that is qualitatively indistinguishable from the state when I see an orange. In light of my earlier distinction between externalist and internalist views (chap. 1, §VI) Jackson isn't entitled to the first interpretation without further argument. Nothing in this state of affairs shows it is unreasonable to hold that *if o* is a cause of a state in which *o* is described as part of the content, that cause is crucial to its identity. If so, nothing lacking the property 'caused by *o*' would be strictly speaking identical with the state S is in when S sees *o*.[10] Of course, this supposed causal requirement for state identity may be incorrect. (I defend it in chapter 7, but that isn't relevant here.) However, it would be premature to *assume* its falsity in setting up the case, as in the first interpretation. Indeed, any promising attempt to prove its incorrectness would appear to need as a premise the claim just quoted, in which case we have an even clearer reason why no one is entitled merely to assume this interpretation. Consequently, by elimination, 'exactly the same' should mean no more here than *qualitatively indistinguishable from.* This is all that can be read off from the intrinsic features of one's own experience, as it were, without first having decided whether it qualifies as a perception. But if seeing is transparent in the way suggested by Moore's remark and my elaboration of it, *what* is being compared with *what?* We are not entitled to assume that we are comparing a single type of subjective content with and without a certain type of cause. This is not to deny that there is such a state, with its own identity conditions, in the case of a hallucination. There may be such, and it may satisfy the conditions for being a sense-datum. But if we are to avoid framing the question so that it presupposes a crucial indirect-causalist article, we have yet to be given a persuasive reason for supposing that the same sort of fugitive entity is present when the object in question is actually seen.

It might be replied that we could not mistake a hallucination for an actual seeing unless the two had a certain phenomenal character in common. J. M. Hinton considers this familiar source of disquiet. I quote at length a passage in which he summarizes what is to be gleaned from the view that hallucinations and suchlike couldn't be confused with seeings unless their contents shared features.

> If things had to have a common property for you to take one for the other then a dagger, or a flash of light (such as may occur unobserved) would have to have properties in common with a 'dagger of the mind' or a 'phosphene': a flash you see when an electric current is passed through your brain. Or else it would have to be, strictly speaking, a sense-datum of the one that you took for a sense-datum of the other. Why, if we don't think that, should events have to have properties in common in order to be mistaken for one another? Why should it not just seem as if they had properties in common? . . . It can indeed be the same experience, but this only means that it can 'be the same' experientially or subjectively or 'qualitatively', i.e., that you can be quite unable to tell the difference. It is no more allowable to twist subjectively indistinguishable events into indistinguishable subjective events than to twist subjectively indistinguishable girls into indistinguishable subjective girls. (1976, pp. 225–26)

The moral is that our vulnerability to mistaking hallucination for perception doesn't commit us to the view that the mistake is founded on a commonality in their contents.[11] It is sufficient that we mistakenly believe they share a content. Moreover, if, as I have supposed all along, seeing is truly transparent, not only are we not driven to the 'common-content' explanation, but it is difficult to see how that view could work. What could be mistaken for what? One twin for another? But then don't we truly have different seeings (on externalism), not a single one under indistinguishable descriptions? Here, again, a useful antidote may be to dwell on the quite apparent difference between sight and phenomena in which an unmistakable double-duty medium, such as a referential description, is present.

VII

Recall the Humean objection: a cause and an effect must be distinct existences. The discussion in §VI largely sidestepped it. Before addressing that objection, I must disambiguate it.[12] Is it about causes and effects or ways of specifying them? What exactly does it claim about either? Certainly, we can accept the view that something cannot cause itself (unless 'self-caused' isn't taken literally). But for that charge to apply to the present case, the distinct existences requirement must demand more. The effect is a state of the form of *S's seeing o* (or *S's visual experience of o*), which is specified in terms of the cause, *o*. But only the rare phenomenalist (or Berkeley) seems willing to suggest that these two specifications pick out only one thing. Nevertheless, the specification of the effect 'mentions' the cause. Is that, then, enough to show that they aren't distinct existences? It is not easy to know. Let me briefly illustrate some of the difficulties in ascertaining just what the Humean insight prohibits.

A preliminary point: it is by now a common bit of philosophical lore that someone can take cause *c* and effect *e* and devise denoting expressions for each in terms of the other. Thus, if we begin with the acceptable sentence 'c caused e' and replace 'c' with its coreferential description 'the cause of e,' the resulting superficial form—'the cause of e caused e'—will not seem to be describing independent causes and effects. Moreover, in the other direction, no matter how natural it may be to describe events as interdependent, different descriptions are always available to disguise this relationship. For example, c might be described as 'the event just mentioned' or 'what I witnessed yesterday just after hearing about the earthquake.' So, if the 'distinct-existences' objection is at bottom about *descriptions* of causes and effects, we must have in mind some set of privileged (or fundamental or canonical) descriptions for which it holds (see Child 1992, p. 306). Such a scheme of descriptions doesn't seem promising: none is in the offing, nor are there compelling reasons for thinking that there must be one. And if the objection is not ultimately about descriptions, we must find a way to determine independence that is somehow free from methods of individuating descriptions of the items in question. Setting those issues aside, let's see if there is something to the condition that would prohibit my candidate visual episode from being logically independent of its visual object.

An initial (minor) glitch is that logical relations of any kind are normally supposed to obtain among propositions or linguistic entities. My 'events'—S *seeing o* and *the visual state of o*—are neither of these. The by now familiar possible worlds semantics for modal logic provides a way of extending logical dependence to them. Let's say that a certain state of o is *entailed by* an S's seeings of o if and only if every possible world (or set of compossible states of affairs) in which the latter occurs contains the former. (This sketch is subject to the usual qualifications: *viz.*, that the possible worlds have the desired accessibility relation, and that this relation may vary with the modal system chosen.) If the seeing entails that state of o, then it is not logically independent of the latter. But if in some possible world this token (or its counterpart) of S seeing o occurs and the causal state of o is not present, that seeing is logically independent of its cause. But, so the objection continues, there is no such possible world. Therefore, unless causation goes through some intermediate effect that is distinct from S's seeing there is no palpable causal relation. (C) by itself does not provide one.

If this is a serious objection, it will cut very deeply into the overall view on offer. I argue later that *if* a token visual episode or experience (say, E) has as its object o *because* a state of o causes E, then a condition of E being just that token and not a different token, E*, is that it be caused by o. Thus, assuming the antecedent is fulfilled, every possible world in which E obtains will be a world in which o's causation of E obtains. This means that every visual episode that meets this necessary condition for being a seeing will have its identity determined in part by being an effect of a particular state of o. Consequently, it obliterates the distinction on this score between a seeing and its contained visual experience, since just the same problematic feature attaches to the visual experience.

Is this really a problem for direct CTP? To begin with the more general issue, it is very unclear that the irreflexivity of causation can be extended so as to interdict causal relations between all items that also have entailment or quasi-implicational relations. Similar and no less justified applications of the principle would interfere with what seems to be a commonplace requirement for certain things, namely, that they be of a certain type, or have their particular identities, only if caused in certain ways. Such requirements are not unheard of, though they most certainly violate requirements implicit in the objection. To begin with an example of type identity, once again it is plausible to suppose that something is a killing only if it is a death *caused in a certain way.* (Even if one were to challenge this account, stronger reasons would be needed than that it violates our causal requirement thus understood.) Thus, the fact that, in every possible world in which K (a particular killing) obtains, it is related to the same origin is no argument for rejecting a causal relation between the origin and the killing.

It might be rejoined that an event could be a killing, even the same killing, if it has a different cause. Both Slim and Lefty are suspects, but either one's causing the death of Stoolie would not alter the fact that this is K. Thus, alternative causes of the same general sort are permissible (so long, say, as the victim, instrument, and general circumstances don't differ), allowing us to escape the Humean restriction. The problem with this reply is that as much may be said of S's seeing of *o:* different states of *o* might have been responsible for this seeing (say, *o* as lit by lightbulb L or by lightbulb L*).

The last reply may be deemed unsatisfactory because distinct killers are of a different order from distinct states of one and the same individual *o*. My next point is precisely that the demand for 'distinct existences' may get applied illicitly just by the failure to sort out the different kinds of distinctness that may be in play. For example, the objection might be demanding any of the following in order to show that the cause and effect are genuinely distinct:

(a) *type-type independence:* that an effect of this type can have had a different type of cause
(b) *type-token independence:* that an effect of this type can have had a different token cause
(c) *token-type independence:* that this particular (token) effect can have had a different type of cause
(d) *token-token independence:* that this particular effect can have had a different particular thing as its cause.

Case (a) seems to provide a natural home for the distinct-existences objection.[13] But to raise it profitably, we must determine which is the proper type of the effect and which the proper type of the cause. Suppose S sees a particular dog, Fido, of such and such a description. This would certainly seem to be the same *type of effect* as seeing another dog from the same litter that is, as we say, visually indistinguishable from Fido. The cause in the alternative scenario would appear to belong to a different type than 'a state of Fido'. But perhaps the objector will demand that, to meet (a), the causal type not be a state of *any* dog. Here, too, it seems easy enough to satisfy the causal view in question. An effect of the relevant type might be caused by seeing a very lifelike wax replica of Fido, or even a life-sized, cardboard, cutout photograph of Fido. Wax figures and photographs certainly do not belong to the same type as dogs.

However, we are not truly interested in causes of *the type* of S's seeings but in its individual tokens. Thus, the cases of greatest concern would appear to be those in which we have a token seeing (S's seeing of o)—cases (c) and (d).

Moreover, it seems we can also set aside (c). Of course, I am maintaining that S couldn't be seeing o if something of a type altogether different from o held o's (alleged) causal place. (That might be challenged from a different source: say, by occasionalism. But it is something the present objector is likely to accept, in a modified form, and to use rather as a reason for arguing that o couldn't occupy a causal role. So we may ignore that challenge here.) But since *this requirement alone* does not prohibit something distinct from o altogether, so long as it is of the same type, from having o's causal position in S's seeing of o, it is not a plausible vehicle for this application of the distinct-existences objection. Thus, I believe we can concentrate on (d) alone.

Althouth S seeing o might have been caused by a slightly different state of o, it must, I have claimed, have been caused by o. Rather than haggling over how slight a difference of state suffices for a distinct (token) cause, I propose to grant the objector her most damaging case: all such states count as the same token cause. In effect, I am granting that the state of S seeing o could not obtain without o's obtaining; or that, when o is its (nondeviant) cause[14] in the actual world, S visually experiencing o could not obtain in any possible world without o's obtaining. Presumably, this is the most difficult circumstance for (C) in light of the demand for token-token independence, (d). If this is no logical barrier to o's state causing either the seeing or the visual episode of the subject, then the distinct-existences objection, at least as applied here, does not capture the Humean insight.

Consider an analogy. Sexual reproduction is a causal process if anything is. Since the publication of Saul Kripke's *Naming and Necessity* (1972), many philosophers have agreed that having certain parents is an essential property of a person. Thus, although we might contemplate a simulacrum of the original person in a possible world in which she didn't have that origin, she couldn't be the very same person in that world. Not everyone agrees with the essentialist result, but I doubt that it would be rejected if its only problem was that it failed to make the child distinct from her parents. Of course, an even less appealing response would be to claim that because of the essential connection, persons are not caused by the reproductive processes that precede them. Thus, even if one has independent grounds for denying this essentialist claim, we should reject any construal of the Humean condition that ruled out these sorts of cases on its basis (cf. Strawson 1979, pp. 51–52).

The situation, broadly conceived, is rather like this. Some effects are described (partially) in terms of their causes. There are various reasons for this. Perhaps our interest in the causes is the chief (or only) reason for our taking note of these effects, or is the chief factor in our desire to produce them, or in those effects having been naturally selected (and thus still occurring). We needn't speculate about which of these explanations, or others, work in particular cases. They are mentioned only to indicate that a sufficient number of natural ones are at hand to dispel any mystery surrounding this custom. Some who raise the distinct-existences objection are troubled by the fact that a description in terms of a cause allows us to infer *a priori* from that effect to its cause (or causal type). They may then ask rhetorically, "What room is left for causal efficacy when the events are already related so that when you have one you have the other by logic alone?" When it is admitted that logic brings off this feat only because of the way in which the effect is described, this only prompts the objector to rejoin that there must then be a different, more fundamental description of the effect that doesn't imply the cause. But the demand itself seems based on a misconception. In the situations imagined, it is not merely that we have two events, of distinct types A and B, and we would have these with just the same regularity and prominence whether we chose to describe them in the causally committed way or any other way. Rather, the whole point of noting the effect, or of its not being lost in evolutionary obscurity, or of our continuing to produce it, or so on, is that it has just this connection with its cause. (We can see how this might be particulary plausible for effects whose chief significance for us relies on their delivering information about their causes: e.g., traces in cloud chambers or chemical reactions when testing for medical conditions.) Thus, the (always possible) redescriptions may sacrifice something vital, may portray the effect as more impoverished than it otherwise would be, in short may be less 'fundamental'. Indeed, the particular effect might not even have occurred (as with current cases of perception) if it hadn't been for the kind of connection with the cause enshrined in the original description. Thus, the kinds of redscriptions with which one could meet the objector's demand might seem disappointing, like the mere trickery of our earlier examples. We may thus be brought around to feeling sympathy for the defender of the causal connection who wants to resist the demand. But when we note the probable bases of the descriptions in terms of causes, I hope we can also see why the objector's demand lacks authority. Our choice of description for the effect may be a matter of the way the world runs, or that in which our interests lie, rather than an easily scuttled taxonomic preference. But it is not, as the objection needs to imply, the following fact about the world: that A and B are not metaphysically distinct occurrences.

S's visual experience of Fido being caused by (a state of) Fido fits this mold. It is characterized in terms of its cause not qua cause but qua object. And it is quite natural that some causes should be objects (think of a portrait, or the position of a dial on any piece of detection equipment). Consequently, it is easily understood why the specification in question should occur, and such a natural relationship can scarcely be grounds for violating a metaphysical constraint on causation.

Where A is a necessary condition for B's identity, the relation between them is by my lights logical: in every possible world in which B appears, A appears. It is far from pointless to remind us that standing in a logical relation is not the same as standing in a causal one. Thus, the relation between the premises of an argument and its conclusion is not, as such, a causal relation. But if the premises and conclusion of an argument express the general kinds of conditions that are found in causal relationships (say, states of affairs), it is difficult to see why such things should be absolutely prohibited from entering causal relations as well. This is not a rejection of the requirement of distinct existences, but only of certain lessons that some have tried to extract from it.

VIII

Let us look at another possible source of the conviction that CTP needs sense-data, one that may tap into a wider discontent about direct realism.

Toward the end of his discussion, Grice (1961) writes, "I hope it will now be allowed that . . . the thesis that perceiving involves having a sense-datum (involves its being the case that some sense-datum statement or other about the percipient is true) has at least a fair chance of proving true" (p. 141). His characterization of sense-data encourages such fond hopes. He "explicitly defines" the notion of a sense-datum by reference to locutions about the way things look, and that may seem to ensure that his notion of a sense-datum will be sufficiently innocuous to merit general acceptance. However, not every way of taking 'looks' locutions provides an alternative to direct realism. Moreover, the multiplicity of such locutions disguises snares that can nullify a suggestion even as modest as the one Grice appears to be making. Let's approach this doctrine obliquely, through a broader survey of 'looks' constructions. Since sense-data are defined in terms of looks, we can, at least in the first instance, go directly to them rather than worrying about sense-data. The conclusion I reach is that none of the initially promising 'looks' constructions shows that CTP requires sense-datum philosophy.

It is emphasized in the next chapter, and is obvious in any case, that truths of the form

(i) o looks to be F to S (or 'looks to be some way to S'),

where 'looks' is taken visually, imply those of the form

(ii) S sees o.

The placement of 'o' in (i) is intended to make it clear that it occurs outside the scope of 'looks.' That is, the construction lends itself to a *de re* interpretation with o referentially transparent. If a particular thing looks some way to a perceiver, then certainly the perceiver sees it. David Sanford (1976, p. 206) deems this principle "questionable." He asks rhetorically, "[If] the fine print appears to me as an undifferentiated blur, do I thereby see the fine print?" Better yes than no. It would be disingenuous of me to say that I didn't *see* it, though I could correctly say that I couldn't *read* it without my glasses. If I did claim not to see it on those grounds, couldn't someone ask pointedly, "How could *it* —that very same fine print—*appear to you* any way, including blurry, unless you saw it?" Moreover, I doubt that we want to commit ourselves to a principle so strong that it allows me to say that I couldn't see a written something (say, a sign) as long as I couldn't (didn't?) read it. I conclude that these misgivings can be overcome. In lieu of other plausible challenges, I believe we are entitled to accept the following implication (with either version of (i)):

(Gr1). o looks to be F (some way) to S → S sees o (i.e., (i) → (ii)).

This is because *o*'s looking a certain way to S just is for S to see *o* (though that may not be all that it is). We must not thereby assume the converse:

(Gr2). S sees *o* → *o* looks to be F (some way) to S (i.e., (ii) → (i)).

Nothing in the intuition behind (Gr1) lends credibility to (Gr2). But it is (Gr2) that must be of prime concern for Grice's thesis. If "perceiving involves having a sense-datum," we want the seeing to imply the sense-datum. (Or, perhaps for symmetry, we want both (Gr1) and (Gr2)—that is, the mutual implication of (ii) and (i). Even so, (Gr2) is the crucial implication here.) This is not to say that (Gr2) isn't credible. Indeed, a large number of writers have found in it no more than the merest common sense. For example, Dretske (1969, p. 9) claims, "I am quite willing to admit that, in a certain sense, D must look some way to S (*not* to be read as: must look *like* something to S) in order for S to see D." And Godfrey Vesey (1965, p. 73) deposes, "if a person sees something at all it must look like something to him, even if it only looks like 'somebody doing something.' " Sidney Shoemaker (1975, p. 299) undoubtedly intends a similar requirement, though stated in the first person, when he writes, "If I see something, it looks somehow to me"; as does John Heil (1983, p. 120), albeit without mentioning a look, when he remarks, "In seeing something, a perceiver must, it seems, take account of, or be affected by, or register in some fashion what is seen." This is but a brief sampling. Sense-data aside, it may even seem that the omnipresent conscious content of the look *accounts for* our seeing. It rests on a promising line of argument. How could someone see something without its looking some way to her?

Faced with such a reflective consensus, perhaps it is prudent just to grant (Gr2). But this tells us only that it is acceptable on some interpretation of (i) or other. It does not indicate that the interpretation on which (Gr2) succeeds also fleshes out Grice's requirement. It is still possible that the only interpretations available for a plausible inference make (i) too etiolated to support even Grice's modest sort of sense-datum. For example, the phenomenon of blindsight (see Weiskrantz 1990), if it is counted as genuine seeing, may demand either rejecting (Gr2) or interpreting it in a way in which looking a certain way doesn't even require a concurrent consciousness of the thing in question. Blindsight patients have gaps in their conscious visual fields. It emerges that they may have information about what occupies that hole only on directed questioning afterwards, for which they show an uncanny ability to 'guess' correctly. But although blindsight patients are normally conscious of something or other when enjoying their visual episodes, the subject matter of their blindsight disclosures are not connected in the right ways (e.g., as sense-data) to that of which they are conscious during those episodes. However, in what follows, I do not try to make capital out of blindsight cases, because I believe (Gr2) fails to support the sense-datum interpretation for other, more revealing, reasons.

On the most straightforward interpretation of (i), a thing's looking to be a certain way doesn't interject anything other than *the thing* that so looks. It is, in brief, the ontological object looking a certain way, and *that* cannot serve as an additional object (a third term for our account). Any sense-datum having a chance of reinstating indirect realism would be at the very least an entity that might have existed without the ontological object to which it belonged. That is precisely why it is alleged that we are guaranteed a measure of certainty for sense-data: their existence is logically, if not causally, detached from how things turn out in the mind-independent world. But if there is a surprised look on Daphne's face, it would be nonsense for someone to say that he experiences the suprised look, but not Daphne's face. Similarly for *o*'s visually looking F. There is no sense to having the experience of looking F, but not of the *o* that so looks. The point here is that although the phrase is relational (so that it may be taken to express a property of more than one thing), the look is a property of the ontological object. A *fortiori*, we should not be tempted by the idiomatic ease of going from '*o*'s looking F' to 'the F look of *o*' into supposing that we can quantify over tokens of F-looks, at least not if such quantification is to have the consequence of licensing identity conditions such that those of the look are independent of those of *o*. The very transparency of (i) presents an insuperable obstacle to that treatment of the idiom.

This reading of (i) is too weak to support anything like the three-term account for which sense-datum theorists contend. (But is it what Grice intended? The interpretation of sense-data secured by (Gr2) is so innocuous that it is hard to see why Grice should have bothered with the claim. Perhaps this is strong circumstantial evidence for rejecting (i) as the idiom with which to elucidate Grice's point.)

The notion of *o*'s looking some way to S and its companions (viz., (i)) are far from pellucid, however. In some ways in which they have been understood, they are incompatible with the plausibility of such implications as (Gr2). For example, (i) has occasionally been taken to imply that S *takes o* to be some way (e.g., Pitcher 1971), an interpretation perhaps abetted by the more committed phrase 'how things look to one' (which lends itself to be understood in part as how one sizes up the situation). But in chapter 4, we encounter serious difficulties with reading any thesis about 'taking' into 'S sees *o*.' It is more appropriate to the construction 'S sees that *p*,' which, I will argue, imports extraneous content into visual reports. For now, suffice it to say that on the interpretation of (i) in question, (Gr2) becomes problematic. It is not the obvious truth to which so many writers readily accede.

More promising for our immediate interest is Dretske's understanding of (i). He glosses it by stating, "D is visually differentiated from its immediate environment by S" (1969, p. 20). This is further clarified a few sentences later, when Dretske reads "visually differentiated" to support "[D's] looking different from its immediate environment." On this quite reasonable, though ambitious, reading I still maintain that (Gr2) fails. If I see a uniformly colored patch of something wholly within my visual field, it is reasonable to conclude that I see all (or many) of its visible parts that aren't distinguished from it. For example, just having seen the margin of this page, can't I pick out some square millimeter of the margin that was also seen, although it was not discriminated from its immediate environment at the time of seeing? Or, consider William Kneale's (1971, pp. 72–73) case of a mended coat, darned so skillfully that a normal observer cannot detect which part was mended. (Cf. Warnock 1965.) Although the threads look like an original part of the coat, doesn't one see the darned patch? As Kneale puts it (p. 73), "to say that the darned part escapes notice by looking like the rest is only to say in another way that people *see* it without discerning it from its background." Such cases seem to me to demonstrate that (Gr2) doesn't go through when (i) is interpreted as *o*'s being (actually) visually discriminated from its surroundings.[15]

This is not to deny all cogency to (Gr2). (For example, it passes on my first interpretation.) However, my only interest here is in whether it is cogent on an interpretation of (i) that would support the objection under consideration. We could continue trying on further interpretations. But at this point I believe another approach is more profitable. Let's ask whether there are minimal conditions an interpretation of (i) must meet to support Grice's claim about the need for sense-data in CTP. We can then ask whether interpretations on which (i) satisfies that condition support (Gr2).

The following condition seems to suit our purposes: if *o* were suddenly to disappear, making no other visible changes to the scene, there would be a noticeable visual difference. Whatever else someone might mean by (i), it appears it would need to meet that requirement if we are to define sense-data in its terms.

Prima facie, this looks promising for handling our counterexamples. If I remove a certain part of the margin of the paper (as it sits on the table), that would be noticeable. If the darned part of the coat were removed, this, too, would make a notable difference. But doesn't this solution depend on my not wearing, under the coat, a sweater of the same weave? Or, taking a case of a moth on the bark of a tree trunk whose coloration blends with that of the bark, mightn't its removal leave the visible situation of the tree unchanged? We might make the point vivid by considering any of a series of paintings by René Magritte, in which an artist's canvass is placed in front of an open window, but doesn't cover the whole scene as viewed from the window. (Let's project ourselves into the larger painting at roughly that visual angle, so that for the remainder of this discussion the painting in question is the one inside Magritte's larger canvass.) The painting is on an easel, and the backdrop outside the window simply extends the scene that is on that painting. Thus, for example, if the right edge of the painting has half of a building, the scene out the window just right of that is of the rest of the building and sky. Of course, viewers of the original Magritte can tell that the painting is a landscape not only because of the prop of the easel, but also because Magritte paints thin lines and shadows to show where the boundaries of the painting lie. But once taken this far, we can easily imagine someone at roughly our imagined angle who fails to realize it is a painting because of the perfect continuity of its boundaries with the real scene. (This is the typical situation at first glance for the viewer of the work—indeed, its intended result—until she realizes that part of what she seems to see as outside the window is really a painting in front of it.) Removal of the painting would make no visible difference to this subject's scene. In sum, in all these cases, a noticeable difference is made only when we imagine the natural scene to have a hole in it of a visually distinct sort. But although that is the situation to be expected, it is not something we are entitled to read into the very defining conditions of the cases used in the counterexamples.

Nothing weaker seems to work. For example, the crucial element in my last condition was discriminability. There are perhaps interpretations of (i) that demand that *S be conscious of* something, though the something might be other than what is taken to look some way in (i). Thus, perhaps the following amendment will supply a minimal 'look' condition for whenever someone sees something.

(Gr2*) S sees $o \rightarrow (\exists x)[(x = o \text{ v } o \supseteq x) \ \& \ (\text{S is conscious of } x)]$

where '$\supseteq$' symbolizes 'is a (proper or improper) part of.' Of course, 'conscious of' is itself in need of further explanation. Even this might be challenged by someone who takes blindsight as a sort of seeing. But the objections to (Gr2) needn't depend on anything as controversial as our evaluation of cases that stretch to the very limit our understanding of sight. Instead, it suffices to note that the right-hand side of (Gr2*) allows the look of *o* (which it purports to interpret) to be unrecognized by the subject, perhaps even inaccessible to her. Whatever one thinks of the much-maligned notion of nonconscious sense-data, nonconscious looks are still more desperate. To recognize how far we have drifted from both the original spirit and the letter of that notion, and how far we are from the role looks were supposed to play in a causal theory, is enough to see why (Gr2*) is insufficient for causalist purposes.

The 'looks' locution that goes with (Gr2*) might be something like the following (which is closest to the type of locution Grice seems, from his examples, to have in mind):

(iii) It looks to S as if *e* is F (or, as if *e* is something).

Unlike (Gr1), the following implication isn't even remotely plausible:

(Gr3) It looks to S as if *e* is F (is something) → S sees *o* (i.e., (iii) → (ii)).

Perhaps it looks to S as if *e* is F while S is hallucinating (and not seeing anything). But recall that the important implication is that which goes in the opposite direction: S's seeing *o* implies (iii). That is the direction of implication needed for the contention that seeing involves sense-data. There are (nonblindsight) cases that make me doubtful even of this, but I grant it for the sake of argument. Thus, we have

(Gr4) S sees *o* → It looks to S as if *e* is F (is something) (i.e., (ii) → (iii)).

Although the implication goes through, (iii) seems (for reasons just given) too insubstantial to support a sense-datum claim. The look needn't be that of *o,* and thus, in the parlance of that tradition, S won't be seeing *o* by virtue of a sense-datum *of o.* In many cases, as when I later reflect that I must have seen the fog because what first struck me as having been seen was hazy, *e* and *o* are neither identical nor related as part to whole. Again, for reasons given above, this will not serve the claim that there must be a sense-datum (describable as the look of *o*) whenever S sees *o.*

Let's summarize the results of my investigation of Grice's claim that "the thesis that perceiving involves having a sense-datum . . . has a fair chance of proving true." Recall that this inquiry was undertaken only because I construed it as a potential source for an objection to any direct version of CTP. Thus, whatever Grice's actual intention, I examined it only insofar as it could serve that end. Since Grice explicitly defines sense-data in terms of 'looks' constructions, though he does not specify which ones, my strategy was to drop direct mention of sense-data to first examine what implication relations subsisted between the canonical form, (ii), and various promising 'looks' constructions. But I could not drop the issue there. The acceptability of implications sometimes depended on specific interpretations of the locutions. Consequently, I had to determine whether the senses under which they were allowed violated fundametal tenets of sense-datum theory, thereby rendering (i) and (iii) useless for indirect CTP. Only (Gr2) and (Gr4) proved crucial for the claim; although both were conceded on some interpretations of their respective implicans, each failed further tests for being definitive of any sort of sense-datum that could restore indirect CTP's main complaint against its direct competitor. In the case of (i), the implication does not work if we imagine a robust 'taking' or 'discriminability' interpretation, and, on the attenuated interpretation(s) still left to us, in which *o* occurs transparently in the construction, there seems little hope for reviving a third term to introduce into an account of vision. For (iii), nothing in the truth of a locution of this form warrants that anything has the look in question, and it certainly doesn't warrant that the look is such that we may say that this sense-datum bears the relation of 'belonging to' or 'being of' the ontological object. The upshot is that, so construed, the Gricean line of argument fails.

IX

CTP has not wanted for commentary, much of it highly critical. Any full defense of the view faces a number of challenges. I have confronted some of them here and in chapter 1; others are taken up later. Thus, it might be useful to have a list of the major challenges that critics have thrown at CTP and how they are to be addressed in this work. In the case of those yet to be explored (that is, most of them), I indicate the chapter in which they are examined.

1."Thus far, we have merely assumed that (C) is correct. We have made some gesture toward clarifying it. But no reasons have been given for its adoption, and noncausal alternatives haven't been discussed." (These matters are taken up in chapter 3.) In chapter 1, I did examine a related criticism to the effect that (C) had no place in an account for which justificatory notions were appropriate.

2."CTP requires the presence of distinctive subjective episodes, reportable by phrases on the order of 'It looks to S as if *o* is F'. These in turn require sense-data, but there are independently good grounds for rejecting sense-datum theories. These are arguments against CTP as well." I have argued that there is a direct CTP that (a) doesn't require sense-data and (b) is nondoxastic (chapter 2). On the usual account of 'distinctive subjective episodes', my alternative is not among them, thereby rejecting the claim in the opening sentence. That aside, on just about all accounts, beliefs are not distinctive subjective episodes, and the presence in the debate of doxastic forms of CTP shows that it is not essential to CTP to have such episodes.

3. "Even if (C) is granted, it is not a sufficient condition for sight (either in general or of a particular thing). A completed causal theory should offer a sufficient condition for seeing." One major obstacle to obtaining one—for many kinds of causal theory not just for perception—is the presence of deviant causal chains, that is, causal chains that are so "indirect" that they disqualify the caused episodes as sightings. Thus, merely having the right cause is unlikely to yield a (composite) condition such that when it is present the subject sees. Thus, a sufficient condition will never be attained (chapter 7).

4. "Another obstacle to achieving a causally sufficient condition for seeing (again, in general or for particular cases) is that the condition must restrict itself *to causal terms.* (C) is only a necessary condition." Appearances are that non-causal clauses will be needed as additions to complete the account. In chapter 8, I reject the notion that a robust CTP must deliver a sufficient condition *for seeing* (or *perceiving*) in exclusively causal terms.

5. "Each perception has more than one causal factor, but only one among them is the object of perception. Even if we don't need a sufficient condition in causal terms for seeing *o,* don't we require an account that selects *o* from among the various causes of sight as the visual object (that is, a sufficient condition for object selection)?" This is a legitimate demand, and I try to satisfy it in chapter 8.

In addition to these general challenges to CTP, I am defending a more specific form of it and thus must address challenges mounted by others who might still consistently be proponents of other forms of CTP. The chief issues that must be faced in this regard are as follows.

6. "The preferred form of CTP in these pages incorporates direct realism. But, even if possible, why prefer it to indirect CTP?" Although a few side comments defend direct realism and direct CTP (e.g., in chapter 2), by and large I ignore this dispute. Because of the independent strength of direct realism (or, perhaps, the weakness of its indirect counterpart), it is more important to indicate how that position is altogether consonant with CTP and sacrifices nothing on the causal issues. (Much of the defense of CTP herein is also available for a sense-datum version.)

7. "There are two leading analyses (more informally, accounts) of perception: doxastic (in terms of perceptual belief) and phenomenal. As the stock account has it, the phenomenal view requires sense-data." My account is, as mentioned above, not doxastic. Whether it is phenomenal, I leave to others to decide. The crucial point, as shown in this chapter, is that its not being doxastic does not force it into being a sense-datum account.

8. "Even if the account on offer is not, doxastic, perhaps it should be." I have yet to disclose anything wrong with a belief analysis of perception. Chapter 4 exposes a fatal difficulty with doxasticism: it requires the wrong form for reporting seeing episodes. In chapter 5, I canvass the arguments for doxasticism. Each is found wanting. In chapter 6, I discuss a master argument employed

against competitors of doxasticism. I call it the "Sellarsian argument" (after Wilfrid Sellars). Here, too, the results are negative.

The present chapter began with the epochal struggle (see item 7) between phenomenal and belief models of visual perception. Doxasticism was placed to one side for our immediate inquiry. Rather, the main thrust of the foregoing discussion has been to show that we can have a direct version of CTP and that doxasticism is not required just for the sake of avoiding sense-datum intermediaries in a causal theory. Whether one wants to count this as a non-sense-datum form of phenomenal theory or a position falling altogether outside the widely acknowledged dichotomy is, to repeat, beyond the scope of the present book. Whatever importance it may have, the direct realist position I assume throughout should be compatible with whichever conclusions on that issue one reaches. However, nothing yet has been said on behalf of or against the eligibility of the only article of causalism to which we have thus far been exposed: (C). Let's now turn our attention to exploring the arguments for, and a few objections to, requiring of our concept of sight that a seeing episode's object be a cause of the seeing.

3

The Case for Causation

Those who imagine Heaven and Hell neigbours, and conceive a vicinity between those two extreams upon consequence of the Parable, where Dives dis-
coursed with Lazarus in Abraham's bosome, do too grossly conceive of those
glorified creatures, whose eyes shall easily out-see the Sun, and behold without a perspective the extreamest distances: for if there shall be in our glorified
eyes, the faculty of sight and reception of objects, I could think of the visible
species there to be in as unlimitable a way as now the intellectual. I grant that
two bodies placed beyond the tenth sphear, or in a vacuity, according to Aristotle's Philosophy, could not behold each other, because there wants a body
or Medium to hand and transport the visible rays of the object into the sense;
but when there shall be a general defect of either Medium to convey, or light
to prepare and dispose that Medium, and yet a perfect vision, we must sus-
pend the rules of our Philosophy, and make all good by a more absolute piece
of opticks.

SIR THOMAS BROWNE, *Religio Medici*

I

Thus far we have taken for granted the causal connection enshrined in (C). Since
many no doubt will find it less than self-evident, let us review the case for it.

Frequently the strength of a philosophical position does not lie in a single,
dazzling master argument, but in the accumulation of (as Mill has called them)
"considerations capable of determining the intellect." With qualification, I think
this is how things stand with (C). To begin with, there are by-now-familiar examples, thought experiments, in which we are compelled to deny that someone saw
something *just because* her visual episode lacked the appropriate causal relation
to the would-be object. I will discuss several such cases. But the foregoing remarks shouldn't be taken to suggest that these are not decisive in and of themselves. Indeed, once misconceptions are removed, they seem to me sufficient to
make the case. But because they have been taken as inconclusive by some—
doubts to be allayed by subsequent elaboration—reinforcement by other considerations is welcome reassurance. In this connection, additional general features of
the perceptual situation may be mentioned. For example, evidence for (C) may be
gathered from the more-or-less-explicit association of certain perceptual idioms
with causal constructions. Moreover, there are restrictions on the spatial placement
of objects of sight vis-à-vis perceivers, which seem to cry out for explanation in

terms of something on the order of a causal connection. Once the restrictions are acknowledged, no one to my knowledge has suggested a promising alternative to it. Each point is elaborated in the sequel.

Shoddy past practice underscores the need to get clear on the relevance of the evidence I allude to. Suppose we ask, "What are we to take it as evidence *for?*" The thought experiments mentioned have generally been regarded as reasons for adopting CTP. Indeed, they are the most prominent arguments for *direct* CTP with which I'm familiar. But, alas, they support no more than (C). That limitation seems to hold as well for other broad defenses of CTP. As noted earlier (chap. 1, §II), although (C) is a major ingredient in causal theories, a number of those who readily accept (C) nevertheless reject CTP. This is indication enough that it falls short in the minds of many of being a robust version of CTP. To the best of my knowledge, there is no clear consensus on what more is required, but on many accounts a causal theory should be able to distinguish the causal contribution of the object from that of any other causal factor, thereby showing how the object's causation makes it the object. This is the notorious problem of object determination tackled in chapter 8. As formulated here, it mildly overstates the requirement, but it captures it closely enough to show why a defense of (C) may be deemed insufficient to establish CTP. At a minimum, if anyone uses these as arguments for (what she calls) CTP, we should note that she isn't entitled to burden the latter view with additional, undefended articles beyond (C). Despite this warning, if correct, (C) yields, as David Pears has put it, "a causal clause" that must be capable of being incorporated into anyone's account of perception (or sight), however uncausal the overall account. That is the spirit in which I propose to take the considerations I am about to present. Acceptance of them is intended to be noncommittal with regard to any further articles of CTP.

II

I begin with the thought experiments. First, per Grice's famous instance (1961, p. 142), I believe I am facing an unoccluded pillar. In fact, the only object I can see is a mirror in which is reflected a pillar that happens to be behind me. Behind the mirror, and hidden from my view, is another pillar, which, from this distance, would have been visually indistinguishable from the reflected one, and which I would have seen but for the mirror subtending my visual angle. No doubt, I see the mirror and the reflection of a pillar. In fact, Grice writes that it would be "incorrect to say that I saw the [blocked] pillar and correct to say that I saw the [reflected] one." An explanation that immediately strikes one is that whereas the first has no appropriate causal role in my seeing, the second does. (Although Grice allows, plausibly enough, that I see the pillar reflected in the mirror, I want to avoid getting embroiled in an arid debate over whether we actually see the thing that we see 'a reflection of.' I needn't insist on it. But I should stress that, aside from the fact that the blocked pillar *wasn't* seen, I did see *something,* whether a pillar, a mirror, or both. That much seems beyond dispute. Its significance emerges later in this section.) Were the mirror slightly distorting, making the misshapen pillar obstructed by it a closer match to my perceptual experience than the one (distortedly) reflected in the mirror, I could still at most have seen only the reflected pillar; this seems to show that match, taken even under the most favorable conditions, is no substitute for causal contribution.

In the next example, *Twelfth Night*'s Sir Andrew Aguecheek rudely encounters Sebastian. He falsely believes he is facing Caesario, who is in fact Sebastian's twin sister Viola in male getup. In that outfit, she was virtually indistinguishable from Sebastian. Unluckily for Sir Andrew, he challenges Sebastian, rather than the timorous Caesario, to a duel. Only Sebastian figures in an account of Aguecheek's enjoying this visual episode. How does Sebastian figure? Once again, the answer comes back, he is the cause of Aguecheek's experience. It is irrelevant that a sighting of the disguised Viola would fit this experience as well as Sebastian, as it is irrelevant that Sir Andrew believes he is seeing Caesario. (Cf. Antipholus and Dromio in *The Comedy of Errors*.)

Notice that in both cases the subject does see something (the image in a mirror; Sebastian), but fails to see what he would have seen (the pillar in front of him; Viola in male togs) in the straightforward, expected situation. Thus, the difference made for S is not *whether* S sees, but *what* S sees. I could have made the same point with a different sort of Gedankenexperiment, one in which the subject doesn't see anything. To wit:

An alert subject, Smithers, has a well-lit blue cube in front of his open eyes. His optic nerve has been severed. However, a clever neural scientist has attached relevant areas of his visual cortex to electrodes, by means of which she produces in Smithers the visual experience of a blue cube. This is wholly fortuitous. The experimenter was merely trying to locate Smithers's cortical damage, not compensate for his detached optic nerve. She is testing his response with a series of laboratory-generated patterns she has, and it just turns out that the one she chooses is indistinguishable from the one that would have been induced by the cube were Smithers's optic nerve intact and her power supply shut off. She may not even know what is in front of Smithers's eyes at the time. Smithers isn't seeing the cube in front of him. Why not? He certainly has a visual experience matching what is in front of his eyes. The absent element is a causal connection between that experience and the visual experience he is enjoying. (A case like this is found in C. B. Martin (1959), p. 109. There is some justice to the claim that it was Martin (1959), not Grice (1961), who rehabilitated CTP, though, for reasons explored presently, the first two cases, in which the subject sees, are more indicative of the true character of the contemporary view.)

I contrast the first two cases with the last one for tactical reasons. The main disagreement between causalists and their opponents has been described as a conflict between disjunctive and nondisjunctive concepts of perception. Nondisjunctivists, or causalists, first seek a 'highest common factor' between seeing something and hallucinating something similarly describable. This, it is commonly supposed, is a subjective experience. One then poses the query "What needs to be added to hallucination to bring it up to actual seeing?" (That is, since ex hypothesi hallucination shares many other elements with seeing, what is it missing that seeing has?) Qualifications aside, the causalist answer is that in cases of actual seeing the (would-be) object causes its correlative subjective experience. On the other hand, the disjunctivist proposes that we start from the normal case of sight, rather than building up from subjective experience. Sight is not hallucination plus appropriate cause; rather, hallucination is sight minus normal circumstances. Thus, we see when our experience satisfies a certain condition, fail to see when it satisfies only a weaker condition (only robust enough to make it an experience)—hence the disjunctive options of the title. (The disjunctivist's starting point seems right. See my remarks on Jackson's sense-datum ploy, chap. 2, p. 42. I dissent only from its later development.) The disjunctivist has two general reasons for her position. One is that the causalist seems to put the object permanently beyond any visual content attainable by the subject. The explanation for this harkens back to problems raised in the last chapter over applying the content restriction to indirect CTP. It is difficult to see how, for example, a sense-datum theorist is warranted in holding that a given subjective content is *of* an ontological object. Placing the object outside the content is an integral part of the initial strategy: to obtain a highest common factor with hallucination. But it places a theorist in a hole from which it is at least far from assured that she can dig out. How does the ontological object get back into the content of the whole seeing episode? (Notice that this is not the skeptical question "How can one ever be justified in claiming that one sees things in the external world?", but a question about how, given all the worldly facts, an experiential content acquires its actual representational features on that account.) The other reason has to do with finding a 'distinct existence' to serve as effect, a problem discussed, and I trust dispatched, in §VII of chapter 2.

We should reject a crucial assumption underlying this description of the differences. Its characterization shares indirect realism's faulty expectations for all versions of CTP. Of course, one *can* approach causalism, as the indirect realist does, with an epistemic prius. But the opening for *direct* CTP is just the thought that this is *not necessary* for a causal view; indeed, it is beside the point as far as the strongest argument for (C) itself goes. The case for causalism shouldn't be seen as a solution to the problem of how we escape from our notional prison into the world beyond—it can also tell us why we see one thing rather than another. Solutions to the latter problem needn't seek a highest factor common to all visionlike experiences. Nor does this imply that the comparison with hallucination isn't revealing. It can claim a place alongside the rest of the evidence for CTP. But it is a mistake to write it, or the notion of a richer common element, into the very conditions of the case for (C). For this reason, CTP doesn't require, as some admirers and detractors have each claimed, subjective experiences. To the extent that Grice shares the critics' assumption, he fails to grasp fully the significance of his case for direct CTP. (I say more in §VIII about the positive thesis of the disjunctive conception. I may remark here that it appears to conflate the sorts of 'looks' constructions I labored to differentiate in chap. 2, §VIII.)

Returning finally to a comparison of the three thought experiments, the first two serve as a useful reminder that we do not need to cast our lot with the nondisjunctivists in order to be causal theorists. Unlike Smithers's encounter with a blue cube, the question in the first two cases is not what we need to add to experience to go from visual episode to vision (or from a nonseeing to a seeing). Rather, it is used to explain why we see one thing rather than another. We thus begin from just where the disjunctivist recommends: a certified instance of seeing. The question about the episode is not why the subject doesn't see anything, but why she can't have seen the thing tantalizingly presented to us as a candidate (say, because of its location or its matching features).

There is another reason for not forgetting, as perhaps some critics have, the full range of conditions under which a causal condition is adopted. Let's return for a moment to the confrontation with which chapter 2 opened: that between those who hold that perception is a form of—possibly incipient—belief (doxasticists) and those who prefer phenomenal accounts of perception. In anticipation of later arguments, in chapter 2 I plump for the second group. For all that, doxasticism is minimally, to the best of my knowledge, a coherent view. It is also widely held. But all doxasticists I am familiar with would accept, more likely insist on, (C) and its conceptual role. Since they generally disparage an ineliminable role for subjective experiences in accounts of perception, in some instances using clinical cases of blindsight to drive home the point, how can they espouse (C), characterized as the nondisjunctivist solution to the 'common-factor' problem? Quite clearly, they cannot. Unless there is a fundamental confusion in the combination of views doxasticists hold we should conclude that the disjunctivist's characterization of the respective approaches of CTP and its opponents slights doxasticism. It thereby restricts CTP within limits much too narrow for both the range of those who hold it and for the evidence on which it rests.

Still, not everyone believes that these thought experiments carry the day. Below I take up challenges to them. But let's provisionally set aside objections in order first to examine other arguments for (C).

III

On occasion, causalists have also rested their case on the need to account for the reliability of our seeing. Strawson (1979), though he calls these 'assumptions', provides a compact summary of this reasoning: "We think of perception as a way . . . of informing ourselves about the world of independently existing things: we assume, that is to say, the general reliability of our perceptual experiences; and that assumption is the same as the assumption of a general causal dependence of our perceptual experiences on the independently existing things we take them to be of" (p. 51). This reasoning encounters difficulties. The very intelligibility of occasionalism, a doctrine in which a third source (viz., God) produces both the objects with their states and our visual episodes simultaneously, is enough to show that we *can* have a true premise or accurate data (reliable visual states) while the conclusion or explanatory hypothesis is false (causation of the states by their objects). It might be replied that in those circumstances we wouldn't really be perceiving anything, our impressions to the contrary notwithstanding. That may be so. Indeed, its truth is important to my defense of the claim that (C) is a conceptual thesis. Still, it would not show, as it must to deflect the criticism, that occasionalism is false. If occasionalism were the case, we would nevertheless enjoy what we now call visual experiences. Our mistake would be only in thinking that they were visual perceptions. However, we would be correct in thinking that those things, whatever we named them, were reliable indicators of our empirical environment. This would not be to say that we could ever confirm their reliability by empirical means. Nevertheless, they would be reliable by inductive standards.

In fact, this is considerably less cut and dried than the foregoing suggests. Because the defense is no doubt intended as an inference to the best explanation, its deductive invalidity is understandable and, by itself, harmless. Moreover, the philosophical difficulties of occasionalism, preestablished harmony, and metaphysical schemes of that ilk, which depend on the activity of a mighty deity, may justify ruling them out as competing explanations. (Remember, once the defense is credited with the status of inference to the best explanation, it is not the mere possibility of God's activity that matters to the argument, but its plausibility.) Or one might simply adopt naturalism, thereby narrowing the criteria for acceptable alternatives. In any event, it is arguable that occasionalism and its kin are no more threats than general skepticism, and thus on those grounds alone are inadmissible given the scope of the explanation. I will not be going into the matter thoroughly enough to see if any of these manuevers work, but it is not perfectly clear as things stand that they don't. Even if the argument is impeccable, we needn't rely on it here. The CTP defended in these pages is not in the first instance the familiar epistemic doctrine. (This is not to deny that it has epistemic implications. See chapter 1. Indeed, whatever CTP's inherent character, it is difficult to see how it could escape having implications, if only conditional ones, for any number of other issues in philosophy. But as defended here, CTP isn't primarily a means of working one's way toward the external world from subjective experience.) Critics demand, and I agree, that we begin our inquiry with perceptions of ontological objects, events reportable by sentences of such forms as 'S sees *o*,' rather than inferring them from something more cognitively primitive. My primary focus is on the implications of ascribing episodes of seeing, not on finding ways to secure visual experience against the threat of skepticism. Given that, I needn't rely heavily on defenses of CTP, typical of indirect realism, that build in the general assumptions about justification. I may leave it to those more interested in pursuing the antiskeptical defense to show how, if at all, their reasoning can evade the disjunctivist's challenge.

Does this concession divide the issues too finely? For example, it has been held that the thought experiments of §II cannot be sharply separated from the nondisjunctivist position (as I have attempted to do). Each is predicated on a conception of what seeing is. Therefore, the judgments our thought experiments were designed to direct us to must rely on our conception of seeing as a means of informing ourselves about our environment, the very same conception that generates the Strawsonian argument just quoted (see Child 1992, p. 299). But this conclusion strikes me as overextended. There is no doubt a sense in which we would not have reached the verdicts we did in the thought experiments were it not for our current concept of vision and all that it implies. But it would be a mistake to suppose that there need be any conscious direction given by that (sketchy) notion in reaching our intuitive judgments. Whatever it is that enables us to grasp the concept of sight, it is only the assumption *that* we understand the words, not the account of *what* it is that we understand when we understand the words, which is the active ingredient in our ability to exercise intuitions in the thought experiments. Otherwise, we would need to possess the very account the intuitions are used to support as a condition of having the intuitions. That requirement is too strong even for the general run of those who hold that our particular bits of evidence are always shot through with theory.

Although the arguments of §§II–III may be the most prominent current defenses of (C), they do not exhaust those in its favor. In §§IV–V, I discuss two further considerations, more subtle perhaps, but no less potent in establishing this core principle of the causal theory.

IV

Various other perceptual idioms quite plainly carry causal implications, and their interaction with standard constructions makes a causal element irresistable. Consider an utterance of 'that horse looks dapple,' what we may call, as in chapter 2, a *de re* 'looks' locution. It is *de re* because on its only unstrained interpretation the subject, 'that horse,' falls outside the scope of the main verb. Of course, not all 'looks' locutions are visual or perceptual. For example, consider 'it looks as if the airlines will raise fares again.' Assuming we can isolate such specimens and concentrate exclusively on the many cases in which 'looks' reports the way things are visually for the subject, I find it difficult to know what it could be for something to look a certain way if it isn't, inter alia, *to cause it to be a certain way* to the subject. What else could it be for that horse to do this (that is, 'look dapple')— or for this to be done to that horse—other than that it be caused to look in that way? If there is a noncausal answer on offer, it has escaped general notice. As Jackson (1977) puts it, "If it should turn out that the orange played no causal role in producing the state I report by saying that the orange looks red to me, then it may be true that it was *as if* the orange looks red to me, or that I *believed* the orange looked red; but it cannot be true that the orange looked red to me" (p. 98).

It may be worth noting that the thought experiments used to support (C) provide, mutatis mutandis, an equally potent argument for the requirement that *o* be a cause of *o*'s looking some way to S. Thus, the pillar blocked by the mirror, Viola, and the blue cube cannot *look* any way to their respective subjects any more than those subjects can see them. There is at least as much an inducement to say in the revised cases that this is due to the absence of a causal link (of the right kind) between experiencer and object experienced.

If we must construe such looks as implying a causal relation of object to subject's visual episode, how can we avoid having such an element in *seeing*? As noted in chapter 2, §VIII, '*o* looks (or appears or seems) some way to S,' where this is a visual comment, implies 'S sees *o*.' That is, in the canonical formulation of the last chapter,

(Gr1) *o* looks some way to S → S sees *o*.

Doubts arose only about an implication in the opposite direction, to wit,

(Gr2) S sees *o* → *o* looks some way to S.

At this point, we might ask, assuming there are grounds for doubting (Gr2)—I will review them shortly—are the doubts transmitted to (Gr1)?

Occasionally, a causal condition is rejected, and (Gr1) with it, because it is part of a larger principle that is abandoned for reasons that do not, in fact, implicate the (Gr1) part. For example, Roderick Chisholm (1957), in one of his early attempts to define what he termed "the simplest of the non-propositional senses of 'perceive',," offered

(i) " 'S perceives *x*' means: *x* appears in some way to S" (p. 149).

Shortly before that, he gives another definition for the right-hand side of this formula:

(ii) " '*x* appears . . . to S' means that *x* causes S to sense . . ." (p. 143).

As in the foregoing, I use 'appears,' 'looks,' and 'seems' in their intended visual interpretations, interchangeably. Chisholm raises doubts about (ii), properly centering on its sufficiency. His exposition concentrates on the problem of object determination: how, out of the multitude of causal connections and conditions, do we select just the perceptual object? We encounter the problem in full regalia in chapter 8. However, in rejecting (ii) as a whole—which can be viewed as a variation of a composite of (Gr1) and (Gr2)—Chisholm gives no hint that '*x*'s causing S to sense. . .' will fail as a *necessary* condition for the truth or understanding of '*x* appears . . . to S.' Although he rejects (ii), this is not for reasons that would count against the part of it that now consumes our interest. Indeed, (if we can make sense of 'sense'), it seems that we have no choice but to accept that part. What could it be for *x* to look, appear, or seem some way to S if not, inter alia, for *x* or its state to cause such a condition in S? In lieu of alternative promising schemes, the necessity of the right-to-left implication seems to me wholly convincing. If the causing is a necessary condition of *de re* appearing and that appearance (for Chishom in (ii)) is a sufficient condition for seeing, then we have (Gr1). This sort of case supplies a useful object lesson, because some apparent rejections of (C) have been bogus. (C) is introduced as part of a single formula with distinguishable commitments, and is then abandoned for reasons directed solely to the formula's additional commitments.

We are still not out of the woods, however. It is not trustworthy (Gr1) but shady (Gr2) that supplies the direct defense of (C). It is the 'looks' locution of (Gr2) that imparts its causal element to seeing. Although in chapter 2, I accepted (Gr2) for the sake of argument, I also noted some problems. Blindsight was one; another might be nonrecognition of what one sees (or even its boundaries), as in the case of the patched tweed jacket; yet another could be subliminal perception (e.g., images flashed too quickly for conscious awareness, but which may nevertheless affect behavior), or 'near-threshold' vision (see Campion, Latto, and Smith 1983). Problem cases might even include 'seeing' an unnoticed clear, glass plate standing between oneself and the scene focused on (e.g., those covering instrument panels in automobiles). Thus, we aren't confident of being entitled to this principle, at least not without further justification. In fact, for the sake of argument, let's suppose (Gr2) is false for one or another of the reasons given. I now wish to persuade you that this concession supplies what may be an even stronger argument for (C). In those rare cases in which an object does not look some way to the perceiver, we have too little left on which to hang a claim that the object was seen if we *also* deny that it was a cause of the seeing.

Recall that we are still entitled to (Gr1), and it tells us that whenever the 'looks' locution in question is true, S does see. Indeed, in those cases the object looking some way not only is indistinguishable from seeing it, but it is difficult to tell what in addition the 'looks' locution conveys other than that this seeing is not a case of blindsight, sublminal perception, or so on. In those cases, the causal condition that attaches to the look attaches to seeing. Moreover, we can regard such cases as the norm; it seems plausible to suppose that if we include some instances in which the object doesn't look any way to the perceiver, they will be the exception.

Thus, the cases that tend to undermine (Gr2) are exceptional and borderline. (This is not to say that they are so for an understanding of the biological mechanisms underlying vision. But they are nevertheless problematic cases for exercising our concept of seeing.) Our remaining grounds for countinuing to count these as instances of seeing are severely limited. Causation by the object is one salient element we expect to find in seeing; the object looking a certain way is another. Ex hypothesi, the second of these is missing where (Gr2) is violated. If we nonetheless regard the cases as sight, we may be relying on such factors as S's subsequent behavior, orientation of her eyes, or her memory, each of which we believe can be explained only by supposing that S saw something on the occasion. Even setting aside that each of these factors may, when traced to its basis, lead us to a new reason for introducing (C), we are still left with too little to make intelligible the supposition that S saw something if *both* the expected look of the thing *and* the pervasive causal connection are absent. Whatever the subsequent behavior (or so on) of S, how is it possible to make it depend on S's perception of *o,* especially in the absence of *o*'s looking some way to S, if *o* did not effect S in some way? In such cases, we must find something other than the distinctive look to count these as cases of genuine seeing. If subsequent behavior, memory, or the orientation of S's eyes is to matter to our judgment, this can be so only because we are assuming the effects an object has on a perceiver.

To recapitulate, the way things look (the sorts of things reported by *de re* 'looks' constructions) is a normal ingredient of seeing those things, indeed is scarcely distinguishable from the seeing in those cases. But in those cases, the object's causation of the seeing is a conceptual factor. The only question, then, is what to do about causation in the other cases I have granted, those in which seeing occurs without the object looking some way to the subject. Once the causal factor has been acknowledged in normal cases, it becomes all the more difficult to maintain with any plausibility that it, along with the look, could be absent in the remaining cases.

V

Finally, (C) supplies a natural explanation for normal restrictions governing sight, to the effect that the perceiver and object be spatially related in such and such a way and that the medium separating them be transparent. To repeat, seeing amounts to more than the mere delivery of information, however accomplished, about visual characteristics. Thus, getting information about the visual features of a mango from a computer readout doesn't count as seeing the mango, or as seeing anything other than the computer readout. Seeing involves a point of view, a perspective, which (at least ordinarily) coincides with the location of the perceiver's eyes. Why should any such restriction enter our common considerations about whether anyone has seen something if we aren't presupposing that the object must have a *real connection* to the state of the subject? And what real connection could we have in mind that isn't a causal one? Of course, it's always possible to regard spatial restrictions as primitive—to maintain that nothing accounts for them. But though anything under the right circumstances may be taken as a stopping point in an inquiry, this is not the sort of thing with which it is sensible to supplant a causal explanation. Whatever the underlying reasons, location in space as such is not inherently explanatory. This is not to say that we cannot explain, say, why something was damaged because of where it was: for example, in the path of a tornado. But the relevance of its relational location in those sorts of cases depends on our understanding that some action took place at that location. (It is no accident that we are concerned with causal explanations as a class, but not with the class of spatial ones.) To impose this kind of locational restriction on perceptual objects without further explanation is arbitrary. The defense that all explanation must stop someplace is cold consolation. Spatial restrictions go begging for further explanation in ways that causal requirements do not. Moreover, whereas the causal relation suggests *how* visual perception comes about, I don't know of anyone who would claim as much for the spatial relation of object to perceiver.

Some philosophers (e.g., Goldman 1977; Tye 1982) contemplate the possibility of clairvoyant perception: say, one's visual experiences covarying with states of visible objects thousands of miles away. Assuming this is intelligible, visual contents would still have to bear the mark of being from a point of view and, moreover, change systematically when an opaque object interposes itself between that visual angle and the object. To bring the point home, ask yourself if there could be clairvoyant vision, say, of a table that wasn't a view of the table *from some angle or other* and *as if unobstructed*. The absence of those features would prevent the proposal from getting off the ground. In this, clairvoyant vision must resemble visualization. Thus, although the subject is deprived of an actual location in an unobstructed line of sight from the object, she requires a quasi-location—a place from which her point of view can be conceived. It appears that even for clairvoyant perception quasi-spatiality would need to be an element of the imagined scene. Of course, the situation is so bizarre that it is difficult to begin to specify the set of quasi-spatial coordinates. But I am not endorsing the intelligibility of clairvoyant vision, merely tracing the consequences of its acceptance.

It is useful to force ourselves to this limit if only to reveal the strong pull of the spatial restrictions. The case, if allowed, also discloses something novel about spatial restrictions. Various writers have recognized the need for a similar restriction (e.g., Geach 1957, p. 25) and attributed it to the fact that the subject's body (more particularly, her eyes) is (are) involved in so many of the implications that constitute a mastery of visual vocabulary. But even this seems to rest on a deeper requirement involving space, namely, that visual perception is always from a point of view (which, assuming the coherence of clairvoyant vision, may not coincide with the location of the viewer's body). This requirement alone is sufficient to establish what I have been calling the spatial restriction. Finally, if we concede this much, it is difficult to see how an explanation of quasi-spatiality will find (C) any more dispensable than we found it for ordinary vision.

None of this precludes the possibility that spatial and transparency restrictions can be incorporated into noncausal theories of seeing. In §VIII, I discuss a potential noncausalist reply along precisely those lines. Indeed, it is perfectly understandable that a noncausalist would want to include spatial and transparency restrictions as an alternative to explaining cases through an appeal to a condition like (C). But this implies only that noncausalist views are compatible with the restrictions, not that they account for them. In fact, on the noncausal view just mentioned, the spatial restriction seems so flagrantly ad hoc in the context that, rather than furthering its author's ends, it might be taken as an ancillary consideration on behalf of (C). This may be reinforced by my earlier remarks about the fact that a spatial relationship does not intrinsically explain how the events in perception would come about. Thus, by itself it is no substitute for causation. On the other hand, requirements that the object bear certain spatial and nonobstruction relations to the viewpoint of the subject are effortlessly integrated into a view containing our causal clause.

VI

What induces some to hold out against this battery of considerations? Objections can be classified under two heads: first, counterexamples to (C); second, competing noncausal accounts of perception. Actual proposals are not quite so neatly divided, but it is useful to collect them in this way. I will discuss prominent instances of both kinds of criticism.

Let's begin with the counterexamples, of which two seem to stand out. First, there is the seeing of perfectly dark things: a black hole in space, or a totally unlit room seen through an open doorway.[1] Since nothing, including light, leaves the scene to our eyes, how is the object a cause of our seeing? Next, there is the case, mentioned recently, of clairvoyant perception, the enjoying of visual episodes whose contents and their changes correlate with objects and their changes, say, three thousand miles away on earth. The bare possibility of such cases, it may be claimed, precludes reading (C) into the very nature of visual perception.

The suppositions implicit in such objections bring us perilously close to opening a full-scale inquiry into the nature of causation, a fascinating topic of truly gargantuan proportions. But we must resist the temptation to divert ourselves (in both senses) here. Suffice it to say that the examples, especially the first, depend on reading into the notion of causation a certain conception of mechanical working to which the causal clause doesn't commit us. In order to show that causation is still operating in the so-called counterexamples, it is sufficient that they not be exempted from certain kinds of continued counterfactual dependencies.[2] This need not commit one to a counterfactual as distinct from, say, a regularity *definition* of 'cause'. It merely registers a widely received view that, on any analysis, singular causal statements *support* counterfactuals. Let me elaborate, beginning with clair-voyant perception.

It is generally accepted that singular causal statements of the sort that A caused B support counterfactuals of the type 'If A hadn't occurred, B wouldn't have occurred.' There are well-known challenges to this, the most prominent be-ing the case of causal overdetermination. Another might be the case in which a powerful demon, though currently inactive, would have brought about the exact same (!) effect had not the normal causal chain run its course. (See David Lewis's Censor case, chapter 7.) Thus, we should claim at most that a causal statement supports a correlative counterfactual *in lieu of special explanations* such as the aforementioned. We may suppose that this still leaves us with a sufficient condi-tion, even if not a necessary one. That is, when the counterfactual is supported, we have a causal connection. But we are also faced with the fact that various counterfactuals hold for other than causal reasons. Fortunately, they belong to well-marked kinds. But they do prohibit us from concluding that, whenever a counterfactual holds, a causal connection is instantiated. The support of count-erfactuals is an insufficient (de facto) necessary condition for an unnecessary suf-ficient condition for causation, what John Mackie (1974) has dubbed an INUS condition.[3] INUS conditions can be excellent indicators of the presence of the phenomenon for which they are conditions. And, when a counterfactual holds that doesn't belong to any of the well-marked exceptions, it is just such a good indica-tion that we have a cause/effect relationship. Furthermore, it gives us a way to separate the question of whether natural causation takes place from that of the specific mechanisms various theories may impose, for one reason or another, on what they will count as causation. As I argue below, the appropriate counterfactu-als deflect the putative counterexamples.

Had it merely been the case that my momentary visual experience fit a con-figuration of (nonastronomical) objects three thousand miles away, it would be either unlikely or impossible (depending on how we are to view the need for special explanations) to maintain that I thereby saw those objects, even if we grant that the experience was otherwise "accurate." What is missing? At a minimum, we would want to be confident that there is a pattern of covariation between my current perceptual content and that configuration. As my point of view, or the objects, changed (at least in certain macroscopic ways), my contents should change accordingly. Moreover, this covariation must be supposed to be system-atic, not random. (This is satisfied when a 'special explanation' is needed for those cases in which the counterfactual fails. It may even be satisfied by less: say, by a statistically significant correlation with counterfactuals.) It is not mere coincidence that my visionlike experience is similar to the one I would have had were I situated at such and such a place with respect to just those things. We may be ignorant about how this works, for it seems to violate our expectations for a certain sort of mechanical palpability. Nevertheless, even a mystery about the principles of working can be overwhelmed by enough evidence that it does occur. And here systematic variation clinches the outcome as seeing rather than as visualization. Thus, although we can remain agnostic about the details of the dependence and still get on well enough using perceptual vocabulary, we cannot both maintain that the distant objects are seen and deny that our perception of them should covary with changes of their placement. That would be tantamount to admitting that the covariation is mere accident and would have taken place just as surely, all other things being equal, if the objects or positions hadn't been altered. We need at a minimum to presuppose that the experience 'tracks' the object, ceteris paribus.

Which counterfactuals are causal? Here are some specimens of the kinds I have in mind for our two would-be counterinstances:

> (α) If the chair had been moved three feet to the left, S would no longer have visually experienced (seen) the lamp in back of the room.
>
> If the bars had been magnetized, they would have appeared to S to repel or approach each other.
>
> If the door had been closed, S wouldn't have seen the unlit room.
>
> If the lens cap had been on the telescope, S wouldn't have seen the black hole.

Prima facie, nothing seems to separate these sorts of counterfactuals from those we would judge supported by a typical singular causal claim. Noncausal counterfactuals are illustrated by the following list:

> (β) If it had turned red, it would still have been colored.[4]
>
> Notwithstanding your noble intentions, had you taken the money, you would have been a thief.
>
> If the clouds had had greenish edges, that would have meant an impending tornado.
>
> If he had another spade, he would have won the hand.
>
> If he had tried to steal third base, he would have been out.

These by no means exhaust the counterfactuals that express noncausal dependence. But they are a fair sampling. Although occasionally—as in the last example—such counterfactuals imply causal relations of other sorts, none of (β) suggest anything like a causal interaction between the states of affairs expressed by the antecedents and those expressed by the consequents. Have the first set of counterfactuals any chance of being similarly understood? The characteristic conventional, semantic, or evidential relations, which would co-opt causal interpretations, don't materialize there. Nor do there seem to be yet other distinguishable kinds waiting in the wings. And it would be insufficient for the objector merely to note that *not all* counterfactual dependencies express causal connections between their antecedents and consequents and leave it at that. The first set of dependencies certainly appear to be causal; thus, in the absence of plausible suggestions to the contrary, it seems only reasonable to hold that a causal dependence underlies the need for covariation in the cases of the perfectly dark object and clairvoyant perception.

In the case of perfectly dark objects (separated now from a consideration of clairvoyant vision), the point about counterfactuals introduces a further difficulty for the objector. The problem the counterexample is meant to expose there is not just how a visual experience could be caused by something emitting no light, but how it could be dependent at all on what seems to be a mere lack. If dependency of any kind can be established here, causal dependency is as good a candidate as any others likely to be suggested. Thus, any form of systematic covariation that cannot be written off as a variety of convention or natural meaning should be equally baffling to the critic who objects to (C). However, it is clear that although the last two members of (α) are of neither of these types, we nevertheless have excellent reason to accept counterfactuals like them. Thus, it would appear that the case against a causal dependency made by the example is no stronger than its case against any counterfactual dependency (save for the restricted types), and the case for such counterfactual dependency, even if it is declared not to be causal, is as strong as such cases are likely to get.

VII

Our defense would be incomplete without a review of leading attempts to replace (C) with a noncausal account of the relation of object to visual episode. I devote this and the next section to examining two particular attempts, by Jaegwon Kim and Paul Snowdon, respectively, that are representative of the most prominent efforts. But I reverse the usual order of exposition, not to say medicine, by delivering the postmortem before showing that the patient is lifeless. I do this in the hope that this brief explanation will reveal more clearly what motivates these efforts and may even aid us in following the exposition.

Both attacks share the indirect realist assumption that the central task for a causal theory is to account for what we perceive from impoverished experiential data. This doesn't mean that they share the assumption that CTP invariably leads to sense-data (though they may), but rather that they accept the view that the outlook underlying CTP identifies what we strictly see with what we can be certain of or have unmediated knowledge of. (They may disagree among themselves about what degree of certainty is satisfactory. Still, each will hold that, for anyone

approaching perception in the manner of CTP, perceptual objects are to be characterized in terms of epistemic transparency.) This working principle is perhaps most
explicit in Descartes and Berkeley, but appears to underwrite the efforts of a broad
spectrum of philosophies of perception up to the present. Kim's critique doesn't
reject the assumption outright; rather, he argues that it is best achieved noncaus-
ally. Snowdon rejects CTP, because he rejects the assumption. On the question of
the assumption, I am with Snowdon. Readers may recall (chap. 2, p. 32) that the
first advantage claimed for direct as against indirect CTP was just that it abandoned this approach. As indicated earlier in the present chapter, §II, the evidence
for direct CTP doesn't require the assumption; indeed, it seems out of step with
the totality of the evidence for (C). Where does this leave us? First of all, if CTP
doesn't need the assumption, Snowdon's assault is easily deflected. Beyond that,
we will also find reason in the details of his substitute account to strengthen the
case for (C). Next, challenging the assumption is an indirect criticism of Kim's
account, because the disappearance of his grounds for rejecting CTP renders superfluous his noncausalist approach. Let us examine his view in greater detail.

Kim (1977) seeks to substitute what he calls *direct cognitive contact* (I hereafter omit 'direct') for causation. The negative side of Kim's argument is that perceiving is "among those [relations] Brentano and others have called 'intentional
relations' "(p. 106), that reference is an intentional relation in terms of which the
others can be explained, and reference (thus perception) can be elucidated non-
causally. Although Kim's views on reference are as much in need of defense as
his views on perception, I must avoid probing too deeply into the former if the
narrative is not to get excessively baroque. Nevertheless, as indicated below, I am
unable to escape noting one or two features of his treatment of reference. Let me
trace the outlines of his argument.

At times it seems as if the chief complaint against causation is that it cannot
explain intentionality (p. 606). But it seems that nothing about (C) requires that it
explain intentionality. We do require that seeing episodes involve objects, but for
(C) we need not decide anything more about the inherent, intentional character of
those objects. It is difficult to see how (C)'s failure to perform a task irrelevant to
its office and strength could impugn it. Kim writes, not unrelatedly, that "the
intentionality of intentional relations does not consist in some form of causal connection"(ibid.). Again, *consists in* may suggest a number of things, the most natural of which go beyond the issues for which (C) is invoked. However, he does
think of his view as at least rejecting (C) in favor of a preferred alternative, and
that is how I will take it.

The argument seems to be that for reference (whose account is assumed noncausal as well) we can fashion a complete account of perception that omits any
mention of causation. Let us see what he believes it is for a sentient being to
perceive an object. Since reference is made a condition of perception, I assume
that Kim is confining himself to language users, or humans, and is ignoring, say,
birds, sharks, and the like, who also perceive things. For example, what would it
be for a scallop to accept a statement or be in a position to refer? Kim writes that
"one natural answer . . . may be to say that this happens just when he accepts a
statement of the form '*a* is F' where '*a*' is a proper name referring to the object.

. . . [T]he basic idea is that when a person perceives an object he is in a position to refer to that object" (p. 609). Given our limited interests, I omit subsequent qualifications. Even with them, the formula leaves much to ponder. In the passage quoted, the first sentence introduces the notion of a *name* referring; in the next, the (distinct) notion of a *person* referring is employed. Furthermore, while, in the first sentence, perceiving implies that the referring has occurred, in the second, perceiving may take place when the person is "in a position to refer," without an implication that actual reference is needed. In this respect, the second sentence is not merely more guarded than the first, it is also more baffling. Suppose we ask rhetorically, "What accounts for a person's being in a position to refer other than that she perceives the object?" Kim seems to have his cart well out in front of his horse: perceiving is usually thought to explain a person's being in a position to refer rather than vice versa. (See Dretske 1977, p. 623.) Thus, one is put into a position to refer to something by having perceived it. The suspicion that this latter is really the connection Kim intends is borne out by the further details of the exposition: sometimes 'cognitive contact' is taken as a loose gloss of 'Russellian acquaintance', which, for Russell, is already an epistemically privileged brand of perception. At any rate, Kim's analysis depends on making good sense of the notion *cognitive contact,* so let us turn our attention to that.

The subject, if not the term, is introduced by Kim with the remark, "[t]o name an object you must be in some sort of *cognitive* touch with it"(1977, p. 614). The remark calls for both additional explanation and defense. Neither is easy to extract from the exposition, but I will try to assemble some clues.

Kim's explanation of cognitive contact is contained in his discussion of reference. There, and in remarks on the related topic of name bestowal, to elucidate the notions he uses phrases such as "epistemological contact" and "to 'pick out' or 'identify'." Each is crucially equivocal in the manner of 'cognitive contact'. Once again, Russellian acquaintance is invoked. This might be thought problematic enough as it occurs in Russell's writings, but it is even less helpful in its present employment, since Kim evinces no predilection for Russell's views about either the possible objects of acquaintance or the reasons for their eligibility. Rather than continuing to founder on a sea of indefiniteness, I will make a suggestion for a core condition, if not a full characterization, of cognitive contact. No doubt it needs refinement, but as far as it goes I think it captures the drift of Kim's remarks.

A relation between sentient subject S and object *o* is a kind of direct cognitive contact only if, if it obtains, S is noninferentially aware that (a) it does obtain, and (b) it obtains with *o,* rather than with anything else.

This, too, provokes queries. Must S be aware of *o* under any description whatsoever? If not, are there some privileged aspects (descriptions) under which S must be aware of *o?* These and other queries beset this sort of requirement; though anyone who, like Kim, needs some such condition must address them, I leave the condition as is for the present. It gives us enough purchase on what is intended to get on with the discussion.

What are Kim's reasons for supposing that each instance of perception (or reference or naming) requires cognitive contact? Other than the obvious, but insufficient, reason that because Kim rejects a causal condition, something else must account for the phenomenon, his support for the contention is not easy to discover. The following passage is as close as I can find to an explicit argument: "when we name an object, there must be some relation obtaining between us and the named object, and this relation must not obtain, within this very same act of naming, between us and some other object as well. If this happened we could not succeed in naming the object we intended to name; either we inadvertently named another object . . . or we didn't name anything at all" (pp. 614–15). The claim here is that, through naming, a unique relation with the nominatum is set up. But this is common ground for the causal and Kim's theories of reference. Nothing in it shows that the relation need be cognitive (viz., satisfy the formula I offered Kim). Have we an additional reason for supposing that the relation must be cognitive? Perhaps the phrase "inadevertently named another object" provides a clue. If the relation weren't cognitive, we might just name something other than what we had intended. Or, we might *not know* what we were naming.

If this is the gravamen of the charge, it is plain why the argument fails. It conflates one's referring to *x* with *knowing that* one is referring to *x*. Normally, a user of a name is not mistaken about what she is referring to, but what is normal is not thereby necessary. We would need yet another argument to rule out such mistakes, but none is forthcoming. Nor do I believe any argument to this effect would be cogent, for such mistakes, though perhaps rare, seem possible. My referential intention couldn't guarantee full disclosure. To illustrate, consider S, setting out to attach the name Φ to an object, in fact ϕ, directly in front of her. She has an intention we might characterize at a first pass as

S's intention to baptize the thing before her as Φ.

Normally, we have no reason to say more about S's intention, and we needn't suppose, because seldom pressed to do so, that the intention admits of further analysis or is ambiguous in any way. But in fact it subsumes (and can be elucidated in terms of) the following two redescriptions.

S's intention to give the name Φ to whatever may be in front of her.

S's intention to give the name Φ to what she takes to be in front of her.

Since what is in front of her may not be what she takes to be there, occasions will arise in which the latter two descriptions cannot be satisfied simultaneously. Imagine a pig, Porky, lying in a pram, swaddled in baby blankets, with a large floppy hat obscuring its face. S takes it for a particular baby, say, Portia. Portia was in the pram a few moments ago, so S may have every reason to believe that it is Portia she is still seeing. S then fully intentionally uses Φ to baptize what? Either baptism, of Porky or Portia, satisfies the first, less determinate intention, but since S believes of Portia that she is in the pram, only one of the latter two can be satisfied. Russell eludes this sort of problem by placing the stringent requirement of full disclosure on what one can be acquainted with. This leads to his philosophy of sensibilia. Kim displays no tendency to follow him down that well-trodden path. But he cannot have it both ways. If he avoids Russell's epistemic commitments, how can he demand full disclosure as a condition for what we are acquainted with?

This is not intended to show that we do not ordinarily know what we are referring to, naming, or seeing. Another philosopher might subscribe to a very exacting standard of knowledge that would preclude our knowing these things. But nothing said here commits *us* to it. The foregoing only shows that we are fallible, and this is consistent with having knowledge, on a host of nonskeptical conceptions of that notion.

Cognitive contact is a poor surrogate for a causal relation in other respects as well. In chapter 7 I take up the vexed issue of deviant causal chains: chains leading from would-be objects to subjects, but in ways that disqualify the visual episode from being a perception. The problem is thorny, but because causation often works in stages, lending itself to talk of causal *chains,* there is some hope of discovering a solution to this difficulty in a more detailed description of the stages through which the chain proceeds. Cognitive contact, on the other hand, focuses entirely on the terminus at which the perceiver is made aware of something. It is thereby ill equipped in this regard to distinguish samples in which the awareness is the outcome of an unproblematic chain from those in which it travels a wholly idiosyncratic route (say, in which God or the manipulator of the brain in the vat induces those states because the would-be object is in the right location). In cases of deviance to be examined later, in which there is a clear inclination to say that no perception has taken place, it is difficult to see why the subject shouldn't be allowed to have the requisite cognitive contact. And if so, why shouldn't Kim be committed to those cases being perceptions? Of course, cognitive contact may seem to violate our considered judgments in such cases only because the notion is not yet well enough understood. But thus far no reason has been given to fuel an expectation that further elaboration might overcome this defect.

Perhaps Kim's initial classification of theories is symptomatic of the conundrum just encountered. He divides them into satisfaction theories, causal theories, and hybrids of the two. Since he rejects the latter two, by his own classification he must be supposing a satisfaction theory that says, "roughly, that something is an object of perception just in case it satisfies a uniquely individuating description involved in a perceptual belief, or in case it is the unique object satisfying a set of existential beliefs" (p. 608). But, as I contended earlier, cases of veridical hallucination (e.g., the hallucinated brain) are instances of this, although the relevant cause (e.g., one's own brain) is not an object of perception. It might be replied that cognitive contact is missing here. But until that notion is spelled out in greater detail, and independently of causal connections, we can make nothing of the claim that these cases are not trouble for this application of cognitive contact.

At bottom, my quandary with cognitive contact—as well as other epistemic substitutes for causation—is that there are limited materials for making sense of it, and I have exhausted the most natural ones without success. As with *match,* we can employ resemblance (or, a first cousin here, accurate description), but, unlike the earlier employments of match, we cannot use causal connection. *Context*, too, may be of service, but it can help only with artificial restrictions that are in dire need of elaboration, and there is no assurance this can be supplied. One difficulty is that the context isn't always the immediately surrounding environment. Much depends on prior assumptions of the relevant thought or discourse. Even if we overlook this, context would not help to secure the aforementioned minimal interpretation of cognitive contact, which has to do more with the informational state of the subject than the location of the object. Without further explanation, there is little basis to expect that a unitary, coherent notion of context, ready to serve this purpose, awaits us.

Of course, much of Kim's case for cognitive contact proceeds *via negativa*. While acknowledging the need for a real connection between object and perceiver, he rejects causation because "we have trouble enough understanding what causation is, without involving it with other difficult puzzles and perplexities" (p. 620). Thus, a slot for cognitive contact is noted, and the unsuitability of the only alternative, causation, may even excuse some of the obscurity in Kim's substitute proposal. However, the sort of doubt raised about causation's bona fides is simply too weak to pose any threat to (C), for at least the following two reasons.

First, Kim has not attempted here (or elsewhere, to my knowledge) to show that there is no such thing as causation.[5] The misgivings about its philosophical employments don't extend to skepticism about causation itself. Rather, the concern appears to be that there are a number of fundamental open questions over the proper understanding of causation. But this alone would not render causation unfit for all analytic employment. A concept is not made illegitimate by being poorly understood, and the fact that its precise interpretation is a matter of ongoing dispute or that there are competing analyses still in the field does not prohibit it from helping to illuminate other matters through its conceptual connections to them.

Second, if causation is not chimerical, we cannot freely choose whether to accord it a role in perception. There may be some limited choice of tools with which to probe a given issue, and the use of certain concepts in a particular understanding of some notion does not preclude another equally good understanding of that notion that contains no explicit appeal to some of the concepts in the first set. But realism about the world demands of us that, by and large, the relevance of one concept to another be dictated by what we seek to understand, not by our preference for well-behaved solutions or our aversion to intellectual bogs. Indeed, I can use these results to turn the tables on Kim. Rather than excusing the obscurities of cognitive contact because of the supposed difficulties with causation, we can regard the problems besetting Kim's substitute notion as a further indication of the indispensability of causation. Despite familiar problems with its analysis, if we need a real connection here—an antecedent that Kim also seems to accept—we cannot scrap causation.

This is not to maintain that causation explains intentionality, whatever that might mean. (C) may require substantial supplementation from noncausal elements before we have anything approaching a plausible account of sight. But in the course of arguing that (C) does not supply this, Kim also denies that a causal connection sheds any light whatever on our problem. On this count, I hope the case has been satisfactorily made that neither in his objections nor in his substitute account has he given us any grounds for overthrowing the strong prima facie case causalists have built for (C).

VIII

A rather different purpose animates Paul Snowdon's effort to show that (C) is, at best, otiose in an analysis of perception. He traces CTP's strategy by focusing on what he calls L-states: states reportable by formulas such as 'It looks to . . . as if . . .'. Then he claims that the causalist's position rests on cases, like Grice's reflected pillar (my first example in §II), displaying the following combination of features:

  (i) S is in an L-state appropriate to seeing *o*,
  (ii) *o* is in S's environment,
  (iii) the L-state is not causally dependent on *o*, and
  (iv) *o* is not seen.

These are called U-cases, 'U' for unseen. We might notice that in at least one of my cases, that of Sir Andrew's nonseeing of Viola, (ii) doesn't hold. Viola is not in S's environment, though it would not matter if she were. More important, this way of setting up the causalist's case, though not outright mistaken, lends itself to a false impression by omitting something. Condition (iv) does not merely leave open the possibility that S sees nothing; undoubtedly, this is the first option it is meant to suggest. That construal lends itself to framing the issue, as mentioned earlier, as a confrontation between CTP and disjunctivism. But it is worth noting that in both Sir Andrew's case and in the one Snowdon cites, Grice's pillar, *something* is seen, though both (iii) and (iv) are satisfied. This difference may seem insignificant, for surely a main point of the examples is to show that the missing causal ingredient prevents only the expected perception. But the fact that these are not failures to see is of great moment if it is going to be assumed or argued that CTP is driven to subjective episodes (that which remains when the causal condition is subtracted). These cases have no such implication. To that extent, if they provide a justification for (C), the overall view is compatible with the putative alternative Snowdon presents below. Consequently, establishing disjunctivism will not in any way weaken the case for CTP. This is something to be kept in mind as we go through the stages to follow.

Snowdon allows that CTP produces an initially plausible "inference to the best explanation" for the U-cases: (iv) is true *because* (iii) is. But, he continues, (a) the existence of some U-cases does "not entail" that there are no cases in which (i)–(iii) are satisfied and S sees *o*, and (b) overlooked factors other than (iii) may explain (iv). The remainder of his essay is devoted to describing just such an overlooked factor, which will then demonstrate how we may have the sorts of cases hypothesized in (a).

For starters, consider the disjunctive truth condition for the construction 'It looks to S as if there is an F.' Sentences of that form are true when either of the following conditions is met:

> (I) there is something that looks to S to be F, in which case S is seeing something (though perhaps not an F);
> (II) it is to S as if there is something that looks to S to be F.

Satisfaction of (II) doesn't preclude satisfaction of (I), but neither does it require it. Each is separately sufficient to render the analysandum true.

The claim is that the first disjunct's satisfying 'It looks to S as if there is an F' takes us from the appropriate L-state to seeing. This is certainly true. Indeed, if (I) adds anything to 'S sees something,' it could only be that this is the ordinary case (not blindsight, near-threshold vision, subliminal perception, or the like). But that much is already implied by the analysandum. Since (I) makes no mention of a cause, we do not need condition (C) to explain why S sees. Moreover, by satisfying (II) alone for a possible L-state, "we can provide an alternative explanation for the status of U-cases" (p. 185). Even if the causal condition does not obtain, as in (iii), it is not this fact, but the fact that (I) does not obtain that explains why S does not see *o* in such cases.

For our limited inquiry, I assume this is an adequate analysis of seeing, ignoring the challenges of what I earlier cited (§IV) as exceptional and borderline cases. Still, readers may be baffled by the fact that the disjunctive account doesn't at first sight appear to be incompatible with a causal theory. To see why these accounts are viewed as competitors, it helps to remind ourselves, once again, of earlier remarks about the way CTP has been supposed to enter philosophical consciousness: as a way to go from subjective experience to the outside world. Among those who take the causal theory as a central topic of discussion, there seems to be some agreement about this. Thus, a contemporary anticausalist has written, "what an advocate of the [causal] theory has to show is . . . that the noisy and colourful things we see and hear do not merely act on our sense organs, but by doing so cause us to have sensory experiences which are correctly reported by saying something like 'It seems to me as if . . . ' " (Hyman 1992, p. 278). Whereas a sympathetic theorist notes CTP's commitment to claims including "there is a state of affairs reportable by a sentence of the form 'It looks to S as if . . . ' " (Child 1992, p. 298). Recently it has been claimed that the metaphysics of traditional realism "involves a causal theory of perception. On that theory, the objects we perceive give rise to chains of events that include stimulations of our sense organs, and finally to 'sense data' in our minds" (Putnam 1994, p. 467). The disjunctive conception, on the other hand, doesn't begin with a state that is more primitive than ordinary seeing: it begins with a state that under normal circumstances (viz., (I)) *is* seeing. Only an L-state's description as a subject for analysis, not its ontological status, is presumed neutral as between seeing and nonseeing. Thus, the choice between the accounts arises only if we lumber CTP with some of the working assumptions of its indirect proponents, assumptions I have already given independent reason to abandon.

Accordingly, suppose I charge that the disjunctivist has failed to capture the force of the first two thought experiments. The remainder of his argument, in direct reply, might unfold as follows. "Even if we accept the point of the first two thought experiments, this won't salvage CTP. Given the theory's foundationalist impetus, it would be pointless to try to retain its causal elements if we couldn't at the same time preserve their foundationalist corollaries (e.g., independently identifiable subjective states). Therefore, any cited causal elements unsupported by the rest of the doctrine could not be part of the concept of perception itself but must rather be part of the body of hard-won scientific, but contingent information about perception. (C) can be no more than an empirical truth." To this I have an obvious reply: once we distinguish the distinctively causalist concerns from their erstwhile epistemic packaging, it is relatively easy to see that this sort of reclassification is without merit.

The disjunctivist's case for viewing himself as being in competition with CTP has been exploded. But there remain questions about Snowdon's positive doctrine. For the sake of argument, I continue to regard the analysis of seeing as adequate, despite earlier challenges. But another question has to do with whether disjunctivism has in fact extricated itself from the causal element it officially repudiates. Earlier in the chapter, I mentioned various features of vision (e.g., spatial restrictions, 'looks' locutions) that any complete account should at least be able to accomodate, and which I argued are best explained by incorporating (C) as a condition of vision. What I will now try to demonstrate with regard to disjunctivism is that when we track down its implications, it either leads back to the causal elements or at a minimum leaves unresolved the sorts of problems they were introduced to address.

The first of the two systematic considerations in support of (C) shows why we cannot rest content with constructions of the form 'something looks (to S to be) F,' a close relative of Snowdon's formula for (I). Placing the term designating the object of perception, or its quantified counterpart, outside the scope of 'looks' cries out for a gloss, and the considerations presented in §IV indicate precisely why that is, in terms of the something's causing a state in S. Furthermore, I averred that these or similar thought experiments could be rephrased to make just as strong a case for '*o* looks some way to S.' If Snowdon wishes to deny that his first disjunct implies this, he owes his readers some account of the matter (and a different one from that for which causation has been invoked).

Toward the end of his essay, Snowdon mentions that a truth-conferring state of affairs—that is, (I)—"involves surrounding objects." This is reminiscent of the spatial restriction supported in §IV. But 'involves' is a rather slight fig leaf behind which to hide the enormity. It does not indicate any serious alternative to *o*'s being the cause of S, and it may be unworkable without the latter's inclusion. Of course, this is not something we can definitely decide in the absence of the author's further elucidation. But at a minimum it sets up the sort of spatial requirement without a hint of a rationale for its imposition. On what basis, for example, short of fiat, can it exclude clairvoyant perception? Certainly, we are entitled to a defense of this requirement. Until and unless the obligation to enlighten us is discharged, nothing in this scheme threatens (C).

We find similar impositions in like-minded critics. For example, Hyman

(1993) claims that "one does not possess the concept of vision until one can deduce the proposition that S cannot see x from the proposition that x is in darkness" (p. 76), and he hints at similar requirements regarding distance and occlusion. (As an aside, we might ask what people could have in mind when they say that rabbits see well in the dark.) Perhaps the author is convinced that these admit no causal accounting because they are already secured by deduction (of a yet-to-be-explained nonsyntactic variety). However, the relationship between sight, on the one hand, and darkness, distance, and occlusion, on the other, is not so wooden, since infrared scopes, magnification, and periscopes, respectively, overcome each of these obstacles. How do they do this? The anticausalist might say that they merely restore an opportunity that the obstacles had removed. But replies of this type seem to me, and I hope readers, paltry evasions: they pitch a characterization generally enough to guarantee that it shares features with all sorts of causal and noncausal overcoming. Since this sort of response would be available even were the causal element fully justified (compare x killing y characterized as x bearing some relation or other to y, rather than x causing y to die), it can be no more than a delaying tactic. When we ask *how* these instruments overcome the obstacles, the causal answer seems irresistable: they permit the object to causally influence our visual system, which it was earlier prevented from doing by prior circumstances.

Thus, when we look past the simplest part of the disjunctivist case, such as the satisfaction of a formula by either (I) or (II), we confront perceptual puzzles that originally drove others to (C) and CTP. The puzzles do not disappear just by taking care not to mention causation. Nor can the causal involvement needed be set aside as mere empirical accompaniment; it concerns the sort of information demanded of ordinary masters of the concept. It seems as if the present view, like the cognitive contact account preceding it, is only a further testament to the difficulty of trying to get along without (C).

IX

A review of any part of the vast scientific literature on the psychophysics, chemistry, or biology of vision exposes a rich and detailed understanding of visual processes. A study of the retina alone supplies a wealth of detail about photoreceptors (rods and cones) and how their stacked clusters of cells are permeated by light quanta. For example, we now know how the quanta alter the cyclic gaunosine monophosphate (cGMP), which would otherwise (viz., in a rest state) inhibit the transmission of quanta by keeping open pores and allowing the cells to fill with positively charged sodium ions. We also know how an intermediate protein, named 'transducin' by the team that isolated it (see Stryer 1987; cf. Baylor and Schnapf 1987), converts cGMP, allowing the quanta to hyperpolarize the cells. And, finally, we have detailed knowledge of the processes by means of which the ensuing electrical cascade proceeds through the retinal ganglion cells, maps relationships on the lateral geniculate nucleus, continues to the precortex, and so on.

None of this storehouse of scientific knowledge gets recorded as such in our very concept of vision. The reason isn't just that it is too esoteric for lay masters of the concept; but equally to incorporate it would come dangerously close to, perhaps cross over into, ruling out even the possibility of novel kinds of sighted individuals with unfamiliar forms of photoreceptors. We can't get too detailed in our descriptions if we want them to be part of a widely shared and flexible system of concepts. Nevertheless, even CTP's critics have generally consented that, as a matter of empirical fact, some causal processes or other are responsible for perception. Thus, the main differences between causalists and their critics haven't been over the truth of such claims as (C), but over its modal status: conceptual necessity or deeply entrenched contingency. But even so modest a summary must be qualified. Although I am unfamiliar with any dissenter who has straightforwardly denied that object causation in fact occurs in perception, some have held views that appear to be inconsistent with its occurrence.

To give an example, those who pursue the claim that the connection of 'veridical' perception to its object is quasi-logical and, thus, that its terms are not distinct existences, seem to want to reject the object causation of perception with their account of the modal status of its terms. This objection was rebutted in chapter 2, §VII.

Others may have concluded that, since seeing something is not a process and causation is, seeing cannot be caused (viz., the causal processes *associated with* seeing are not the causes *of* seeing). Thus, Ryle writes that "seeing a tree is not an effect—but this is not because it is an eccentric sort of state or process which happens to be exempt from causal explanations but because it is not a state or process at all" (1960, p. 102). (However, Ryle's target seems to be physiological reduction rather than causation per se. Very likely he isn't committed on reflection to the view that seems to be stated so baldly in the quoted remark. See pp. 101–9.) The argument (even interpreted narrowly) rests on a faulty assumption. Winning a race, to use Ryle's example, isn't a process but a product. Nevertheless, products involve processes, such as running the race, and can be effects of them. However, it is not my primary purpose to discuss the plausibility of such objections, but their nature. They form the only kinds of basis for challenging even the empirical truth of (C), namely, a philosophical (e.g., metaphysical, semantic) principle that would bar this sort of causal interaction. As for, say, Browne's theologically motivated repudiation of (C) in the epigraph, so far as I can tell, even he doesn't claim that Heaven's "more absolute piece of opticks" is intelligible by human standards.

For the rest, the disagreement with critics comes to whether causal information such as that encoded in (C) belongs to our concept of vision. Certainly, causalists will agree that any causal component belonging to that concept will not contain anything like the detailed information with which this section opened. Indeed, our concept can survive natural discoveries and changes of mind about virtually all the specific processes involved in visual perception. But the causalist will insist that intuitions that we share (highlighted in the thought experiments) and restrictions we impose on the relative locations of perceptual objects and uses of 'looks' locutions all attest to the operation of causal thinking in the way we wield our visual judgments. Against this, critics have tried to show, through the imposition of different sorts of requirements (viz., direct cognitive contact, the disjunctive conception), that the admitted facts of causation can signify no more to possessors of the concepts in question than empirical truths. My rejoinders were aimed to show that the objectors have not made out their case: rather than displacing the conceptual role of causation from vision, their schemes have the unintended consequence of highlighting the need for it.

That the causal link is part of the very mastery of our concept shows up not so much in the common use of 'cause' and its congeners in our workaday conversational reports about what we perceive (though it may show up there as well), but in our considered judgments about cases of perception—about when something is seen or prevented from being seen. That, I maintain, is a more solid indicator of the embedding of a causation here. I don't know what the data would look like if implementing a reformed educational scheme led, say, to abandoning the very notion of natural causation. In such a topsy-turvy world, I find it hard to conceive what to make of vocabulary that may sound similar to what we now use. But given that people—even skeptics in their off-duty hours—do now operate freely with such a general notion, I am claiming that it infects our perceptual judgments. As I argued earlier in this chapter, when anticausalists have sought to rest their explanations of perception and nonperception elsewhere, they have prematurely cut off the inquiry. Instead, they leave such explanations as 'because it is dark' and 'because it is close by' hanging in the air. Such reasons cannot stay aloft without support. As endpoints of a line of inquiry they merely raise a further puzzle about why they should matter at all to vision if they don't indicate some underlying connection between the object and the perceiver's enjoyment of that episode. It looks as if causation is at the very heart of our mastery of *perceiving,* not just a bit of generally accepted lore about a matter that might have turned out differently.

PART II

Perception, Cognition, and Belief

4

Visual Data

DUKE. If there be truth in sight, you are my daughter.
ORLANDO. If there be truth in sight, you are my Rosalind.
PHEBE. If sight and shape be true, why then my love adieu.

WILLIAM SHAKESPEARE, *As You Like It*

I

Let us turn our attention to the form of visual objects, a topic that also falls under that of the logical form of perception sentences. Many kinds of phrases following forms of the verbs 'to see' and 'to perceive' (and their translations) give syntactically acceptable objects, but two in particular concern us. The first is the propositional clause, an independently evaluable proposition, usually, though not invariably, preceded by 'that.' (Indeed, we can call this construction 'seeing that.') Its significance for us is to express something sentential in structure. Although I am employing the term of art 'proposition,' the classical importance of this form is that visual contents have the snytactical complexity of sentences. The other form is the direct-object noun phrase, coming closest to signifying what commonsensically might be regarded as a thing or entity (but including scenes, events, and items of unbounded complexity). We may call the first specification *propositional,* the second *objectual.*[1] An example of the former is "Daphne sees that a bird is in the nest"; an example of the latter, "Daphne sees a bird." As will soon be made manifest, these constructions permit different sorts of implications, thereby lending themselves to quite distinct philosophical theories about perception. There are a number of other constructions, some of which will also concern us to a lesser degree, but the central issues of this chapter play off the two just noted.

Is either construction more perspicuous or strictly accurate for reporting what we see? A number of concerns prompt this question. Indeed, the question is intrinsically so important to understanding perception that we needn't yoke it to a further issue to vindicate its study. If we regard these forms as our best, albeit rough, guides to the ways in which we carve up the world, when properly qualified it is a natural approach to determining the broad ontological types of what we can see: things or facts (about things). The question also bears on the place of causation in perception. Just as there is a live issue about the logical form of perception sentences, there is also one about the logical form of sentences that report singular causation. Certain types of specifications are suitable for causes and their effects (results), others may be eliminable by form alone. Both propositional (factative) and objectual (eventlike) clauses have been cited as promising candidates. As mentioned in the last chapter, I will not be delving deeply into questions concerning causation itself, although, as readers may have noticed from related discussions, the topic is hard to repress. I return to it briefly at the end of this chapter. In any case, it is essential to CTP, inter alia, that the ontological object of vision be of a form suitable to serve in a causal relation. To that limited extent, the logical form of causal sentences bears on the present inquiry.

There are sundry other ways in which one's choice of a preferred syntax for perception reports affects one's total views. Influence is often surreptitious. For example, occasionally philosophers assume, without further argument, that the topics of perception and perceptual knowledge are identical, or at least they treat the subject of perceptual knowledge as if they were treating perception itself. This both enhances and results from taking certain forms as perceptual data. Later, in §X–XI, after I have sorted out more basic issues, I give a few examples of the ways in which neglect of the logical-form question creates pitfalls for further projects or leads an argument astray. But the subtle effects are so pervasive that it is simply not feasible for us to try to do justice to the subject here. We aren't likely to find perceptual topics of serious concern in which the influence of the question of logical form hasn't been felt.

One of the chief interests in the logical-form question results from what I earlier called 'doxasticism': the doctrine that perception is itself a distinctive form of belief.[2] This is an influential view, if only a minority one.[3] Our present issue is joined because thinkers, doxasticists among them, frequently maintain that what is believed is, from the point of view of form alone, propositional. In other words, if proper reports of what is believed are given in propositional clauses, then the appropriate idiom for belief is 'believes that'. Accordingly, on doxasticism the 'perceives that' or 'sees that' idiom would also be most accurate for explicitly displaying the form of what we perceive or see. Of course, what we see is never literally a proposition, and, with the exception of the most avid readers, usually not a sentence. But on this account it would be what a proposition expresses: say, a fact or state of affairs. This conclusion about perception—I henceforth feel free to use 'seeing' interchangeably—is reinforced by another current view: seeing is inferential. If we infer to what we see, what we see must have a form suited to inferential relations, and it is a popular thought that this form is propositional or sentential. (Once again, I must enter a qualification, because what we see, if seeing is propositional, is never a proposition as such—except accidentally, if propositions are visible—but something factlike: say, a state of affairs.)

On some accounts, the objects of belief or inference need not have propositional form. Perhaps my belief that it is raining consists in nothing more than a set of behavioral dispositions, for example, to open my umbrella when I step outside. Nevertheless, there is ample reason to connect doxasticism to propositional seeing reports. This is partly due to the way doxasticism is standardly developed. The view that seeing is propositional has been a mainstay support of doxasticism; so much so, in fact, that it would be unthinkable to undertake a review of doxasticism that didn't examine the status of seeing that. Perhaps even more crucial, few have questioned that beliefs, when reportable, *can be* accurately reported propositionally. (The apparent exceptions, when not reportable at all—due either, say, to want of vocabulary, ineffability, or analogue pandemonium—aren't genuine counterexamples. They don't lead to the conclusion that some other form of expression is preferable.) *A fortiori,* those beliefs that are seeings must be accurately reportable propositionally (and without loss of content when translated from other forms). For such reasons, the most prominent and promising versions of doxasticism are those that comport best with a doctrine about propositional seeing described below.

I examine doxasticism in greater detail in the next chapter; my focus in this one is the supporting doctrine about the propositionality of seeing, a view we may call 'cognitivism' or 'the cognitive thesis.' Briefly, cognitivism is the view that the proper objects of seeing are propositional. It is defended by John Searle as the view that "all seeing is seeing *that,* whenever it is true to say that x sees y it must be true that x sees that such and such is the case."[4] Contrary to appearances, this way of stating cognitivism need not mark a confusion of seeing with its reports: rather, let us say it takes advantage of an analogy between familiar ways of reporting seeing and the units into which objects of sight may be articulated. The latter are divisible in roughly the way we tend to parse linguistic components of sentences, which, it is assumed, provide the structures of the propositions they may express. We needn't regard this as rock-bottom metaphysics. It is consistent with this approach to admit that we would not divide objects in this way were we not influenced by forms of expression. Nevertheless, we may use our current constructions, subject to correction, as rough guides into the metaphysical issue. Thinkers of all stripes haven't been shy about doing so. After all, where else could our inquiry begin if we didn't take seriously our current perceptual idioms? Using this newly minted terminology, Searle's contention can be restated as, "all seeing is propositional, whenever a statement of objectual seeing is true, a (correlative) propositional one is true."

Notice that it would distort Searle's obvious intent to couple his earlier remark with its inversion: "all seeing *that* is seeing." Cognitivists will want to claim that more is to be discovered in the propositional idiom. Nevertheless, we can distinguish two forms of cognitivism. In weak cognitivism—henceforth intended, unless otherwise indicated, by the simple title 'cognitivism'—the claim is that whenever a seeing (by a belief-forming creature) takes place, a full propositional report of it is available. Strong cognitivism adds that the propositional report is the best, most revealing, or canonical way to report a seeing (relative to whatever philosophical purposes generate the comparison). By and large, our discussion will concern only the former version, although the bias toward propositional seeing should always be kept in mind. However, the differences between the views will be narrowed when we examine further requirements for propositional reports. For not just any propositional report will do. To satisfy the cognitivist, the correct propositional report must attain a certain level of substantial content.

The view could use additional fleshing out. I plan to clarify it further only as needed to evaluate its basic claims. But for starters it will help to note the following.

First, although there is no reason why propositions shouldn't count as (nongrammatical) objects on some taxonomies, the foregoing distinction is meant to mark off a narrow sense in which objects are directly signified only by nonpropositional noun clauses. Thus, bricks, red bricks, falling red bricks, and red bricks with 'garde' painted on them in large white letters are all potential objects in this sense, but that a red brick has 'garde' painted on it is not.

Second, the simple distinction drawn above is not intended to exhaust visual idioms. For example, following elaboration of the current distinction, I will turn my attention briefly to another construction, 'S sees __ to be __,' which has intriguing homologies with both objectual and propositional seeing. Furthermore, there is a host of other notions, including seeing how, seeing which, seeing as and seeing why, whose introduction at this early stage would only complicate the exposition without profiting it. (Though later, I will need to compare the features of some of them to my initial prototypes.) Despite this, the simple contrast presented here is valuable in clearly framing the focal issues. To grab a useful label, we may call someone who holds that seeing is primarily objectual a noncognitivist. I do not directly defend that view, but I do offer reasons for rejecting cognitivism and, subsequently, doxasticism. To that modest extent, it might be said that noncognitivism, in the absence of yet-uncharted constructions, is credited with whatever plausibility attaches to sole survivorship.

Careful attention to Searle's formula also yields an adequacy condition for both cognitivism and doxasticism, one that is vague but nonetheless indispensable. Notice that Searle does not maintain merely that each objectual seeing implies some propositional seeing or other, but that each seeing *is* a seeing that. That difference seems to me to portend, above all, that a propositional-seeing translation should capture in its specification whatever would be contained in as canonical a formulation as one could obtain of the correlative objectual seeing. That is not yet very clear; perhaps the best way to understand this heavily qualified claim is to see what motivates it.

As explained more fully shortly, the objectual idiom tolerates a wide range of substitute specifications of its objects *salva veritate,* with little regard for whether the subject is actually in a position to describe the object that way. Not so for propositional seeing. A garden variety propositional construction dictates that its reports contain a feature we may characterize as the recognizability, under that description, of the visual content. Thus, many acceptable substitute descriptions for the objectual construction will lack propositional counterparts. It is unreasonable to demand of cognitivism that it be able to find some rephrasing of each objectual report, one which captures with an equally thick description what has been reported objectually. Thus, consider once again, in slightly modified form, Austin's famous example (1962, p. 98). Suppose someone reports that S saw a man being shaved in Oxford. We may also report, with regard to the same man, S saw a man born in Jerusalem. Both reports of this single sighting are permitted by objectual seeing, although S may be aware that the man was being shaved in

Oxford, but not aware that he was born in Jerusalem. We would be holding cognitivism to too high a standard to require that S be reportable, roughly, as having seen *that* a man was born in Jerusalem, or even *that* a man born in Jerusalem was being shaved. In the most naturally imagined cases, something on the order of "S saw that a man was being shaved in Oxford" would suffice. Despite this, there will be some objectual reports of what is seen, although they may not satisfy everything required for propositional reports, that do not violate *seeing that*'s restrictions on recognizability. For those descriptions, cognitivism requires that there be a propositional construction that captures just as much detail, or the identical detail, as does the corresponding objectual one. Not only is this required for strong cognitivism, but it seems suggested by any requirement that seeing simpliciter *be* seeing that.

The vagueness of the condition should not thwart all application. Of course, some differences between propositional and objectual reports stem from ineradicable differences in the kinds of noun clauses each admits. Let us adopt a policy of maximum tolerance here. (Short of altogether ignoring the facts. The propositional nature of a report carries with it both advantages, fastened onto by cognitivists, and disadvantages, presently elaborated, which are important to the dispute.) Nor do we possess any refined standard to measure 'thickness' of description. That notion remains fuzzy and intuitive. But there are clear cases in which a shift from one of these idioms to the other is made possible only by draining the original of all interesting content. To give an example, I report myself as seeing Nelson's Column. Any cognitivist proposal that could do no better than produce the propositional report "GV sees that something is something or other" fails to satisfy this condition. What better way could there be to discredit cognitivism than showing that in some cases it is capable only of such impoverished redescriptions of the visual information reported objectually? The absence of crisp standards doesn't weaken the demand for an adequacy condition that restricts propositional glosses to those that are not so woefully inadequate.

A similar requirement is in force for doxasticism. To achieve its typical claims, proponents must maintain that each instance of seeing something *is* a case of belief. This entails not only that seeing *o* implies believing something, but also that what is seen (when cast in its proper, usually propositional, form) is identical with what is believed. (For example, see Armstrong's formulation in note 3.) Thus, if the only relevant beliefs at hand contained drastically impoverished reports of what was seen (after compensating for the aforementioned differences) or a clearly distinct content (say, amounting to nonvisual presuppositions for seeing such things), this would count decisively against that version of doxasticism.

A certain artificiality attends this way of separating cognitivism and doxasticism. Although they are not identical theses—thereby subverting a host of writers who confuse them—they are more closely related than may at first appear. As presented more precisely below, a condition of propositional seeing (viz., recognizability) implies that the subject believes the content (= takes it as such), and, as recently stated, doxasticism requires that what is seen at least *can be* formulated propositionally without loss or addition of content. Nevertheless, treating them separately is justifiable. Although I have maintained that cognitivism implies doxasticism, doxasticism implies what seems to me only a very weak form of cognitivism. Doxasticists needn't insist on any primacy for the propositional form of reporting belief (say, if one holds the dispositional theory of belief mentioned earlier). Moreover, depending on which thesis is one's target, different though overlapping sets of considerations will be emphasized. Thus, cognitivists and their opponents stress considerations of form, whereas doxasticists and theirs stress the relations (or lack thereof) between perception and cognitive states or behavior. Because of this, the issues are more likely to be clarified if we don't hastily make a stew of these two positions. I rely on the subsequent exposition to vindicate me in this. Implicational relations between the views will be dealt with as they become relevant.

II

Consider the following. I am hovering high in a helicopter somewhere offshore, and I see on the otherwise deserted stretch of beach what the unwary might take for an oil slick. In fact, it is a beached whale. Thus,

(WO) GV sees a whale

is true, though it need not be true that

(WP) GV sees that it is a whale (or, that there is a whale).

Even if I had known that it was a whale at the time I saw it, (WP) wouldn't be true if I could not tell by the particular sighting that it was a whale. Suppose (WO) is true but (WP), for whatever reason, is false. I will refer to this combination throughout as the 'whale example.' It shows that we cannot assume in any simple fashion that seeing something is always a case of seeing that something, at least not if cognitivism amounts to the proposal that this happens by a content-preserving transformation of, or mere addition to, the object specification in true statements made with sentences of the form '[Subject] + see(s) + [Direct Object].' No doubt seeing, in either guise, is intentional in the minimal sense that it is a mental phenomenon directed at, about, or of something. The something is its intentional content. The foregoing point may then be restated by saying that we cannot always replace the intentional content of objectual seeing with a propositional one, at least not if this is to be accomplished straightforwardly by embellishing the former in the prescribed manner.

As embodied in 'see that' constructions, there are three salient features of propositional seeing to account for these and further difficulties.

(a) *success-verb status:* 'x sees that p' implies (the truth of) 'p.'
(b) *recognizability:* 'x sees that p' implies that x both experiences and takes what is seen in the way expressed by clause 'p.'
(c) *accuracy:* The way x takes what is seen is correct.

In the whale example, it is (WP)'s failure to satisfy (b) and (c), for which (WO) has no comparable requirements, that accounts for the difference of truth-value between the two. ((a) is not applicable to (WO) without further assumptions.)

Some readers may suppose that objectual seeing merely rebaptizes Dretske's (1969) nonepistemic perception, only now confined to sight. I have no wish to minimize the marked similarities, although I did not have Dretske's (or Warnock's or Kneale's) views in mind when contemplating the implications of the whale example. Anyone who finds the comparison helpful is welcome to it. I avoid it for a few reasons. In part, I am anxious to take a fresh look at the issue, without the baggage of whatever Dretske and his critics go on to say about nonepistemic perception. Part of that baggage consists of the labels 'epistemic' and 'nonepiste-mic' themselves, which encourage reading the issue indifferently as concerning cognitivism or doxasticism. But, in addition, Dretske subscribes to the principle that S nonepistemically sees D only if "D is visually differentiated from its imme-diate environment by S" (1969, p. 20), a principle about which it is possible, and wise, to remain uncommitted for present purposes. Moreover, Dretske qualifiedly supports a principle for nonepistemic seeing to the effect that if S sees X, and X is identical with Y, then S sees Y, the only problem cases involving the possibility of misleading, but not false, ascriptions resulting from ambiguities in the substi-tuted clauses. He allows, largely on this basis, that S may see a bunch of mole-cules; say, if a seen table is identical with such a collection. Once again, there is no need to take strong exception, but it is another tangential matter whose support would only distract us from the main issue here.[5] On that and a number of other minor points where Dretske's exposition either parts ways with mine or goes far-ther, it is unnecessary to ascribe to objectual seeing features other than those highlighted in the present comparison. With that warning, let us press on with the implications of the difficulty just raised.

The whale example poses a major challenge to cognitivism.[6] Can we salvage a more careful version of that thesis? One suggestion might go as follows: "If (WO) is true, although GV must be seeing that something, the something need not be identifiable in the same terms or even at the level of description in which (WO) is specified. A promising candidate for a propositional seeing report to capture this experience is a locution along the following lines:

(WP*) GV sees that there is something in front of him.

It should strike us immediately that this modification violates the adequacy condi-tion discussed at the end of §I. Rather than appealing to that condition outright, let us see how it naturally arises from pursuing the present line of inquiry.

For starters, the view adumbrated seems to rescue the cognitivist thesis from easy refutation by counterexample. But it exacts a heavy toll. The thesis now amounts to the weakened claim that whenever a subject sees, it sees that some-thing. Does this capture the thesis that all seeing *is* seeing that? Certainly it pro-vides no support for the view that what we see on each occasion is manifest in the correlative 'see-that' report. It thereby falls short of what seems to be cognitiv-ism's *Grundanschauung:* propositional seeing is the more fundamental notion—'*x* sees that p' discloses more about the nature of particular seeings than 'x sees y.' Even if we abandon this strong version of cognitivism, a minimally ambitious cognitivism will still require that the propositional form yield as much about what is actually experienced as a straightforward objectual form. (WP*) clearly fails that test. Although I was mistaken about the oil slick (which is what I would be inclined to say that I saw), that erroneous report occurred at a level of description far more detailed than that attained by anything in (WP*). I had to notice a good deal more to make the sort of mistake I did. Cognitivism's correlative see-that construction purports to supply a definite specification of what was (properly) seen. That task cannot be discharged by anything as etiolated as (WP*). Furthermore, it is significant that (WP*) does not enable us to distinguish one instance of seeing from any other on the basis of what is seen, whereas this is routinely achieved, say, for cases of seeing a whale and seeing a ship. Finally, nothing in cognitivism thus amended suggests a motive or grounds for initially adopting it. I suspect the view would never have been so eagerly embraced had its defenders not been able to assume that the propositional phrase gave as thick a description as the perceiver would be in a position to give with its corresponding direct-object clause.

If cognitivism has a direct response to this sort of a problem, it has escaped me. (Toward the end of §III, I discuss one effort to address the issue of the multifariousness of descriptions allowable for objectual constructions. However, that reply skirts the question of the subject's misidentifications.) But cognitivists do have something further to say on their behalf: they have additional, overwhelming positive reasons for their view. Those are confronted later. But I have yet to explore fully the terms in which the issue has been defined. Let us now turn to that matter.

III

As previously noted, the two idioms being contrasted do not exhaust those of interest. Let us look at another construction, 'S sees x to be F,' which has a foothold in each of the competing idioms. Much of the dispute seems to have centered around it. For convenience, let us call it 'the predicative construction (idiom)' and speak, with the same deference, of predicative seeing. Various writers, when considering analyses of simple seeing (or, mutatis mutandis, perceiving), prefer this idiom to either the objectual or propositional. Thus, instead of the clearly objectual "S sees a blue thing," Shoemaker (1975, p. 299) opts for "S sees something to be blue" as a candidate analysandum. And John Heil writes, "I shall consider only cases of simple 'direct' perception, cases, for example in which we should say that Lucy sees a lemon or Henry sees a cat. Such cases instantiate the schema: 'S sees x to be F' " (1983, p. 119).

We can fashion a view parallel to cognitivism from such instances, only about the predicative rather than the propositional construction. Let's call it 'property perception'. It would say that all seeing is predicative (or that all seeing is seeing of something that it is somehow). At a minimum, this view is committed to holding that a predicative report adequately captures what may at first seem at least as straightforwardly objectually reported. The one looming certainty is that advocates of property perception cannot simply ignore objectual reports. The worst that can be said about objectual seeing here, as opposed to certain other current idioms, is that it is insufficiently explicit. No one claims that it is off-target, that its reports fix on something other than what we seek to characterize. Thus, property perceptionists must show that a predicative construction can always replace some objectual one (though certainly not *every* objectual one). A potential advantage of the former for this task is that its constructions have both affinites to, and differences from, each of our other idioms. We should examine these at closer quarters. I begin with comparisons to objectual seeing.

Like objectual reports, predicative constructions allow room for S to misidentify what she sees. S may take the wind-tossed branches for a lurking figure, and this does not impair her having seen the branches blowing in the wind. Similarly, a report of the form 'S sees that *x* is F' allows room for her to misidentify *x*. There is also this important difference: however badly S mis-takes *x,* she must correctly take it for an F. This immediately goes beyond an objectual report for two reasons. First, it discloses a way in which things seemed to S, which, say, 'S sees a G' does not. Second, statements made with sentences of this form convey that S *correctly identified* something predicable of what she saw. If the report is true, although S may be mistaken about the particular thing that is F, she cannot have been mistaken about its being F (or an instance of an F).

With regard to the first point, it should not be supposed that I am relying on earlier doubts about the principle 'if S sees *o, o* looks somehow to S.' Let's accept it for the sake of argument. Even so, 'S sees *o*' discloses neither how *o* looked to S nor how S took *o*. But 'S sees *x* to be F' does disclose at least how S took *x,* if not how *x* looked to S. For this reason, if no other, Heil's remark that 'Lucy sees a lemon' instantiates the schema 'S sees *x* to be F' is mistaken. Lucy may not have taken the lemon to be a lemon, and it might not have looked like a lemon to her. (She may not even know what a lemon is, though this wouldn't prevent her from seeing one.)

The dissimilarity is only heightened by the second point above, for Lucy may have taken the lemon to be a cactus flower, in which case her misidentification is not captured by something of the form 'S sees *x* to be F.' There are many perceptible things the lemon is, thus many ways to report objectually what Lucy saw. But we can imagine a case in which none of those she is prepared to offer—and which is of comparable thickness (recall the adequacy condition, pp. 86–87)—can be captured by the predicative construction. The latter requires some correct predication on Lucy's part, and the characterizations she is prepared to offer (without going altogether bland) may all be incorrect. If, as I have suggested, the property-perception view needs to replace objectual reports without introducing any of the not strictly perceptual implications that the latter avoids, it fails. It is difficult to see how a set of predicative judgments, as currently understood, can be relied on to maintain the truth-conditions or contents of objectual reports.

As I have described property perception, it claims not only that its constructions are to be chosen in the study of vision, but that they can be used to report, without nonperceptual addition, just what is reported with the objectual construction. I have nothing to add to my earlier justification for imposing this condition. But it may be imagined that the view's defenders would regard the matter differently: that I have laid on them an undeserved burden. It is worth a brief remark to explain why this is not so.

What is displayed here as a conflict of explicit doctrines does not usually occur as such in the literature. It is more a matter of adopting one practice rather than another without much stage setting. Writers occasionally make passing remarks about other options, but there is seldom a sense of a field of carefully framed positions from among which one is to be chosen. However, insofar as the practice of property perception advocates can be summarized, it is the custom for them to begin with the most straightforward perceptual reporting, objectual, and then to slide into the predicative style without comment or to employ the two styles interchangeably. (The quote from Heil is one instance, another from Paul Churchland is given in §XI. Specimens abound. Those familiar with the literature can easily check for themselves that this is a fairly standard practice.) This indicates that, at a minimum, the advocates of property perception do not discern any major differences between the idioms. They certainly do not supply reasons, much less compelling ones, for not taking into account seeing as reported objectually. From the pervasiveness of this procedure, I can only conclude that such writers do not believe that the change from objectual to predicative idiom involves significant alterations.

Next, compare predicative with propositional seeing. In spite of some minor differences of syntax and scope, the predicative idiom's object clause is already propositional. But its propositional construal cannot be anemic. It has the vital implications for *being F* that separate propositional from objectual reports. Thus, once again, Heil: "What, then, must be the case in order for it to be true that S sees x to be F? First, of course, x must *be* F. Unless this condition is satisfied one has only a case of supposed or presumed perception. Given that x is F, however, it must be the case as well that S *believes* x to be F" (1983, p. 122). When confined to the predicate position alone, these are perfectly parallel to conditions (a) and (b), respectively, for propositional seeing. We may compare this with Shoemaker's proposal for an analysis of 'S sees something to be blue,' which includes a clause to the effect that S believes "that there is something blue before him."[7] The formula differs from that for propositional seeing only in that there is no implication that the term replacing 'x' describes how S took it. Of course, on this interpretation, predicative reports are wholly unsuited as terminological equivalents of objectual ones. The whale example shows as much. Quite emphatically, GV doesn't see that the thing (blob) before him is a whale, nor does he see that it is an oil spill (since it isn't). Were we allowed to assume cognitivism or doxasticism, we might be able to use either of them to mount an argument for the property perception view. But it is highly unlikely that things can be decided in that order; that is, the plausibility of cognitivism (or doxasticism) seems to rest on the choice of data, and thus on the idiom encapsulating it, rather than the choice of data and idiom resting on the strength of cognitivism.

This is not to say that adherents of the view being criticized are simply ignorant of differences among the various constructions. But attempts to overcome them have fallen sufficiently short of the mark to lead one to surmise that their full significance hasn't been grasped. Heil, for example, asks us to distinguish characterizations of a cognitive state's *content* and its *object*. As noted earlier, objects of sight can be redescribed in too many ways for any single subject to notice them under all permissible descriptions. It is unreasonable to demand of the doxasticist (or cognitivist) that she hold that the subject believe something about the object (or 'take' the object) under each of its possible descriptions. According to Heil, by reporting objectual seeings only under *contents* of which S was aware, and avoiding descriptions that have nothing to be said for them other than that they accurately describe the object, we can avoid the by-now-familiar difficulties. He writes, "I may see a burglar yet have no beliefs about burglars, only beliefs about a man dashing down the street. Here my perceiving is characterized not by reference to its content but simply by reference to its object" (1983, p. 120).

The solution works, if it does, only because it addresses a relatively mild problem. It misses the chief lesson of hard cases, such as the whale example. The man dashing down the street and the burglar are identical. Thus, my perception is still correctly described when I say, "I saw a man running down the street." Furthermore, the level at which I can offer the description doesn't appear to violate the adequacy condition on p. 86. Therefore, we can also generate a suitable belief that I have about a man. But the whale is not identical with an oil spill. In that case, not only do I lack total information, but my identification is downright mistaken. This is what I have taken to be revealing about objectual seeing. No description of the whale retaining roughly the same level of informativeness provides a basis for ascribing a propositional or predicative seeing to me. And if I try to describe the seeing in terms of its content (that is, as I am aware of it), I obtain not what I see but what I erroneously think I do.

Thus, it would appear, the predicative construction has nothing new to contribute to our examination of the objectual and propositional ones. It neither legitimately promotes the cause of cognitivism nor aids clarification. It is more flexible than propositional seeing because it introduces a referentially transparent slot and thus a place at which some error and ignorance can be accomodated. But it still requires just the sorts of implications that make propositional seeing an inadequate substitute for objectual seeing. I conclude that one is justified in sticking to the original dichotomy in the further examination of cognitivism and doxasticism.

IV

The broad influence of cognitivism is attested by the popularity of the term 'veridical' in evaluating perceptual episodes. Though usually not adopted tendentiously, the term seldom fails to introduce a bias in favor of a propositional idiom, and not without reason. Characteristically, a veridical perception is not only genuine, as opposed, say, to a hallucination or a dream, but is also a correct identification of what is seen. Consider, for example, what Searle says about veridicality: "[W]hat must be the case in the station wagon case in order that the experience be a veridical one? At least this much: the world must be as it visually seems to me that it is."[8] This gives the innocent appearance of explaining a neutral term of art. But, as its last clause indicates, veridicality incorporates requirements of propositional seeing, (b) and (c), which have no counterparts in objectual seeing. This is how the notion is customarily understood. On its interpretation nonveridicality lumps together miscellaneous flaws—say, misidentification and hallucination—and simply excludes from being a perception anything that has any one of them.[9] Nonveridical perception, thus understood, is nonperception. But in lieu of reasons to the contrary, the whale example would appear to force on us a distinction between *accurate* perception and perception *tout court*. Accuracy requires, over and above simple perception, that there be a correct identification by the perceiver, (c), and, if reporting is relevant here, that the episode be acknowledged by the subject in whatever terms are used to characterize it as a perception, (b). These certainly aren't conditions of objectual seeing. Clearly, a cosmos in which all genuine seeing is veridical has no room in it for the singularities of objectual seeing.

Cognitivists are obliged, moreover, not only to explain which of several potential propositional locutions correspond to a given objectual seeing, but also to disclose how their correlations are determined. Cognitivist writings rarely contain guidance on this. We should look into the issue, if only because on closer inspection the most natural choices aren't very appealing. Although Searle also fails to address the problem, we can illustrate how cognitivist practice tends to be haphazard by drawing general lessons from his attempts at paraphrase (which, although not systematic, are quite representative). The substance of his suggestion for translating

(1) I see a yellow station wagon

into a propositional seeing is

(2) I see that there is a yellow station wagon in front of me.

But it is unclear why we should prefer this to, say,

(3) I see that a station wagon is yellow.

Although it may be true that something with the structure of (2) is generally available, whereas (3) is possible only because (1) contains a compound noun, it is unclear why this should matter to the acceptability of a paraphrase. To what guidelines should we appeal? For example, is the likely or actual response of a queried perceiver relevant? If not, what does matter? These uncertainties are merely symptomatic. One might adopt a "multiple-drafts" model for paraphrase, analogous to the one recommended by Dennett for thought contents (1991, pp. 111–43). Or one might reject any general procedure; paraphrase is to be achieved on a case-by-case basis (as I do later with some putative counterexamples to the centrality of objectual seeing). Thus, these misgivings aren't likely to render the cognitivist speechless. But the choices seem so unmotivated and unpromising (in light of such snags as the whale example) that we are entitled to some rationale. Supposing paraphrase is a case-by-case matter, I have been unable to uncover a single detailed justification for a specimen.

Consider again paraphrase (2). It involves a supposition about the placement of objects of vision that, at the very least, goes unstated. If I saw the station wagon in a mirror, (2) would be false, and if I knew that I saw it in one, I would not be tempted to affirm (2), even if I would affirm (1). If I were on a planet whose dense atmosphere bent light rays in unaccustomed ways, I might be disinclined to affirm (2), but I might accept (1). (Kinaesthetic, vestibular, and tactile sensing might still yield the same notion of *being in front of me*.) Thus, the availability of paraphrases like (2) depends, inter alia, more on the medium through which ambient light normally travels than on elments more naturally associated with the concept of vision.

Moreover, (2)'s suitability depends not on the mere truth of (1), but on my inclination to report it as such. If I held the eccentric belief that creatures from the planet Celib disguised themselves as yellow station wagons, then though (1) may be true and nothing is wrong with my visual system, I do not *see that* there is a yellow station wagon in front of me. Of course, neither do I see that there are Celibates in front of me, though I may mistakenly believe otherwise.

Finally, perhaps only a few would be dismayed by the fact that the paraphrase of (1) into (2) or (3) immediately implies doxasticism—for conditions (b) and (c) of propositional seeing both require that I take what I see in a certain way, which in turn seems to imply a form of belief. Nevertheless, anyone, whatever her commitments, should be uncomfortable about this following merely from our paraphrasis routine. A cognitivist might try to avoid the commitment by holding that certain of the implications of our current 'see-that' idiom need revision. On such a view, the *seeing that* that is claimed to be basic will retain the critical element of being propositional, but it will no more imply that S takes the propositional object seen in the way described than does a correct report of objectual seeing. Although this is a possible view, no one to my knowledge has worked out its details. Thus, to the extent that this effortless route to doxasticism induces a bad intellectual conscience, it is advisable to avoid it.

V

The two most explicit, and succinct, arguments for cognitivism I am familiar with are found in Searle's *Intentionality* (1983). Unfortunately, they emphasize technical notions whose proper explanation would take us far afield. I will settle for a thumbnail sketch of those notions, exposing just enough of their detail to enable us to grapple with the arguments.

Recall Searle's version of cognitivism: "whenever it is true to say that x sees y it must be true that x sees that such and such is the case" (1983, p. 40). The first argument for it runs, "[t]he fact that visual experiences have propositional Intentional content is an immediate . . . consequence of the fact that they have conditions of satisfaction, for conditions of satisfaction are always that such and such is the case" (p. 41). A state or event is Intentional (distinguished by the author from intensional) if it is directed toward, is about, at, or of something. Presumably, it is a sufficient but not a necessary condition for being Intentional that the state (or event, hereafter understood) have conditions of satisfaction. Such conditions are invariably propositional, and all Intentional states *with propositional contents* have conditions of satisfaction. For instance, conditions of satisfaction for belief are the truth conditions of what is believed.

Let us look again at the foregoing argument. We may ignore the potential for confusing the content/object distinction in talk of 'Intentional contents'. Nevertheless, we have not been told just what the relation of an Intentional content is to the sort of content we express when we answer the question "What did S see?" (call the latter 'visual content'), and we have not been told just what it is about the propositionality of satisfaction conditions that makes their correlative Intentional contents themselves propositional.

Readers may be surprised by these remarks because the answers seem so obvious from the drift of this exposition: Intentional content *just is* the relevant visual content (and answers questions of the form "What did S see?"), and the propositional content of conditions of satisfaction just is or provides the Intentional content. Of course, the Intentional contents mentioned in Searle's remark are contents of "visual experiences," not of seeings. But his cognitivist thesis, for whose support the argument of the passage is introduced, is about seeing, not about visual experience. Given that the remark is an argument for cognitivism, the distinction—should there be one—between visual experience and seeing must be negligible in the cases in which the visual experience does not occur without a seeing. That is, the move from visual experience to sight does not require modification of content. Thus, in cases of seeing, propositional conditions of satisfaction *are* or supply the visual content. Unfortunately, thus understood the argument fails miserably. I proceed to explain.

To begin with, specifications of conditions of satisfaction that are then read back into Intentional content threaten to violate the recognizability condition, (b), for propositional seeing. As Searle himself admits, more must be included in the conditions of satisfaction for see-that reports than the subject is likely to *take* as seen, or even to take as having obtained. For example, compare conditions of satisfaction for my seeing that a station wagon is in front of me with those for my believing it. My belief is true if a station wagon is in front of me, but my visual experience may not be a seeing, although this condition is met. I may be veridically hallucinating. Recall the neural scientist's blue-cube experiment of chapter 3. The causal connection between object and experience, (C), is necessary for sight, although there isn't a comparable condition for belief. Searle cites this as a reason why *a station wagon's being in front of me* is only a partial condition of satisfaction. The completed condition may be summarized as

I have a visual experience (that there is a station wagon in front of me and that the station wagon in front of me is causing in an appropriate way this visual experience).

When Searle writes, "when I see a car I have an experience, part of whose content is that it is caused by a car" (1983, p. 73), the content he has in mind is clearly Intentional.

If we count everything going into the conditions of satisfaction as part of the specification of *what* someone 'sees that', then she cannot see that such and such if she is ignorant or mistaken about the role of causation in seeing. Something has gone awry with this line of argument. I may see a station wagon in front of me although I hold that an emanation from my eyes, rather than the ontological object, is causally responsible for it. Or perhaps I am an epigone of Malebranche and hold that when I see a car it is because God simultaneously causes both the car to be in front of me and my experience, no causal connection subsisting between those two effects of God's activity. No doubt, I wouldn't be seeing were either account true. But my erroneously accepting such accounts, or no account, shouldn't be held against my seeing a car or seeing that a car is in front of me. Otherwise, of two subjects having similar experiences caused in similar ways, one of which harbored such a false notion, only the other would see the car, though the only relevant difference between them was in their metaphysics. It is difficult to believe that this can make so fundamental a difference to one's ability to see.

The sensible alternative is to avoid reading just any old thing from the specifications of conditions of satisfaction into the Intentional content of visual states. Searle (1991, pp. 183–84, 228) later says as much. But this deprives him of the reason I earlier gave him for insisting that seeing be propositional. Let us look at the problem from a slightly different angle. First we have cognitivism. Next, this is supported by the view that Intentional contents are propositional, which is itself finally supported by the view that seeing has propositional conditions of satisfaction. But we are not finished. Cognitivism would appear to be a consequence only if Intentional content were the same as visual content. How else could the form of the first dictate the form of the second? Searle seems to rely on the fact that the Intentional content, by way of conditions for satisfaction, contains various elements that add up to a proposition. But bearing in mind that visual content as such, when accurate, reports what S sees—not what she recognizes, what she thinks she sees, the conditions for her seeing it, or anything else—it is difficult to discover any warrant for inserting that information into visual content.

Cognitivism demands that visual content be displayable in reports of propositional seeing. But the only reports of propositional seeing we are familiar with contain a recognizability condition. Perhaps Searle has in mind something other than our familiar propositional idiom. That would have two significant drawbacks. First, we can no longer understand his original and straightforward statement of cognitivism, that "whenever . . . . x sees y it must be true that x sees that such and such is the case"; that depended on construing these phrases in our accustomed way. Thus, we lose whatever basis we had for apprehending, without special explanation, the claim's intended force. Second, as I mentioned earlier, no one to my knowledge has worked out the details of this novel idiom. Thus, we do not know enough about this option to see what the claim (and contrast) amounts to on the novel construction, or even to know that it is a coherent alternative to the older form of expression.

If one attempts to avoid this by denying that the propositionality of conditions of satisfaction make Intentional contents propositional simply by being imported en bloc into the latter, then we are owed a further account of how the former brings about the latter. Nothing remotely promising seems on the horizon. On the other hand, if it is said that Intentional contents, though propositional, are not to be identified with what I have been calling 'visual contents' (= what gets reported in reports of what one sees), then not only do we now have a new and mysterious relation between sorts of contents, but it is no longer clear what this information about the forms of conditions of satisfaction and Intentional contents has to do with the cognitivist thesis.

Abandoning the argument for cognitivism restores some flexibility to Searle's account of satisfaction conditions. We might supply the missing ingredient by saying that the conditions of satisfaction consist of a specification of what is seen plus what he calls 'the psychological mode' (e.g., seeing, believing, wishing, remembering). The specification 'a car in front of me' may disclose which thing is the cause of the experience, but it is the specification of the mode as sight— rather than, say, as belief—that determines that there is a particular causal element. It is now plain why elements of a state's conditions of satisfaction need not figure in their psychological realization: they fill out the psychological mode instead. We need not endorse the analysis. But, given Searle's starting point, this is a natural direction for the account to take. It would also show why the inference pattern from "Φ belongs to the conditions of satisfaction for Σ" to "Φ belongs to the Intentional content of Σ" will not work. The psychological mode need not be part of the content of that mode. That, in turn, undermines the first argument for cognitivism.

Once this is untangled it is easier to see how objectual seeing might have conditions of satisfaction, including a causal component, without collapsing into propositional sight. Daphne sees a car. A rough approximation to a sufficient set of conditions for this might be as follows.

Daphne has a visual experience caused (in the appropriate way [10]) by a car.

Propositional contents fashioned only from these materials may include ingredients that are irrelevant to reports of what she saw. For reasons just mentioned, she need not have seen *that* a car caused her experience. And it is precisely because objectual seeing has nothing comparable to features (b) and (c) of propositional seeing that we may omit clauses for them, which are designed solely to interject those features and are included in Searle's earlier statement of roughly the same conditions of satisfaction. (Searle's conditions are given in the first person, an unfortunate twist that, as demonstrated soon (p. 101), further confounds the matter at hand.)

Nothing in these objections challenges the view that conditions of satisfaction are propositional. If true, the view appears to be unaffected by the forms of visual contents. Conditions of satisfaction form a species of requirement or rule, and we would not expect that sort of thing to be specified other than either propositionally or in a form from which a propositional clause is easily recoverable. But it is difficult to see why we need any direct connection between a condition for something to take place and the forms that must be displayed in reporting what took place on that condition. An analogy may bring out the oddity of the demand that there be this connection. A condition for kicking a football is *that a football exists,* which is propositional and, speaking loosely, represents a state of affairs. But it does not follow that, when I kick a football, I kick a state of affairs or that what I kick is propositional in form. The nonIntentionality of kicking shouldn't distract us. The parallel is so striking in all other relevant respects that it should compel us to wonder why, if the inference works in one case, it should not work in the other.

VI

The argument just rejected relies directly on conditions of satisfaction. It introduces Intentional content only for those properties that are supposed to be derivable from satisfaction conditions. But the relationship between conditions of satisfaction and Intentional content, on the one hand, and that between such conditions and sight or visual experience, on the other, are more vexed than Searle's direct approach suggests. Let us look more closely at this.

Visual experiences are Intentional just by being *of* something. But Searle claims they are Intentional only because they have conditions of satisfaction "in exactly the same sense that beliefs and desires do" (1983, p. 39). Various Intentional states (e.g., adoration, hate) don't have satisfaction conditions, so having conditions of satisfaction (at least of a certain sort) cannot be a necessary condition of Intentionality. At most, having conditions of satisfaction is sufficient for Intentionality. But is every state or event that has conditions of satisfaction Intentional? We might make the answer affirmative by definition, but doing so would gloss over important differences in the range of cases. For example, speech acts have conditions of satisfaction, but it is unclear that they are Intentional.[11] Certainly statements, a class of speech acts, seem to lack one prominent feature of Intentionality: their truth conditions do not have to be framed in just the way the utterer would have taken them (viz., as their 'experienced aspect' is made manifest). Moreover, there are a number of decidedly nonIntentional phenomena (in the technical sense being employed), such as killing, inventing, expediting, and being later than, to which are attached requirements suspiciously like conditions of satisfaction. If we choose to call them such, then having conditions of satisfaction is not sufficient for Intentionality. On the other hand, if we choose to make satisfaction conditions sufficient for Intentionality, how can we know that the satisfactionlike conditions that appear to underlie visual experience really are such without determining in some other way that visual experiences are Intentional? If we need to repair to another method for detecting Intentionality, that would render problematic Searle's argument from conditions of satisfaction to the Intentionality of visual experience.

We may conclude that Intentionality plays no essential role in Searle's argument. Rather, the latter rests on conditions of satisfaction. This makes it all the more urgent to discover whether visual experiences (and thereby seeings) have conditions of satisfaction. The answer is not as obvious as it may at first seem. The one reason given for saying that visual experiences have conditions of satisfaction is contained in an analogy drawn with belief and its elaboration in the following passage: "In both the cases of belief and visual experience I might be *wrong* about what states of affairs actually exist in the real world. Perhaps I am having a hallucination. . . . But notice that in each case what counts as a *mistake,* whether a hallucination or false belief, is already determined by the Intentional state . . . in question" (1983, p. 39, emphases added). A belief may be true or false, correct or incorrect; this is determined by the truth (correctness) of what is believed. But how does a hallucination render its experience 'wrong' or 'mistaken'? *I* may be wrong in *taking* the experience for an actual sighting, but qua experience it has yet to be shown that hallucinating involves taking. This detail wrecks the comparison with belief. The culprit disguising these crucial differences seems to be a conflation of two conceptions of visual experience. It also lends bogus authority to the view that because visual experiences have conditions of satisfaction, they must have propositional contents. Here are the details.

First, there is a psychological notion of visual experience that we may call 'phenomenal experience'. It is this sort of visual experience, having an independent mental status, that Searle has in mind when he writes, "the claim that there are visual experiences goes beyond the claim that perception has Intentionality" and that perception is "realized in conscious mental events" (1983, p. 45). Remarks such as the following seem geared toward this sort of notion: "It is a bit difficult to know how one would argue for the existence of perceptual experiences to someone who denied their existence. It would be a bit like arguing for the existence of pains: if their existence is not obvious already, no philosophical argument could convince one" (1983, p. 44). But merely taken as a phenomenal component of perception, how can visual experience be either correct or mistaken? Phenomenal experience *sans phrase* is no more *a taking such and such to be the case* than is having a pain. On this conception, the comparison with belief cannot be sustained.

The second construal of 'visual experience' may be obtained by, as it were, strictly analytic means: by subtracting the implication that makes 'see that' a success verb. Thus, Searle remarks, "If I see the table what is left over if I subtract the table? . . . [W]hat is left over in the case of visual perception is a visual experience" (1983, p. 87). (Bear in mind, "see the table" must undergo Searle's cognitivist treatment before subtraction.) This conception may be useful for stating conditions of satisfaction should we wish to speak of visual episodes while remaining neutral about the success implications of our idiom. Shoemaker (1970) solved a similar problem for the success verb 'remember' by introducing quasi-remembering and quasi-memory. Quasi-memory is like memory save that '*x* quasi-remembers that *p*' does not entail '*p*.' In the same spirit, we may introduce quasi-seeing for this kind of visual experience. '*x* quasi-sees that *p*' does not entail '*p*.' In other prominent respects, quasi-seeing is like *sees that*. In particular, since seeing that is a form of taking such and such to be the case, so is quasi-seeing. Let us overlook recent doubts I raised about the procedure. Nevertheless, it will come as no surprise that this treatment violates ground rules of the current debate.

First, we have been given no reason to conclude that quasi-seeing is identical with phenomenal experience. It is only the common title 'Intentionality' that binds the two notions, and we have seen how weak a basis that is. Second, by modeling quasi-seeing on propositional seeing, it assumes rather than establishes that seeing has conditions of satisfaction. As an argument for cognitivism, it's too flagrantly question-begging to escape even the casual reader.

VII

Searle offers a second argument for cognitivism: "[T]he verb 'see' takes spatial modifiers that under natural interpretation require us to postulate an entire proposition as the content of visual experience. When I say, for example, 'I see a station wagon *in front of me*', I don't normally just mean that I see a station wagon that *also happens to be* in front of me but rather I *see that* there is a station wagon in front of me" (1983, p. 41).

Let us begin with the supporting example in the second sentence. One should be immediately struck by the fact that our willingness to go along with the interpretation has nothing to do with this being a case of seeing, but with its being a *first-person* report of the seeing. But, although being in the first person is vital to the conclusion, it shows precisely why the conclusion doesn't support cognitivism. No doubt, if I am in a position *to say* the first of these things, I shall be in a position *to say* the second. Thus, if I am able to say

(4) I see a station wagon in front of me,

I am normally—say, if I don't suspect foul play—willing to gloss this with

(5) I see that there is a station wagon in front of me.

But suppose someone else says of me

(6) GV sees a station wagon in front of him.

We forfeit the earlier inducement to infer its parallel to (5),

(7) GV sees that there is a station wagon in front of him.

It is because I am in a position to say (4), not because (4) or (6) happens to be true of me, that we glide so effortlessly to the 'see that' construction.

The supporting example fails, but what of the main argument (contained in the first sentence of the quoted passage)? Searle had stated earlier that desire always takes a propositional content despite grammatical appearances to the contrary. His reasoning was that specifications of desire contents take temporal modifiers that cannot be construed as modifying the state of desire itself. One may desire something at a given time, where this cannot be understood as expressing that the desire occurs at that time, but only that the current desire be fulfilled at that time. To account for such modifications, he concluded that we must introduce propositional contents for desires. Whatever the merits of that reasoning about desire, it cannot be extended automatically to the spatial modifiers of seeing. *Some* spatial modification does attach to the seeing itself, as in

(8) GV sees, in front of him (or, from the balcony), a station wagon.

for (8) to be true, GV needn't be aware that the station wagon is in front of him (or that he is on a balcony). Consequently, the fact that 'see' takes spatial modifiers does not lead to the cognitivist consequences, whatever we think of Searle's argument about desire and time.

Reflecting once again on the two arguments for cognitivism, it is curious that nothing in them so much as addresses the difficulty produced by the earlier whale example. Recall that its point is that I see something that I misidentify. What *seeing that* can I be assigned? Where '*p*' is a propositional clause that expresses a correct identification of what I see, as distinct from the description I would offer, I do not see that *p*, for (b), recognizability, is absent from my experience. Nor can we specify what I *see that* in the inaccurate terms that would satisfy (b), for that violates both conditions (a) and (c) of propositional seeing. The foregoing arguments for the cognitivist thesis imply that there must somehow be a correlative propositional seeing, but they neglect to show so much as that this is even possible.

At the risk of wielding the proverbial thermonuclear flyswatter, I cannot overemphasize the importance of cognitivism's failure even to come to grips with such commonplace phenomena as the whale example. This is not to say that there isn't an explanation for this neglect. For example, current discussions of perception are rooted in earlier ones dominated by a subjectivist slant. A cardinal presupposition of such approaches was that there is available a neutral, basic language to express precisely the content of our experiences, and its vocabulary could be used accurately to describe our experience even if we chose to expose ourselves to error by venturing descriptions that go beyond its limits. Thus, theorists of this camp would be confident that there is a perfectly adequate way for me to describe what is in fact a whale without erroneously attributing notions to the perceiver. Such views no longer dominate philosophical thinking. But one thing a study of past disputes teaches us is that when a view is no longer prevalent or at the forefront of concern, presuppositions accepted as too platitudinous to reopen during (and largely because of) the view's ascendancy may still remain embedded in philosophical consciousness, Perhaps this helps to explain a tendency to overlook the sort of problem the whale example raises. Even so, such an explanation does nothing to reduce the impact of the case or to diminish its threat to cognitivism.

VIII

Earlier, pp. 89–90, I deemed inadequate a potential cognitivist ploy of supplying at least a minimally descriptive propositional report corresponding to each instance of objectual seeing. But I did not question the assumption that such a minimal description was available in each case. Let's do so now. Imagine that an experimental subject is aware that she has been given a perception-altering drug. We may initially suppose she sees a table and identifies it as a table. But since she does not know whether her visual experience is a drug-induced hallucination or a genuine sighting, she declines *to take it* for either.[12] What does she see *that?*

A potential answer might start by trying to separate the implication of the table's *identification* from that of its *existence*. Perhaps the formula 'S sees that the experience is of a table' (rather than, say, an aardvark) will work. But even this, granting for the sake of argument that it fends off the immediate objection, is ultimately futile. For now, we can drop another assumption I made: that S takes her experience as tablelike. Let us suppose S misidentifies what she is experiencing as an unfamiliar animal. The success condition of propositional seeing, (a), prevents our saying of S that she sees that it (either the furniture or the experiential content) is other than tabular. Perhaps our subject sees only that this is an experience of something. But have we said anything more than that S realizes that she is having a visual experience?

As we will see, the doxasticist might retort that S must have at least a suppressed inclination to believe that this is, say, an animal (See Pitcher 1971, pp. 92–93). Indeed, the fact that doxasticism and cognitivism haven't been clearly distinguished in the past may induce some readers to believe that a standard doxastic handling of these sorts of cases solves the present problem. But whatever relief that maneuvre may afford doxasticism (and I will argue that it is not much), it is cold consolation for the cognitivist. The latter must maintain not that there is a belief (or an inclination toward one) in the offing, but that there is a 'see that' sentence that accurately and completely reports what S sees. Given requirements (a), (b), and (c), the cognitivist is hard-pressed to produce such a sentence. Given the further requirement that the propositional content not be less informative than the normal level of perceptual reporting, the task becomes even more daunting. The only path I see open to the cognitivist is to propose a revised propositional idiom, whose reporting omits one or more of propositional reporting's current commitments, (a)–(c). But, once again, there don't seem to be serious proposals of this sort at hand, and I haven't any reason to believe that they stand much chance of success. In robbing propositional seeing of implications central to its current semantic force, it is difficult to see what there remains for such an idiom to convey.

IX

The demise of the cognitivist thesis has left an explanatory vacuum. What are the connections between objectual and propositional seeing? Perhaps neither is conceptually prior to the other. In this section I venture the following three claims, though the reasons I can produce here are no doubt too sketchy to pretend to definitive treatment. First, the converse of Searle's claim—that all seeing that is really objectual seeing—is equally unacceptable. Briefly, this is because 'see-that' constructions report more than what is strictly visual in cases in which reports of objectual seeing do not. Thus, we could not expect to capture the former by the latter without remainder. This consideration also leads to the next claims. Second, *visual* 'see-that' reports involve in their analyses clauses that specify objectual seeings. In an important way, this shows that the latter are the more distinctively visual construction. Third, following trivially, given that objectual seeing has this station, it is the member of this pair deserving greater interest in philosophical treatments of vision.

The argument for these claims starts from the fact that 'see that' is not an exclusively visual idiom at all. It is now perhaps a commonplace in discussions like this that nonperceivers, or even the blind, can *see that* Carruthers murdered Colonel Hargaves, Daphne's mood has improved, one shouldn't play the downstairs piano after midnight, the economy has taken a downturn, the Cold War is over, or the filter should be changed every six months. But it is less often appreciated that we have a choice between at least the following two attitudes toward this data.

(i) 'See that' has (at least) two senses or uses, only one of which is strictly visual. Discussion of the cognitivist thesis must begin by isolating the visual sense/use and employing it exclusively in our inquiry. The foregoing examples can then be dismissed. They don't bear on the visual sense.

(ii) 'See that' is used in precisely the same sense in visual cases as it is in the foregoing examples. And its wide range of application is a clue to its invariant features in both contexts, as well as to the fact that it is not used primarily to report visual perceptions.

For whatever reason, the explanation in (i) seems to have gained general acceptance. Thus, although it has been noted that the 'see-that' idiom occurs in a wide range of cases—many of which have little or no connection with the visual perception of what is reported—not much has been made of this. But of our two options, (i) is conspicuously less attractive. Despite the primitive state of our current understanding of polysemy, on the crude tests we are accustomed to employ, little evidence for two senses of 'see that' has emerged. The simple fact that 'see that' can be used either visually or nonvisually is insufficient to plausibly ground such a distinction. I admit to being mystified about why this evident gap in the defense of (i) has not been more prominent in discussions. In both visual and nonvisual contexts, 'see that' retains its salient implications: (a) through (c). If we choose (ii) to explain these constancies, we can exploit the wide range of cases in which 'see that' is appropriate as an indication of what it *always* expresses: accurate recognition. We might then venture the promising suggestion that this element is so fundamental to what the idiom conveys that it is understandable why its use is warranted even in cases in which the visual component is totally absent. No doubt, all of this needs refinement. But in it we may discern the lineaments of an explanation of nonvisual occurrences that avoids the embarrassment of having to admit that, although we are confronted with different senses of 'see that' (for which there is also a dearth of persuasive evidence), those senses are intimately related by the commonality of their most salient implications.

On the other hand, with the exception of one sort of case, which, I will argue presently, can be explained without damage, 'S sees *o*' is above all a visual idiom.[13] In such cases as those of the drunk seeing pink rats or the patient seeing spots before her eyes, the construction marks a visual experience if not a perception. A troublesome case, at least superficially, is that of prophetic utterances, such as 'I see a world without war.' But here I believe we encounter a metaphor: an extension from vision to visualization, adopted just because it associates the latter with the former.

If these were the only tough cases, we would not have to worry about a systematic extension of the objectual construction beyond instances of vision, visual experience, or visualization. Not so for 'S sees that *p*,' which has standing uses broader than the visual. Unfortunately there are also nonvisual examples of the objectual idiom that may appear at first less tractable to my claim, to wit, 'I see the point of his remark' or 'I see his problem.' I believe we have well-motivated grounds for paraphrasing these into other idioms, including the propositional. But the case is a delicate one, for we don't just want to be high-handed in offering options never scouted for a cognitivist defense of (i). Thus, let me develop the case for paraphrasing in three stages.

First, it is important to bear in mind that '*x* sees *y*' and '*x* sees that *p*' are not intended to exhaust our resources for reporting visual detections, but only to provide an interesting contrast with which to probe a specific issue. A number of potential visual idioms, including 'see what' ('who,' 'when,' 'where'), 'see if,' and 'see how,' have not been treated. Thus, for starters, we are not confined to considering only these two constructions. Others that may overlap with those I have spotlighted cannot be placed off limits to our deliberations.

Next, although I have used the superficial grammatical form of 'see [+ direct object]' or 'see that' as a basis for collecting instances, it was never intended to be more than a rule of thumb for sorting our two types of cases. Nothing is sacrosanct about this exact phrasing. To give a trivial example, were I to say 'S sees the ship is docking,' this would have to be counted as a propositional construction despite the absence of the normal connective 'that' between the verb and the propositional clause. Ultimately, there is no recipe enabling us to avoid making case-by-case decisions based upon the particulars of each case.

This leads directly into the last point: the objections to cognitivism were not intended to rule out well-motivated rephrasings into other idioms in individual cases. They were designed to show that the cognitivist hasn't justified the method of wholesale analysis she needs, and considerations like the whale example deliver a potent prima facie case against her being able to do so. Perhaps for a host of individual cases, a report of a seeing in the direct-object idiom can be glossed by a propositional idiom. Despite this, the fact that instances must be decided case by case is itself a renunciation of cognitivism. If the latter view were correct, there would be a general argument showing in advance that for each objectual seeing some propositional paraphrase or other will be available.

Fortified by these points, we can set out to discover whether our troublesome examples merit rephrasals that show that they are not embarrassing instances of the objectual idiom after all. We don't need to seek very far, for a brief consideration of what such utterances would purport to convey makes it plausible to claim that they may be taken as unguarded versions of 'see what' reports: 'I see what the point of his remark is' and 'I see what his problem is.' Slightly more ambitiously, but in the same vein, we might say that they are incomplete interrogative transforms of 'see that' forms, which—could they be finished—would report 'I see that the point of his remark is __' or 'I see that his problem is __.' There is also some reason to think of these propositional reports as alluding to an answer to a 'what' question: 'What is the point of his remark?' 'What is his problem?' thereby connecting the two proposals. However, it is sufficient for my purposes if 'see what' provides an acceptable gloss on these particular examples. In addition to a grasp of the particular idiom, which makes this proposal appealing, there are more-or-less-generic considerations supporting an understanding of this type. For one thing, both examples incorporate an element of recognition—which (I have noted) objectual seeing as a rule omits—that accounts for its compatibility with ignorance or mistake, as in the whale example. The suggestion is strengthened by the fact that no content or force seems lost (or added) if we retranscribe the originals as 'I *understand* the point of his remark' and 'I *recognize* his problem.' Of course, I must be careful here, since the same might be claimed for some 'see-that' constructions, and there this fact was used to reject the central role of that idiom. But unlike that case, my two sentences do not exemplify a standard or regular use of the objectual idiom, but seem rather specialized and to occupy that unruly semantic penumbra where one can no longer clearly distinguish the literal from the figurative. Furthermore, it is quite clear that any use of 'see' that implies the recognition condition, (b), could not be just a special case of the objectual construction. That implication is foreign to the construction as such. On the other hand, it suggests that the sentences belong with propositional rather than objectual seeing. On the whole, it appears safest to regard such reports as 'I see his point of view' as synecdoche in which 'what . . . is' is deleted but recoverable (in much the way that 'that' is recoverable from 'I see the ship is docking').

My third claim, that objectual seeing is the more distinctive of the two visual conceptions, emerges directly from this contrast. The propositional idiom is suited more generally to detection. It just happens that visual detection is a prominent variety; thus, usual instances of this idiom will be used to report visual detection. Objectual seeing, on the other hand, is more intimately tied to reporting nothing extraneous to vision.

The earlier contrast also supplies my first claim: propositional seeing cannot be reduced to objectual seeing. The former always contains an element of accurate recognition not strictly found in the latter (or in visual experience), and thus the latter is unable to account for this element in its constructions. Just because '*x* sees *y*' reports nothing more than a visual perception (when it does report one) it is, once again, the more distinctively visual of the two styles of expressing apprehension. We cannot exclude the bare possibility that neither construction is a perfectly precise way of reporting such occurrences or that what is needed is another, hitherto-uncataloged idiom, which may include an element of recognition. Let us view this possibility as a challenge to a neocognitivist: flesh out the details and explain, in the process, why thus far the language community does not seem to have sensed the need for it in its everyday practice of reporting visual episodes.

(If a current idiom other than those canvassed were more distinctively visual, it would be puzzling why it hasn't appeared elsewhere in the literature to challenge our other candidates. Here I assume there is none, pending, of course, its unlikely presentation by a more thorough microglot.)

My second claim, which only serves to increase the burden on our already staggered mythical cognitivist, is that visual 'see-that' reports require clauses that specify an objectual seeing in their analyses. Because 'see-that' reports are not invariably visual, when they are, a method is needed in their analyses to indicate that the content taken has been visually generated. That is, we must be able to mark off visual from nonvisual takings, either of which may have been present in a given case of x seeing that p. To achieve this, 'x sees that p' must be analyzed, inter alia, with a clause of the form 'x sees y' (see Jackson 1977, chap. 7, esp. p. 164). This seems unavoidable. How else might one flag the visual element in relevant occurrences of 'see that'? Of course, we cannot assume that any particular formulation of an analysis is the only acceptable one; alternative formulations always seem to be in the offing. But I cannot conceive how any analysis that did not explicitly mention objectual seeing could avoid implying or presupposing such a clause, for it will need a way to mark off the strictly visual. Consequently, whatever the further details of the analysis of 'x sees that p,' when the propositional seeing is appropriately visual, it is committed to a clause that reports or presupposes an objectual seeing. This is one natural way of expressing a thesis that tends in a direction away from cognitivism. That is, it shows that propositional seeing relies for its full understanding on objectual seeing.

It might be asked, what philosophical progress has been made by settling this matter? Earlier I mentioned that one's choice of perceptual idiom may strongly influence both the approach one takes to the issues and the results one is likely to obtain. The subject is a large one, unsuspectedly seeping into crevices in our theorizing about perception. For the remainder of this chapter, I try to supply a few illustrations of this broader significance.

X

Throughout much of this century, it was often considered sufficient for a treatment of perception to start with perceptual *judgings*. Moreover, these were not judgments of the sort 'Daphne sees a car' but, presumably, a subject's judgments that purport to give only the content of her own perceptual experience, such as 'There is a pen on the desk.' Explicit justifications for this procedure were rare. Essays, treatises, lectures, and so forth, simply commenced with the unstated supposition that this was a legitimate way to approach standard philosophical problems of perception. (This may have been abetted by the widely disseminated attitude that philosophical conundrums were at bottom all problems of language.) Whatever its explanation, in light of my earlier discussion, it can be seen how that practice prepares the way for theorists to substitute discussions of perceptual knowledge for those of perception. For example, A. J. Ayer does not hesitate to read "the content of my present visual experience" as saying no more than "my [visual] judgment" (Ayer 1973, p. 81). Given properly rigorous standards for knowledge, this is no doubt an added encouragement to sense-datum theories.

How does this preconception get embroiled with the distinction I have been at pains to expound? Let me take Ayer's most notorious argument for sense-data in two steps. In the first, he announces that ordinary perceptual judgments carry implications that "go beyond" what we are entitled to claim that we perceive on a "strict acccount." Put otherwise, the vocabulary in which we describe the ordinary objects of perceptual judgments already commits us to an object's having a status and constancy not discoverable in our particular experiences of it. We cannot refer to objects other than, say, as persisting solids, belonging to kinds that have parts and qualities not all of which can ever be visually transparent to the subject at once. The first step may seem innocent enough, but the next one seals our fate. We arrive at an accurate description of what appears in perceptual experience by, as Strawson (1979, p. 43) puts it, cutting out "that heavy load of commitment to propositions about" independently existing objects. Both steps make it plain that this is a question of trimming the description to what we *know* that we see—that is, to what we are entitled to say we *recognize* without incurring a certain epistemic risk—which is then identified with what we see-in-all-strictness. No doubt, the perceptual idiom that supports such descriptions is propositional, or at least predicative (that is, quasi-propositional). Of my two focal constructions, only the propositional contains a recognition requirement, and indeed a requirement to recognize the object accurately. Had the argument started from objectual seeing, neither stage would have proceeded smoothly. Let me elaborate.

Regarding the first step (that visual judgment reports more than vision can disclose about the object), for objectual seeing there is little basis for the presumption that first-person judgments about what is perceived must be careful, or minimally venturesome, to be (in the strictest way) true. That aside, let me consider the matter from the vantage of objectual seeing. On that idiom, the fact that what I do see 'goes beyond' *what I am entitled to claim that I see* doesn't appear to be relevant. Ignoring conversational implicatures (e.g., of first-person present-tense reporting and informational expediency), objectual reports of what S sees bear no fruitful implicational relations to what S knows she sees. We can report what S sees in just about any way we think the visible object is describable.[14] Consider the whale example, or someone saying 'She saw the hat Daphne's uncle bought in Singapore.' Staying with the perspective of objectual seeing, my hand is still not forced when I turn to the second stage: elimination of the commitment to independently existing objects. Such excisions concern not what I see, but my *knowledge* of what I see. Whatever the ensuing account of objects of perception, taking the logic of objectual seeing as our starting point deprives us of a basis for reasoning as follows: "Whenever the perceiver's knowledge about, or acquaintance with, an ordinary object of perception might be enhanced, there must be a more scrupulously described object of a (stricter) experience, knowledge of which cannot be similarly enhanced."

Nothing in these objections should be construed as ruling out the thesis that whenever S sees something, S *takes* something to be the case. Doubts about that thesis were raised earlier. But the present objections do not rest on them. Where objectual seeing is focal, how the subject takes the scene is not a determinant of what is actually seen. However S mis-takes an *x*, it is still an *x* that S will be seeing. Thus, although what one sees and what one knows that one sees usually overlap, they don't come to the same thing.

Again, my critique quite deliberately neglects a familiar approach to perception in this century, earlier identified via the special case of indirect realism. On the neglected account, we begin not with seeing, as it were, but with *visual experience,* the primordial soup out of which visual perception emerges. Continuing, a visual experiencing has its own object. The event is a sort of embryonic seeing, perhaps called 'sensing'. But it is invariably arrived at by taking what we know we see for what we see. On the other hand, on the same account, what we vulgarly regard as seeing is more like what we would pretheoretically think of as surmising. Although this is a common picture for certain traditional approaches, it is much more difficult (perhaps impossible) to marshal compelling arguments for it once we abandon perceptual *judging* as our starting point. Our task should be to go back and ask (not a little rhetorically) how the standard argument gathers any momentum without taking for granted features that perceptual judging doesn't share with the objectual construction.

This is not intended to suggest that the earlier approach accounts wholly for the popular impulse toward treatments of perception via perceptual judgment. That would be a caricature. But neither should we overlook the role that the concern with risk-free apprehension has had in making it seem natural to substitute 'perceptual judgment' for 'what we perceive' as a way to gain entrance into our topic.

The bias I have sought to expose requires only the weaker version of cognitivism (p. 85). That is, it is sufficient for this approach if propositional seeing *is just as good as* objectual seeing for collecting perceptual data, even if it is no better. But, since a sine qua non of the approach's success requires that it ignore the actual logic of objectual reporting for purposes of data collection, it must be supposed, at a minimum, that the deliverances of objectual seeing can be fully squared with the formal features of propositional constructions, a supposition vigorously attacked throughout this chapter. In fact, we are more likely to discover adherents of the approach who suppose that the data of objectual reporting is secondary, of less vital concern than that of propositional reporting. But even the present approach does presuppose, at a minimum, that (concerning form alone) for any occasion a propositional report adequately captures what has gone on perceptually. That is sufficient to illustrate the significance of the cognitivism issue for this one.

XI

Let us briefly consider the question of the penetration of observation by theory. Suppose we ask whether we unavoidably read into our descriptions of perceptual objects our various current theoretical commitments, commitments that are clearly nonperceptual.[15] This (cluster of) issue(s) is doubtlessly no less complex than cognitivism itself, and it should be possible to arrive at various conclusions about it quite apart from commitments with regard to cognitivism. Not much is to be gained by raising it here as a side issue. Nevertheless, theoretical penetration is of some concern to both cognitivism and doxasticism, and certain discussions of it again illustrate how an incautious commandeering of an idiom as data can make or break an argument for a conclusion about it. I choose as my setting a scenario that Paul Churchland (1979) takes to illustrate the massive theoretical penetration of what we see.

We are to imagine a race of creatures whose eyes are sensitive to the middle-range temperatures of spatial objects. Churchland argues that such creatures might *see* hot objects where we would see only white ones. He writes of his creatures, "As they see it, the visually perceivable world consists not of middle-sized and variously coloured material objects, but rather of middle-sized and variously *heated* material objects. That is, they perceive hot objects *as* hot (warm, cold) they can visually perceive *that* they are hot (warm, cold)" (1979, p. 9).[16] He concludes that they see heat just as we, so to speak, see white. Basically, the whole of the argument for this is contained in the quoted passage. The remainder of the exposition relevant to the argument surveys potential objections and responds to them. The main thrust of Churchland's subsequent defense is that the objections manifest nothing more than a parochial outlook about visual qualities or meaning.

Two aspects of the passage from Churchland should command our attention:

(i) the contention that we are entitled to claim that the creatures see temperature *because* what they see is a function of temperature;
(ii) the ease with which the chosen idioms—that they perceive (see) an object *as* hot, or *that* an object is hot—are used to report the desired results.

(i) is explored in greater detail in my discussion of object determination (chap. 8). Here I note only that Churchland employs a less subtle version of a principle rejected there: roughly, that if what one perceives is a function of X, then one perceives X. No doubt, what we perceive is a (partial) function of a number of things, including the state of our perceptual organs and the ambient light, but we don't perceive our sense organs while using them save under special circumstances (and perhaps never perceive the ambient light). We needn't consider that further here. But there is another interpretation of the claim in (i), more directly related to (ii), which I should say something about.

Perhaps Churchland isn't ultimately concerned with our current notion of perception (and thus with the fact that, on that notion, we don't perceive whatever our perception may be a partial function of). He might just be enjoining us to call 'sight' whatever concept preserves this evidentially useful relation. The real claim then would be that, if the operation of our perceptual faculties is sensitive to such and such, allowing us to infer that such and such, an improved concept permits us to say that we perceive such and such.

This type of reform does not engage issues with which we are immediately concerned. But it suggests a justificatory role for (ii). Even a recommendation for rational reform should have a foothold in current conceptions. Unadorned suggestions are cheap; programs that lay claim to serious attention subsist on the improvements they offer to currently flawed notions. This in turn demands, at a minimum, that the reformer accurately assess the current conceptions that, ex hypothesi, are to be discarded. 'Improvement' is a relative notion: from something to something else. A program that rests on a distorted notion of current practice is a nonstarter. It is at this juncture that the quoted examples are revealing. They are a prime indication of what Churchland takes to be implied by the current concept. He suggests this by his choice of idiom for reporting results that he supposes readers can acknowledge as evidence without presupposing that they have been converted to his conclusion by other means.

The evidence that the creatures see temperature is contained in the two clauses of the last sentence of the quoted passage. It is flagged here as (ii). The crucial expressions must be taken as examples of acceptable usage, indicating how easily our current modes of speech admit these novelties. Thus, even pursuing the current reformist interpretation of Churchland, part of the case must be that this view is continuous with current practice to the extent of admitting such data without violence to familiar reporting practices. If what I have said above is fair, it will be a significant part of his defense to use such utterances to show that the creatures are visually perceiving heat (and not merely inferring it from visual clues of a different sort). Thus, let us apply what we have learned elsewhere in this chapter to these alleged perceptual reports.

It should be abundantly clear by now why being able to say that a creature sees *that* Xs (hot objects) are hot should not be enough to show that it sees (an instance of the property) heat or hotness. Propositional reports as such do not imply objectual ones. Indeed, Churchland's way of reporting what has gone on is perfectly compatible with the creature merely surmising that the object is hot from the sight of something else, just as someone may infer that her house has been robbed by seeing her personal belongings strewn about.

The construction according to which the creatures see hot objects *as* hot may seem more persuasive. The topic of *seeing as,* or aspectual seeing, goes well beyond the scope of the present inquiry, and, in any case, it is altogether too intricate a subject for the sketchy treatment I can accord it. Various writers (e.g., Vesey 1965; Runzo 1977) have supposed that whatever else seeing may be, it is seeing as. However, even were this accepted, it would not support the claim in question. Churchland's example needs its contrapositive: all seeing as must be (plain) seeing. Only then are we entitled to infer that just because the creatures saw the hot objects *as* hot, they saw the heat. Lacking this we have yet to be shown the relevance of being able to report the infrareds to seeing a hot object as hot.

In explaining his view that all seeing is seeing as, Vesey writes "if a person sees something at all it must look like something to him" (1965, p. 73). This purports to show that whenever there is an objectual seeing, it can be reported as a seeing something *as* something. Vesey does not even try to show the converse, that whenever we see something *as* something we are visually perceiving it. We are well within our rights to demand extra support for this second proposition. It is clear that, as a rule, 'seeing as' is not sufficient for seeing. Thus, 'seeing as' is occasionally tantamount to nothing more than *regarding* something as something, even if this is not visual. For example, consider 'Though he is a credit to the profession, his colleagues see him as a disruptive influence' and 'Blücher's advance may be seen as the turning point of the battle.' Ordinarily, the question 'Can you see *x* as *y* ?' may be read as 'Can you *take* *x* to be *y* ?' and *taking* is a notion that I have argued prevents propositional seeing from collapsing into objectual seeing.

I can find nothing in Churchland's claim that the creatures see hot objects as hot to suggest more than that the creatures have made such an inference. It is even unclear, as we are asked to understand the case, that the creatures objectually see anything. Thus, even if, as has been claimed, 'seeing as' can be a basic perceptual idiom, it would not follow that all occurrences of that idiom are perceptual. In the case of (ii), it is crucial to show that it is an instance of the perceptual idiom. But it is also the sort of case for which that claim is likely to be most controversial. What Churchland must demonstrate with his case is precisely that his infrareds are not merely inferring the heat of an object from seeing something else. The examples in (ii) are designed to allay the natural suspicion that precisely this is going on. But when apprised that the form of construction chosen is not used exclusively for perceptual reporting, but also for reporting precisely the sorts of surmisings he needs to rule out, the reports lose their polemical heft. The evidence summed up in (ii) cannot carry the day, and for reasons of just the kind I have detailed in this chapter.

What further conclusions are we entitled to draw from this? Certainly not that Churchland's view is false or that his (perhaps) intended reform is unworthy. I have not demonstrated that he is wrong to maintain that the only obstacle to saying that the creatures saw the heat is our dogged attachment to antiquated forms of expression. But if one is out to revise a current conception because of its blemishes, we may be excused our suspicions when one hasn't first discharged an obligation to grasp the rudimentary facts about the notions to be replaced. The supposition that any of the idioms chosen had the force of showing these incidents to be visual certainly abetted, to a large degree, the implicit claim that the adjustments made for the new creatures are much less disruptive of important principles that underlie our understanding of perception than they might otherwise seem. This may, in turn, be taken as evidence that current views about visual objects are merely clumsy, scienifically neolithic attempts to delineate what seeing is a function of, thesis (i). Thus, the carelessness with which this supposition is defended cannot be ignored. (This may be especially so in the present case, since Churchland has presented so little reason to accept (i), other than the idioms just reviewed and the attack on his opponents as philosophically reactionary.) Indeed, it is still an open question whether it is possible for creatures to see the hotness of the object in the straightforward way in which they see, as we would put it, color. The fact that the words are, in some generous sense, sayable should not lead us to discount the evident awkwardness needed to state it. That may suggest that there is more to the distinction between the visual and nonvisual than Churchland seems willing to credit. At a minimum, it undermines the intuition his choice of example seeks to invoke in his readership. Even if I am mistaken in this, we have another instance in which propositional and related constructions have supplied a claim with resources to which it would be evident it was not entitled if it strictly adhered to the direct objectual construction. And that is what I set out to illustrate.

XII

The discussions in §§X–XI help us to see another valuable point. Rarely is cognitivism defended as explicitly as in Searle. Nevertheless, it is a widely shared assumption, manifested simply by appropriating propositional reports of vision and perception as the standard. Occasionally theorists claim, without further argument, that propositional reports can capture whatever gets reported objectually, without decrement of visual content or introduction of the nonvisual. The last two sections highlight how these and related assumptions about acceptable forms of visual reporting can make certain substantive conclusions seem inevitable or highly plausible. Thus, although the distinction between objectual and propositional seeing I began with may have sounded parochial, I hope it is now clearer how it has been influential in deciding (frequently illegimately, sometimes unawares) classical disputes in perception theory.

Although I have clarified a number of issues and examined the arguments for and against cognitivism, our obligations don't end there. Pressure has been exerted from below (causation) and above (belief) to adopt one or another position. I indicated earlier how doxasticism gravitates toward, perhaps with some plausible assumptions requires, cognitivism. I discuss that influence in greater detail in the next two chapters. But before closing this one, I will briefly remark on the influence of causation, which inclines much more subtly toward objectual reports.

The dispute over the logical form of singular causal statements (and causal explanations, not to be confused with the former) concerns the proper way to fill in the blanks in sentence frames such as '__ caused . . .' and '. . . because __.' Let's concentrate on causes rather than effects. Two contenders for exclusive or canonical form for causal clauses are factlike (propositional) and eventlike (objectual) phrases. Since CTP claims that the ontological object of sight is also its cause, there is the pressure of economy of theory to match the logical forms of causes and visual objects. If they were not strictly identical, we would require an additional means to get us from the form for its objecthood to the form for its causal efficacy without damage to (C) and suchlike principles.

The issue regarding singular causal statements is still largely unsettled. However, the tradition of conceiving of causes as more objectlike—events, or properties or features of events, or perhaps even processes—seems to be in more robust health. At least theorists feel comfortable talking about event causation, whether or not they have views about fact causation or the priority of one form over the other. Hume, for example, gives as one of his famous definitions of cause "an object precedent and contiguous to another, and where all the objects resembling the former are plac'd in like relations of precedency and continguity to those objects, that resemble the latter" (bk. 1, pt. 2, sec. 14). Other writers, including

Donald Davidson (1967), have also argued, if not unassailably, for the objectual over the factative form. As it fortuitously turns out, this is also the idiom I have favored for visual reports.

The matter may be worthy of passing note, but I don't believe it carries much weight. Even if one's total view produced a different form for the one than the other, it seems that there would be various means for CTP to work its way around the mismatch by inserting further stages of conversion in the causal process. Thus, it is doubtful that any outcome with respect to causal statements will force our hand on the cognitivism issue. Of much greater concern, perhaps, is the influence of doxasticism. There the pressure on a positive outcome for cognitivism seems a good deal more intense. I now turn to the arguments that support doxasticism.

5

The Credulous Eye

"Man alone understands, while [other animals] perceive but do not understand"

ALCMAEON OF CROTON

I

Perception is a central mechanism of belief fixation; that is undisputed. The issue between doxasticists and their critics is not over whether perceiving is normally and systematically connected with belief, but over whether perceiving should be understood, in whole or part, in terms of perceptual belief. I take it for granted that its proficiency at fixing beliefs is one of the most interesting things about perception. Nevertheless, perhaps this remarkable capacity does not disclose very much about what it is to perceive something. That, at any rate, is the position I am defending.

However we decide that issue, its affect on the ultimate fortunes of CTP will be minor. This is not to say that its outcome makes no difference whatsoever to certain ways the causal theory may be formulated or defended. For example, the popular notion of 'matching content' among causal theorists, which we are seeing has serious difficulties, would improve its prospects markedly were visual content identical with a correlative belief content. (See chap. 7, §V.) This is an in-house quarrel between comparably plausible competing versions of CTP. But because doxasticism's fate is so central to the shape of so many topics in the philosophy of perception, we do well to continue pursuing the topic.

The last chapter gave us a good start: cognitivism is a useful initiation into our current issue. Not only has it been a mainstay in the defense of doxasticism, it has also been adopted largely for its utility in defending forms of doxasticism. (With the help of such rubrics and phrases as 'the cognitive nature of perception' or 'perceptual cognition', advocates occasionally don't even differentiate the theses.) Conversely, there are some short arguments from doxasticism to cognitivism. Recall that even if a belief content is regarded as no more than a behavioral disposition, and thus needn't be encoded propositionally, reports of that content *can* be given in a propositional form. This combined with the view that seeing is a form of believing yields the conclusion that what is seen can always be reported propositionally. That amounts to what I called the *weak* form of cognitivism (chap. 4, §I). It claims only that an equally substantial propositional report is always available, but makes no claim for the priority of propositional reports. But we may also take a giant stride toward arguing for the stronger form by adding to the doxastic premise the widely received, indeed eminently reasonable, view that belief, whatever else it may be, is a relation of a subject (or its state) to a proposition—taking 'proposition' here broadly enough, say, to cover not only certain concrete sequences of (mental, spoken, or written) tokens, but also abstract entities. Seeing then becomes, inter alia, the acquisition of such a proposition (or an inclination toward one) on the equally reasonable supposition that for doxasticism the objects of the relevant pairs of beliefs and seeings are identical.

Belief all by itself has presented philosophy with a host of vexing problems. Given its role in doxasticism, one might be expected to begin by clarifying belief. For example, to list but a few queries that may become relevant, there are questions about whether every sort of perceiver is capable of having beliefs, about how far the implications of our other beliefs are also beliefs, about the conditions for ascribing beliefs not consciously entertained, about relations between occurrent and dispositional beliefs, about belief and conceptual competence, about the applicability of familiar logical and sentence-forming operations to the contents of beliefs, and about requirements of acquaintance and coherence for having certain beliefs. However, to avoid getting bogged down in matters marginal to my main concern, I have chosen to sidestep such issues and simply to grant doxasticism those answers most favorable to any version of it I happen to be discussing. In this connection, let us assume that doxasticism may employ both occurrent (episodic) and dispositional beliefs, without prejudice to a potential behavioral analysis of belief; that all perceiving creatures have at least sufficiently low level beliefs to satisfy doxasticism; that belief can be represented as a relation of a cognizer or its state to a proposition; that there are tacit beliefs (though, as becomes clear, their ascription must be strictly limited); and that whatever restrictions there are on belief do not restrict anything we could be independently said to perceive. Should anything turn on these assumptions, they can be modified at the proper time. Otherwise, none is vital to my reasons for rejecting doxasticism. They are all assumed here only to allow the narrative to proceed with fewer qualifications.

I begin by summarizing and then scrutinizing various of the reasons for doxasticism found in the philosophical literature. The view's sponsors haven't delineated their arguments very sharply, so attempts to collect them runs the disjunctive (perhaps dual) risk of either repetition or omission. I choose to risk repetition to better avoid neglecting something a doxasticist might deem essential.

For exposition's sake, at the start this survey employs an oversimplified version of doxasticism: one stating that seeing is a form of belief. As we have seen, doxasticists qualify this in various substantial ways. One such qualification is that seeing (perception) is not merely believing but the acquisition of a belief (or sustaining one already acquired). For another, doxasticists don't always require an actual belief for their analyses of seeing, but perhaps only an inclination to believe—in a pinch, even a suppressed inclination may do. Such qualifications loom larger when we consider reasons militating against the doctrine itself. But in initial arguments for establishing the view, their roles are minor. In making their case, doxasticists are more intent to emphasize the connection to belief than to modulate that relationship to accomodate hard cases. Qualifications may be introduced as they prove necessary; but unless advised otherwise, I write in terms of the simpler version. On to the arguments.

II

First, once again, there is the contention that doxasticism is the only (reasonable) alternative to sense-data (Armstrong 1968; Pitcher 1971), and, for whatever reason, sense-datum analyses of perception are fatally flawed. The only remaining hope for a satisfactory account is via the generation of beliefs.

The first part of this argument was briefly examined in chapter 2, where a serious weakness was exposed. The argument relies on there being no phenomenal notion of sight other than one captured by a sense-datum analysis. The moral drawn by doxasticism is that with the removal of the sense-datum option, analysts must seek something other than appearances, phenomenal experience, or the distinctively visual character of qualities. Should we accept this? Suppose all forms of sense-datum theory have been decisively refuted. Even so, the attacks on sense-data which I, and many other naysayers, find persuasive—both those that reject arguments for sense-data and those that raise problems with the concept itself—target the theory's understanding of visual experience. They are not designed to attack the indispensability of visual experience itself, though they may very well be compatible with such an attack. In fact, sense-datum theory, although not dead, is moribund. But the grounds for its abandonment needn't question phenomenal experience per se, but only its sense-datum explanation: its explanation in terms of intermediate, mind-dependent objects of experience.

Once the sense-datum option is eliminated, the contents of visual experiences that don't fall short of being actual perceptions must be filled by the objects of those perceptions. I have already suggested, via my direct realism, that by and large these will be the familiar, mind-independent things, states of affairs, and events of ordinary perceptual reporting. This isn't meant to imply that this class of objects cannot enter as terms in analyses of *experience*. That they do enter them may be reinforced by the fact (elaborated in chap. 7) that such experiences, when they have objects, are individuated in part by those objects: nothing can be identical with a chosen experience that doesn't share its ontological object. Nor does the collapse of sense-datum analysis rule out our speaking of appearances in this regard, so long as it is understood that it is the appearances *of* the objects that are in question. (Of course, it must also be shown that the relation we intend to express by 'of' is taken in a less unnatural way than sense-datum analysts take it. But that poses no special difficulty.) In sum, the notion of an appearance is not discredited solely by the refutation of its sense-datum analysis (see Alston 1990). This argument for doxasticism fails because the two choices offered in its initial premise do not exhaust the options.

It may be rejoined that doxasticism need not draw the dichotomy quite so severely. We can imagine a proponent claiming instead that even if the nondoxasticist option is not strictly a sense-datum theory, the phenomenal content it supplies is nevertheless a type of Given (in the sense in which it figures in the phrase "the Myth of the Given"); a Given, whatever else it might be, is perceptual content below the level that our conceptual apparatus reaches. Thus, by accepting a phenomenal rather than a doxasticist treatment of perception, one places the strict objects of perception beyond the grasp of belief contents and makes it virtually impossible to show how perceptual content can fix belief.

The charge is serious. Although I have denied that perceptual content as such *is* belief content, I certainly wouldn't want it to be inaccessible to being transformed into a belief or to serving as evidence for beliefs. That not only fails the doxasticist pattern, but prohibits perceptual content from playing any role in fixing belief. However, the issue raised by this rejoinder is a sprawling one, and I must limit it strictly to my concerns if I am to avoid having (what is for me) a side issue overwhelm my focal interest. (In full blossom, it opens a very large issue dispute, raging for many years, between foundationalists and coherentists.) Insofar as it bears on my claims, I have dealt with part of it in chapter 1 (§V). There I argued that just because our perceptual contents enter our receptive faculties from the external world, they do not have to enter as a nonseparated, indescribable mush (say, Anaximander's *apeiron*). As external objects, they may already come packaged fully divided into roughly the types, features, and masses that at least some of our linguistic-conceptual apparatus is poised to register. Thus, there is no call to suppose that *this* Given, just because it isn't itself belief, is not already divided in such a way that it is unreceptive to belief. In the next chapter, I make some additional comments that indirectly reinforce this outlook. But once it has been shown how perceptual content as received can already be available to the categories of our thought, we must forgo any temptation to encroach further on this vast issue.[1] Thus, we needn't accept the 'doxasticism or disaster' option to which this argument tries to direct us. A number of controversial assumptions, standing in need of support, lie behind the claim that nondoxasticism is confined to so thin and primitive a notion of content. Exposing the lack of credibility of some crucial ones is enough to overthrow the argument.

III

Nondoxastic alternatives consistent with direct realism can be *purely* phenomenal (qualia) or materialist, or virtually any shade in between (e.g., phenomenal features supervening on the physical). I will say something more about them here, if only to remove any basis for a lingering attachment to the original dichotomy. But I will not say enough to satisfy some, because it is important to the position I take to leave things open for competing nondoxastic views. (Liberally construed, all of the views contrasted here with doxasticism, including materialism, might be considered phenomenal. I reserve the title 'qualia' for what is supposed to be *irreducibly* mental.) Let's see what can be said within those limits.

Commencing with the most provocative formulation (qualifications can be entered later), *doxasticism neglects 'what it's like' to see things*. This isn't intended as a self-standing argument, but more as a specification of a thesis to be defended. It is a familiar refrain, but I have written some unfamiliar lyrics. I will proceed to add a series of loosely woven explanatory, polemical, and qualifying comments to this bald assertion. I trust that, at their conclusion, the reasons these underdescribed options elude the competence of doxasticism will be clearer.

The remainder of this section proceeds as follows. First, I outline the most general reasons for supposing that perception has a phenomenal character. Second, I discuss a few phenomenal specimens and explain just what import they have for the immediate issue. Finally, I return to the issue from what traditional perception theorists would have regarded as the wrong end of the phenomenal continuum, that is, with fully public and objective characteristics of perceptual content. This is done in order to show just how little one has to prove about phenomenality to make the case against doxasticism.

Doxasticists and their opponents can agree that our visual equipment is basically *a means of gathering information*. But in that phrase, doxasticists emphasize the expression 'gathering information' to the neglect, if not the deliberate suppression, of whatever is conveyed by its earlier part, 'a means of.' All detectors obtain information through specific modes. In some cases (e.g., artifacts), we are a good deal less concerned with particular modes. Thus, at a certain level, we can appreciate the force of the remark, even if we ultimately disagree with it, that any device we build to detect temperature is a kind of thermometer. The case is more difficult to make when we drift farther from clear instances (even when it is something in which we believe we have identified a definite function). Consider, for example, a tree, among whose likely candidates for distinctive function is performing photosynthesis. Granting it, still not every conceivable thing that frees oxygen molecules from an intake of carbon dioxide by converting carbon atoms to starch and cellulose counts as a tree. (Perhaps none of them is if, say, it is manufactured by us.) Function isn't everything. Similarly, vision detects things in a distinctive way. But not every way of gathering just that information counts as seeing. Earlier (chap. 3, p. 65) I mentioned a computer printout that describes a particular mango in rich visual detail. Quite simply, seeing that isn't seeing the mango, and this result has nothing to do with the amount of information available. (The reasons for this, as well as the notion of phenomenality, are developed further in chap. 9.) Similarly, hearing the bell ring or seeing the light go on may be a perfectly reliable indicator that the prey has fallen into the trap, but it isn't seeing the prey fall into the trap, just as seeing bear tracks in the snow is not seeing a bear (however reliable an indicator of a nearby bear). Nor are these matters of seeing 'indirectly' rather than 'directly', which might be an appropriate way to mark the distinction were information gathering the only thing at stake. A finely graded instrument may turn out to be more reliable than sight in gathering just the same sort of information also gained by 'eyeballing' (say, a heat-sensitive device in a spy plane). Nevertheless, its detecting may not be a kind of seeing. Thus, seeing appears to be modal specific. The means by which the information is gathered cannot be discounted.

An important underlying reason for harping on this point, both here and below, is that doxasticism tends to drive all else out of its account of perception and always poses at least the implicit threat of doing so. Some accounts of perception have managed to mix information processing with phenomenal components (e.g., Dretske 1979, 1981). But for doxasticists, part of whose case is to emphasize in a distinctive way the information-processing nature of perception, the phenomenal component is at best a distracting annoyance, more likely an unnecessary accompaniment of sight (e.g., Heil 1983), possibly a (Cartesian) superstition (e.g., Churchland 1979; Dennett 1991). The belief-generating function and the what-it's-like do not comfortably coexist inside a single account. It is not uncommon for more recent doxasticists, when they develop their case in detail, to spend a good deal of time considering phenomena in which the pick-up of characteristically visual information is accomplished without any prima facie grounds for the discovery of supporting visually phenomenal constituents. I discuss a few of these shortly. Here I want to emphasize only the direction in which such accounts point—not so much to criticize the view as to highlight some important implications of the conflict.

Of course, if this is supposed to be a problem for the doxasticist, she might solve it by adding to her account that the distinctive kind of belief must involve the eyes, or the information must originate photologically. The former reply is weak if not supported by some deeper justification for the requirement. Why should we demand that the eyes be involved? The latter reply looks less like an arbitrary imposition, since it seeks to characterize the source of the information. That appears to be a relevant basis for carving out a distinctive kind of belief. But it, too, by itself, doesn't seem enough. On this basis, we still cannot distinguish seeing an *o* from reading about it on a computer printout that describes images captured by an attached camera.

The manner in which our visual apparatus detects is distinctive, and it happens to be subjective at first approach. Being subjective, it is more difficult to approach in certain ways, but talk of subjectivity in this context shouldn't be supposed to have certain of the more radical implications some have drawn from it. For example, I do not mean to imply that the what-it's-like is ineffable. There are two ways in which descriptions may be said to be ill fitted to seeing. First, description is one medium, sight another. On an intelligible, though rarefied standard, one medium cannot in the fullest possible manner replicate another. Thus, for just the reasons that we say (independently of appeals to physiology) that one cannot hear green, see thunder, or taste a symphony, apprehending a syntactically structured object, such as a description, is not tantamount to seeing what is described—save for the odd case in which the description is self-referential. But precisely the same limitation, and for the same reason, attaches to describing something like a photograph or a painting, neither of which is subjective in the usual sense. Second, there is a sense in which what we see will always be more detailed and specific than our ways of describing it. For example, our few shape terms, even when exquisitely elaborated, and though adequate for all normal purposes, 'fall short' in obvious ways of the irregularities manifested in our perceptual information, just as even such qualified sortals as 'large, grey stallion' invariably do not exhaust the specifics made manifest to sight when we see a large, grey stallion. It is the manner in which (what happens to be) information is picked up by this sensory mode that makes it phenomenal.

No doubt, we could also add *qualia*—roughly mind-dependent properties of mind-independent perceptual objects. At best, they are perceiver-relative. They are often what thinkers have in mind by 'phenomenal'. There is no need to take a stand on their inclusion here. They aren't needed to describe a phenomenal element in the sense just given. The two ways in which seeing something outdistances its verbal description are sufficient to establish the point in question. They illustrate a perceptual 'what-it's-like' of just the sort that doxasticism has a stake in downplaying.

Even so, it should be noted that we do not require this much for an alternative to doxastic specifications of content. An account in wholly physicalistic terms would suffice, so long as the specification of the state was not to be identified with a belief (or an inclination-to-believe) content. Of course, whether such identification is permissible is not likely to be determinable by neurological data alone, but at the conceptual level at which our discussion is proceeding. Thus, for example, David Marr's (1982) descriptions of the early stages of vision, up through 2 1/2 and 3D sketches, detecting such primitives as edges, blobs, bars, and terminations in terms of relatively strong light contrasts is first and foremost in phenomenal terms, despite its material underpinnings. And we require neither reduction nor an overlay of perceptual belief to complete the description. (This is no accident. Marr gives reasons for it: e.g., p. 99.) The point is broached here to enable us to note that questions of physicalist or token materialist reduction, or even supervenience on a material base, are neutral with respect to the present issue. Talk of the phenomenal features of vision, because of past discussions of this subject, should not mislead readers into believing otherwise.

I can drive home the point about the phenomenal component with a couple of representative cases, both about color. Normally sighted humans are trichromates. That is, among the photoreceptors of our retinas are three types of cones, each optimally sensitive to a different part of the visible sprectrum—from shortest to longest wavelength, blue, green, and red. There is no strictly logical reason why the combination of cones shouldn't exceed this number, so imagine a genetically mutated tetrachromate. She has a type of cone the rest of us lack and distinguishes sharply between two similar shades of red in the way we do between colors such as blue and yellow.[2] For her, these reds are two distinct colors, which in our incapacity we fail to capture. (Grice [1962] similarly asks us to imagine a Martian with a sense modality that we lack. This exercise is easy enough, since we can more simply imagine our own race lacking one of its current sensory modes. There the comparable task would be for these sensorily impoverished counterparts to figure out from the physical data available to them what our experiencing such things is like. If, within the current limits of their physiology, they successfully developed a system for describing and even detecting the presence of features that that modality had detected in its distinctive way, would we say that they actually developed the missing sense?)

In another case (modified from Frank Jackson 1982), we may imagine Mary, a perfectly instructed student of color and its perception, who has had from birth flexible contact-lens implants (perhaps to protect her from a rare disease) that make her see everything in grey scale. As an ideal scientist, she knows everything her science can disclose to her about the causes of color and its perception. Presumably, given all the initial conditions, she could even predict the color of the car she will be seeing just after the lenses are eventually removed. But when the implants are removed, she comes to 'be informed about' (whether or not we wish to call it knowledge is unimportant) something she hasn't been taught in her studies, namely, how it seems to her.

It is important to stress that given complete information about the conditions, she might be able to predict *which* color she will eventually enjoy. Many of those convinced by Jackson's case also accept the view that mental content is (at a minimum) supervenient on physical conditions. That is really all that is needed to make a case for the potential predictability despite Mary's disadvantage. Nevertheless, there is something of which she becomes apprised that isn't contained in the information on which her prediction is based.

Daniel Dennett (1991) rejects the case. However, the fact that she can predict the color is virtually the only specific objection he has for doing so. Since every 'fact' about the case can be demonstrated without the what-it's-like, he declares that Jackson's description doesn't prove its existence, leaving us only with an intuition of uncertain provenance. "It doesn't prove anything, it simply pumps the intuition that she does [have something not contained in the physical description]" (p. 400). Dennett's dismissal is too breezy. Its inadequacies would be even more striking if, instead of just commenting on Jackson's description, he were forced to provide an alternative characterization of the circumstance. The problem is this: If we imagine Mary after the lenses are removed, she'll still be able to distinguish cases in which she sees a color from those in which she uses her former method. It is hard to imagine that this isn't precisely how she will describe that difference. Similarly, it is now commonplace for sighted individuals to predict the colors of unseen objects based on other knowledge. (E.g., based on your knowledge of my past behavior, you reason that my new car is blue.) Removing the air of exoticism from the Mary example shows that there is a perfectly ordinary and robust distinction to be accounted for: one that won't go away so easily.

What are Dennett's options? So far as I can tell, there are only two: either he can reject the distinction even for the ordinary cases, or he can claim that the distinction cannot apply (as in Mary's preoperative condition) where there is no contrast with other sorts of cases. Neither choice seems promising. As for the first, it doesn't leave us with so much as the means to distinguish the case in which I learn the color of your walls by seeing them from that in which you inform me of their color. As for the second option, it is difficult to see how the lack of contrast in Mary's early condition dispatches the description of the cases Jackson suggests. There have been attempts to use contrastive arguments to show that we couldn't apply one sort of description without a realistic ability to contrast it with another sort. But this case is unlike that between, say, real and counterfeit money, in which such arguments have gotten some mileage.

I have foisted on Dennett only desperate countermoves. My defense is that I do not see how it is possible for him to acknowledge the ordinary facts in individual cases—that not every successful judgment of this sort is a seeing—while at the same time refusing to recognize them if in the general case what Mary has is *as reliable as* sight. I conclude that Jackson has done more than merely prime our intuition pump. Dennett's high-handed treatment, on the other hand, once deprived of the advantage of its sketchiness, seems to run roughshod over clear distinctions that are simply highlighted incidentally by Jackson's example.

Staying with the argument would take us too far from our main business. Thus, I satisfy myself with noting that Dennett's response rests on two related and highly contentious notions: a restrictive (behaviorist?) conception of knowledge and a form of verificationism (Dennett, 1991, pp. 461–2; see Block, 1993, for details). Both have been the targets of heated philosophical controversy, and their shortcomings have been so thoroughly exposed that philosophers nowadays generally avoid them without mention. Nevertheless, each gets overtime employment in Dennett's philosophy, without, so far as I can tell, much of an attempt to show that they are, *pace* the critics, available for use as plausible premises. At any rate, given the vast area Dennett dismisses by labeling it 'intuition', I believe many would be happy to setttle for it.[3]

The remainder of Dennett's discussion largely concerns attacking further implications regarding epiphenomenalism that Jackson draws from the example. Since this is beside the point, we could agree (for the sake of argument) that given the supervenience base mentioned, there can be no token effects which could not be characterized physically via their supervenience base. But, then again, when the supervenience base is satisfied, neither will there be any effects of a completed supervenience base which couldn't be characterized with a mental cause. As John Mackie (1985) puts it, "members of a pair of causally inseparable items cannot compete with one another for a causal role" (p. 144). One's choice here for specifying a cause (as distinct from an explanation) cannot be grounded in anything firmer than current interest.

Given that the issue of the reducibility of experienced content has been set aside, there is no need to dwell on the supposed ineradicable subjectivity of perceptual experience. Perhaps it is best to make the point about what is left to doxasticism by beginning with the sort of case not usually supposed favorable to illustrate a 'what-it's-like.' So let's start with a distinctively perceptual feature that all parties can regard as an unlikely candidate for subjectivity: the property of *being behind something*. Without perceivers there would be no place in objective reality for one thing to be spatially behind another.

Seeing one thing sticking up from behind another is a perfectly natural sight. Better yet, it is robustly intersubjective (no group of behind-blind subjects), and it has nonperceptual, strictly spatial consequences for motions a body must undergo to reach such things. But it is easy to overlook the fact that were it not for visual perspective, the whole notion of being behind wouldn't have much of a foothold. The property of being behind something is not tactile, and the property of one thing being beyond or past (farther than) another—which, although also perspectival, may still be instantiated in a world without the sense of sight—is not tantamount to its being behind another. One reason is that to be behind another, the second must be (partially or wholly) fronted by whatever subtends the visual angle from the perspective in question. This is not an implication of 'beyond.' The thing behind another can be, although it needn't be (think of a plate of glass), occluded by what fronts it. Clearly to say that *x* is behind *y* says more than that *x* is past or beyond *y*. (Nor is this a matter of being close by. Venus is behind the Sun at certain periods.)

This must be heavily qualified because workaday vocabulary defies neat slots; usage almost always strays from its original home. Thus, we sometimes use 'behind' loosely for 'beyond' or 'past,' the latter two being strictly more appropriate when we are considering fetching something rather than merely eyeballing it. Moreover, we might say that the broom is behind the cupboard without reference to our current visual angle, for a cupboard has a front and a back. It is a fair speculation that this has to do with the customary position, and thus visual angle, one would have vis-à-vis the cupboard. But although we could still use 'behind' as a rough equivalent for 'beyond,' it seems clear that not much of its distinctive informational contribution remains without its visual associations. If we were suddenly bereft of sight, there would be little point to preserving the word, even as a term of convenience. There seems to me to be no alternative to considering it primarily a notion of visual perspective.

From there we can work our way to seeing things as being of a certain size and at a certain angle. Although the features themselves are no longer inherently perspectival, some of the same sorts of perspectival phenomena are present. When things look cubic to us at normal angles, it is not because they look the way we would describe cubes geometrically. A perfect still life of our scene might be rhomboid or, if seen head on, square, or as if the top part had been lopped off of a triangle. These what-it's-like qualities are not part of a total description of the world without perceivers. The description is from a subject's perspective and has a quality that can of course be described or sketched (it is not in any way ineffable). Still it appears to be more than a belief.

Color is, of course, a more extreme case of the same thing. I simply allude to the previous cases to indicate the phenomenal character of color. The mutant with four types of chromatic cones, and Mary, our neural scientist, with her greyscale lenses removed, not only draw more distinctions than before, but they do it on the basis of qualitatively distinct experiences.

Recall that the immediate point is not to demonstrate the indispensability of phenomenal components, but to explain what they could be. Nevertheless, if the availability of direct realist, phenomenal alternatives is important to the case against doxasticism, the account of this collection had better be at least plausible. To that end, I offer what I regard as a firm, albeit defeasible, intuition (of an Aristotelian cast; see *De Anima* 418a24–b2) that our current concept of sight is so bound up with the ways in which distinctive features like color and shape visually strike us that any account that is incompatible with this faces a tough uphill struggle for credibility, perhaps even for intelligibility.[4] As I remarked earlier, doxasticism is generally unreceptive to, if not incompatible with, inherent phenomenal features. Although neither that account nor mine need mention the particulars of the phenomenal qualities of sight, mine is fully compatible with such a definition. It is simply that my view does not aspire to be a complete account of visual perception. Aside from articles of the causal theory, the only views I am defending are negative in nature: noncognitivism and nondoxasticism. The importance of this is that, although there is something to which I can appeal in (C) as the effect of *o* whether or not doxasticism is the case, the doxasticist's attack on phenomenal features leaves her with no version of (C) she can accept if she cannot make out her doxastic thesis.

(There is a point to invoking Aristotle here, if only to cut off the weak, though apparently persuasive, claim that the 'intuition' I have tried to induce is nothing more than a stubborn relic of Cartesianism (e.g., the image of the Cartesian Theatre, the lingering effects of Cartesian dualism, Cartesian privacy, the ghost in the machine). It is in Aristotle that we discover the first influential account differentiating sense modalities via the sorts of what-it's-like's proper to them. Of course, the noble ancestry of phenomenal characterizations is no evidence for their plausibility, but it does allow us to take off the table a certain shallow bit of historicizing.)

IV

Before resuming this survey of the direct arguments for doxasticism, let us pause to look at some of the unusual phenomena its defenders cite to support the view that visual detection can take place with no, or very different, phenomenal experience. Two favorite cases are blindsight and prosthetic tactors for blind subjects. Do they serve the purposes for which they have been introduced?

First, blindsight. Its sufferers lack a normal visual experience of some of the objects that send the required amount of photologic information to their retinas. This is due to a subtotal lesion or ablation of a major visual pathway leading from the lateral geniculate nucleus to the visual cortex. Since geniculo-lateral and cortical projections contain maps of the retinal information, in which neighborhood and continuous areas are preserved (Kandel 1981), it is understandable that partial impairments in those regions would prohibit visual fields from including certain angles subtended by a subject's normally working eyes. Indeed, on questioning, patients sincerely deny having seen things falling in their blind areas. But, remarkably, when asked to 'guess' about some rather unspecific visual information (motion,[5] direction, light, gross shape) in their blinded hemifields, patients are uncannily accurate (Perenin and Jeannerod 1975). Earlier, it had been supposed that this information is restricted to impulses from retinal rods, but more recent evidence suggests that patients also give accurate answers about color opponency—normally a function of cones (see Stoerig and Cowey 1990). Moreover, patients are not that much less accurate than the normally sighted at detecting certain interactions between their sighted and blind hemifields, although poor at guessing about the same information confined to the blind hemifield. Finally, they continue to display pupillary reflexes and galvanic skin responses to objects in their blind hemifield (Weiskrantz 1990).

In the second sort of case, researchers constructed a device to enable blind subjects to detect at a distance objects in their environment. They attached to eyeglass frames tiny, low-resolution video cameras, which sent signals to electrical vibrating "tinglers" attached to the front or back of the subject's torso (see Bach-y-Rita 1972). These *tactors* (as the tinglers were called) were arranged in matrices (say, twenty by twenty) to project arrays of pixels in black and white onto the subject's torso, creating digitalized images of what the cameras recorded. After some training, subjects were thereby enabled to detect objects, read signs, and recognize faces. Because of the low resolution, there were severe limits to what subjects could detect, but after acclimation to the device, subjects seemed to ignore the medium (the tactors), which became as 'diaphanous' for them (recall Moore and Grice, see p. 40) as phenomenal aspects of sight do for the normally sighted. (We may assume that in the more than twenty years since these experiments were first reported, advances in digitalization would permit much higher resolution tactor imaging.)

How might doxasticists utilize such cases? First it should be noted how the cases are not used. I do not know that any doxasticist has claimed that patients unqualifiedly see things in the special circumstances mentioned. (Some researchers have spoken unguardedly of blindsight as "unconscious vision" (e.g., Young 1987, p. 121). But this is not in connection with our issue.) They are more likely to use the cases to break down any sharp distinctions between seeing and non-seeing. (See Dennett 1991, chap. 11; and Heil 1983, pp. 78–81.) In this they may be seeking to expand our notion to include such cases, since what is vital (viz., information intake) is preserved, or at least to convince us to jettison any principled distinction between phenomenal and nonphenomenal seeing, thereby discounting the importance of the presence of phenomenal features. At any rate, the cases would appear to be useless to them unless (a) they can be made out to be akin to seeing (something like seeing) in crucial respects, and (b) they are instances of belief pickup (or belief-inclination pickup). Employing (a) and (b), let us see how each case fares. I begin with (b).

Tactor subjects certainly appear to believe that they have been enabled to detect things. They show little difference from sighted subjects in this respect. But consider blindsight. Blindsight patients explicitly deny that they see anything in their blind hemifields. Rather, they respond to requests to guess. Often this is forced guessing, since their first inclination is to deny that they saw anything at all at those locations. Their honest belief that they are guessing, and are forced to guess at that, presents what seems to me a nearly insurmountable case against attributing to them either a visual belief or even an inclination toward one. This common result clearly defeats the presumption of (b) for blindsight. Of course, they might be trained to drop this outlook on learning of their success rate (Weiskrantz 1990, p. 257). But that affords no relief to the doxasticist; her claim is that *all* cases of seeing are forms of belief (or inclinations to believe), and she must still account for blindsight subjects before they were given this injection of confidence. (On the other hand, the nondoxasticist can accept with equanimity the fact that people usually instantaneously believe what they see. No exception need be made to accommodate the newly confident blindsight patients.)

Turning to (a), it is unclear (despite my earlier explanation) how these cases can be relevant to the dispute without presupposing the position they set out to support. Suppose we regard them as showing that the information we now gather by sight could be gathered in other ways (as by, e.g., cameras, spectroscopes, touch). This doesn't seem far-fetched, but it doesn't advance the cause of doxasticism one iota. On the other hand, it would beg the question to claim baldly that the cases show how sight takes place, despite the absence of its usual phenomenal accompaniments, because its information-gathering task is discharged. The issue now is precisely whether accomplishing that makes these legitimate cases of sight. What, then, can the cases be taken to demonstrate or befuddle? Perhaps they are meant to reduce the distance between these exceptional methods of information pickup and normal vision. But this sort of assimilation is unlikely to faze anyone convinced by the reasons given in §III for requiring a phenomenal constituent of perception. It appears they are only compelling if we concede, in advance, a crucial assumption to the effect that the distinctive way in which vision goes about its business is dispensable. However, isn't that assumption a large part of what is at issue?

Sticking with (a), the way in which blindsight and tactor cases are reported deserves closer scrutiny. It would be shoddy practice to be influenced in our description by the fact that these devices compensate for information-gathering faculties their subjects lack. Officially, that is an intervening variable and therefore irrelevant to the assimilation of the cases to sight. The fact that a wall is detected, say, by both sight and touch isn't the slightest evidence for breaking down the distinction between these sensory modes. Similarly, if blindsight is to approximate normal vision, our judgment shouldn't be influenced by the fact that the blindsight patient is impaired in some ways from the usual means for apprehending information in that quarter. Of course, in the case of blindsight, it is impossible to imagine what it would be like for it to operate alongside, rather than in place of, normal sight. Still, our inclination to assimilate it to sight should not be influenced by its compensatory status. Defenders of the assimilation must take into account that a sort of nonphenomenal informational pickup (even if via the light traveling through the retina) might not so easily be taken as a type of sight if it were redundant and supplemental to normal seeing rather than a compensation for defective sight. This is not to say that there aren't other reasons for calling it a kind of seeing. But its compensatory function no more makes it a type of sight than it would the white cane of a blind person.

The point emerges most clearly for tactors. We cannot discount the testers' interests in approximating a source of information that the sighted have and the blind lack. It is because of this interest in any positive result in restoring (or discovering) ways in which that gap can be closed that we, the readers, as well as the testers, may be so willing to regard this as a kind of vision, if only a quirky kind. But there are very many instances in which the comparison with the (normally) sighted is not in question, a few of which I have already discussed (e.g., seeing bear tracks, gathering information via computer-printout descriptions). Those who appeal to the tactors on behalf of doxasticism appear oblivious to the implicit lessons of such cases. But the previous instances are important if for no other reason than that they do not rely on compensating the subject for a loss of vision. Similarly, if the tactors create sight for the blind, they should also do so for the sighted. But suppose a sighted person were also given tactors. Would we be as likely to maintain that she, given her usual way to detect visual information, would also be *seeing* via the tactors? There appear to be principled reasons for not assimilating the examples to sight when viewed as a supplemental way of gaining information for the sighted. If this counted as seeing, why not count reading about something (or the other exemplified cases of coming upon information about visual characteristics) as another way of seeing that thing?

(Incidentally, Dennett 1991, p. 341, agrees that the tactor results are "inconclusive," but here is a case he takes to show it. Two blind, male college students were "shown" for the first time photographs from *Playboy*. Though they could describe much of the content, they were disappointed at not being aroused, or at the absence of pleasant feelings. The suggestion is that it is at least inconclusive that they could have been said to *see* the photographs in the manner of their sighted peers. The conclusion is premature. Whatever the what-it's-like of sight may be, pleasant feelings or arousal is not an ingredient of it. If this is an argument against the tactor-assisted actually seeing the centerfolds, then it is an argument that heterosexual females, homosexual males, and children under six can't see them either. We have in this a small hint that Dennett's phenomenal opponent may be more straw than flesh. For further evidence of a similar sort, see ibid., pp. 379–80, 383–88.)

Not much stands out in these muddy waters. That is bad news for doxasticism. The best use the doxasticist might have made of such phenomena—to show that the alleged phenomenal features of sight are marginal or disposable—can be achieved only by presupposing that these are types of proto-seeings. And to do that one must already adopt, in defiance of the arguments of §III, disputed articles of the view it is being used to demonstrate.

V

I return to the review of arguments for doxasticism. A second argument begins from a claim that perception and belief alike are intrinsically related to behavior. First, belief is definitionally connected to behavior, at least via inclinations to behave in certain ways. So, too, is perceptual awareness, which, in the words of Gareth Evans (a died-in-the-wool antidoxasticist), is "imbued with . . . a necessary, though resistable, propensity to influence our actions" (1982, p. 123). These connections aren't meant to foreshadow a reductive analysis of belief or perceptual awareness to behavioral dispositions. We can leave open the details, noting only that such connections are compatible with a wide variety of theories about their more exact nature. Next there is a connection between perception and belief: all parties can agree that perception fixes belief. We may conclude that, since perception has basically the same relation as belief to behavior, it is reasonable to conclude that perception, and vision in particular, is merely a form of belief. In addition, this conclusion may be dictated by theoretical simplicity. Other views demand a generation relation between perception and belief, thereby, first, multiplying steps and, second, fostering an enigma about the indirect nature of perception's relation to behavior. Neither complication arises for doxasticism. Thus, as an attempt to account for the conceptual connection of perception to behavioral propensities, doxasticism delivers the more streamlined explanation.

For the sake of argument, I grant the evident propensity of both belief and perception toward behavior, though there is ample room for doubt about Evans's claim that it is *necessary*. (Indeed, since perception is habitually belief-fixing, the propensity of belief toward behavior is all that is needed.) Moreover, the behavior is not only resistable, it is in fact on most occasions resisted. No one I have ever encountered is hyperkinetic enough to behave on the basis of *most* of what she sees, unless we count noticing or physiological reactions as instances of behavior. (Of course, *the propensity* to it may not be resistable, but I'm not sure what sense it makes to talk of being able or unable to resist a propensity as distinct from the behavior evincing it.) Still, this qualified admission does nothing to settle the dispute between doxasticists and their opponents, for it is the common ground of both sides that perception ordinarily, unceremoniously leads forthwith to belief. Their differences are over how to explain this relationship. So far as I can tell, and momentarily setting aside the addition about theoretical simplicity, this argument does nothing more than note the existence of a perception-belief nexus. It doesn't give grounds for preferring any of the competing explanations of it. (No doubt, some nondoxastic views may not even accept the existence of this close relationship. If they do not, this fact may explain why doxasticists emphasize it. But although it may bring us to better appreciate why a doxasticist argues in this way, it doesn't improve the argument for that view. We can sympathize with the direction of the doxasticist corrective while maintaining that it goes too far and thereby oversimplifies the relationship of belief to perception.)

We turn now to the the central role of theoretical simplicitly in the argument. It is said that rejectionists require an additional, and unexplained, relation of generation to take us from perception to belief. Doxasticism dispenses with it, thereby presenting a simpler taxonomy of relations and explanans. Simplicity is so overused and poorly understood an appeal, it is difficult to know what weight to give this sort of claim. Of course, it is always qualified by 'ceteris paribus,' but in practice matters are rarely equal. In the case at hand, it must compete with the virtue of completeness. And the facts in this and the last chapter that have led me to insert the extra stage can be said to be ignored by the 'simpler' explanation. For realists about explanation, simplicity cannot be a virtue that answers to nothing else, but must serve as a clue to having got things right. Overlooking salient facts cannot be lightly brushed aside. Otherwise, although the greater simplicity of theory A over theory B (assuming it could be satisfactorily measured) may be a sufficient reason *for wanting* A to be true (or plausible or warranted), it would be a weak consideration for believing in or adopting A in a situation in which the evidence doesn't otherwise favor A over B.[6]

However, when we look more closely at the details of this particular doxasticist justification, we see that the matter needn't be left to rest on the extent of one's confidence in appeals to simplicity. Heil, once again, writes that perceptual states "ought to be the sorts of state that can both enter into the production (hence explanation) of behavior *and* serve as justificatory epistemic *relata*. These properties are commonly associated with beliefs. It is beliefs, in conjunction with desires, that largely determine the course of what we should call intelligent behavior" (1983, p. 121). The reasoning, reduced to its bare bones, exhibits the pattern: perception issues in behavior (and justification) in way z; belief issues in behavior (and justification) in way z; therefore, (it is reasonable to believe that) perception is belief. We may safely assume this is intended not as a deduction (which would make it fallacious), but as an inference to the best explanation. However, such similarities are explained equally by either doxasticism or the view that perception normally generates belief. To strengthen his argument Heil remarks that "one is, on occasion, inclined to justify beliefs about how things stand by linking these to what one has seen, heard, or felt" (1983, p. 121). However, this consideration doesn't advance his case. One can justify a belief by citing the *kind of* belief it is (e.g., perceptual) or by citing the evidence for it (e.g., perception). On either appeal, what is important is that one can cite having perceived something. That it is also classified as a belief does not contribute to the justification. In fact, even were this an appeal to a kind of belief, what is crucial about it would be the perceptual content, not its also being a belief. Quite the contrary, the fact of its being a belief would, if anything, seem to weaken its status as a justification. Suppose we ask whether an appeal to perception could still justify a belief if this took place only because the former was an instance of the latter. It is difficult to see how that fact could have any tendency to justify. That something is the case, or is probably the case, counts for justifying; that something is believed, with no further information about its epistemic credentials, does not. The features of perception, considered apart from a belief classification, supply the justification. Thus, the few considerations brought forth to strengthen this argument for doxasticism lack any tendency to do so.

Of course, if it is supposed that the only *evidence* for belief is behavioral, and that this is the same type of evidence for what one has perceived, avenues for distinguishing perception from belief are narrowed. If they cannot be distinguished by the kinds of evidence for their ascriptions, perhaps it makes no sense to try to distinguish perception from belief. I do not know whether Heil has anything like this in mind, but there is at least a whiff of his relying on our being driven to a(n) (unstated and vague) strong assumption of this ilk. This emerges from his practice, as when he considers the following example. Suppose S looks at a bookcase with 143 books on it and reports seeing books, but no specific number. To those non-doxasticists who would claim that S has seen 143 books (though S doesn't have the corresponding belief) Heil replies, "It is not enough that S's eyes be open and that the books be in S's field of view. S may be blind, or hallucinating, or distracted, or in some other way cut off from the scene before him. So long as S sincerely denies having noticed the books, there is no obvious way to rule out such possibilities and, in consequence, no guarantee that S has seen the books in any sense" (1983, p. 68; cf. p. 72). Consider carefully the last sentence of this passage. It affirms that we cannot "rule out [the] possibility" that S's denial is correct and that there is "no guarantee" that S has seen the books. Both points are unassailable. But the mere possibility that S hasn't seen 143 books does not preclude the possibility that he has, and the lack of a guarantee is not an argument that S hasn't seen 143 books. In fact, most of the truths (on any subject) that we assert cannot rule out the possibility of their falsehood or guarantee their truth. They are no less acceptable for that. The critic needn't even claim this much: it suffices if it is plausible that the relevant cases fall on both sides. An objector only needs good reason to believe that in *some* cases like this, a specific number of items are seen (though, regrettably, we may be in no position to say which they are). On the other hand, Heil seems committed to arguing that the mere possibility that S's denial is correct, or the lack of a guarantee that S saw 143 books, is enough to dismiss the claim. If we were to generalize the grounds on which this case is being overturned (to grounds for anyone's seeing anything), any principle I can discover as emerging would be ruinous for the ordinary extension of perception.

Suppose a doxasticist digs in her heels and continues to insist that one cannot see *x* without noticing that very same thing, quite independently of the foregoing failed argument. (This may not be Heil's view, but it may tempt others.) A worthwhile examination of this view cannot be conducted without considering further arguments for it, and no specimens of those are before us. Moreover, the following points, though they may not be major, bring out obstacles to finding any such argument. First, the 'no seeing without noticing' view can't be true in quite the strict form presented here. Just to mention one sort of complication, it is common for perceivers to remark about things they didn't notice at the time (because they were too distracted, distraught, or otherwise unattentive), "I wish I had paid closer attention to that, because. . . ." And following 'because' they go on to give some perceptual virtues the scene had, indicating quite clearly that they did see it, even if, as we say, they paid no attention to what they were seeing at the time. Any defense of the thesis will need to explain how it can accomodate such cases. Second, it might seem natural to defend the strong 'no seeing without noticing' view by appealing to doxasticism. But in the present context this is an inadmissible response. 'No seeing without noticing' was introduced precisely to defend doxasticism. Together with the argument of the quoted passage, this seems to me to exhaust the likely reasons for holding the strong 'no seeing without noticing' thesis. To reiterate, defending doxasticism against the objection is a steep climb. Without that thesis, strongly interpreted, where is one to look for support for the claim that S couldn't have seen 143 books in these circumstances?

Concerning the specific case, it is easy enough to confirm to our satisfaction in an imagined case that none of the conditions in the author's second sentence prevent S from having seen the books. For example, S may have other, quite specific, information about that shelf of books, showing that he isn't blind, hallucinating, distracted, or otherwise cut off from the scene. The random possibility of such interferences cannot motivate Heil's response; for what is to prevent us from stipulating that none of them are present in our case?

VI

Next, an argument, more often insinuated than featured, is based on the evolutionary role of perception in our mental economy. The key idea is that our perceptual faculties have developed only because they deliver belief. This is perception's evolutionarily prescribed *function*. From this vantage point, the particular mechanisms perception employs, and its current phenomenal incarnation, are "inessential"; the task it performs is "intrinsic" to it (see Heil 1983, p. 17; Armstrong 1968, p. 209).

For the sake of argument, let's grant the first step: that visual perception has a function. My main contention is that this doesn't support the doxasticist lesson the argument draws from it. But first I wish to make two preliminary points about the strength of the argument.

First, we appear to have a wide selection of functions among which to choose. At a minmum, for the purposes of definition, these would need to form some sort of hierarchy, vision being identified only with the highest distinctive function attributable to it. For this purpose, doxasticism chooses the creation of belief. Granting the argument's basic assumption, I believe it is still more sensible to take as its most basic function the provision of specific sorts of information (say, about color, shape, and some other features, such as distance, as well as various features that may be constituted by configurations of these basic properties, such as danger or food). In short, this sense (as the others) supplies a source of information for belief formation. Since information is not yet belief, but rather a basis for forming beliefs, this could yield a nondoxastic account of vision that is still functional. Dretske makes the point using the following analogy.

> Typically, [the experience of seeing X] embodies information about the colour, shape, size, position and movement of X. The role or function of the sensory system in the total cognitive process is to get the message in so that a properly equipped receiver can modulate his responses to the things about which he is getting information. The sensory system is the postal system in this total cognitive enterprise. It is responsble for the *delivery* of information, and its responsbility ends there. What we *do* with this information, once received, whether we are even capable of interpreting the messages so received, are questions about the cognitive-conceptual resources of the perceiver. If we don't take the letters from the mailbox, or if you can't understand them once you do, don't blame the postal system. (1979, pp. 10–11).

No doubt, one could add the earlier doxastic function to this one: the two functions aren't incompatible. However, the argument seems to appeal to a principle to the effect that since visual faculties are products of natural selection, like all other evolved organs, they must serve some function. The informational function satisfies this demand: it needs no complementary belief function. Therefore, the doxasticist cannot argue from the claim that visual perception must have some function or other to her preferred conclusion. Further argument is required to show not just that perception has a function to certify its evolutionary status, but also that it has to have the more specific function doxasticism claims for it.

Second, what is the basis for supposing that vision has a function at all? There are certain facts it seems we could all agree on. For example, had it not been for perception's being a source of reliable belief, perceptual faculties would probably have withered rather than flourished. Minimally, this is a plausible conjecture. What mechanism would propel the refinement of simple photosensitive cells into complicated eyes, or their perfectly happenstance linkage with freakishly elongated nerve endings into an efficient optic nerve, and the subsequent development of these features into norms for species in which they developed, other than the usable information for survival that this system supplied its possessors: in brief, what other than natural selection? Since the last century, when God went out of the business, no one seems to be vending an alternative explanation.

What are we to make of these admissions? Only, I believe, that gathering information useful for the organism is a salient necessary condition for that faculty's having developed and for its becoming prevalent. Whether this is, intuitively speaking, sufficient for the display of this sort of behavior being a *function* of the faculty is controversial. Those regarding it as sufficient to be a function will claim it is obvious and will build their notion of something's (proper) function around it. Thus, Martin Davies writes, "[i]t is sufficient for a mechanism to have *F*-ing as its function that it was *selected for* its *F*-ing" (1983, p. 421–22) (cf. Millikan 1984, esp. pp. 28–29). Those regarding it as insufficient to be function may see this not so much as bridging the gap between the facts cited (about necessary conditions) and function talk, but as starting on the function side of the gap—sans euphemism, as begging the question. For example, imagine the following fictitious, but realistic, scenario. There is a plant that, due to selective disfavor under the current changed environmental conditions, appears destined for rapid extinction. But it bears a fruit that humans find flavorful. Thus, humans go to extremes to build artificial environments to cultivate this plant in great numbers: it not only survives, but flourishes. (The case could be made even more vivid by beginning with the statement that until recently humans found the fruit repugnant, but, due to a sudden massive gene mutation, now enjoy it.) Certainly, the plant's survival is dependent on its selection, domestic selection. And it is domestically selected for its sapor. But what account of the plant would give its appeal to humans as among the plant's or its fruit's functions? None, I venture. Cases like this incline opponents to see a conceptual gap between necessary conditions for a thing's survival together with salient behavioral characteristics and its function. Opponents will want to draw a sharp distinction between paradigm cases of artifacts, where there is the clear intention to build something for a purpose, and cases like the evolutionary ones mentioned. Functionalists, on the other hand, will cleave to the original intuition, wanting instead to frame stricter definitions to overcome problem cases that beset formulas such as Davies's.

However, I am setting aside whatever scruples I may harbor about this, because the situation does seem to me to be aspectual: a matter of competing intuitions rather than something that can be decisively settled. Some see the shape of the elephant in the cloud, others don't. My main objection rests on the fact that the relevant conclusions we can draw from this rely altogether on further details. Given our liberality with the notion *function*, it seems that whether O's function deserves a place in a conceptual account of O, much less is capable of driving out all the other (viz., phenomenal) features of O, depends on whether the function *is designed*. Given that 'function' is being taken so broadly, I maintain that we cannot infer from 'x has function F' to 'x is designed to have function F.'[7] Although some things with the former property have the latter, this is not invariably so.

It will perhaps ease the way for me to make my case if we look briefly at one way functional explanation has been regarded since, say, the 1960s in the philosophy of science. Robert Cummins has stated, "[t]he point of functional characterization in science is to explain the presence of the item . . . that is functionally characterized" (1975, p. 49). Now, as Larry Wright (1974, p. 158) has made clear, 'presence' is a tricky notion, covering why something has a certain placement, why it has flourished, why it exists at all, why certain larger systems contain it, and perhaps other things as well. But Cummins's assessment seems accurate to the extent that, in some sense or other, functional explanations were devoted to showing why a thing was 'there', as opposed to not there at all or somewhere else. (See, e.g., Hempel 1965; Ernest Nagel 1961. Wright supplies further citations.) The crucial point here is that this falls decidedly short of claiming that the identified function belongs to the intrinsic characterization of what its bearer *is*. The characteristic appeal to a function to explain the presence of things having it (in a rather loose sense of 'presence') is considerably less ambitious than using a function to explain the intrinsic nature of its possessors. But the doxastic argument under review requires the stronger sort of appeal.[8] My current interest is in seeing how one might be warranted in going *from* a feature that explains something's presence *to* what it basically (essentially!) is. My contention is that this cannot be done for vision. But to reinforce the point, I also want to explain why the second sort of appeal is a further step, standing in need of additional support.

There are no hard and fast rules to guide us here, but on the whole those things with definitely identifiable designers and creators—roughly, the class of artifacts—admit having their design accomplished in radically different ways and with an array of different materials, with minimal disruption to our concepts of them. Thus, we can imagine knives that are laser beams, chairs of a variety of different shapes and materials. Even here, our tolerance for recognizing radically new forms of familiar objects isn't unbounded, and the function cannot be described at too general a level. For example, a commercial airliner is not simply a souped-up carriage, and a space ship is not an airplane. Occasionally, for commercial or ironic ends, the limits of sensibleness are violated even in informal discourse. But there is a good deal more latitude in these cases for new Os that don't visually resemble old Os. Explanations are at hand for this. If something is specifically created to do a certain sort of job, we can imagine an object created with a very different form as an improvement on the original rather than a new kind of object. For example, radios may contain vacuum tubes or printed circuits. That is why the unmistakable identication of a designer/creator is important. The things so named, though they have a certain look, have very little standing independently of the reasons for which they have been so shaped.

Let's turn our attention to natural selection. The ruling fact about it, seldom figured in the equation by philosophers who use it in functional accounts, is that *natural selection doesn't design or build anything*. "Unless favourable variations be inherited by some at least of the offspring, nothing can be effected by natural selection" (Darwin 1859, p. 78). Natural selection promotes a process on organisms (or genes or populations or organs)[9] brought into existence by other processes—in this instance, heritable variation. Were no eyes around—produced by genes, novel alleles, genetic mutation, naked chance, or whatever—natural selection would be impotent to create one. Natural selection operates on phenotypes and adjusts things so that effective traits (on the applicable standard) flourish in and even dominate populations. Biologists often allude to natural selection "directing" a process (e.g., Buss 1987, p. 4).This is a helpful trope. Think of a civil engineer redirecting the course of a river. The direction is imposed on an already-flourishing river *and* its natural activity (flowing). Domestic selection, which Darwin also discusses at length, differs vitally from natural selection in this regard; it is arguable that here designers really construct new organisms from raw materials, although perhaps only through a laborious process.

This is crucial for us, because (say) the organs that are the raw material for natural selection already have a sort of standing that cannot be ignored. Thus, disputes over form versus function. Creatures have an ontological standing before the forces that give them their current shapes operate on them. Consequently, whatever the evolutionary tale, birds are not dinosaurs. Gold, too, has a function: say, as a standard of exchange. But in the order of things, the features of gold precede the functions for which humans covet it. Similarly, the features of the eye seem to have preceded the functions for which natural selection influenced its development. Perhaps artificial eyes are more akin to real eyes than artificial diamonds are to real diamonds. But there is enough independent status for the former to question whether it could actually be an eye if it doesn't gather its information by means of inducing the kinds of episodes enjoyed by the normally sighted.

There are some revealing scattered facts that may be connected with the distinction I have been drawing. Although we may have little compunction about claiming that sight has a function, we show greater timidity in attributing design to it. Helmholtz is reported to have said that if one of his workers had presented him with a human eye in his laboratory, he would have rejected it. While this may at first seem like sheer bravado, there are features of visual perception that, although they don't effect our willingness to attribute functions to sight, do give us pause about them as products of design. For example, why should photons entering the retina have to pass a forest of retinal ganglion cells to get to rod and cone cells from whence they are rerouted as impulses back through the ganglion cells? From the 'design stance', the retina looks as if it has been mounted backward. (To the best of my knowledge, no one has a clue about this: that is, an evolutionary or engineering explanation about why it is advantageous to do things this way.) Moreover, we detect electromagnetic radiation only of wavelengths roughly between 380 and 760 nanometers, though this is only a fragment of the electromagnetic radiation band. Why would a designer place such limits on us? Actually, here there is a pretty solid, if speculative, historical explanation. These are the wavelengths in which light doesn't disperse under water, where our ancestral eye undoubtedly originated. But although this makes sense for a fish eye, it makes no design sense for ours. Although the eye does execute certain useful behaviors well enough within its limitations, and thus may provide strong evidence for these being its function, the claim that it is designed raises questions about its seemingly arbitrary architecture that may be ignored when considering function alone. It is extremely unlikely that those questions can be answered effectively from a strict design stance.

Thus, although we grant that vision has a function, and that the evolutionary history of sight is relevant to its discovery, two things about this 'designerless' function are worth noting. First, although I have not undermined a place for a function in an explanation of why sight "is present" (in one of the several legitimate interpretations of this phrase), we have seen why in this instance the ascription of a function seems incapable of being read into the very nature of seeing. Second, connected with this, functions that attach to sight aren't sufficiently central to chase out of the concept all of its the strictly formal elements. For example, the structure of the optic system, its morphology, is too well entrenched to consider anything that fulfills that belief-generating function but operates on altogether different principles from being considered an eye. If what was said earlier about the place of phenomenal features is correct, they, too, would seem to be resistant to displacing.

The distinction between function and design is connected, in various ways, with further questions about the type of argument I am examining. Stephen Jay Gould and Richard Lewontin (1979) have launched a notorious attack on adaptationism in evolutionary thinking: roughly, the view that any trait that has survived a long process during which natural selection was operating must have done so *because* of an adaptive advantage (in its environment or over competing organisms). If there is no obvious candidate, then there must be a hidden one we can eventually unearth. Their attack is hotly disputed by some; but we can extract from the foregoing distinction a reason why, as they painstakingly catalog in a number of cases, the supposition that there must be a design explanation for each relevantly evolved feature leads to speculations that strike us as so clearly ad hoc. Various factors other than advantage must be taken into account when explaining the development of a mechanism, including the availability of parts, history, and what is compatible with the remainder of the system. Occasionally, a system developed for altogether different reasons generates a faculty that is then capable of making use of independently existing material. But this later use may be epiphenomenal (in the sense of a mere byproduct), not the driving force (or cause) of the system. (Gould and Elizabeth Vrba (1982) have called this 'exaptation'.) This is indeed pertinent to the development of our visual system, which, like the jaw, seems to have arisen through a conjunction (and subsequent development) of separate organs—photosensitive surface cells connecting to an elongated nerve from the central nervous system—rather than through a protracted refinement of a single one. Why should this matter, since we can still recognize a definite current functioning of the system? The obvious reason is that the adaptationist argues that the system developed this way *because* it performs this function. This sort of explanation drags in its wake a tendency to drive out all other explanatory factors. But the explanation of perception arrives too late to attain this imperial status. Were natural selection a true designer, we might see the current function of the mechanism as so basic that questions of morphology or typical characteristics would seem peripheral. Since it is a mistake to view natural selection as a kind of inventor in a workshop, it is similarly a mistake to drive out nonadaptionist (nonfunctionalist) considerations in understanding relevantly evolved features.

The point might be reinforced by asking why, in the long course of evolution, certain common enough and useful structures *haven't* evolved. Is it just that the process hasn't been given enough time? For example, despite the fact that wheels are a very useful mode of locomotion, it is no accident that no creatures have evolved them. They require parts that are juxtaposed, but without physical connection, whereas physical connection seems to be an indispensable feature of living systems. What grows in nature is strictly accountable to biological possibility. Its adaptive advantage may tell us something about its thriving thereafter, but, if I am correct about the function/design distinction, adaptationist explanation is not (at least not ordinarily) in a position to disclose the nature of the mechanisms or faculties whose persistence or presence it may explain.

VII

Finally, there is the view (Pitcher 1971, chap. 3; Heil 1983, pp. 32, 105) that the way things look to us is profoundly influenced by our background beliefs, values, and so on. A short way with this claim is to grant it, but to insist that it does not warrant doxasticism. For we are interested only in beliefs that have a chance of being identical with what, under some favored system, is seen. And nothing in the foregoing claim shows that an influencing belief, value, or so on, has a chance of being identical in content with what is seen. If seeing is to be a form of belief, we must have an identity of *what* is seen and *what* is believed. (More about this in §VIII.)

To elaborate, I distinguish two batteries of beliefs: influencing beliefs, which together with values, and so on, provide the background for what we see; and content beliefs, which are supposedly generated by the particular perception. As stated, the argument indicates no more than that the influencing beliefs, values, and so on, influence how we take what we see. But even if I have general beliefs about, say, the kinds into which the world is carved, it remains very unclear how those categorial beliefs bring it about that I have particular (demonstrative) beliefs about what I am seeing on a given occasion. It may even be admitted that, because of the beliefs I have about the way the world is divided, normally when I see I 'take' things a certain way. But what power has this argument to show that the seeing *is* the taking, rather than that the former generates (habitually and normally) the latter? In brief, the evidence leaves room for both doxasticism and the alternative to it under consideration.

Let us look more closely at the sort of thing a doxasticist might have in mind. Pitcher cites an impressive body of empirical evidence for the claim that things of greater value (e.g., coins) will, under various circumstances, appear brighter and larger than similarly sized objects of lesser or no value. There is already a plausible explanation for this in the psychological literature, and it doesn't lead to doxasticism. The more interested we are in something, the more we notice it, the more our pupils dilate, the more light from that object enters the pupils, the brighter it appears. If the relevant size differentials in these experiments are explained by the amount of light entering the pupils, how does that induce doxasticism? Indeed, imagine the following fantasy. Suppose a race of perceivers genetically wired to have their pupils dilate when fixing on light green objects. Light green objects will then appear brighter to them. Why couldn't a nondoxasticist offer just this explanation of the phenomenon? The origin of pupillary dilation in greater interest or value is irrelevant. It is the dilation, not the value, that creates the disparity. And the disparity itself supplies no argument for doxasticism. The phenomenon has a purely mechanical explanation and stands in no need of influencing beliefs or values.

What about size? To some degree, brighter things look larger. Thus, we can again appeal to the previous explanation to help account for this phenomenon. But let us set that aside. The point I want to emphasize here is that Pitcher's appeal to 'how things look' is inconclusive; 'how things look' can be understood in various ways. As Pitcher uses it, it seems to mean nothing more than 'how things are taken.' But if the argument is that value can effect 'how things are taken,' this presupposes, rather than argues for, doxasticism. (Recall, *taking* implies *believing*.) To repeat, it is granted by all parties that there is a well-established nexus between seeing and believing on its basis. The only issue is whether these intimately related items are distinct. It is at this point that an objector will want to insist that if we do accept the maxim "if S sees *o*, *o* looks some way to S," we are not thereby committed to a question-begging interpretation of *o*'s looking some way in terms of belief. Thus, to settle how things are taken by the perceiver is of no use unless we have already decided that seeing is a form of taking (viz., that doxasticism is correct).

VIII

None of the arguments just canvased establish the doxastic thesis. I know of no others. What about the doctrine itself? Is there additional reason to doubt it? We may have our suspicions. For example, I'm suspicious of any account of perception that turns virtually everything about it, other than its tendency to generate a subclass of beliefs, into so much information-receiving porridge. But that isn't much of a refutation. There may also be grounds for suspicion just in the fact that it is likely to inherit weaknesses from its close polemical connections with cognitivism. Are there also more definite shortcomings? Let us pause to see if we can sniff some out.

As I mentioned, some of the faults of cognitivism exposed earlier are also defects of popular varieties of doxasticism. If we apply specifically to doxasticism the earlier experiment of the subject who falsely believes herself to be hallucinating (pp. 102–3), further vulnerabilities are uncovered. They don't surface for cognitivism alone. Of course, some points will depend in part on the details of the specific doxasticist thesis. But there will be profound difficulties aplenty for all versions. I briefly sketch a similar example.

S realizes that she has been given a drug to induce hallucination. S, in fact, sees an opposum on the ground (sleeping or "playing possum"), but she supposes that she is hallucinating. In fact, S doesn't even take her experience as being of an opposum, but as being of a rock. Thus, even as far as identification goes, if S did believe she was seeing she would say she saw a rock. Pitcher offers a roughly similar challenge to his own first formulation of doxasticism: "A man is stumbling across the desert when suddenly there looms before him what he takes to be a mirage, or better yet, a hallucinatory vision, of an oasis. He is absolutely sure that his senses are deceiving him, or that his mind is, because that has been the case on the forty-three very recent occasions when he thought he saw an oasis. This time, however, the oasis is genuine. Surely it cannot be denied that the desert traveller sees the oasis" (1971, pp. 82–83). My example contains an additional difficulty for doxasticism: that is, not only a mistake about whether S is seeing, but a misidentification of *what* she is seeing (and mistakenly thinks she's halluci-nating). Either one may be problem enough for the position.

Two articles, implicit in the most popular version of doxasticism—in fact, the only version that proves viable—exacerbate the difficulty. (Remember, doxasti-cists identify perceptions not only with beliefs, but also with acquisitions of beliefs and inclinations to believe. I state these articles in terms of beliefs, but they can be reformulated more precisely if needed.) There will always be a certain belief content in terms of which a given instance of seeing is to be understood. I repre-sent it with the schematic letter 'B.' I may then characterize the two articles as follows:

(i) B must, in some sense, be the same as what is seen.
(ii) B must be true.

Article (i) needs qualification. Even on cognitivism, what is seen is a fact or state of affairs, but what is believed is a proposition or sentence. Here the differ-ence between the presentational nature of sight on direct realism and the *re*presen-tational nature of belief cannot be ignored. Thus, it may not even be intelligible to claim what can be seen or to see what can be believed. Those who tend to collapse whatever gets introduced via 'that' clauses into a single category may be prone to overlook this difference. Nevertheless, belief and sight contents should correlate in the following way: the proposition believed will express just the fact (or state of affairs or thing) seen. Of course, as with (ii), we can imagine a form of doxasticism without this requirement. Nevertheless, it does embody an im-portant part of the doxasticist outlook. A leading doxasticist motive is to supply an account of the content of visual experience (= of what is seen) that will avoid what they (doxasticists) take to be the pitfalls of phenomenal accounts. How can a belief do this if the only true descriptions of the propositions believed don't express *any* true description of what is seen? Under these circumstances, isn't there some visual content for which the belief analysis gives no accounting? This problem may not prove fatal. But even if doxasticism can find a way out without adopting (i), it will require at least a complication of theory to coordinate the description of what is believed with that of what is seen. In the process, the view may also begin to look less convincing. Nor do I believe this is a problem only for those doxasticists who rely on the 'only alternative to sense-data' argument. Any doxasticist theory whose belief contents do not match up in the required way to visual content leaves an opening for a different, phenomenal, approach to occupy its unclaimed territory.

As long as 'what is believed' is a candidate for truth-valuation, it would appear that (ii) follows from (i). Since what is seen cannot be false as long as the statement that it is seen is true, it is difficult to conceive how what is believed can be anything but true.[10] Nevertheless, doxasticists have substantially qualified their acceptance of (ii). This is in part dictated by their general methodology. Since that can lead to a misunderstanding of the main point, perhaps the matter should be addressed before putting aside the topic.

For doxasticism, it is generally perceptual experiences, not perceptions, that initiate beliefs or their inclinations. Thus, just as some perceptual experiences are hallucinatory, delusive, and so on—rather than genuine perceptions—so some perceptual beliefs are erroneous. (Unfortunately, the confusion of genuine perception with veridical perception infects these distinctions. I stated in chap. 4 that these categories do not coincide even if they overlap. And it is in part their area of nonoverlap in which we find the tough cases in which the connection unravels.) I am *not* claiming that (i) commits doxasticism to the view that all visually generated beliefs are true. For example, some of these beliefs will be generated by visual experiences that are neither identical with actual seeings nor ingredients in them. They can be hallucinatory. But in cases of actual seeing, *if* what is experienced is identical with what is seen, *and* what is seen is the same as ('matches' in the sense described earlier) what is believed, the unavoidable consequence is that the belief is true, even after allowance is made for distinguishing the kinds of intentionality that may classify different 'what's. However, Pitcher explicitly accepts (ii) only for what he calls 'The First Case' (1971, p. 86), and other doxasticists have barely begun to plumb the depths implied by such a commitment. In any event, perhaps it is a commitment we should keep in mind for later consideration, for it also follows from doxastic positions that take cognitivism as a basis. (Recall the success-verb status, (a), of *seeing that,* p. 88.)

Against this backdrop, what are we to make of the case of the drugged experimental subject? One reply has been that such cases are "not conclusive," because it may be that S "forms at least a suppressed belief (or inclination to believe)" that there is a rock in front of her (Goldman 1977, p. 258). At a minimum, this forces the doxasticist to give up the view, (i), that the content of seeing and believing are identical. By thereby leaving a very important element of a seeing episode, its actual content, unexplained via the belief, it sacrifices a central inducement for adopting doxasticism in the first place. Even if we can, on some occasions, find a suppressed inclination to believe accompanying a perception, it remains a mystery how its content could be an ingredient in an analysis of the wholly divergent thing that is seen. It also abandons (ii). S has misidentified the opposum as a rock, and thus if she had to believe something was in front of her, it would be that it is a rock—a false belief.

Perhaps it will be complained that the discovery of a suppressed inclination to believe in such cases looks suspiciously ad hoc. Ultimately, I think the charge is not wholly unjust. (I return to it in §IX.) Moreover, if the mere possibility of a suppressed inclination is enough to render a counterexample "not conclusive," we may suspect that we are being held to an unreasonably high standard of conclusiveness. Certainly, if there is any point to testing sweeping claims by trying to find counterexamples, this seems to be as clear a case as one could find of a successful negative result. However, giving doxasticists their due, they have not been oblivious to these sorts of problems and have attempted to handle them. For all that, I believe the most valiant of those efforts fail. Let us look at those that seem to be most responsive to the problem.

Armstrong (1968) and Pitcher (1971) both recognize degrees of tractability in the range of perceptual cases. In the first case, there is no problem. What is seen just is what is believed. But there are hesitant cases also, in which we recognize immediately that the scene cannot have the properties we are inclined to ascribe to it. Pitcher offers the case of a driver on a hot, dry day who sees what looks like a wet spot ahead on the road, but realizes it cannot be wet. In such cases, we have "an inclination to believe", but nothing more (Armstrong 1968, p. 221; Pitcher 1971, p. 92). But the cases opening this section of the would-be hallucinator or the desert traveler cannot be dispatched so handily. Here it does not seem plausible to suppose that the perceiver has even a (straightforward) inclination to believe something based on present visual experience alone. At this juncture in the dialectic, the views of Armstrong and Pitcher diverge.

Armstrong holds that all cases of what he calls 'perception without belief' are 'potential beliefs'. They would have been beliefs but for the presence of contrary beliefs inhibiting them. How is this to be explained? Armstrong attempts to bring potential belief into line by understanding it via a counterfactual: "[b]ut for the fact that the perceiver had other, independent beliefs about the world, he would have acquired certain beliefs—the beliefs corresponding to the content of this perception" (p. 222).

For starters, let's pose a loaded question: Why shouldn't we take this as an explanation of the failure of doxasticism rather than a defense of it? Armstrong's counterfactual seems to suit this unsympathetic explanation quite nicely. It explains why some perceptions are not beliefs, and thus why perceiving cannot be a species of belief. To prevent the appropriation of Armstrong's counterfactual for nondoxastic ends, more is needed: say, not only that the counterfactual is true, but that Armstrong's account of it supplies the best (or only) way to understand the particular perceptual episode. This would tie the nature of the episode to its capacity to become a belief. But that seems to reintroduce at the next step a trace of an inclination to believe, which is precisely what the counterfactual sought to elucidate. Even so, making out that the counterfactual is crucial to understanding the perceptual episode will be a formidable challenge. I will explain.

A basic problem with that line of argument is that even if an actual event is a potential belief, it is difficult to see how it can be *only* that. [11] An actual something that is also a potential F must be more than just a potential F. Otherwise, how does one account for its actuality (as something else)? And, ex hypothesi, we are dealing with an actual perceptual event.

The point, in generalized form, might go as follows. If we allow that some actual G is a potential belief, it must also be an actual something over and above its being a potential belief. Call this additional character it has 'being F'. Presumably G is a potential belief *because* it is an F, for a thing's potentiality depends in an obvious way on its actual features. *Non entia non sunt effectus.* Perhaps G might never have developed the capacity to become an F had it not been for its ability to become a belief. (More on this in §X.) Even so, it is difficult to see how the potentiality for belief could explain the present constitution, as opposed to the origin, of F. Whatever F might be, it would appear that it is more reasonable to discover visual content in it, since, unlike belief, it is present in each case of sight. (Of course, we are limited in our choice of F if we want something that will both support the counterfactual and still credit this as an episode of seeing in the absence of an actual belief. If it is not, among other things, a phenomenal content, what else could it be?)

This line of thought, if plausible, should be particularly demoralizing for doxasticism, a prime selling point of which was that the only remaining candidate for perceptual content is unacceptable. If, to salvage its own view, doxasticism must let other features of visual content into the picture, what has become of that advantage? Of course, to say that there is little left for Fness to be if it does not include phenomenal features is not to say that it is a sense-datum (as in the doxasticist's dreaded prediction).

This is not the only problem with Armstrong's solution. Even for those of us nondoxasticists who agree that perception is belief-inducing (through cultivated habit), the counterfactual fails to capture the essence of this relation. Which *independent* beliefs about the world must be ruled out for the belief condition of perception to be met? We must have some such independent beliefs or other: it is difficult to imagine what beliefs perception would generate were our minds totally blank slates at the time. Must we rule out, for example, the belief that the deliverances of perception are normally reliable? Filling in the details of Armstrong's counterfactual, either in the general case or in particular cases, is a prodigious task. And, as Frank Jackson (1977, pp. 40–42) has shown, this path is filled with dangers against which there is no obvious defense.

Up to a point, Pitcher's solution is like Armstrong's. He appeals in the hard cases to a suppressed inclination to believe (1971, pp. 92–94). Unlike Armstrong, Pitcher does not seek to elucidate it counterfactually. To better account for a variety of cases, Pitcher's solution is proffered in the context of an analysis of the locution, "It looks to S as though there is an x at place u." In the most challenging cases—those of the desert traveler or the would-be hallucinator—even an inclination to believe, say, that this is an oasis (or a rock) doesn't seem to be present. Nevertheless, he maintains that we have reason to ascribe to the perceiver a *suppressed* inclination to believe that this is an oasis (or a rock), *viz.*, that there is an x at u, suppressed because of the presence of conflicting beliefs.

What reason is there to hold this? If it looks to me as if the railroad tracks are converging in the distance, am I suppressing a belief that they do converge? I realize right off, without any hesitation, that they don't converge. This is certainly an indication that I am not suppressing a belief to the contrary. It might be assumed that in my callow youth I had such a belief about similar structures. If that were the case, or if there were palpable hesitation in my reaction, there might be at least a shred of a basis for the ascription of a suppressed inclination. But the assumption about my youth is pure speculation, and no hesitation is ordinarily detected. (Do we have inclinations to believe whatever youthful fancies we have since been disabused of?) Thus, the existence of such a suppressed inclination lacks independent confirmation.

If we lack evidence of a suppressed inclination to cover all the cases for which it is needed, have we at least some indication of what to look for in trying to detect one? Pitcher's only clue is an analogy, and it is more confusing than helpful. He mentions the case in which we want to believe a child's story, but find the evidence against it overwhelming (1971, p. 93). The problem with this is that *wanting* to believe something is not the same as having a suppressed inclination to believe it, or at least not a suppressed inclination of the right kind. My wanting to believe something is not evidence for even a proto-belief, and it can operate as a cause of genuine belief only when it is sufficiently suppressed into my subconscious that I no longer realize it is operating *as a want*.

If we impose on the view the conditions that the belief and visual content must be the same and that the belief must be true—(i) and (ii) from earlier in this section—it becomes even more difficult to satisfy the demands of a suppressed inclination to believe in the case in which S falsely believes she is hallucinating a rock. She has an inclination to believe two things that are incompatible with the supposedly suppressed inclination we are ascribing to her: that she is hallucinating and that, if she weren't, she would be seeing a rock. For either (i) or (ii) to be true, S must somehow also have a suppressed inclination to believe that she is seeing something other than a rock. But the best candidate for a suppressed inclination to believe anything perceptually here is that she is seeing a rock. What independent motive is there for targeting a suppressed inclination to believe something other than this?

Suppose, as in my recent thought experiment, S has a belief tantamount to not-*p*. How can S also have an inclination, suppressed or otherwise, to believe that *p*? Well, people do have inconsistent beliefs. But I am supposing S to be aware at the time of the inconsistency, and as a rule people do not hold inconsistent occurrent beliefs while at the same time being aware of the import of their inconsistency. Moreover, we have just seen that believing one thing while wanting to believe something else will not elucidate this. Perhaps we can say that S may have *a reason to believe p,* despite her belief that not-*p*. I think this may be the kernel of truth in Pitcher's claim. But if this is what he has in mind, it is no help toward refurbishing his proposal for a suppressed inclination to believe. A reason to believe, even one in possession, does not add up to an inclination to believe. I have many relatively minor reasons to believe things that I surely have no inclination to believe, such as that any arbitrarily selected one of my comrades will betray me. (That someone has betrayed some comrade in the past is some inductive evidence, though surely very little, that this one of mine will betray me.) People sometimes weigh reasons on both sides of an issue before concluding what to believe, but each reason on a given side is not in effect a miniature inclination to believe. In the case of perception, the outlook is even more meager for this variety of reason to believe. I do have a reason to believe my visual experience, namely, its general reliability. But as an explanation of how perceptual belief is normally fixed, it appears to suit nondoxasticism even better. The connection thus explained, running through reliability rather than belief, seems to be empirical and contingent. (See §X for a fuller development of this point.) It presupposes no suppressed inclination to believe and would explain the general connection of perception and belief without one.

IX

I have concentrated on the problem of ascribing to a subject the appropriate belief, or an inclination to it, in rather special circumstances. But let us suppose we can somehow overcome the ascription problem. It is worth at least brief attention to see whether, again in the special circumstances, the resulting belief (or suppressed inclination to believe) could satisfy conditions (i) and (ii) of the preceding section, that is, whether it could be the same as what is seen or whether it could even be true. Dealing with (i)—the belief must, in some sense, be the same as what is seen—requires sorting out some possibilities.

Considering only my earlier two 'see' constructions, we seem to have at least several alternatives for what sameness of belief and visual content could amount to. Objectual seeing is a tough case because, unlike standard representations of belief content, it lacks propositionality. Thus, if doxasticism attempts to satisfy (i) with respect to objectual seeing, perhaps the best corresponding belief we could come up with would be one framed in the earlier predicative idiom—S believes x to be F—understood in such a way that F provides a description that could be given in a true objectual report of the seeing (but not necessarily one the subject could give). I shall let this much pass. Even so, in the earlier case in which S saw an opposum, the only description of a belief she was likely to be inclined to give is that there is a rock in front of her, and these contents do not match up as (i) requires.

The case of propositional reports is a bit more complicated. I divide it into two cases. At one point, Armstrong (1968) writes that a belief is identical with the content of a *seeing that* report, but he suggests paranthetically, as if to guard against just this sort of difficulty, that a 'seem to see that' report will do (e.g., 1961, p. 228). I treat each construction in turn.

In the earlier example, had S not believed she was hallucinating, she might have been inclined to report that she saw that a rock was before her—precisely what she would have believed. Thus, it seems we have just the right sort of coincidence between her reports of belief and seeing content. The problem is that, although the report would truly disclose the content of her belief, it would not truly disclose the content of her seeing. She does not see that there is a rock before her. The content of her seeing is identical with its object, and, ex hypothesi, there is no rock to serve as object; thus there is no rock to serve as content. The only thing capable of serving as the content of her seeing is 'that there is an opposum before her' or, perhaps, 'the opposum before her.' The former she doesn't see *that,* for she doesn't take it for an opposum, and neither is identical with (or matches) the belief content.

I now turn to what S 'seems to see that'. When, as in the present case, she seems to see that there is a rock before her, what is the content of her seeming to see? A natural answer might be 'that there is a rock before her,' but that can't be right. Recall that the episode is one of seeing, and ultimately the connection mediated by 'seeming to see that' is to enable us to match up the contents of the seeing and the belief. For a direct realist, the content of the seeing cannot be other than what is in fact seen, and no rock is in fact seen. S sees an opposum. She takes it for a rock. The phrase 'a rock' should not therefore be taken as a (partial) description of S's visual content, but as a description of *the way she takes* her content. But, again, the way she takes her content, in fact an opposum before her, is not an element of the visual content. It is rather a relation she bears to it. To make 'that there is a rock before her' a description of her actual content, we would need to introduce something other than what she sees (that) as a more immediate object (of, perhaps, a more immediate episode), and the opposum would then be an inferential object of the familiar kind in indirect realism. If it is substantial enough to serve as part of her content, it is a *something* that is in her experience.

There is another very general supposition, however, that might be used to get around the counterexamples. Imagine the claim that although none of the beliefs I have produced can be identical with what is seen, seen that, or seems to have been seen that, another belief, phrased in terms neutral between rocks and possums, is also present. I call any such neutral rephrasings 'sterilized descriptions.' The seeing can also be reported with a sterilized description, thereby insuring the coincidence of what is believed and seen.

Although sterilized descriptions concern only the physical world, the method harkens back to the older empricist doctrine (discussed in chap. 4, p. 109) of an unadulterated language in which sense-data (or whatever occurs at the purely 'observational' level) could be sharply insulated from the unwanted implications of theoretical add-ons. I have no inkling whether this notion, confined now to physical description, is workable. In any event, the attempt to use it to rescue doxasticism is fraught with all sorts of perils. For one thing, it must be applied on a case-by-case basis, with no further guidance about the type of description wanted. There is no neatly delineated level of description at which all cases of relevant perceptual misdescription or error occur. For another, we would need to countenance a very generous practice of belief ascription to ensure a supply of relevant beliefs for all cases like the whale example or the opposum/rock confusion. Sterilized descriptions do not, as a rule, replicate the way someone is likely to report her beliefs, and it is highly speculative that a believer would ordinarily be willing to accept the restatement. Thus, we would need some assurance that the believer indeed had such a belief, despite the fragmentary operation of the usual tests. If these are not the ways our beliefs are reported, and behavioral tests are likely to be too crude, why are we so confident in supposing that preceivers have such beliefs? Is it, once again, an appeal to a purer level of language, in which all things can be reported accurately? That bit of philosophical orthodoxy stands in serious need of defense. Finally, in reaching for a suitably sterilized description of a belief a perceiver might have, what assurance have we that this is likely to avoid violating the adequacy condition of content retention discussed in chapter 4, pp. 85–6. Although S sees an opposum, she would not describe it that way. But any way she would describe it is likely to be at a level of comparable richness. Although none of these may turn out to be true descriptions of what she saw, they may be all she can sincerely offer. In sum, there is no guarantee that there is any available description of the content of S's seeing or visual experience other than 'a possum before her' (or something similarly complex). Since this is not an instance in which she just lacks the right vocabulary to express her true beliefs, what remaining reasons have we for warding off the unhappy conclusion that she is incapable in the circumstances of having any belief whose content coincides with it?

X

There is perhaps another way to test the doxasticist hypothesis, but it requires a preliminary explanation. Since both sides admit that there is a systematic, normal relation between sight and belief fixation, a mere correlation of these will not decide the issue. What we want to know is whether the connection between perception and perceptual belief is, to put it crudely, contingent or conceptual. Toward this end, there is another feature of perceptual beliefs that may be more useful: that they are generally *reliable* or *justified*. Our current situation, then, is that we have something correlated with perceptions, call them 'Gs,' and they have two features that interest us: being beliefs and being (normally) reliable. If the correlation depended solely on Gs' being beliefs, this would be strong evidence in favor of doxasticism. If beliefs were generated along with perceptions, independently of the former's normal reliability, it is difficult to see what explanation a nondoxasticist might offer of how a (contingent) correlation of this sort would come about. But if the correlation depended on Gs' being *reliable* beliefs, nondoxasticism has the advantage. If we then asked how it is possible for two contingently related items (perceptions and perceptual beliefs) to be systematically connected, an answer would be forthcoming: the continued reliability of the beliefs reinforces a habit of automatically accepting perceptual information. We might even, if one's taste runs that way, couch the explanation in the language of natural selection. I am not claiming that this sort of test is conclusive. If sight's connection with Gs is through their being justified, the doxasticist, too, might use the link of normal reliability. For her, it could form the basis for a historical account of how primitive photosensitivity developed into epistemically understood vision. However, by leaving open the possibility of an explanation for indicating how a contingently related perception and perceptual belief might be systematically correlated (and, under the circumstances, a less contrived explanation than the doxasticist's alternative), this option places the burden of proof squarely on the shoulders of doxasticism.

Thus, it would be instructive if we could devise an experiment to distinguish the plausibility of these two hypotheses about Gs. We might begin by noting that it is strictly a contingent fact that the beliefs we get from seeing are reliable. It is easy enough to imagine a world in which they would not be. Let us do so. The world is either different from our actual one, or we are imagining a future change in our present world in which this contingent connection no longer obtains: perceptual beliefs are not (or are no longer) reliable, indeed are to an equal extent unreliable.

The next step is a sterner test of the reader's tolerance of contingent absurdity. Even if we are granted that perception *could* continue to evolve in this linear fashion without perceptual belief being reliable, it is difficult to imagine that creatures with just our faculties in every other respect would survive long enough to note the fact. (That is why it may be easier to imagine that our perceptual beliefs suddenly become unreliable than that they never were so, though the former supposition raises more questions for the purpose to which I want to put it.) But I now ask you to imagine just that. Somehow—perhaps through the development of a supplementary reliable faculty—our species continues to survive over an extended period of time, long enough to become familiar with the nearly total unreliability of the deliverances of perceptual experience. Would we continue to believe what we 'see'? It certainly doesn't seem so. Why would anyone continue to accept the contents of a so-called faculty with no rational expectation of justification? Any habit we might have formerly cultivated to believe what we take ourselves to see would atrophy. For this reason, it is easier to accept the view that seeing generates belief because of the contingent fact that such beliefs are, as a rule, justified than that seeing *is* belief.

The doxasticist is not without resources for this eventuality, but they strike me as ineffectual. For example, she may hold that the experiment is impossible, for when the inclination to believe disappears, so does the seeing (perception). Indeed, hasn't this been her position all along? However, despite the extravagance of the scene, I find it difficult to convince myself that it is impossible. Little in the details of the doxasticist's actual position is designed to wean us away from the intelligibility of belief and the other factors in sight to come apart as imagined. (In fact, some of what I discover in just about every doxasticist seems to make it quite intelligible: e.g., Heil 1983, p. 63; Armstrong 1968, p. 212.) It may be easier to accept that, with the disappearance of perceptual belief, our very perceptual abilities will degrade until we are no longer aware of their deliverances. But it seems quite likely that for some time we would continue to be able to train ourselves to note them, just as we can come to notice so-called white noise (say, of a chorus of cicadas on a summer evening) with a bit of effort. This is sufficient to assure us that the imagined division of belief from sight is intelligible.

Another potential reply is that, although actual beliefs are no longer generated by perceptual experience, we will retain a suppressed inclination to believe, thwarted only because it has become overgrown by a new habit of not heeding perceptual deliverances. This line has little to recommend it. What are we to make of an inclination that is forever dormant and that, over time, is quite effortlessly resisted? Such a claim strikes me as empty.

I return to my original point. The beliefs to which perceptions are currently attached are justified beliefs. Therefore, we should ask whether the relation (which, in the case of doxasticism, is subsumption) results from their being beliefs or from their being justified. My fanciful scenario was designed to show that justification, not belief, accounts for the relation. This, in turn, suggests that perception normally and automatically generates belief through long-established habit. That conclusion is the nondoxasticist alternative to saying that perception is a form of belief.

In light of the problems with doxasticism, the phenomenal features of sight, assuming that they aren't vulnerable to comparable objections, supply the default position. This doesn't mean that there isn't further work to do. Accepting phenomenal features as such doesn't even begin to address issues concerning qualia and materialist reduction. Chapter 9 goes part of the way to allay these concerns, but no doubt not far enough to satisfy certain critics. Moreover, this does not mean that functions have no place in the concept *vision,* although they will have no tendency to drive out other candidate intrinsic features unless we can identify a designer that imposed the function. But even the plausible function I conceded to sight (and that only for the sake of argument)—the delivery of certain types of information—falls short of what the doxasticist needs. That so little progress has been made toward a full-blooded account of visual content may disappoint readers. But nothing more was promised. My modest goal was to evaluate doxasticism, and I have accomplished that. In the next chapter, I explore what I take to be the last stand of both doxasticism and cognitivism. I also offer some broad hints about the more specific nature of the relationship between sight and belief.

6

The Generation of Perceptual Belief

[W]hen the decisive facts did at length obtrude themselves upon my notice, it was very slowly, and with great hestitation, that I yielded to the evidence of my senses. . . . That this was the case, I attribute to the force of prejudice, which, unknown to ourselves, biasses not only our *judgments,* properly so called, but even the perceptions of our senses: for we may take a maxim so strongly for granted, that the plainest evidence of sense will not intirely change, and often hardly modify our persuasions.

JOSEPH PRIESTLY, *Experiments and Observations on Different Kinds of Air*

I

It may seem that the exposition so far has deprived perception of any of its traditional significance. In chapter 1, the focal conceptual issue (and the role of a causal component) was sharply distinguished from direct inquiries into perception's contribution to knowledge. This places to one side a central motive epistemologists have had for the study of perception. The past few chapters have rejected a popular explanation for the close relation between perceptual episodes and belief, that is, the doctrine that perceptual experience is subsumed under belief or belief inclination. This puts yet a larger gap between the present treatment of perception and the topic of perceptual *knowledge* with which it had formerly been joined. Moreover, my examination of cognitivism has concluded that we cannot use the most straightforward way of showing how a single thing might serve as a content both of a perception and of a belief. Hitherto, cognitivism had been a common assumption on which doxasticism was erected. Finally, although an intimate connection between perceptual episodes and the generation of beliefs has been remarked, very little has been done to clarify that relationship. Thus far, one might complain, all the action takes place in a black box. Indeed, to this point, efforts have been bent almost exclusively toward blocking the most direct avenue for explaining how their crucial interaction comes about.

In this chapter, I set out to restore the balance by offering some positive suggestions about perceptual belief fixation; commencing with the elaboration of a theme (introduced at the close of the last chapter) that the connection results not from perceptual belief's character *as belief,* but from its being, by and large, *justified* or *reliable.* But there is not much high drama in the sketchy and somewhat prosaic account on offer. In this instance, as sometimes happens (to the amazement of a certain breed of cognoscenti), widely held homely intuitions are reliable pointers toward a solution.

After outlining the basic view and attempting to dispel a few misconceptions about it, I examine what I take to be the most pervasive and ultimate objection to any nondoxastic account of this relationship: the dual contention that nothing can justify a belief except another belief and that nothing can be justified that isn't already in the form of a belief content. Thus, perception can neither be justified nor justify anything else unless it already possesses the essential character of belief. Actually, this is more like a family of contentions, since its core insight is developed in a number of different directions. But although the details often lack sharp focus, the complaints stem from a single outlook. Before probing that issue further, I outline a familiar and humdrum tale of one relationship between seeing and believing.

A clear alternative to doxasticism must explain not only how perceptual belief is generated by seeing, but also why the two are so closely yoked as to seem blended. I hold that these projects can be easily combined into a single, elaborated account. Before undertaking that task, let's raise what will seem to some a prior question: If perception is objectual and belief propositional, how is such a relation even conceivable? Put otherwise, how does the one sort of content generate the other? Although there may be a number of ways to get at what it is, more precisely, that bothers someone who raises this question, I will jump in by offering a short answer: in much the same way that an explanation is drawn from any nonlinguistic evidence. This is to construe the question as being about what may seem to be an insurmountable barrier separating the forms of object specifications in the things that are supposed to interact (viz., sight and perceptual belief). Of course, *explanations* are always at least potentially propositional. But phenomena that display widely diverse structures may contribute the labor that gives explanations their weight. Similarly, the phenomena of perception do not have to be cast already into a certain structure in order to generate their correlative beliefs. It would be fallacious to suppose that just because our reporting takes a certain form, what we are reporting must be of a similar form. The fact that, normally or canonically, sight is objectual, belief propositional, is by itself no cause for alarm.

Even if we don't preclude *the possibility* of belief generation, what explains its actual occurrence? A seeing episode causally generates a perceptual belief. But the central part of the tale has yet to unfold. The content of the former is responsible for the content of the latter. The causal relationship is mediated by *understanding*. But, although causation via intentional content is a rather special sort of causation, it is not peculiar to sight and belief. It occurs when one person understands the words of another, when someone acquires a belief based on another's evidence, or when intentions issue in behavior. I assume the principle on which it operates is, minimally, no more problematic than the least worrisome cases of this group. This is not to say that there isn't further room for elucidation of this variety of causation. (For a summary of them, see Kim (1993), essays 14, 15.) But any problems it may conceal are not confined to the perception-belief nexus. If problems at all, they more broadly infect a familiar type of causation. Given the limits of this inquiry, I simply rely on the consensus that this sort of causation occurs, even if further analysis of it is badly needed.

However, there are special features of this relationship that warrant further comment: namely, that a typical belief is generated so regularly and unobtrusively as to make it difficult to distinguish it from the perception, and that the beliefs so generated are normally reliable. The latter feature results from the fact that perceptual contents (as distinct from belief contents) have been reliable indicators of the environment, transmitting their reliability to the beliefs they fix. Once again, this is a contingent fact. If perceptions hadn't been reliable—and their subjects still somehow survived—perceptual contents wouldn't have led to beliefs. And if such creatures had had compensating methods for obtaining survival information, it is a good guess that over time their perceptual faculties would have atrophied. At the very least, those faculties would have been likely to recede in consciousness, like certain ordinarily unnoticed kinaesthetic sensations that we can be trained to heed. But, as a matter of fact, perceptual belief has proved so reliable for ordinary purposes that tendencies to act on perception (hence to believe its deliverances) are constantly reinforced, and the step from seeing to believing has become habitual and nearly instantaneous.

Thought experiments presented in chapters 4 (p. 103) and 5 (pp. 138–9) distinguished visual episodes from correlative beliefs. There is also some revealing clinical evidence in rare disorders, such as agnosia, a neurological recognition deficit. (Prosopagnosiacs have this deficit for face recognition in particular.) An agnosiac can scan the scene, but, due to a local impairment, may utterly fail to recognize or identify it. It seems clear that the subject sees what is in front of him in these instances, not only from what he says (e.g., that there are such and such features or that he can see it but can't identify it) but also occasionally from his ability to sketch in detail what he has seen (Levine et al. 1985, esp. pp. 1011–12). Even in these cases, the absence of automatic perceptual identification is never total and usually manifests itself most clearly in an inability to recognize faces. As one articulate agnosiac has remarked, "If I recognize [the face], it is by means of an addendum, such as glasses or a beard. I rely on these and on where I see the person. . . . I run through the people it might be and then use addenda. It's a logical process rather than a visual one" (ibid., p. 1011). The authors add that the agnosiac's wife had to wear a distinguishing item, such as a hair ribbon, for him to identify her at parties. Of course, a died-in-the-wool doxasticist might insist that, insofar as the subject had visual episodes, there must have also been *some visual belief or other,* if not the generally expected recognitional one. Despite some early misleading nondoxastic language, I don't know that anyone denies this. But the crucial question is still whether the perceptual beliefs are identical with what is seen. In the present cases, this is precisely what is missing. If even some of what the subject sees is not encoded as a belief, then that much of the visual episode is not a visual belief. Any part of visual content left over after the belief element has been exhausted should be a problem for the doxasticist explanation of the nature of such content. Still, I am not pressing this in the present context as a knockdown objection. Rather, it is intended as an illustration of how we may shed layers of habit to uncover what it is like for seeing to be sharply separated from certain sorts of recognitional, perceptual beliefs, which, under normal circumstances, we unhesitantly identify with our perception. This is all in the service of making it palpable how the stages of vision and visual belief may be pried apart.

The foregoing thesis, then, is that perception causally generates perceptual beliefs, that they are distinct, and that their close connection is accounted for by the fact that the beliefs have been generally very reliable and thus advantageous to believers. Let us call it the *natural thesis,* or NT for handy reference because I venture that it will strike most readers as perfectly natural. It would hardly be worth stating with such ceremony but for the fact that some have denied it. Its greatest drawback isn't its initial credibility, but subsequent problems that can arise in implementing so self-evident a suggestion. I know of no dramatically decisive argument for NT. The most striking evidence on its behalf is the *close relationship* between perceptual episodes and perceptual beliefs. Perception effort-lessly, instantaneously, and with only extremely rare exceptions, yields perceptual belief. By itself that doesn't distinguish NT from doxasticism. But with the demise of doxasticism, urged in the last two chapters, it leaves the field to NT to explain that close relationship.

However, although the reliability of perception is evidence for NT, it doesn't seem to be evidence of the same sort for doxasticism. If we were to assume doxasticism from the outset, perception's general reliability might provide a sup-plementary confirmation of it. For example, it might help explain why perceptual believers have survived. Or it might form part of an explanation of why the whole system would have flourished in the course of evolution. But although reliability may indicate why a connection subsists between separate things, it has no ten-dency to show that perception is a form of belief. Thus, by itself perceptual relia-bility can be evidence for NT alone. Since this data can be absorbed by doxasti-cism, should we have independent reasons for holding that view, I would not claim that it is evidence *against* doxasticism. But neither is it evidence for it.

In outlining the present view, we should note that causation enters at two stages: once for CTP and once for NT. Let us call the causation inherent in CTP, that of object to visual episode, 'causation$_1$'. Object causation is not only a condi-tion of visual perception, it is also a de facto necessary condition of perceptual episodes being reliable indices of the environment. Were it absent, then, in lieu of the intervention of something on the order of The Benevolent Designer, there would be no reason to have expected that our episodes would be sufficiently regu-lar to rely on. This causal condition is not sufficient for reliability. But then again neither is it *merely* a necessary condition: it is also central to understanding why perceptual belief is in fact reliable. In the absence of speculations about pernicious influences that would not only distort the signal but even make it irregular, the presence of causation$_1$ indicates why such episodes should be capable of generat-ing reliable belief. In this qualified sense, the causal connection embodied in prin-ciples like (C) underwrites the reliability of vision.

At the second stage, a more complicated event or state of affairs involving the perceptual episode causes$_2$ perceptual belief. The cause comprises the perceptual episode plus the particular causation (the relation between the cause and effect) of its object. All are factors in generating the perceptual belief. It may help to draw on Dretske's (1988, 1993) distinction between triggering and structuring causes. (For our restricted issue, we can set aside the question, for which Dretske invokes the distinction, whether it accounts for the eligibility of causation via content.) The title 'triggering' is suggestive of the phenomenon: instances include turning a handle to draw water from the faucet, a hurricane damaging a home, depressing of a key on a computer keyboard to make a letter appear on the monitor, turning a knob to play the radio, one billiard ball moving another through contact, walking to one's destination, swatting a fly, and firing a pistol by pulling its trigger. Object causation, cause$_1$, of vision is another instance. But a triggering cause takes place against background conditions that have a cause themselves, and the causes of the background conditions are, narrowly constued, structuring causes. S (an arbitrary structuring cause) is the cause (either structuring or triggering) of B (a correlative background) in which T (a correlative triggering cause) is able to trigger E (the effect of T). Extending Dretske's nomenclature, I refer to the constellation involving S, B, and the causing of B by S—that is all of S → B—as the *broad* structuring cause. This will later allow me the (merely) terminological convenience of considering B as a constituent, rather than an effect, of the structuring cause. One might demand that in strictness S, broadly or narrowly construed, is not a cause of E but of T's causing E. But conversational practice also allows us to cite it as a cause of E. Other than the relativity of causal *explanation* to interest, one reason for this may be that the conditions it creates can make the operation of some T or other very dependable. (More on this to follow.) Another reason, as Dretske notes (1993, p. 125), is that hallmark, nonbacktracking,[1] causal, counterfactual dependencies hold for S and E just as they do for T and E. Thus, filling the tank with petrol (narrow S) creates a full tank (B), which enables the car to run (E) when the ignition is turned on (T). Similarly, lining the logs with tinder (S) creates flammability conditions (B), in which introducing a lit match (T) triggers combustion of the log pile (E). When, in later chapters, I discuss causal chains, the primary interest is in triggering causes, though examples of chains given here and elsewhere typically include nodes of each kind.

Cause$_2$ is a more complicated story, involving a constellation of causes rather than a single stroke. Part of cause$_2$ that interests us is a triggering cause: the perceptual episode triggers a belief. But this does not exhaust the whole, or even the core, of the explanation NT envisages; NT should account not only for occasions of belief causation, but also for (a) its near-universal connection with perception and (b) the automatic or habitual, almost imperceptible way in which it operates. The background conditions of broad structuring causes have an explanatory advantage that we may exploit in explaining (a) and (b): their tendency (or at least possibility) to persist beyond bringing about a given token effect. Narrow structuring causes are triggering causes of (or relative to) the background conditions in place that permit the triggering cause of E to operate. Thus, my filling the tank is a trigger for the background condition of the tank being full, against which my turning on the ignition triggers the car to start. Background conditions such as the full tank, unlike triggering causes, typically continue in place past the time of at least some of their natural effects, and thereby enable a number of token triggers—in principle without limit—to operate. In the present case, once generated by narrow S, the background conditions that permit the generation of perceptual belief remain in place for the operation of object causation without limit.

We need take no stand on the more specific origin of the perception/perceptual belief relationship. Perhaps it is to be discovered in our genetic makeup. The reaching reflex of newborns is some evidence of this. For the sake of argument, we may grant that the rock on which the perceptual fixation of belief is founded is genetic. Then our genetic makeup will be (at least part of) our background condition, B, and whatever may be the causes of creatures with that genetic inheritance flourishing will be (at least part of) narrow S. Nevertheless, as studies have shown, the impulse to form perceptual belief (or the reaching reflex) can be quickly extinguished by frustration. The reliability of the belief generated (e.g., the fact that the infant does normally catch the object seen) accounts for the absence of frustration and sustains the connection. Consequently, the successful run of past instances is another part of S, since reliability, too, is a part of B. Thus, although the object seen may trigger the belief, it is the fact that the object is the source of this impulse, which has proved reliable in the past, that is the structuring cause of the perceptual belief—cause$_2$.

Just as a background condition makes possible a trigger of E, it can also increase or diminish the efficiency of T. More tinder speeds up combustion; higher-octane petrol makes the car start more easily. Reinforcing background conditions may turn triggering causes into hair-triggering causes. The presence of oxygen makes material flammable; pure oxygen is highly flammable. Not only has the past overwhelming reliability of percerptual belief allowed a broad structuring cause—one whose background conditions persist for an indefinite period of time—to be a structuring cause of triggers of perceptual belief, but it has turned them into structuring causes of *hair-triggers* for perceptual beliefs. Moreover, their action governs not only the various perceptual episodes of a single perceiver; but also the various episodes enjoyed by wide groups of perceivers, since another's perceptual history can also be a source for reinforcing or extinguishing the impulse for a trigger to operate. (Even doxasticists note that when our confidence is shaken, as in an experimental setup, the transition to belief is not as smooth.) The increased facility owed to reliability's strengthening of structuring causes accounts for both the near-universal and automatic nature of the generation of perceptual belief: in brief, for (a) and (b) above.

To remove possible confusion, the appeal to reliability here is not to the seeing of some particular things, but to the general deliverances of sight. I may never before have seen a lizard on a rock, but I can trust the reliability of my vision to assure me that this is what is in front of me. Of course here, as with *any* reliable device, if the content is outrageous or miraculous, an appeal to reliability may be insufficient to fix belief. It is easy to believe in a lizard encountered on the desert adjoining Tucson, not so for one encountered on the streets of Reykjavík. But this doesn't detract from the fact that it is the contents of perceptual experience in general, not particular contents, whose reliability figures in NT's cause$_2$.

There is also a normative payoff to this account of belief fixation: its continuing relationship does depend on the generated beliefs being *reliable* indicators of subjects' environments. We are vulnerable to many other nonevidentiary ways of fixing beliefs. Among them are indoctrination, beguiling rhetoric, and the surreptitious influence of profound hope (vulgarly known as wishful thinking). Such phenomena amply demonstrate (were it needed) that what accounts for a belief need not also be even a remotely plausible candidate for evidence for its truth. But belief may also be generated by the evidence for it, and the same type of relationship persists *just because* of those features that, if we chose to cite them, count as evidence for a belief's truth. I suggest that this is the current relation set up by cause$_2$. Precisely that which makes perception a reliable indicator of the environment allows it to serve as evidence for belief.[2] Reliability triggers and reinforces the background, accounting for the longevity of the relationship; but the content of the perception (without consideration of its recurrence) delivers the evidence. This is independent of the fact that, on the very first occasion of perception (supposing it to be identifiable), a believer couldn't be in a position to recognize its deliverances as evidence for belief. Thus, to originate this linkage, there must be something on the order of either genetically encoded disposition or trial and error, about which we needn't speculate. Reliability sets up the conditions under which perceptual episodes trigger beliefs and, in the limited sense in which NT by itself may be said to preserve and strengthen the connection, shows how the contents of visual episodes *ground* visual beliefs. Grounding is more than a relation of generation; it is the sort of generation that contributes to what it grounds being evidence.

For whatever use it may be in dispelling misgivings, this is not the only case in which it seems that something plays a causal role because it also plays an evidentiary one. When one infers a conclusion from premises, there must be more than the implicational (or evidential) relation between premises and conclusion. There must also be an appreciation of the force of those premises, which in turn *gives rise to one's acknowledging*—in other words, causes one to acknowledge— the conclusion. That the contents are inferentially related is no bar to the mental states containing them being related causally. And we saw earlier that there is an even broader class of cases in which causation operates only via the *understanding* of contents. Some may be wary of describing causal generalization in mental terms. But my use of it should be relatively uncontroversial, since I am prescinding from consideration of the level at which the causation is implemented. To illustrate by analogy, it is no objection to phenotypical causation that the causal work is implemented (if it is) at the level of genotypes. I merely note that the perceptual situation is not singular in this respect, and that this eliminates one basis for suspicion about it.

The foregoing may strike some readers as consisting of nothing more than tiresome platitudes. Why on earth would anyone want to reject such a view? Roughly, the reasons are twofold. First, it is incompatible with doxasticism as well as with most versions of cognitivism, arguments for which may be marshalled as reasons against NT. Second, there are independent objections to some of the materials needed in the construction of NT. In the last two chapters, I disposed of challenges to NT that emanate directly from cognitivism and doxasticism. That seems to leave only objections to notions endemic to NT. In particular, one rather sprawling objection seems to me to be the lone serious remaining difficulty of this type. Roughly, it is the joint contention that the only thing capable of grounding a belief—that is, providing a basis for an inference to it—is another belief, and the only thing capable of being justified is belieflike already. In the past, the objection's most immediate targets have been not NT, but foundationalist theories of justification and externalist theories of knowledge (e.g., reliabilism). But NT shares with those doctrines the tenet that although something (visual perception in this instance) is the justifier of perceptual beliefs, its justificational content is neither a belief per se nor justified by further beliefs.

It should be noted that, although the argument to be examined provides an almost irresistable inducement to doxasticism, it seems not to have been an especially prominent motive for adopting that particular view. One reason is that the argument is a special case of a broader form of reasoning that divides philosophers and philosophies in a much more basic way; many doxasticists and nondoxasticists alike fall on the same (first) side of that divide. On that side, are philosophers who suppose that, despite obstacles and indirections, the observations on which one bases her metaphysics and epistemology are ultimately tested before the tribunal of the world. In the end, theses are justified by, checked against, or modulated to aspects of reality they purport to describe. On the other side are philosophers who hold that such confrontations of supposedly entry-level observations with undistorted reality are a myth. The latter sort may hold that we are unable to carry out the independent check because the apparatus with which we attempt it is already so soiled by our prior judgments, concepts, and so on, as to contaminate the evidence. This is oversimple, lumping together into a single camp thinkers who sharply disagree with one another on the details; but it describes, at its unspecific level, two general attitudes toward the nature of knowledge. Many doxasticists and cognitivists belong to the first group, and thus would not avail themselves of the argument I am about to discuss. Nevertheless, other things to be said on behalf of doxasticism have been exhausted, and eventually this has been hit on this as the last line of defense against NT. (I commented in chap. 1, p. 16, that its conclusion enabled its proponents to collapse what are now known as cause$_1$ and cause$_2$ into a single causal relation.) Since my defense would be glaringly incomplete if NT remained vulnerable to this objection, the remainder of this chapter is devoted to its examination.

II

There is no special problem about how something nonpropositional, such as perception on this account, can *cause* a perceptual belief. After all, a belief could conceivably be caused by something as eminently nonpropositional as eating a dodgy mushroom or suffering a blow on the head. But the causal relation I am interested in is (a) mediated by the contents of perceptions and (b) causal (at least habitually so) because it is evidential. Still, there may be some problem in appreciating a difficulty (a blind spot for which I have sympathy). What could be more commonsensical than the (nonpropositional) detection of a lizard on a rock giving rise to the belief that a lizard is on a rock? Some may be mystified about how the information detected gets transformed into the propositional belief content. (There is a hint of this in Sellars 1956, p. 255.) I have little to say about it here. The only more definite source of perplexity I can imagine is founded on certain suspect principles. Thus, until presented with a clearer basis for it, I will ignore it. (It will probably be of no solace to the perplexed to learn that the justifier can be encapsulated in a factative clause, e.g., that S sees a lizard on a rock: that is, it is the seeing of this thing, not the thing without the seeing, that serves as justifier here. It is not this whole clause, but only 'a lizard on a rock' that enters into the clause specifying the content of the perceptual belief.)

Others may profess bafflement about how the deliverances of perception, if they are not already at least proto-beliefs, can *justify* anything (see, e.g., Davidson 1986, p. 310). If I happen to entertain a set of propositions that I neither believe nor disbelieve, how can I deploy those propositions as premises or evidence to justify anything else? Thus, nonpropositionality aside, how does perceptual 'information' justify perceptual belief?

The literature contains a frontal assault on all such forms of justification, from which I may fashion a version aimed directly at NT. Because it is inspired by an attack launched by Wilfrid Sellars against the perceptually Given, I call it the "Sellarsian argument." Its direct targets, foundationalism and epistemological (rather than psychosemantic) externalism, share with NT a claim to ground certain beliefs (called 'basic beliefs') on an evidential basis that is not itself another belief. On that understanding, perceptual beliefs count as basic. The thrust of the Sellarsian argument is to indicate that, as far as justification goes, there is no way to break out of the circle of beliefs. Ancestral forms of the argument may be traceable to Hegel and Bosanquet. One problem is finding a formulation potent enough to do justice to its insights and clear enough to enable us to evaluate it. For that, I draw mainly on a version presented by Laurence BonJour (1985, chap. 4).

A basic belief (or 'knowledge', hereafter understood) is frequently called non-inferential. That is too broad for present purposes. Rather, I shall say that if a belief is basic, its justification is not a matter of inference *from other beliefs*. This is not tantamount to claiming that there is no evidence for it; in some sense, yet to be fully explicated, I contend that basic beliefs are justified by the perceptual contents that generate them. Should one wish to call this sort of a relation *inferential*, it seems futile to rail against such a reasonable extension of so imprecise a term. What is significant here is that there are *no other beliefs* from which a justified basic belief need be inferred.

One factor that contributes to confusion on this topic has been the insistence, by a group of foundationalists-cum-sense-datum-theorists, that sensing itself be the requisite knowledge (or belief). In those circumstances, there is nothing further (save the external situation, which, for a variety of reasons, they regard as an unacceptable evidential base) on which the justification of a sensing could draw. Basic beliefs of this kind must be noninferential, period. But it would be a mistake for the Sellarsian to take such a view as representative of the whole collection of antagonists. It is clear that a noncognitivist could hold that something can count as a source of information, even appreciated information, without thereby being a belief. The Sellarsian must, therefore, account for the other forms of NT in any frontal assault on basic belief.

III

Belief is representational and intentional. BonJour seems to be proclaiming nothing more than this when he states (repeatedly) that belief is "cognitive or judgmental." But for Sellarsians, the converse also holds: whatever is representational (much less, cognitive or judgmental) is already a kind of belief—or at least close enough to one not to be capable of explaining how basic beliefs arise. On this reading, strictly objectual seeing could not be representational. This is not because, as stated in chapter 1, §VI, seeing is *presentational*. Rather, it is because, if seeing were representational on this understanding, it would be belieflike and thus proto-propositional—thereby ruling out objectual sight. Now, there are some accounts on which perception consists of nonconceptual, or incompletely conceptual, content (see chap. 9). I provisionally set aside that matter, taking it up again on pp. 174–7. It is mentioned here only to point out that, although defenders of nonconceptual content could enthusiastically support the objections initially raised against the Sellarsian argument, those objections do not rely on anything resembling the various notions of nonconceptual content in the literature.

Recall that by a basic belief I mean one that is justified, but not by being inferred from another belief.[3] It is justified either intrinsically or by something not essentially belieflike. For the Sellarsian, there are no basic beliefs. On NT, perceptual beliefs as a class are typically basic.

The above tenets lead immediately to a dilemma for the perceptual grounding of belief (and for basic beliefs). Either perception is already cognitive or judgmental, in which case it can justify perceptual belief, but is already belieflike itself (and so not an independent ground of belief), or perception is not cognitive or judgmental, in which case it is impossible for it to provide justification for something else. To wit: "if [the foundationalist's] . . . immediate apprehensions are construed as cognitive, at least quasi-judgmental (as seems clearly the more natural interpretation), then they will be both capable of providing justification for other cognitive states and in need of it themselves; but if they are construed as noncognitive, nonjudgmental, then while they will not themselves need justification, they will also be incapable of giving it" (BonJour 1985, p. 69; cf. Davidson 1986, p. 310). To elaborate, to achieve what is claimed for sight (BonJour's "immediate apprehension"), two things must be true of it:

(I) that it not need justification from something else;
(II) that it be capable of providing justification for other things.

Not to put too fine a point on the matter, it must be an (externally) unjustified justifier. But it cannot be unjustified by failing an applicable standard. It must be either self-illuminating or of a form that prevents it from being the kind of thing for which justifications may be sensibly offered. I opt for the latter (see §V). How can it then serve as a premise or evidence from which something else—a perceptual belief in this case—can draw justification? This is the dilemma: possessing one of the necessary features seems to disqualify visual perception from possession of the other.

As BonJour anatomizes the perceptual situation, there are certainly the following two elements:

(a) an external situation;
(b) a perceptual belief (or judgment).

We may say that (a) is the situation of a lizard on a rock (*l* on *r*), and (b) is the (occurrent) belief that a certain lizard is on a certain rock. (a)'s obtaining is ontologically indifferent to its being perceived. But this is not sufficient for (b)'s being justified: for that to occur, the subject of the belief, S, qua percipient being, must consciously grasp the situation in (a). For the Sellarsian, this awareness is itself a judgment or belief, indistinguishable in status from (b). It is typically allowed that (a) may be the *cause* of (b), but not its justifier. By elimination, nothing is left to justify (b) other than S's other beliefs (including perhaps the belief that (a) causes (b)), and we are well along the path to a coherence theory of justification. For the foundationalist and, more importantly, the NTist, there is a third item mediating the first two:

(c) the (visual) perception of *l* on *r*.

We might replace 'perception' with BonJour's terms 'intuition' or 'direct awareness' (the latter of which he takes from Anthony Quinton). I continue to use my version for this discussion. According to this stripped-down Sellarsian argument, if the content (object) of (c) is objectual, it admits no external justification, but then it cannot justify anything else (if (I), then not (II)); whereas if the content of (c) can justify something else, then it is 'cognitive or judgmental'(if (II), then its form rules out (I)). This argument is the sternest direct challenge to NT. Can it be met?

IV

Consider the following:

(S) S sees a lizard on a rock;
(L) C_s(lizard *l* on rock *r*).

(L) is the content of S's visual episode, and since S *sees* what is in question, the content, (L) happens to be identical with the object, *l* on *r*, on this occasion. I will attack the Sellarsian argument by showing how (L) may justify a perceptual belief, that a lizard is on a rock ((b) from the last section), although

first, (L) isn't itself justified (not being of a form to take attributions of justification), though it is—and this is what counts—properly related to something
that is justified; and,

second, (L) can be relevantly nonbelieflike: that is, it has the capacity as it
stands to be a justifier, despite lacking the (propositional) *form* or *structure*
of a belief (typically (II) is developed to imply that this much is needed to
serve as a justifier).

I go about this in reverse order, by first explaining how (L)'s role as justifier is
not impaired by its not being of the required form (by Sellarsians) for occupants
of this role. To simplify the exposition let's provisionally place off limits the first
issue: that is, why (L) itself is not justified. No doubt, this separation of the issues
slices things too finely for some purposes. The Sellarsian argument maintains that
being justified is a necessary condition for being a justifier; this is explicitly rejected in the first point. So the Sellarsian might complain that in treating these
two issues as if they are independent usurps a point of contention. It is precisely
for this reason that I return in §V to see how the tenets in the first point are used
to argue that (L) cannot be a justifier because it is not in fact justified. Nevertheless, the separation of issues is provisionally warranted, since my current concern
is only for (L)'s form. I propose to establish that not having propositional form—
not being suitable to serve as a premise in a classically formulated deductive or
inductive argument—does not by itself disqualify a justifier. This is quite apart
from whether the occupants of those slots are duly certified as justifiers in other respects. Even if (L) were not a justifier, it would not follow that its form alone prohibited it from occupying that slot. To that limited extent, we may consider the
second point before settling the first. Thus, I return to the loaded question with
which Sellarsians may be expected to confront us: How can a perceptual content
qualify as a justifier for belief despite being noncognitive and nonjudgmental?

My answer proceeds by maintaining that once we have collected all the elements Sellarsians typically acknowledge, and which could fit in classical argument
forms, particular justifications are still incomplete. Their completion requires the
inclusion of a step that various present and prior considerations show cannot be
shoehorned into a classical propositional form. Moreover, even if this basis for
justification could be reconfigured in the favored way, *pace* Sellarsians, that would
do nothing to account for its contribution to the justification. But before getting to
those issues, some preliminaries are in order.

As a first step, let's see what more we can say about 'cognitive' and 'judgmental' as they figure in the particular objection. BonJour uses these terms nearly
interchangeably to describe the contents of perceptual experience. (Later, I examine a slight opening for a distinction he mentions, but it doesn't affect the discussion at this stage.) In the limited role for which they are used, both appear to
amount nearly enough to a third term, 'propositional'. One indication of this is
contained in BonJour's understanding of a related dispute that broke out earlier in
the century between Moritz Schlick (1934–35) and Carl Hempel (1934–35; Bon-
Jour 1985, pp. 61–64). Skipping many details, Schlick held the anti-Sellarsian
view that he could confirm a statement in a travel guidebook by checking it against

reality. He might do this simply "by looking." In reply, BonJour, following Hempel, maintains that what Schlick is really doing is comparing the first proposition with a second: that is, the one in the guidebook with "the one which represents the content of Schlick's experience." He adds that such a justification "only raises the further issue of how this new proposition, *or rather the perceptual judgment which embodies it,* is justified" (p. 64, my emphasis). Not only is the propositionality of a content sufficient for it to be (or embody) a judgment (or cognition), but the reverse seems to be the case as well: all judgmental (cognitive) contents are propositional (or embodied by what is propositional). Thus, on this account, a nonpropositional content is not judgmental (not cognitive). We also have adequate independent grounds for this conclusion; as we have seen, what is not propositional (by which I mean 'not equivalent to something propositional,' whatever its surface form) cannot be a belief content. And by saying something is cognitive and judgmental, BonJour certainly means to suggest that it already satisfies the conditions for being a form of belief. Moreover, this fits the general use of the first two terms as they have entered the debate.

As a rule, Sellars does not use this set of terms to carry his point; but his pivotal expression, 'representational', seems designed to play the same role, though a good deal more problematically. As customarily understood, something's being representational does not preclude its being nonpropositional. I noted in chapter 1 (p. 24) that standard accounts go no further than stating that a content is representational if it is intentional (*of* or *about* something) or has conditions of correctness (satisfaction conditions). A portrait or an 'x' scrawled on a napkin can do that; thus it is no small mystery to assimilate the representational right off to what is judgmental. It appears that there must be missing, or merely assumed, steps if the inference from representationality to what is judgmental or belieflike is to stand any chance of success. No doubt, representationality can be a murky notion in discussions of this ilk. But however it is understood, nonpropositionality is not a standard contrast for it and scarcely enters the discussion when that topic is center stage. For example, consider representational lexical items. Our rough but serviceable notion applies as much, say, to proper names and other nouns as to whole utterances in which they occur. The contrast between the representational and nonrepresentational does not even seem to overlap significantly with the focal one, *objectual* versus *propositional,* of the past few chapters. Thus, we should resist framing the issue, as Sellars seems to favor, as being about the representational nature of perception. The Sellarsian argument must draw whatever strength it has elsewhere.

Since this whole class of stipulations appears to beg the question, we might be curious about its motivation. This trespasses on the grey area of speculation. But I believe we can be fairly confident that cognitivism—the view that all seeing is seeing *that*—makes its unacknowledged contribution. As we have seen, taken as a premise cognitivism guarantees that visual contents are beliefs. On the other hand, occasionally it looks as if cognitivism is the conclusion of, rather than a premise in, the argument. We are confronted by a small group of mutually supportive tenets, and it is often unclear which is being used to support which. That aside, enough has been said in chapter 4 about the failure of cognitivism to assure us that any defense of Sellarsianism that requires it is in trouble. Henceforth, I am concerned only with other sources of support.

We might begin to approach the question whether (L)—C_s(lizard l on rock r) —can justify S's belief that a lizard is on a rock, by asking what does the justifying in such a simple case. I maintain that there are general and specific aspects to an answer; and that, although the general aspect conforms to Sellarsian restrictions, it is invariably insufficient. The specific aspect is needed to render a satisfactory explanation, but it cannot always be recast propositionally. Or, at least, the only reasons on the horizon for so recasting it themselves presuppose the Sellarsian conclusion.

The preceding claims concern ordinary justificatory practices; they have no authority over a reformed notion of justification. Although I have no detailed account of this process to place before readers, my contentions do imply a strong adequacy condition for any final account of perceptual justification. In particular, the belief in question *requires* as data the content of a lizard on the rock, rather than a propositional transform of it, for its justification. Consequently, however many other propositional elements also figure in the justification, there will always remain an indispensable feature of it that eludes treatment as just another premise or step in a classically formulated argument.

So much for a preliminary overview; I now proceed to explore the details. I begin with the general component of perceptual justification. This is the part the Sellarsian finds unproblematic, but let's review some crucial features of it just to assure ourselves that my defense of a nonpropositional element doesn't inadvertently ignore or even underestimate resources at the opposition's disposal.

S certainly wouldn't be justified in believing there is a lizard on the rock if perception hadn't been reliable, or if she were not justified in believing it reliable, in the past.[4] Thus, the reliability of perception is one aspect of the justification, at least in the sense that a challenge to it is a relevant challenge to the justification of its perceptual belief. Put otherwise (but see note 3), we are confronted with the challenge, "why should we believe our [perceptions] are reliable, that is, why should we trust our senses?" (Davidson 1986, p. 310). If a good answer is not forthcoming, we should be puzzled why anyone should regard her deliverances, however striking in other respects, as evidence for beliefs. And *that* our perceptions are reliable is propositionally encoded information, *eo ipso* cognitive, as demanded by Sellarsians.

No doubt, in contexts in which justifications are offered or are in question, the issue of the past reliability of (S's) perception is seldom raised. There is good reason for this. It is not just the generation of some belief or other that is in question, but the justification of a belief with a specific content. To justify *this* belief, we must appeal not to facts about perception in general, but to what is perceived in the present circumstance. To so much as mention the general elements of justification in workaday contexts conversationally implicates that the method is risky or, if reliable, that the particular device used to pursue the method might be defective. In typical contexts, to answer the call for a justification with such general features misses the point of the inquiry. The situation is analogous to that of a panel instrument. If the altimeter is unreliable, I may not be justified in believing that the plane is flying at thirty thousand feet; if the sonar is unreliable, I may not be justified in believing that a large object is moving through the water. But customarily when I claim that the plane is flying at thirty thousand feet (or that a large object is moving through the water), I appeal not to the general reliability of the instrument or its kind, but to what it has detected on the occasion in question. We should also note that citing the evidence of the instrument is not the same as citing the episode of instrumental registration, although I use the instrument to make my appeal and both appeals may be present or appropriate on a given occasion. To appeal to the registering on the instrument would be akin to citing a sense-datum, something from which the state of affairs I mention can only be inferred. I may of course do this by stepping back from the standard routine. But it distorts actual practice to assume that this is how we behave in nonexceptional cases. Rather, I cite the altitude of the craft, period! Similarly, when S believes there is a lizard on a rock, she is appealing to the deliverances of perception, not as such to her perceptual state.

This is not to claim that general reliability isn't an implicit part of the whole justification. But since the target is a particular belief, with a quite specific content, the particular state of affairs perceived as well as the perceiving of it are also needed to justify *this* belief. General considerations don't begin to touch the main issue of concern when concrete questions of justification are raised.

One effective way to meet a demand for justification of one's visual report is simply to say to your interlocutor, in the spirit of Schlick, "Look!" Of course, Hempel and BonJour have questioned the nonpropositionality of this appeal, but neither one questions its particularity. Thus, if we have independent reason for not accepting the claim that the content must be propositional, we are left with an appeal to something that is undeniably particular without any prejudgment about the syntactical form it must take. In the right location and at the right moment, it is a *relevant* response. The response may *assume* that S's eyes are reliable, but it requests her merely to gather information. Even if the reliability of her faculty stood behind the utility of this request, the cardinal point is that it is not what is being probed here. If she doesn't gather the information of a lizard on a rock (or that a lizard is on a rock), there is little point to this way of meeting the challenge.

But (and this is the crucial point) we do have independent reason for rejecting the view that the content is propositional; namely, the whole line of argument of chapter 4 against cognitivism. I have demonstrated not only that the arguments on behalf of the view that all seeing is *seeing that* are unsound; but also that not all seeing can be seeing that—perhaps none is. Thus, as just shown, the particulars of the circumstance disclosed by perception are required, but they will not invariably (or even usually) have propositional form.

Granting for the sake of argument the Sellarsian contention that an appeal to perception is futile without a general certification to the effect that perception is a reliable source of information, the general element will still not be sufficient to justify any particular belief. For example, in the circumstances under consideration (in which I see a lizard but not a coyote), it will be insufficient to justify the belief that this is a lizard rather than a coyote. There are general elements of justification, no doubt including such precepts as that perception (vision) is generally reliable, that must be factored into any justification. But these are insufficient to justify any particular visual belief. Such a belief must have a content that pertains to the immediate environment, and nothing in the canvassed general considerations supplies that concrete element. Sellarsians are prone to call attention to the fact that the foundationalist's announced basis typically falls short for want of a justified belief in the general reliability of that kind of apprehension and of a conceptual knowledge of the classificatory notions employed in the appreciation of those deliverances. None of this is being disputed here. But the knowledge (or justified belief) in question is all general, whereas the beliefs supposedly justified on this basis are quite specific. Accordingly, justification would be equally incomplete without the particular state of affairs to which the reliability test and that conceptual appreciation were applied. This ingredient is essential, central, and, I claim, not yet a belief. Thus, however the total justification, with general and particular factors combined, is construed, it cannot be on the model of a deductive or an inductive inference. We do not simply have a set of premises, but rather a number of propositions *plus specific visual input.* When things are optimal, that input is an object or complex of objects; under certain less-than-optimal circumstances, it is misinformation, perhaps the mere appearance of things.

Of course, there are also other elements in a complete justification, some of them particular in ways that the general reliability of perception is not. For example, Sellarsians would no doubt claim that justification is incomplete without a step on the order of (S), but less committally phrased. Thus, referring again to *l* on *r,* we require 'that S visually enjoy an episode of it' or 'S's visual enjoyment of an episode of it.' It is simplest here to grant to the Sellarsian the former, propositional, phrasing of this step. (When the visual episode fails to be a seeing, we may replace 'it' by 'the appearance of it.' The crucial point is that both are nonpropositional. For simplicity of exposition, I henceforth omit the qualification.) In one way, the subject matter is perfectly particular, for the 'it' is replaced by a particular lizard on a particular rock for some cases, a mountain lion on a hill for others, and so on. In another way, the step is generic, for it will always contain a sentence frame of the form 'that Σ visually enjoys an episode of ____,' for any Σ. Even if this much is granted, I do not see how the justification can be complete without also including the specific 'it' as an independent element. The remainder of that step is formulary: it doesn't matter what the subject matter of the seeing is. The critical work of bringing any particular justification down to earth is done by the thing experienced. It must enter either as a visual object or as an apparent object. And the long argument of chapter 4 showed the overwhelming implausibility of supposing that this could be accomplished by what is propositionlike.

The notion that all justification requires totally truth-evaluable premises or steps dies hard, so let's elaborate a bit further the moral of the preceding discussion.

The Sellarsian maintains the following conditional: if perceptual content isn't propositional, consideration of the nature of justification alone shows that it cannot serve to justify anything else. Justification is by inference, and inferences demand steps. Steps, in turn, are propositional. Thus, by showing that the object of perception is not propositional, we would have shown it was disqualified by form as a justifier.

Given the pressure to include (L) as a separate ingredient, there is no question here of validly deducing a conclusion from justified premises or inductively inferring it from justified steps. Of course, I can always approximate in propositional steps the theoretical induction, or inference to the best explanation, that leads from seeing a lizard on a rock to the belief that there is a lizard on a rock. For example, I might include the propositions that I perceptually receive what I would describe as a lizard on a rock, that the experience occurs under optimal conditions, that perceptual experiences under those circumstances have proved very reliable, and a number of other things (such as that it is not uncharacteristic for there to be lizards or rocks here) that defy handy enumeration. Grant that one may infer from this that there is a lizard on a rock. Even if a reasoning can be reconstructed in the above manner, it is moot whether the crucial premise gets its evidential force from being able to be formulated as such, or rather that its ability to be thus formulated gets its evidential force from what it represents—(L). Nothing in the reconstruction itself shows that the derivation doesn't get its force from the detection of this content, and earlier considerations incline me to believe that it does.

Let us say that the conclusion of a standard argument is "derived." It may be that what is derived from justified steps is generally justified.[5] The unqualified converse—that if it is justified, it is derived—is much easier to question. An appeal to the many instances of justification that are propositionally derived is to no avail. Principles supported by an impressive enumeration of paradigm instances are suited for being sufficient conditions, but not yet for being necessary ones. But this does not leave us with a mere standoff. We have before us, in the example presented, a perfectly natural and commonplace sort of situation in which we acquire a justified belief without this sort of orthodox derivation. In a more liberal sense, this belief might be construed as derived, just as I claimed earlier that all such beliefs might be inferential. But it is not derived or inferred *from other beliefs* or from anything that is itself a candidate for being justified. Thus, it is not a derivation in the sense stipulated earlier in this paragraph. It is the task of the Sellarsian to show either that such a scheme cannot work alongside derivation, or that the state of affairs I have attempted to sketch warrants reconstrual in a way that will bring it under the umbrella of derivation. I have canvased a few attempts at such reconstruals and found them wanting. Further plausible suggestions, if there are any, should issue from the Sellarsians themselves. In their absence, why isn't it reasonable to hold that some justification isn't derivation?

Before passing on to the next stage of this defense, I explore a bit further some of the maneuvers that, by obscuring this point, have assured Sellarsians that they needn't encounter nonpropositional contents.

When BonJour insists on the third term, (c) of §III, as the justifier, he uses such phrases as 'the apprehension of a lizard on a rock' ambiguously to suggest that it is the apprehending, rather than what is apprehended, that procures the justification. This in spite of the fact that elsewhere he properly distinguishes what is apprehended from the apprehension itself (1985, pp. 75–76). Confusion is also abetted by the dubious employment of an old nemesis, the term 'cognitive'.

It is appropriate to say that what is apprehended is *cognitive* in at least the minimal sense in which being cognitive amounts to no more than being apprehended. On this interpretation, if we are direct realists, it makes perfectly good sense to say that what is cognitive is only contingently so. That is, what is cognized may be item (a), the state of affairs itself. And this would have obtained were it never cognized. It amounts to no more of an admission than that made for our content (L): although it is nothing beyond the object seen, had it not been a content as well (i.e., been seen), it could not have played its justificatory role. But certainly BonJour, and less obviously Sellars, take the admission that an apprehension is cognitive to imply three other things about the content cognized:

   (i) that it is 'in the mind',
  (ii) that it is (at least implicitly) propositional in form,
 (iii) that it includes conceptualizations contributed by the cognizer rather than by the immediate environment cognized.

Discussion of (iii) must be deferred until §VII. As for (i), it is uncertain how it would aid the Sellarsian cause without further premises. But since it is part of a general outlook in which those premises are available, let's examine it briefly. Although it is unsurprising that Sellarsians would tacitly assume (i), given the heavy emphasis on sense-datum varieties of foundationalism (although one of BonJour's targets, Anthony Quinton, is a direct realist), it is far from clear what good reason there is for supposing that what is cognitive is always 'in a mind'. Certainly what is perceived is *apprehended*. But in the sense of 'mind-independence' explained in chapter 1—the favored contrast for 'being in the mind'—the direct realist will insist that much of what we apprehend is mind-independent. Nothing in the Sellarsian argument as such seems to conflict with this direct-realist account of perception. Pending further notice, we must conclude that the insistence on (i) as an element in our intuitive understanding of 'cognitive' is unwarranted.

Turning to (ii), consider again the pairing of 'cognitive' with 'judgmental'. Suppose we agree that if a content is judgmental, it is propositional. Although a judgment may be assertive in a way that a proposition needn't be, and on occasion a judgment may be delivered in a form so syntactically slight as a nod, I will not challenge the implication from judgmental to propositional. The problematic move is that from cognitive to judgmental. BonJour seems to recognize that this requires support, as when he hypothesizes that we might consider an immediate apprehension as "cognitive, at least quasi-judgmental (*as seems clearly the more natural interpretation* [of cognitive])" (1985, p. 69, my emphasis). But nothing else in the text suggests a recognition of the need to support this elaboration of 'cognitive'. Moreover, BonJour says that a cognitive grasp is "propositionally formed, capable of being true or false, and capable of serving as a premise in an inference" (p. 76), but there is no evident support for these declarations.

All this, I suggest, facilitates the neglect of the possibility that in an apparent case of seeing, what is apparently seen may be nothing epistemologically fancier than a lizard on a rock, or a whale on the beach. This possibility isn't wholly ignored by BonJour, but the identifications in (i) and (ii) make it easy for him to overlook such cases, despite their familiarity. For example, when he proceeds to discuss something that may be cognitive but not judgmental, he disparages it as a mere effort to say that it is half-cognitive and half-noncognitive: not a very appealing option. Even when he plays along far enough to agree that perception is a species of confrontation, he holds that "this by itself provides no very compelling reason for attributing epistemic justification . . . to the cognitive states, whatever they may be called, which result" (p. 77). Unfortunately, he provides little in the way of further clues about the compulsion that this confrontation lacks. I can only guess that it has to do with one or another of the elements of the Sellarsian outlook, and I hope to show by the end of this discussion that, in each case, a demand for more than this sort of a confrontation is unsupported. In any event, from what has been said thus far, it should be clear why NTists are entitled to believe that such a scene supplies a paradigmatic "compelling reason" for ascribing justification to a cognitive state. Furthermore, thus far, the reasons against it have been patently inadequate.

If the sources of the objection—with the exception of (iii), to be addressed later—are eliminated, the first part of my task is accomplished. I have shown how it is that a nonproposition, and thereby something that cannot be represented in a formal inference, may become crucial to justification: in other words, how it may be a justifier. A perception with an objectual content is not *ex vi termini* propositional. Therefore, it need not be a belief. Moreover, on direct realism, the content of an actual seeing is a state of the world, l on r. A bit more adventuresomely, another Sellarsian article is that only beliefs may be justified. Adding it, two conclusions inimical to Sellarsianism become apparent: first, the formal requirements for being a justifier do not indicate why it needs to be justified, and, second, the object of perception does not need to be inferred from beliefs in order to play its fundamental role. These findings have important implications for the view being examined.

V

Let's take stock. Given the limited options under discussion and the relevant notion of justification in the context, the Sellarsian maintains the following propositions:

All justifiers must be beliefs.

All justifiers must themselves be justified.

Only beliefs may be justified.

In §IV, I attacked a main pillar supporting the first claim: the thesis that only what is capable of being cast propositionally could serve in a justification. But my work isn't finished until I can make a case for discarding at least one of the last two propositions, for it is easy to see that together they imply the first proposition.

I have mentioned that the first proposition is a formal issue, since it imposes a structural requirement on the nature of the steps in a justification. The second and third are substantive, since they directly impose requirements on the content of justifying steps, considered individually. (I interpret 'belief' in the third proposition to mean *belieflike contents* not *things actually believed.*) In this section, I will accept the third proposition (qualifiedly) and offer reasons to reject the second one. Though sundry small points remain to be discussed (in §§VI–VII), that should be sufficient to explode the Sellarsian case.

My total defense set out to show two things about (L), the content: *l* on *r,* in its position as potential justifier:

that it is not necessary that it be itself justified;

that it is not necessary that it have the form of a belief.

The second of these is to deny the first article of the earlier Sellarsian view; the first denies its second article. §IV amounted to a defense of the second denial. It is now time to turn to the first one. But on the face of it, the first denial (corresponding to a denial of the Sellarsian first article) may seem preposterous. Appearances are that "nothing counts as justification unless by reference to what we already accept" (Rorty 1979, p. 178). Replacing "justification" by "reason" and "what we already accept" by "belief," we obtain (near enough) "nothing can count as a reason for holding a belief except another belief" (Davidson 1986, p. 310).[6] In other words, the justifier must itself be justified, and to be even a candidate for being justified it must already be something the subject believes ("what we already accept"). We can easily appreciate the kinds of absurdities its defenders would claim to follow from rejecting that view. I use *p* to justify *q:* when pressed for my reasons for affirming *q,* I cite *p.* But, save for conversational restraints, it is equally appropriate to interrogate *p.* Suppose when asked for my reasons for *p,* I respond, "I needn't defend *p* as well. It's not another thing I believe, but only my justification for *q.* And if it is not among my beliefs, then it doesn't also require that I justify it." If that is so, why should I take *p* to lend any credibility to *q?* Wouldn't this manifest an appalling ignorance on my part of what it is for my beliefs to be justified? *A fortiori,* if *p* isn't a belief of mine, it cannot serve as a justifier for any of my other beliefs. Such constraints on justification lead directly to a coherence theory of belief, for "[w]hat distinguishes a coherence theory is simply the claim that nothing can count as a reason for holding a belief except another belief. Its partisan rejects as unintelligible the request for a ground or source of belief of another ilk" (Davidson 1986, p. 310).

Notice that what is most directly brought out by these reflections is the need for *p*'s justifiability, not the need for its being believed. It is the lack of justification that matters in the previous exchange, and the issue of belief enters only because defenders such as Davidson and Rorty hold in addition that in order to be a subject for justification *p* must be a belief, or belief content. But it is justification that is at the core of the difficulty. This may be disguised in the foregoing because, once again, the scenario has been conducted in the first person. That inevitably confuses the issue of what justifies my belief with that of what I am *in a position to cite* as my justification. Of course, it is possible to maintain that nothing can justify my belief unless I am in a position to cite it as my justification. But that view cannot be assumed. It requires further argument of just the sort undergoing critical scrutiny here. That aside, we are left with a genuine problem of justification. Somehow we must discover a way to give *p* the value that attaches to something by virtue of its being justified. If it does not possess this virtue, how can it lend any credibility to (other) beliefs?

In the example under consideration, however, it is difficult to see how *p* can be justified, not because it isn't a belief, but because it isn't of the propositional type that takes this sort of attribution. Remember that our *p* may be just (L) of p. 159: the content of S's seeing *l* on *r*. 'Justified' and 'unjustified' don't seem to take root here. Of course, it would be equally inappropriate to treat (L) as if it *lacked* justification in the ordinary way. It doesn't fail a standard that governs it; it doesn't fall under any such standard. Nevertheless, something would be awry if we could not say more in defense of (L)'s worthiness as a justifier.

I suggest the following. (L) can serve as a justifier, because it is the visual content of an episode—(S), that S sees a lizard on a rock—which is itself justified. (S) is justified by being an instance (perhaps of a certain more specific kind) of perceptual experience, which is justified in turn by its reliability (or, if one prefers, by our knowledge of its reliability). Recall that this is the reliability of perception, or perhaps sight, in general, not the reliability of sighting lizards on rocks. Does this imply that (L) is also justified? Unless we want to coin a novel form of justification, I don't see the point of taking this further step. As claimed above, (L) isn't ordinarily the sort of thing that takes such attributions. But it bears a certain relation to what is justified—being the visual content of a justified perceptual experience—which is sufficient to qualify it as a justifier. What is to be gained by insisting over and above this that (L) itself be justified? Such a decision has no power to convert (L) into something judgmental or propositional, and it doesn't affect the mechanics that qualify (L) for its evidential role. Moreover, calling (L) justified on the basis of its relation to (S) alone does have a downside: it misleads some with coherentist preconceptions to conclude that, robust appearances to the contrary notwithstanding, (L) must be belieflike and propositional.

In this we have an explanation of how a perceptual content itself can both justify beliefs and, at the same time, not be another thing that is justified, much less a justified belief. No more is being claimed than that this is a sufficient condition. A wider class of visual episodes than seeings will of course be justified, for one can be mistaken and yet justified in appealing to what it seems to her that she sees (cf. §VI). Moreover, on some occasions, she will see something, but it will not generate a perceptual belief, because she doesn't realize she is seeing that thing. The whale example illustrates this. It does not mean that I wouldn't be justified in coming to believe that a whale is on the beach. It is simply that I am not in a position to generate the belief, because I don't realize it is a whale. Moreover, I may even be justified in believing it is an oil slick, for we can imagine circumstances in which it would be warranted to take my content in this way.

This would mark yet another kind of case in which someone's (unseen) visual content may justify a visual belief. But it is not my present task to delineate the class of visual justifiers as a whole. I need only insist that the relationship of (S) to (L) supplies a sufficient condition for (L)'s being a justifier.

At this point, I grant for the sake of argument that something cannot be used as a justifier unless one supposes or takes it for granted that it is a justifier. This should not lead anyone to suppose that it is *the realization,* not (S) or its content (L), to which justification may be attributed here. The realization has to do not with the justification as such, but with one's knowledge of it, and thus one's ability to utilize it. Realizing that what one is perceptually experiencing (under the circumstances) is *l* on *r* doesn't add a whit to the justification already inherent in (S). But, like anything else I may have with or without knowing that I have it, realizing I have it enables me to put it to use.

To head off possible misunderstandings, I am not claiming that perceivers consciously employ arguments of this sort. As speculated earlier (p. 154), perhaps (but just perhaps) through selection, we are genetically encoded simply to jump to beliefs from visual contents. This would be more instinct than policy. Nevertheless, on reflection we do think that our perceptual life affords us good reason to continue to react this way. (If we found the course of behavior harmful, it might be largely under our control to inhibit it.) If this crude outline of the situation is accurate as far as it goes, the account can serve as the background explanation of how such reflections are supportable.

A potential Sellarsian reply is that since it is (L)'s relation to (S) that accounts for its authority, we should take (S) as the real justifier here. This is similar to a move made in §IV; but, like that one, it is too weak. Even if admitted, it won't dislodge the perfectly good alternative interpretation in which (L) is a justifier. (S)'s worth still relies on its constituent (L), however we choose to disguise that relationship. And to show that my first point is mistaken, one must show not only that some sufficient justifications omit unjustified justifiers, but that no set of minimally sufficient justifications include them. Moreover, the very presence of an alternative set of minimally sufficient conditions that incorporate (L) as a step indicates that alternatives that omit it are somehow less illuminating: they work, if they do, only by fudging (inside a larger clause) an indispensable justificatory element. But I will let the dialectic play out a bit before developing this point, for its later application will enable us to appreciate it better. For now, let me cite a different response, namely, that it changes the subject. The content of the belief is not S's seeing, but *what* S has seen: *l* on *r*. The latter, and it alone, is relevant evidence. What S saw may be counted as evidence pure and simple. But *that* S saw it, as distinct from what S saw, could be relevant to there being this lizard on this rock only if this episode of seeing had been somehow involved in bringing about *l* being on *r*.

This may motivate the Sellarsian to show that she has not, as I have suggested, avoided the particular subject; she may achieve this by making her reply more specific. We can reconstruct the reasoning propositionally to show how this particular belief may be derived from those premises, all of which may be plausibly considered evidential. To give a hint, suppose we reason as follows:

Perceptual contents of type T are reliable.
(L) is an instance of T.
Therefore, (L) is reliable.
What is reliable is justified.
Therefore, (L) is justified.
What is justified is a propositional entity.
Therefore, (L) is a justified propositional entity.
For S to use (L) in a justification, S must believe (L).
Therefore, that there is a lizard on a rock is a justified *belief* for S.

Both the fourth and sixth steps—"What is reliable is justified" and "What is justified is a propositional entity"—are, for reasons made evident in this chapter, highly questionable. Moreover, the reasoning leaves the working part of (L) enigmatic. Its introduction in the second step doesn't make any reference to the detail of the content or to how that detail performs its job to bring about the justified belief. However, at present the issues I want to raise are not affected by the details of the reasoning. We need only note here that one can consistently accept the reasoning while adhering to the nonderivational view of basic belief I am defending. In my initial characterization of basic belief, it was explicitly stated that even if we found a candidate for a basic belief, it would not be a belief that *couldn't* be arrived at via other justified belief (cf. note 2). If we ever manage to stumble onto something that needs no support, that would not prohibit it from entering another discourse in which it had support. Therefore, we must look elsewhere for something to threaten the alternative view.

It would appear that what the model reasoning above must be designed to show is either that a non-Sellarsian account is impossible or that, despite appearances, its *real* structure is something on this order. There are philosophers whose practice seems to betray adherence to the maxim that showing that a language fragment *can* be treated in a certain way is enough to show that it *should* be treated in that way . But 'can be done' no more implies 'should be done' here than it does in morality. However, what more plausible grounds are available to defend this reconstruction as a way of showing that the justification for using (L) is impossible or elliptical, or even confused in any way? Certainly, one cannot invoke the very Sellarsian principles being challenged. Nor can Sellarsians be content to argue that their reconstruction is just as good; if you recall, the point of offering it is to *rule out* other forms of belief justification, not to *rule in* theirs. And it is hard to see how the presence of the reconstruction shows that the connection of contents to something justified isn't sufficient to make them justifiers in their own right. Thus, nothing remains of the Sellarsian position other than a brute preference for its own version. (I must also confess a brute preference for my own, since it seems to make such good sense of how what we apprehend, as opposed to our apprehending of it, fixes belief directly—a commonplace sort of occurrence eluded rather than explained in the Sellarsian scheme. But the point of this rejoinder doesn't require the reader to place confidence in my preference.)

In sum, the defense of NT against the Sellarsian argument requires only that we produce an intelligible scheme of justification employing visual contents as primitives. The Sellarsian reply is to produce a derivation of the justification of the same proposition without employing visual contents as primitives. That is inadequate, since it has no tendency to supersede or drive out the NT scheme. However, someone might claim I have overlooked more promising interpretations of Sellarsian remarks. The remainder of this chapter is devoted to examining further interpretations and implications that may be worthy of comment.

VI

Sellars has more than once (1973; 1979, p. 171) raised the following difficulty to treating a perceived object as a justifier. For the object to play this role, it must be present. But then its presence needs to be guaranteed: "[T]he state of affairs being of the kind it is, it is *evident* if and only if it is *true* (*i.e.*, obtains), even though being evident is not the same thing as being true" (1973, p. 618). Its being evident is crucial to its being a justifier. We may construe the argument as maintaining that if the state of affairs (object) is indeed a justifier, it follows that there is no larger epistemically accessible class, such as the class of appearances, that is in reality playing that role. But without false appearances there is no way to account for mistakes. (This is what I take to be the significance of its being evident if and only if it obtains.) Since there is no room for mistake on this view, there must be an epistemic guarantee of the state of affairs' occurrence, contrary to what we know to be the case. Consequently, the state of affairs (ontological object) cannot be the justifier.

But what prevents us from appealing to a larger class, including both objects of perception and mere appearances? The trick is to avoid collapsing everything belonging to this class into a mere appearance, indeed to resist blandishments for viewing the entire class as characterizable in any way that goes beyond acknowledging that its members are all justifiers. At the level at which Sellars seeks to delineate the class, and given the adequacy condition of being present in perception, it will be a ragbag of things consisting of some worldly states of affairs together with a miscellany of misperceptions (e.g., illusions, hallucinations, delusions, dreams, and whatnot). It is the felt need to find some single, simple notion covering all these cases that drives us either to regarding sense-data as the only justifiers or to restricting the evident to what actually obtains.

The challenge, though subtle and serious, rests on an assumption rejected in the discussion at the end of §VI of chapter 2. The claim that there must be a broader (and distinct) class of things—appearances—playing the role of justifier seems to focus exclusively on the case of perceptual mistake in which one takes something for something else. Mistakes of this type commonly do occur; particularly when we literally mis-take one *physical* thing for another similar one. Generalizing this paradigm for the whole of perception, we would need a class of appearances to ensure a ready supply of comparable entities to be mistaken for one another. Indeed, even if we admit other kinds of mistakes as well, isn't the mere presence of this sort enough to require us to devise a class of appearances to cover both erroneous and mistake-free cases, which will then be the sorts of intermediaries whose failings lead us to embrace coherentism?

Suppose we ask, "What follows for NT's justification scheme from the assumption that a *mistaken* appearance is nothing more than an appearance?" I answer, "Nothing about the ability of actual things (ontological objects) to serve as justifiers!"

In cases of perception without mistakes of this kind, the fact that the object appears in a certain way is not sufficient to transform it into a mere appearance—the kind allowed in classifying mistaken appearances. Without the aid of the dubious sort of inference rejected in chapter 2, p. 43—the inference that, if I mistake one thing for another, they must share properties—there seems no warrant for elevating *an appearing object* to *an appearance*. When it is the object that we perceive, why not maintain that the object serves as the justifier rather than as its mental proxy? This does not by itself prevent what may be a mere appearance (say, a hallucination) from being mistaken for it on occasion, thereby accounting for error even on the agreed model. But it does stop us from being stampeded into explanations in terms of appearances for every case just to accomodate visual error.

A natural rejoinder is that the subject will not be in a position, by use of the means through which the original justification was obtained (viz., perception), to distinguish a genuine object from a mere appearance. True, but not to the point. Grant that a subject is unable to discern through the very same visual experience that her experience is not erroneous: the experience is not self-certifying. However, this is not a question of the nature or legitimacy of the original justification, but of its metajustification. It may still be the object, rather than an appearance, that plays this particular role in the justification. Demand for a metajustification does not abolish the need for the original justification. When the perceptual experience is not erroneous in a justification-defeating way, it will be the perceptual object that plays that justificatory role. The issue is not whether the original evidence would, were it genuine, suffice to justify the belief, but whether the type to which it belongs satisfies further standards of purely epistemic goodness.

Sellars's complaint, it seems, has more to do with the subject's knowledge of what she sees than with her seeing of it.[7] I have been arguing that we can have the latter without the former. I don't know that there is enough textual evidence to pin down Sellars's explicit views on the matter. Nevertheless, the general line of argument seems to commit him to disagreeing. Unless he runs together seeing something with knowing that one sees it, this objection to NT doesn't appear to get off the ground.

I hope the introduction of these considerations also helps to undermine the very paradigm of mistake it takes for granted. Without it, I needn't make the concessions granted earlier for the sake of argument. And quite independently of this issue, it cannot be extended to all perceptual mistake. Not all mistakes are hallucinations. More often, one misidentifies what one nevertheless genuinely sees. Mistakes of the kind involved in the whale example are much more commonplace than total visual delusion.

The rejection of the objection does not place on me the burden of supplying an alternative account of perceptual mistake. Aside from the fact that I do not have anything I would advertise as one, I suspect that there are a variety of circumstances, perhaps not easily bound under a useful title, that account for an equally wide assortment of perceptual errors. But even if I possessed such an account, it could only confuse matters to implicate it with the main issue. Sellars's objection, I have argued, is mistaken about how visual objects enter the justificatory stream, about the consequences the existence of mistakes have for other experiences, and about the whole range of perceptual mistakes that resemble (what is in fact) one not particularly significant variety. Each is sufficient to doom the objection.

VII

I have yet to consider a third property, (iii), which our montage Sellarsian ascribes to all cognitive apprehensions: that they include conceptualizations. We might add to it the view that the classifications and discriminations implied by conceptualizations are taken as contributed by the cognizer rather than by the immediate current environment. According to this view, the mere fact that the scene has undergone this processing by our faculties makes it belieflike, and thus in need of justification. In answer to a foundationalist claim that immediate apprehensions are prior to language, conceptualization, and predication, BonJour replies: "no matter how preconceptual or prepredicative such a state may be, so long as it involves anything like a representation, the question of justification can still legitimately be raised: is there any reason to think that the representation in question is accurate or correct? And without a positive answer to this question, the capacity of such a state to confer epistemic justification is decisively undermined" (1985, p. 78). This reasoning ignores the possibility of nonconceptual experiential content: that is (roughly), content whose *representational* character is not explained by the perceiver's possession of the concepts of what gets represented. Admittedly, the notion cries out for clarification. I do place any reliance on it myself because, as explained more fully in chapter 9, adequate specifications of it do not seem to yield the sort of extension intended by the disinction, while such specifications as have been offered to approximate the intended extension are more problematic.[8] However, unlike BonJour, I do not maintain theses that make it incumbent on me to reject nonconceptual content in order to avoid employing it. If BonJour has reasons for ignoring it here, I suppose we must discover them in his remarks on the Schlick case, although it is doubtful that that version is very close to what recent philosophers have in mind by nonconceptual content. At any rate, BonJour excludes it without offering his readers anything to show that he is entitled to do so.

But my chief difficulty with this reply is rather different. When, in the passage quoted, it is asked "is there any reason to believe that the representation in question is accurate . . . ?" the accuracy in question is not that of something like (S), but that of something like (L). If we can apply such tags as 'accurate,' 'inaccurate,' 'correct,' 'incorrect' to (L) and its kin, then, according to the argument, they must be postconceptual and postpredicative. However, this is a nonsequitur. Eligibility for such epithets, as the passage makes clear, turns only on the contents being representations. And, to repeat an earlier point (p. 161), nothing in the notion of representationality requires that the form of the representer be propositional. It may seem as if the author acknowledges this when he writes hesitantly on the same page, "assertive *or at least* representational content" (my emphasis). But if being minimally representational is a step down from being assertive, the claims in the earlier passage do not support the larger thesis about the structure of justifiers. A postconceptualized and preconceptualized simple object can have the same structure, whatever other differences conceptualization makes. Furthermore, bearing in mind my remarks about nonconceptual content, even if we allow that only a user with concepts could have representational content, it doesn't follow that what is conceptualized is the evaluable content. Conceptualizations may be in the form of background conditions and not be part of the perceptual content (that is, of what is evaluable) itself. There is no warrant for using those conceptualizations to flesh out the content from its (potentially) nonpropositional form into a propositionlike phenomenon.

The polemical situation, as I see it, is as follows. Certain things represent accurately. But there is little motivation for a desideratum that they be propositional contents other than allegiance to a Sellarsian restriction. Suppose we search of grounds for that extra step. Prima facie, its prospects aren't bright. Consider maps. Mapping is (accurate or inaccurate) representation. This example alone renders BonJour's reasoning doubtful. Although a map represents, say, Utah bordering on Nevada, whether this entitles us to claim that it *states that* Utah borders on Nevada is just as vexing a question as the one raised about the cognitive thesis. Thus, comparisons with cases likely to show that what is representational is (or always can be) evaluated for accuracy are less likely to show that what is representational is always propositional. It has not been shown that contents are propositional *because* they are representational.

Another possibility is to claim that contents are representational because they go proxy for something else. Aside from the fact that this assumes that all forms of perception are indirect—a view already criticized, and one with little attraction for Sellarsians—it doesn't yield a sense of 'representation' that advances the objection. To declare that a content is representational in this way is not to settle whether it is propositional. The state of affairs it represents needn't be one that can be encapsulated in a propositional form. A sense-datum theorist can be a noncognitivist as easily as can a direct realist.

For yet another interpretation of what might be intended, I pounce (rather heavily I'm afraid) on a clue in the initial contrast with what is prelinguistic, preconceptual, or prepredicative. On this understanding, BonJour can be taken to be claiming that the minimal level of representationality involves the application of concepts and that this (in a way yet to be explained) implies that whatever is involved with it is propositional or infected by belief. There are a few proposals here—one ambitious and one modest. Each stands in need of elaboration.

The ambitious proposal is that to recognize objects as such and such is to bring them under classifications; to bring them under classifications is to describe them; to describe them is to apply concepts to them; and, perhaps since no descriptions are perfectly 'neutral' (whatever that portends), to apply concepts to them is *to project* something from our constitutions onto the world. (Thus, the notorious projection versus discovery issue.) Once established, it is but a short step to holding that belief—in the form of 'taking to be a such and such,' where the 'such and such' is filled in by the projected feature—enters into whatever we see. Although this type of argument seems to have an inexhaustible supply of philosophical lives, I cannot find much merit in it. It provides little evidence to show that the categories into which we divide the perceived world are not as much a discovered, cognition-independent part of that world as any class of perceivable qualities one chooses. The argument occasionally makes an appeal to certain truisms, such as that if we had different or altered faculties things would appear differently to us. Although an impeccable observation, it takes some imagination to figure out how it purports to settle the issue. It is possible to take it as saying no more than that without certain faculties we would be incapable of detecting certain qualities. This is true for any detection device and tells us nothing about whether to classify the features in question as detected or projected. Nor is it to the point to mention that creatures with other faculties or a different set of concepts would carve up reality in different ways, failing even to notice some of the features we currently claim to detect. We may conclude from this no more than that things can be cross-classified in a multitude of ways, that nature is richer than any cataloging of it operating on finite list of principles of division; but it says nothing about whether any of those ways of classifying things are discoveries or projections.

Perhaps the most damaging point against the ambitious version of this argument is that if we accept everything thus far proclaimed in its premises, it would still not show that the products of its projections were propositional rather than objectual. There is a perhaps less aggressive interpretation of this argument on which contents could still be considered cognitive: that is, they are products only of cognizing beings. And such beings, it might be assumed, couldn't see anything without a body of beliefs. But even if the concepts employed in our contents presupposed that we possessed some propositionally representable information about *them* (a stronger supposition than called for by the preceding steps), it would not show that the contents themselves were so representable. Not every bit of knowledge underlying my ability to grasp a content is a part of that content. If it were, it is difficult to see how any assertion could be made explicit; to convey it would require stating its underlying knowledge, and the underlying knowledge of that underlying knowledge, ad nauseam. To infer directly from a content's being cognitive to its being judgmental would mark a serious confusion of senses of 'cognitive'.

A modest proposal, related to the ambitious one, is that a subject would not have the ability to use concepts in perception—that is, to subsume objects under them—unless she were already capable of at least an inner language. Concepts enter our mental economy only by way of bits of information, and these are at least quasi-linguistic. Any time a concept is applied, such conceptual information is presupposed. This form of objection suffers from the last fault ascribed to the ambitious version. The fact that, say, the description under which I see presupposes that I have a background of propositionally representable information does not show that the particular application of the description is itself propositional. The form a product takes needn't duplicate the form taken by the wherewithal needed to obtain it.

Of course, whenever someone *takes* what she sees in a certain way, what is taken is transcribable propositionally or predicatively. This is because it requires reporting by such forms as "S sees that *e* is F" or "S sees *e* to be F." But to begin with either idiom presupposes the cognitivism or doxasticism whose faults have already been exposed. It is also true that the issue of justification, and therefore of NT, arises for perception only when a subject *takes* what she sees in a certain way. But that, too, has no tendency to rescue this line of reasoning. It can be maintained that the taking is itself the perceptual belief that the (independent) perception justifies. In other words, the reason that taking is ubiquitously present in such circumstances may be due not to the fact that perceptual contents are propositional or predicative, but to the fact that the contents of perceptual beliefs are. The difficulty for NT vanishes.

This exhausts the, at least minimally, hopeful uses of 'representational content' that I can muster for the argument under consideration. On none of those I am familiar with is the argument cogent.

VIII

The Sellarsian argument posed the last formidable threat to NT. But its challenge dissipates on scrutiny. Earlier in the present chapter, I maintained that NT offers a perfectly adequate account of the relation between experience and perceptual belief. Put very briefly, the object we are aware of (at the perceiving stage) is the basis for fixing a belief about the state of the perceived environment. That this basis is almost universally exploited for belief is explained by habits nurtured through the mediation of its past reliability. That perceptual believing is nevertheless a further step to be taken, and not wholly automatic, is brought out clearly only in those peculiar instances in which collateral information leads us to withhold it (see chap. 4, p. 103; chap. 5, pp. 138–9) or in which the belief system breaks down while the visual system remains intact (chap. 6, p. 151). Nevertheless, we have good reason—including the failures of the alternative—to maintain that the relevant pairs of seeings and believings differ. On the other hand, some may still be bothered by the generation of a propositional content for belief out of something that is not essentially propositional to begin with (the perceptual content). There are indeed questions to be raised about the way this gets accomplished, but the solutions are empirical details. As for the remaining philosophical anxieties about any such connection, those that I have been able to articulate clearly strike me as holdovers from the general Sellarsian outlook.

Finally, I return, by circuitous route, to my main buisness: the causal theory of perception. As mentioned earlier, since causation is not usually regarded as factative, it is easier to integrate the causation of perceptual episodes if their causes can be seen as having the structure of objects or events: things canonically describable via nouns and nonpropositional noun clauses rather than as incipient beliefs. Having cleared away this debris and earlier obstacles to causal accounts in general, there remain a number of serious concerns about the details of CTP. The problem of deviant causal chains is one such; the question of how the object of visual perception is chosen is another. The next two chapters take up each in turn.

PART III

Completing the Causal Theory

7

Deviant Causal Chains

"What is it you want to buy?" the Sheep said at last, looking up for a moment from her knitting.

"I don't *quite* know yet," Alice said very gently. "I should like to look all round me first, if I might."

"You may look in front of you, and on both sides, if you like," said the Sheep; "but you ca'n't look *all* round you—unless you've got eyes at the back of your head."

But these, as it happened, Alice had not got: so she contented herself with turning round, looking at the shelves as she came to them.

Lewis Carroll, Through the Looking Glass

I

Let's chart our progress on the causal theory. A first principle, (C), to the effect that *o* is seen by S only if it is a cause of S's perceptual episode, has been established, and various considerations for allegiance to a direct-realist version have been adduced. Chapter 4 makes it clear that whatever else is accomplished, we had better be able to deal with objectual seeing. Now let's jump ahead to the problem of the next chapter. Suppose it had been shown that *o* had a distinctive causal mark, one that makes manifest why it, out of a multitude of causal factors, is the thing seen. Would there still be serious problems to bedevil CTP? No doubt, there are other delicate questions to be raised about visual perception. For example, we could always revive the issue of Aristotelian proper sensibles—characteristics proper to, and only to, vision—so that nothing could be seen save by detection of those characteristics, and whatever *things* were directly detected through those characteristics would *eo ipso* be seen. But let's suppose that this and other minor matters are resolved without detracting from the causal character of the larger theory. Do we now have before us a finished CTP? If an affirmative answer to this question implies a set of *sufficient,* causally driven (though perhaps not precisely causal) conditions for S's seeing *o* (or even for S's seeing), the answer must be a resounding 'No!' The culprit I have in mind is causal deviance.

Speaking geometrically, a man in my direct line of sight is operating an exotic device: a cerebrograph. With it, he induces all sorts of visual experiences in me that, without background knowledge, I could not distinguish from my experience when actually seeing things. For the most part, the induced contents bear no pertinent relation to what is in my line of sight. But on one occasion, he induces a scene of a man operating a cerebrograph. The setup and man look very much like what I would have seen were he in the same position but not in fact inducing this experience in me. Given the facts of the case, we should conclude that I am not seeing that scene. (It is similar to Strawson's case [mentioned earlier in chap. 2, p. 33] of a man veridically hallucinating a brain that happens to look very much like his own brain, which in turn is a cause of the hallucination.) My diagnosis is that the causal chain is deviant: the only potential object is the man operating the cerebrograph, but the causal chain running from that occurrence to my episode is of the wrong kind. Although he may be inducing that scene because he knows that is what I would be seeing were I seeing, my explanation for the deviance is that the chain runs through his intention. But that is of secondary importance to the claim that, for whatever reason, the chain is in fact deviant.

Others who agree that no seeing takes place may abjure the diagnosis that it results from causal deviance. For example, some may say that the causation of the episode doesn't run through my eyes, and seeing requires that the eyes be on the chain. Until we clarify what counts as an eye, such claims threaten to end up as no more than terminological preferences. (It take it that all parties allow that there may a wide variety of natural and artificial photosensitive devices that transduce light into electrical impulses. Are they all, *ex vi termini,* eyes? Is it even necessary that the experience be generated via photons bleaching rhodopsin? Indeed, other than that performance of a function described at a rather abstract level, why even consider the multichambered 'eyes' of many creatures (e.g., squids) as of the same sort as our own eyes? These questions aren't merely rhetorical, but raise serious doubts in my mind about the advisability of such a requirement.) At any rate, the requirement of having (much less, using) eyes is seldom spelled out in greater detail and is thus insufficiently specific to consider further here. In fact, at this stage, I will dismiss all the various alternative explanations that a fertile imagination could produce. The deviance of the causal path certainly looks like a promising place to begin a search; alternatives can wait until we have satisfied ourselves that the cases cannot be straightforwardly explained as deviant.

The problem has analogues in other topics in which causal analyses have been tried. Consider memory. It is plausible to require that S remembers (a personally experienced) event e only if e is responsible for S's current knowlege of it. But suppose S told T about the event, subsequently forgot about it, but later regained knowledge of e by having been told by T about it. I am assuming that T doesn't merely jog S's memory, but causes S to acquire the information anew. S's current knowledge is causally traceable to S's original experience, but it only recurs in S through a deviant causal route: through T's storage of it. (T may be a diary instead of a person.) Most would agree that S doesn't remember, and causal deviance from experience to current knowledge is an enticing explanation. Similar problem cases can be produced for causal clauses in accounts of intentional action and knowledge.

This does not mean that a solution to the deviance puzzle for visual perception will have application, mutatis mutandis, to all the areas in which problem cases can be found, or even that it will be a clue to resolving similar puzzles facing other sensory modalities. If the solution proposed below can be extended to the analogous problems, that is a welcome bonus. But in lieu of further argument showing otherwise, we may take it that a failure of similar solutions elsewhere is not an argument against one working for vision. I will not attempt to explore here the implications of an eventual solution beyond the issue of present concern.

II

Let us then examine causal deviance with respect to sight. Unfortunately, it is difficult to characterize the problem without assuming too much. This is understandable. A solution is a way to segregate such cases for elimination, say, by a clause tailored to exclude them. Once a characterization isolates the relevant cases, the desired clause is at hand. Thus, a detailed characterization of the problem would seem to contribute much of the real labor toward its solution. This is indicated by the way in which those offering different solutions disagree on the nature of the problem itself. I try to stave off the inevitable as long as possible in this section by giving what seem to me clear instances of the phenomenon on which all parties can agree, and then asking whether we can find a clause to eliminate them all through a characterization that covers their range. (Even the range of relevant cases is in dispute. Ultimately, the only justification for one's choice of a range is the persuasiveness of a solution combined with the ability to handle cases ignored or misread elsewhere.) However, even at the outset, my characterization departs from that of some others. By a deviant causal chain, I do not mean merely a quirky or unusual one, but one singular enough to disqualify a would-be perception. And this cannot be merely a question of *degree* of peculiarity. S may see with the aid of an abnormal chain running through a prosthetic implant, or even through a device outside S's body that boosts otherwise weak neural impulses (just as telescopes, and some microscopes boost physical signals). Unusually enhanced chains may still be nondeviant or, as I will frequently call them, *standard*. In my patois, there is no such thing as a seeing that has occurred despite a deviant chain. (Here, too, as we will see in §X, there is disagreement. At least one author holds that, where it is possible to link two scenes in a certain way to a single visual episode, that episode may be a perception relative to one scene while, due to deviance, not relative to another scene.) With that in mind, let me add two prime examples (the second just a tarted-up version of the cerebrograph case) to that of Strawson's veridical hallucinator.

First, at a public demonstration of hypnotism, H places S under a spell, telling S that he, S, *sees* a woman in a red dress seated in front of him. S thereupon enjoys the appropriate seeinglike state. Let's suppose that S's glazed and inoperative gaze is fixed on a woman in a red dress seated in front of him, so that, were he in that attitude but not in a trance, this is precisely what he would be seeing, down to as fine a detail as one likes. Indeed, we may imagine the following two further sorts of causal involvement with the actual woman. First, H chooses to induce just this scene because, as H observes, it is what S would be seeing had he been able to look at things from that perspective. Second, S is the woman's escort, he knows her well, and her being seated there is the last thing S saw before succumbing to H's spell. Thus, we may suppose, whichever details of S's content are not explicitly induced by H's command are fleshed out from S's short-term memory bank of a scene appreciably like the one he now conjures. Despite all this, I believe it will be generally agreed that S is not strictly seeing—as opposed to visualizing—this or any other scene while obeying H's command.

Throughout the present chapter, I use this example ('the hypnotist case') as a touchstone for various proposed solutions.

Second, consider one of the thought experiments of chapter 3, p. 58. A well-lit, blue cube is placed in front of Smithers, and his eyes are open. But his optic nerve has been severed. To compensate this loss, a clever neurologist has his brain attached to a device with sensitive probes, enabling her to produce a seeinglike state similar to the one Smithers would have been in had he seen the blue cube from just that distance and angle. But in the present scenario, unlike that of chapter 3, she causes this particular content just because she knows it imitates what he would have been seeing. Indeed, other than the long-term unreliability of her procedure, the neurologist stands in much the same relation to Smithers's experience that is assigned to God by a Malebranchean occasionalist.

(One salient difference is that the neurologist has been caused by the cube to produce just that experience in Smithers. Thus, the causation runs *from* the blue cube *to* his seeinglike episode, although he doesn't see it. On occasionalism, God is the cause of both the cube's being there and the experience: the causation does not run from the cube to the experience. Nevertheless, I claim that Smithers wouldn't see the cube in either case. Supplementing the neurologist with Godlike reliability wouldn't help, for reasons to follow.)

These are typical specimens of deviance. (This might also be true in the veridical-hallucination and cerebrograph cases, but with less certainty. One might claim in those cases that there is nothing that, but for the deviance of the chain, would have been seen. They appear to lack candidate objects. Nevertheless, they are the sorts of examples that a solution to the current problem might account for incidentally.) In neither of the two most recent examples is anything seen, and, very broadly, this seems explained by the visual episode's not being caused in the right way by the only thing that could be the object of sight. Before proceeding to inquire whether we can discover a rule to exclude such cases while not violating our concept of vision, the natural next step in the investigation, a few more preliminaries are in order.

III

Compare the preceding case with a straightforward, unproblematic one in which Sue actually sees something, say a tree in the forest on a sunny day. The causal chain that accounts for Sue's seeing runs well past the tree, to the source of illumination (the sun), and in various other directions (e.g., to the causes of the tree's being planted or those of Sue's being at that location). Nevertheless, if we imagine the sorts of changes that would have introduced perception-defeating deviance, the only segment of that chain that matters is the one running directly from the tree to the visual episode. Nothing outside that part of the chain could have produced deviance. For example, suppose there were at that moment a total eclipse of the sun. The whole chain would be terminated, and there would no longer be a perception. But it would not be because there was a deviant causal chain: there would be *no* (relevant) chain to be tested for nondeviance. Moreover, if, at the moment of eclipse, a flash of lightning were to illuminate the tree, that very perception might have taken place, however unusual the source of illumination on the occasion.[1] No illumination in which the luminous source is not itself the perceptual object, however irregular or unusual it may be in other respects, is sufficient to render a relevant chain deviant.

We shouldn't rest satisfied with this characterization, however. Although the relevant part of the chain runs only from the object to the visual episode, where there is no seeing (as in cases of deviance), there is no object; thereby invalidating my way of selecting the relevant part of the chain. A minor qualification eliminates this inconvenience. If we are to judge that an episode fails *because of* deviance, something must be identifiable as having the slot usually accorded the object. It is only in cases in which something present fails as object that worries about deviance can arise. Other visual episodes that are clearly not seeings all seem to fail to satisfy (C), thereby obviating a need to appeal to causal deviance to explain their failures. This seems to open the prospect of forming a class of those things that are either objects or, in the case of deviance, ersatz objects. Let's use the noncommittal expression 'candidate object' to refer to that sort of node on a causal chain. General characterizations are, as usual, elusive. But in practice there is no problem in identifying the candidate object, if there is one, of a given visual episode. In the case of the hypnotist, the woman in the red dress is the candidate object; in the case of the neurologist, the blue cube serves. If the veridical hallucination of the brain counts as causal deviance, the hallucinator's brain is the candidate object. Once again, for emphasis, the only part of a causal chain we need be concerned with is that whose termini are candidate objects and visual episodes.

In what follows, I propose a way of segregating cases of deviance by satisfaction—or, more properly, nonsatisfaction—of a certain counterfactual. There have been various other suggestions for accomplishing this end. Some of them anticipate that no account will exclude all clearly aberrant cases; they proceed to commit themselves to jettisoning certain solid judgments for (what they take to be) the compensating virtues of their solutions. They are unabashedly revisionary. In contrast, one of the chief virtues of my account, or so I claim, is that it avoids this uneasy resolution. To the extent that we have clear cases, this proposal divides them up in the way that our strong, pretheoretical commitments do. But before setting it out, I will canvass several other counterfactual accounts. They may at first seem more natural than mine, so their failures are instructive. However, because their failures have been taken by at least some writers to show the hopelessness of this whole approach, it may also be worthwhile first to state briefly why a counterfactual account of nondeviance has strong initial appeal.

The subjunctive-conditional construction is often viewed as philosophically mischievous. In some circles, dragging in a subjunctive conditional to salvage one's view will be thought of as too desperate to deserve a hearing. Nevertheless, this form remains the clearest way to express a nonaccidental covariation between two events, episodes, or states of affairs; it is covariation, not conditionality for its own sake, that is crucial here. The two states of affairs whose covariation I have in mind are the termini of the relevant segment of the causal chain: the candidate object and the visual episode. It appears that any solution to the problem of nondeviance ought to be able to express a relationship between such states of affairs without entangling us in the scientific details of actual, familiar perception. If we have a conception of vision worthy of the specialist attention of philosophers, it should be compatible with the discovery, or the invention, of very different sorts of sighted creatures, with unfamiliar physiologies (or none at all), and living in a world in which light rays bend in unusual ways. Thus, it seems advantageous to confine any philosophical solution to a consideration of the interaction between sensory episode and candidate object. Covariation that extends beyond actual cases presents itself as a promising way to represent that relationship. The most natural way to represent that is with a subjunctive conditional or, more specifically, a counterfactual (that is, a subjunctive conditional whose antecedent, we assume, is unfulfilled).

Readers should be warned about the inherent limitations of the project. If we ignore the physics and physiology of vision, then unless the phenomenal nature of the visual episode is spelled out in more detail than would otherwise be needed, nothing in the present account will distinguish the deliverances of this sensory mode from those of any other. That is, the account will not distinguish, say, seeing from hearing. This shouldn't be regarded as a shortcoming. I am attempting to understand one thing about vision, not everything. Thus, there is no reason why further distinctions, however legitimate, need be introduced into the present inquiry. On the other hand, such a restriction does make the present account more easily adaptable to the other sensory modalities, thereby snatching a virtue from necessity.

IV

Christopher Peacocke (1979) reviews prospective counterfactual solutions, and each comes up short. (This is a prelude to his own solution, discussed in §X in this chapter.) He identifies a counterfactual theory as "any theory to the effect that there is a certain collection of counterfactuals the holding of which is necessary and sufficient for nondeviance" (p. 75). But these requirements are of unequal weight, for "counterexamples to the necessity of counterfactual sensitivity can be seen as more important than counterexamples to sufficiency, since if we do not have necessity then counterfactuals will not be part of a uniform account of nondeviance" (p. 78). This sound advice must be tempered by the following admonitions.

Beginning with sufficiency, for seeinglike transactions it is easy to confuse two sufficient conditions: one for *nondeviance* of a causal chain from *o* to S's visual episode, the other for *seeing o*. Our concern extends strictly no farther than sufficiency for nondeviancy. Of course, it may happen that, combined with what has already been settled—say, (C), a content restriction, a solution to object determination, and certain minor items—the condition will be sufficient for 'S sees *o*' as well. But it is no part of the task of someone seeking to solve the deviancy problem to show this; an overly ambitious effort to do so may embroil one's proposal in controversies that are strictly superfluous to the task at hand.

There is another distinction to be noted. Were we still interested in sufficient conditions *for seeing,* they might be conditions for intransitive or transitive seeing. A condition for intransitive seeing, seeing simpliciter, may not yield a condition for transitive seeing, seeing *o.* (Of course, no seeing is really intransitive: all seeing is seeing something. These are merely shorthand for discussing two elucidation targets within a single subject matter.) At first, it may seem as if there is a comparable distinction between sufficient conditions for transitive and intransitive nondeviance. This would be possible if a visual episode could be deviant for one object, but nondeviant (and thus a potential seeing) for another. However, my way of characterizing deviance leaves no room for such a distinction. It requires that we first identify a unique candidate object for the visual episode. This in turn rules out relativizing deviance to one or another causal chain. (This decision is independently justifiable. The issue is taken up later in the chapter.) Thus, the only sufficient conditions for deviance of concern are those for transitive seeing. And, by and large, when I consider sufficient conditions for seeing, they will be for transitive seeing. This is the view that gets put into play when I later consider object determination and, but for the admonition of the preceding paragraph, would flow from restrictions on the nature of deviance.

Returning to my earlier remark that the only sufficient conditions directly relevant here are those for nondeviance (not those for seeing), it may seem easy enough to confine ourselves to their pursuit. But the situation is complicated by competing demands on the standard of proof we must employ. In test cases likely to be of interest, S would have seen *o* but for the deviance of the causal chain that delivers the content. Accordingly, solutions that cover problems of that nature will discover, say, the absence of a desideratum *f* such that the addition of *f* to the original case would yield a set of sufficient conditions for S seeing *o.* Of course, if the distinction just drawn between the different targets of sufficiency is on the right track, it ought to be possible, in principle, to have instances of deviant chains in which S would not be seeing *o* even were the deviance removed. Such visual episodes would fail to be seeings for more than one reason, and it is understandable why they would be inferior examples on which to hone our intuitions about deviance or to test solutions to it. (If we want to be sure that our characterization covers deviance, Mill's method of difference dictates that we fix attention on a single defect and that our correction of it be precisely targeted. Multiplication of intervening variables defeats that prescription.) Thus, the strategy mandated by describing and treating cases encourages philosophers to suppress conditions other than the one needed for a solution to deviance in assembling a sufficient condition for seeing. It is no wonder that we are lulled into forgetting about conditions that aren't salient in the focal circumstances. I will have occasion in the next chapter to see how writers have fudged this difference, or one roughly similar.

We can protect against errors that arise from the vice of overextension by labeling solutions as conditions for nondeviance rather than for seeing. This can also simplify the search for sufficient conditions. Where doubts may surface about suggestions for a sufficient condition for seeing, they may not arise for a less ambitious set of sufficient conditions for nondeviance.

Turning to necessity, though perhaps more important than sufficiency, a necessary condition for nondeviance (or for seeing, the difference here being negligible) may itself be excessively modest. Analytically, it may be unimpeachable but yield little of use to an illuminating account of visual perception. Thus, if we are to forswear the indispensability of necessary *and sufficient* conditions, we should at least demand something meatier than bare necessity. It is not easy to state with precision what, short of sufficiency, is wanted. But it is clear that it should contribute to our understanding. At a minimum, it would appear that such a condition should shed light not only on why certain irregular chains defeat seeing, but also on why the extraordinary character of others *need not be* incompatible with sight. In short, it should select among unusual chains for a particular feature that accounts for standardness *in those circumstances*. Perhaps this isn't full-blooded sufficiency, but it is a gesture toward it. Among candidates will no doubt be the INUS conditions of chap. 3, p. 67, Insufficient Nonredundant parts of Unnecessary Sufficient conditions (see Mackie 1974, p. 62). They are necessary conditions of *a* sufficient condition, but the latter need not be necessary as well. INUS conditions, though not always informative and falling short of the frequently announced aspirations of philosophers, include many of the most fruitful results of philosophical efforts to elucidate concepts (viz., when the sufficient condition is prominent and the part is substantial).

I now commence the inquiry into a counterfactual solution, starting with Peacocke's saga of failures. To summarize his first effort,[2]

> (8) (a) A causal chain from an array of objects to a visual episode is nondeviant (standard) only if
>   (b) if the external scene were to change (in ways to be specified in the particular case), (c) the experience one has would be correspondingly different (1979, p. 76).

Although this initially seems to explain why the hypnotic subject does not see the woman, its shortcomings are quickly exposed. Any case in which any one of a wide range of visible alterations of the scene would completely darken it, thus preventing one from having *any* experience of it, is a counterexample. The perception of a hand on a sensitive light switch suffices. A perceptible movement of the hand (in certain directions) will darken the scene and not result in a correspondingly different experience, although the chain before the movement is certainly not deviant and normally results in a perception. That is, the hypothesis would make (b) true where (c) is false, thus rendering subjunctive conditional (b)–(c) false. But (a) is hypothesized as true (viz., the chain starting from the hand on a switch to the episode is standard), thus the instance of (8) as a whole would be false. Peacocke devises a case in which an array of objects in an artificially lit studio is arranged so that if any of the objects is "perceptibly moved or visually altered . . . all the lights would go out and nothing would be perceived" (p. 76). This violates (8) in like manner.

We might attempt to salvage (8) by adding to (b) "and (if) any experience were produced under the circumstances." Another slight amendment is also in order. We must be careful not to phrase the requirement so that its current nondeviance depends on what will, or might, happen at some future time. It is difficult to comprehend how that could matter to whether one sees *now*. I amend the suggestion accordingly:

(9) (a) A causal chain from an array of objects to a visual episode is nondeviant (standard) only if
    (b) if the external scene had been different and an experience had been produced under the circumstances, (c) the experience would have been correspondingly different.

(It might be thought that, similarly, what is merely possible does not matter to what is actually seen. This would misconstrue the role of counterfactuality in the formula. The truth values of simple counterfactuals are not determined by what happens elewhere, but by what happens here. Cf. Stalnaker 1987, p. 163.) Unfortunately, a simple modification to the earlier conditional nullifies whatever gains this reformulation promises. Peacocke claims that (9) "would not be true [of genuine perception] if, for instance, an alteration in one of the perceived objects [had] caused the release into the air . . . of some hallucinatory drug" (p. 76), causing us to hallucinate a scene like the one we would have experienced before the alteration. This shows that counterfactual (b)–(c) fails to capture what is distinctive of standard chains, and this flaw is transmitted to (9).

V

David Lewis (1986a) offers a somewhat similar counterfactual view, on which, "if the scene before the eyes causes matching visual experience as part of a suitable pattern of counterfactual dependence, then the subject sees; if the scene before the eyes causes matching visual experience without a suitable pattern of counterfactual dependence, then the subject does not see" (p. 281). In effect, two conditions have been given for an instance of a matching visual experience being a seeing (or not being a seeing):

(a) that the scene before the eyes causes matching visual experience;
(b) that the matching visual experience caused is (or is not) a part—or, as we might say, an instance—of a pattern of counterfactual dependence.

Although these are sufficient conditions for seeing and not seeing, respectively— rather than merely for nondeviance or deviance of the chain—that is unlikely to be problematic here; built into the antecedents are enough putatively noncausal conditions to satisfy the most exacting critic. For example, the requirement that the scene be "before the eyes' " ensures the involvement of the eyes. Furthermore, in requiring that a *visual* experience be generated, Lewis has left room for someone to limit experiences to those of a distinctive sort (say, with the proprietary quality of visuality). These additions may in fact import too much. Fortunately, we need take no stand on such prodigality. Moreover, although the formula makes no mention of what is seen, Lewis has already stated that he intends his analysandum to be "seeing in the intransitive sense, not seeing such-and-such a particular thing" (1986a, p. 276). Thus, the conditions are intended for 'S sees' not for 'S sees o.'

Condition (b) warrants amplification. What pattern of counterfactual dependence provides a background against which the causation of a visual experience can count as a seeing? Lewis answers: "There is a large class of alternative possible scenes before the eyes, and there are many mutually exclusive and jointly exhaustive subclasses thereof, such that (1) any scene in the large class would cause visual experience closely matching the scene, and (2) any two scenes in different subclasses would cause different visual experience" (1986a, p. 283). How large a class, how many subclasses, and how close a match are all matters of degree. In the central case, something is seen, say, in broad daylight without the good offices of gnomes or other potential interveners. From there we must choose, in the face of much indefiniteness, how far we may deviate without losing the concept of sight.

In Peacocke's last test case—in which any perceptible changes would release into the air a drug causing one to hallucinate just that scene—condition (b) is violated. The causation is not part of a pattern of suitable counterfactual dependence. Perhaps other scenes viewed with that perceptual equipment would be part of such a pattern, but this one isn't because no scene in a relevantly distinct alternative subclass would cause a relevantly different visual experience. Nevertheless, the subject sees. Clearly this appears to violate the present proposal. But Lewis remains undaunted, insisting in a relevantly similar case that the subject doesn't see. He dubs the case 'The Censor.'

> My . . . eye is in perfect condition and functioning normally, and by means of it the scene before my eyes causes matching visual experience. But if the scene were any different my visual experience would be just the same. For there is a censor standing by, ready to see to it that I have precisely that visual experience and no other . . . . So long as the scene is such as to cause the right experience, the censor does nothing . . . . But if the scene were any different, the censor would intervene and cause the same experience. (1986, p. 285)

His, perhaps uncomfortable, assessment of the case is that the subject does not see *just because* (b) is not satisfied: the visual experience is not part of a suitable pattern of counterfactual dependence. A "friendly" critic, Bruce Le Catt, claims that the subject might be said to see, making a conservative amendment to the original view in order to remove its counterintuitiveness. Despite accepting in outline Le Catt's way of mapping possible causal interventions, Lewis adheres to his original verdict that the subject doesn't see in The Censor case (1986b, p. 290). Le Catt's modification goes roughly like this. He imagines that briefly before the occurrence of an (arbitrarily chosen) intermediate stage in the chain leading from the original scene, S_o, to the experience, E_o, a monitoring signal, M_o, must intercept and disable another chain that would have led from the censor, C, to an indistinguishable experience, still E_o. The mechanism of the second chain is disabled, because the monitoring signal indicates to it that E_o will be produced if the first chain goes through, rendering superfluous the censor's action. Thus, although there is still no global counterfactual dependence of the experience on a variety of scenes, there is—taking a leaf from Peacocke's earlier notion of stepwise recoverability—a kind of *stepwise* counterfactual dependence of the experience on intermediate stages. That is, where '>' symbolizes an appropriate counterfactual dependence, we have

$$S_o > M_o > \text{ and } M_o > E_o,$$

although we must forgo

$$S_o > E_o.$$

There are other important details in this modified account, but none that wouldn't be more distracting than useful here. The lesson we may take from it is that, when seeing occurs, the causation must still be part of a pattern of counterfactual dependence, although it is now stepwise dependence. Thus, S sees the scene, despite the presence of the censor as part of the visual machinery.

To repeat, Lewis rejects this salvage attempt. It is unclear how deeply entrenched his conclusion is, or even where he actually stands, for he is not very forthcoming about just why "the essential feature of seeing is altogether missing" (1986b, p. 290) from Le Catt's stepwise dependence. However, since my qualms about the view have to do not with the rather rarefied dispute between Lewis and his cat, but with shared basic assumptions of both theories, I will be brief about my reasons for plumping for what seems to me the only sober answer here: the subject sees, despite the presence of the standby censor. Brian McLaughlin (1996) seems to have got it just right: the censor is not an intrinsic part of the machinery of perception. As Lewis notes, it doesn't prevent normal causation. As such, it is like any number of standby failsafe procedures, ready to perform if the primary system fails. There is every reason to believe that the subject succeeds, as McLaughlin puts it, in exercising a capacity to see. And this, beyond our intuition (or perhaps accounting for it), makes it well-nigh irresistible to judge that the subject is seeing. When we view a result that is at odds with this judgment, it must count more heavily against the battery of background assumptions or perceptual theory supporting it than it does against seeing taking place. Le Catt's role is merely to provide an easy expedient by means of which we may retain Lewis's theory while heeding the outcry of offended intuition, namely, accept stepwise dependence in place of simple counterfactual dependence. In either variety, counterfactual dependence is central. Thus, if there is a serious basis for disagreement here, it would appear to lie not with our preferred answer, but with questioning the central paraphernalia of the theory that generates both positions. That is the sort of criticism of Lewis I eventually introduce.

The conservative modification momentarily diverts our attention because of its facility in handling problems already encountered. For example, it would satis-factorily explain the case of the hallucinogenic vapor. We can imagine the original chain's leading to its matching experience by having the production of the vapor derailed at its very inception, through the scene's not having changed. The moni-toring signal here is the nonalteration (or constant state) of the scene. (This is no assurance that there aren't further counterexamples to the amended view. I will not pursue them here. My chief concern is to question the conceptual tools used. Highlighting its extensional inadequacy doesn't pinpoint the culprit.)

We have seen that Lewis's original conditionals are *sufficient* for seeing and not seeing, respectively. As I also noted, sufficiency without necessity will guar-antee no role for the proposal in a uniform account of nondeviance. Do Lewis's conditionals also supply necessary conditions? If we could transpose them, this would suggest as much, for then not seeing and seeing, respectively, would appear in the antecedents of the two resulting conditionals. But the availability of transpo-sition will depend on the sort of conditionals we take to them to be. For example, consider Lewis's earlier formulation: "if the scene before the eyes causes matching visual experience as part of a suitable pattern of counterfactual dependence, then the subject sees" (1986a p. 281). Although phrased in the present continuous tense, its force seems accurately conveyed by a subjunctive conditional: "if the scene before the eyes *were* to cause matching visual experience as part of a suit-able pattern of counterfactual dependence, then the subject *would* see." And Lewis has himself shown that subjunctives are not transposable.

Let us suppose we can overcome this obstacle, just to view what a completed and precise formulation of this position would look like. Thus, by transposition of the second conditional and combining it with the first, we obtain

the subject sees if and only if the scene before the eyes causes matching visual experience with a suitable pattern of counterfactual dependence.

The point I wish to emphasize here is that this retains the two crucial elements of (a) and (b):

(i)   matching visual experience (from (a));
(ii) (i)'s being an instance of (a suitable pattern of) counterfactual dependence (from (b)).

(ii) fails, or so it seems to me, because of its essential relationship to the notion of 'match' used explicitly in (i). Thus, my critical remarks concentrate on (i).

Lewis maintains early that "visual experience has informational content . . . , and it matches the scene to the extent that its content is correct" (1986a, p. 274). And he holds that visual experience typically produces belief and that "[t]he content of the experience is, roughly, the content of the belief it tends to produce" (p. 274). Is the belief in question here *de dicto de re, or de se?* If *de dicto* he is committed, at a minimum, to cognitivism. And indeed it appears that Lewis is committed to either propositional or predicative contents (see chapter 4, §III) for visual experiences. As before, belief contents needn't in fact be encoded propositionally. (For example, they might be features of dispositions.) But when the content of a belief is reportable at all, it should be able to be captured without loss or addition propositionally. For beliefs are truth-evaluable, and it is what is propositional, or equivalent to what is propositional, that has this capacity. If the content of a visual experience just were (even roughly) a belief content, it, too, should be the sort of thing that is truth-evaluable. But, as the qualifications in the last quote indicate, Lewis is less than definite on the relation of perceptual belief to visual episodes. This has the virtue of not committing him to doxasticism, a view we have been given ample reason to reject. It also places a serious obstacle in the way of interpreting his use of 'match'. If we don't know what to make of the contents of visual episodes, we certainly can't tell what it is for them to match the scene. Ultimately, I believe there is little choice but to ascribe to him a propositionalist or predicativist notion of visual content. Thus, matching will be the relation of a truth bearer to its truth-constituting conditions on a correspondence notion of truth. Although this opens too large an issue to examine here—I discuss it at length elsewhere (1988)—in the end there seems to be nothing seriously wrong with this sort of relationship. In that sense, it is progress. The difficulty is in viewing visual content as propositional or quasi-propositional. The cognitivist thesis was rejected in chapter 4 (and additional considerations counting against it were adduced in chapters 5 and 6). Thus, it is no longer available as a promising interpretation of *match*. Without it, both (a) and (b) are in jeopardy.

A further complication merits notice. I have claimed that direct realism is an attractive view, and fully compatible with CTP. As I noted in chapter 5 §VIII, doxasticism, in its purest form, takes visual contents to be belief contents, and belief contents may be either true or false. (Thus interpreted, in light of the previous discussion, (i) of chapter 5, pp. 139–40, is false.) One implication of the whale example was just that a belief content may be false even when one sees something. In that case, even if we allow that what is seen has a factlike (propositional) structure, the belief content cannot be identical with the sight content, for the propositional seeing content must be a fact or at least a truth. As a consequence, although the result is not a classical sense-datum view, it, too, is barred from being a direct-realist view in the following sense: it is committed to the view that what is seen (but perhaps falsely believed to be otherwise) is not a constituent of the visual episode that is, on the occasion, a seeing. Recall that the object enters via its identity with the content, which is an impossibility on belief-content accounts. The question is whether this standard consequence applies to Lewis's form of the theory as well, if, as seems appropriate, we take into account his view (1983) that all belief is, at bottom, the self-ascription of a property to the believer (belief *de se*). I judge, with a misgiving to be mentioned shortly, that it does. Consider, Lewis's statement, "As it might be: I self-ascribe staring at something furry (and at nothing else); I am in fact staring only at Bruce, staring is a suitable relation of acquaintance, and that is how I believe *de re* of Bruce that he is furry" (1983, pp. 156–57). We may take this as Lewis's suggestion for treating paradigmatic cases of visual content. But although I self-ascribe staring at something furry, it may not really be furry. (Consider that azaleas in large groups, say in a bush, looked at from a natural distance, seem to have velvety surfaces. They aren't velvety. Bruce might just have been shaved and painted to look furry.) Nevertheless, I see what seems to me to be furry. Thus, the belief as a unit cannot be identical with my visual object. My misgiving is that Lewis never says outright that visual experiences *are* beliefs; indeed he speaks with an indirection that hints that he is deliberately avoiding this identification. If that is so, I don't see how matching *belief* can matter. The problem of deviant chains is about visual perception, not about contingently related beliefs generated via such perception.

Of course, Lewis has only (roughly) identified experiential content with belief *content,* not with belief itself. But as long as this commits him to holding that the experience is accurately represented in a propositional or predicative idiom, it has the foregoing consequence. As demonstrated in chapter 4, pp. 88–93, ascriptions of these contents imply forms of belief (i.e., that the content is *taken* in a certain way).

Given that Lewis's notion of match can't be used, is there perhaps another one that we might plug into Lewis's formula? Let's begin with a roughly pictographic interpretation, something like the comparison of copy to original. Using it, nothing in the original formula would need rewriting. What's wrong with that?

The obstacles to devising any usable notion of qualitative match are familiar and formidable. The literature is rife with instances of seeing through distorting lenses, seeing lighthouses or oncoming cars at night experienced as nothing more than beams of light, seeing a ship by spotting a dot on the horizon, seeing things through a thick fog, seeing (spotting) something by detecting only a small piece of it through the trees, seeing the forest when one in fact views only a few of its trees, and seeing despite considerable visual 'noise' (in the information-theoretic sense). In light of the multitude of recalcitrant cases of this kind, this carbon-copy version of matching looks very unpromising.

Are there other plausible interpretations? One that we hear from time to time is phrased in terms of isomorphism. A musical score matches a performance not because of (nonstructural) similarities between ink marks and the notes sounded, but by a (rough) one-one correspondence between them. This is the usual case for sight, but not, I believe, essentially so. If I can see something by seeing it in a mirror, I can see it by seeing it in half a dozen mirrors at once. Hume and others have said that, by pressing an eyeball, one can see double. (I confess to being unable to make the experiment work on myself. Nor can I remember having ever suffered from double vision. But undoubtedly there are such cases.) In the past, such phenomena were used to argue for sense-data. The pointed question was 'Which object is the real one?' and the forced answer was taken to be 'neither.' I argue that both are. The case is really no more problematic than if you closed your left eye, I closed my right one, and we both looked at a candle. Which of us sees the real candle? A natural answer is that both of us do. The only difficulty in the pressed-eyeball case is that one is forced momentarily to have two visual fields (since one cannot focus to consolidate them into a single stereoscopic field), and thus one sees the object twice. Many creatures do not have their eyes located the way humans do. Many fish have each eye facing off in a different direction, ruling out stereoscopic focus. Thus, they must daily manage more than a single visual field of the type familiar to us. There seems to me no more difficulty of principle here than that in the double-vision case. If so, it seems to count against any vestige of essential isomorphism on which a 'match' theorist could rely.

Moreover, it is unclear how isomorphism would operate. For example, is isomorphism preserved in the cases mentioned earlier (chap. 2, pp. 50–1) of seeing the darned part of an "invisibly mended" coat, or seeing an arbitrarily selected square centimeter of a larger patch of the margin of this page? Any reason we have to suppose that any answer will be arbitrary or conventional deprives the suggestion of its force, for visual perception (for which nondeviance is needed) is neither.

There is yet another wrinkle. Lewis suggests that a kind of nonmatching experience *might* work in the absence of match if the failures of match were systematic enough. Alongside match, we now have another test: degree of systematicity. Thus, match is not the only relevant comparison between episode and object; room must be left for systematicity as well. It is unclear what is meant by systematicity, but it would seem to convey a regular and reliable relationship, one that would support counterfactuality. Indeed, it seems to be just the sort of thing David Pears appeals to under the title *match*. After rejecting an interpretation along the lines of resemblance or "any other concept of a natural relation founded on the properties" of the object and episode, Pears explains that "E [visual experience] matches O [object] perfectly if and only if E is the sort of visual experience that in normal circumstances justifies P in making a claim about O and that claim is true of O" (1976, p. 26).

Whether we regard this as a nonmatching but systematic relationship or as a variant of match is relatively unimportant . However, it is a match that doesn't light. It quickly falls out of the picture, replaced by a kind of reliabilism. We can raise questions, as I do in §IX, about how we are to take "under normal circumstances"; whether we must know, or even be capable of knowing, that they are normal; and whether specifying the circumstances need be (under full disclosure) repeatable or can be one-off. These questions directly concern our ability to apprehend O, circumventing any need for an intermediary. 'Match' remains simply as an unrevealing cover term for whatever works.

Have I overlooked yet other interpretations of match? I won't foreclose on the possibility. But I have already gotten down to interpretations that stretch the sensibleness of the notion, and we might expect further efforts to retain even less of what is distinctive about one thing's matching another. Pending novel suggestions, let's declare such appeals dead (at least as ways of determining when we see something).

As for supporting counterfactuals, in The Censor seeing takes place without any (noncausal) counterfactual dependency. And there are additional counterexamples even to stepwise dependency. The difficulty, as I suggest in the next section, is not with the notion of counterfactuality, but with the antecedents and consequents used (viz., with what is tracking what). Ultimately, I think this is traceable to a reliance on 'matching content' in all counterfactualist solutions (and some noncounterfactualist ones) with which I am familiar, because that introduces a second level of tracking. Not only is the visual episode tracking the scene, but this is accomplished through a second tracking: that of the content of the visual episode (propositional or otherwise) following the scene. Introducing this second relation requires an explanation of the relationship between that content and the scene. The present group of resolutions is shipwrecked on the shoals of this second level of explanation. The move to Pears's notion of match, alternatively to Lewis's systematicity, doesn't improve matters, because it still requires a second distinct sort of subjective entity, although it is not explained in detail what this is, to conform to the scene. On the direct realism I have proposed, the scene is itself the object—and thus the only relevant part of the content—of the visual episodes incorporated into seeings. On the above proposals it is not. I will now argue that this difference is vital.

VI

By now it should be abundantly clear that if a counterfactual solution is to succeed, it must be rescued by a rather different kind of expedient. I presently suggest that Peacocke, Lewis, and others who have considered counterfactuality have looked in the wrong place for their covariants. That is, they have fixed on the match between a (distinct) experiential content and a scene. We should concentrate instead on the interaction between the *identities* of the scene and the visual episode, respectively. By avoiding the quagmire of levels of comparison between the intrinsic features of scene and episode, this promises to give us a streamlined way to capture the intuition that, despite distortions in our experience, a normal visual episode is able to *track* the scene. First, I briefly summarize the view and explain how its crucial notions are to be understood. Following that, I put forth the explicit solution to deviance that these notions make possible.

An instantiated perceptionlike state, what I have been calling a visual episode, is a token of some kind. As such, it has identity conditions over and above its mere similarity to another intrinsically described token.[3] Call one such token E, and the particular array of objects seen A. (For simplicity, I consider only visual episodes that are constituents of seeings. In the present case, this implies that A itself is a constituent of E's content. But what I am about to say holds for all such episodes that are *of* something.) Changing from A to another array, A*, always results in a different token, say, E*. It follows that E is also altered (to some E*) if A changes its role to other than candidate object, even though it still occupies a position on the causal chain. In sum, when E is an episode involved in a seeing of A, that fact is essential to the identity of E. No otherwise-similar episode E* could be identical with E.

Let's illustrate how a token episode may change or remain the same. Imagine a spider crawling across your arc of vision. As you watch it, you enjoy a series of—perhaps arbitrarily individuated—sensory episodes. Whichever way you choose to divide them, also imagine that the actual spider is replaced by a different but visually indistinguishable one, and so smoothly that you cannot detect the switch. This may be accomplished in various ways. One is by magic. Less outlandishly, we could use a mirror (or a screen) to cover some part of the spider's path, so that when the spider disappears behind it, another one begins to be reflected or projected, making it indistinguishable to the observer (you) from what would have happened had the mirror or screen not been there. If we may count the case in which the spider is replaced, by any method, as the counterfactual state of affairs, we may also say that counterfactually one's visual episode would have changed from E to E*. E* is not a seeing of the original spider. No doubt, this much will be granted. Nevertheless, the original spider, the one that disappears behind the mirror or screen, may show up on the causal chain leading to the visual episode; we can imagine that the mock-up was produced solely to convince you to believe that you were viewing the original spider and no other. The original spider thereby plays a causal role, via the intention of the designer of the sham, in your enjoying E*. However, the change of object (the spider) has caused a change of E, thereby nullifying your seeing of A. Moreover, the reflected or projected spider may be perceptually indistinguishable from the original one, thereby neutralizing any role for the absence of qualitative identity (or similarity) in explaining this result. But notice that the contrary-to-fact occurrence of a different state of affairs that affects only the intermediate stages of the causal chain—those between the two previously identified termini—is unlikely to alter judgments about the identity of E. If a freak of nature had caused the impulses originating from photons that hyperpolarized chemicals in your retinas to be routed through different clusters of retinal ganglion cells, ceteris paribus that would not change the identity of E. Whereas the identity of the visual object is crucial to that of the visual episode, alterations in intermediate stages are not. (Massive changes in intermediate stages may be another matter.)

Notice how this introduces a measure of externalism into visual episodes. Not all visual episodes are ingredients in seeings. When they are not, and don't fail only because of a deviant chain, we may remain uncommitted about their identity conditions. But for those visual episodes that are ingredients in seeings, they have objects by way of the actual objects of the seeings that contain them. The case I have prepared attempts to show that having a certain object in the candidate position is a sine qua non of token episodes that have them; so that a numerical change of object is sufficient for change of episode.

The spider example doesn't illustrate deviance, but only the dependence of the token identity of a perceptual episode on that of its object. It wouldn't be a case of causal deviance for at least the following two reasons. First, deviance prevents an episode from being a seeing, whereas in my experiment both E and E* are seeings, though of different things. Second, in the counterfactual case, the displaced original spider, though still a causal factor in the seeing, is no longer in a position to play the role of candidate object. Equally worthy of note, it remains possible that considerable qualitative change in the object, while the same object remains, is also sufficient to change E's token identity. These principles leave room to argue that a certain degree of qualitative distortion would change E to E*. The example is designed to show only that a necessary condition for the identity of individual experience is identity of object. Thus, total qualitative similarity of objects is not sufficient to retain the identity of the token experience, whereas numerical difference of the former is sufficient for the latter's being different.

It may be tempting to object that this whole scheme of identification relies on the dubious assumption that we have a meticulous method of identifying, reidentifying, and individuating token episodes. However, the objection continues, there is little to go on here other than our impressions, which fail us on presentation of even the simplest problem cases. Isn't this enough to show that such individuation is not the key to a systematic understanding of causal deviance?

It is true that we have little reason to suppose our methods of identification are very refined here. However, I'm not seeking a criterion to allow us to classify each token as the same as or different than a given target episode, but only a test to match decently with, and thereby elucidate, two kinds of defensible commitments: those with regard to deviance and those with regard to the verdict 'nondeviant despite unusual circumstances.' Thus, it is significant if the remarks about the absence of a refined method of identification apply with equal force to our ability to classify cases of causally deviant visual episodes. Classification of chains as deviant also does seem to break down in some cases. It is my contention that assessments of visual-episode token identity and causal deviance hold and fail to hold in roughly the same ranges of relevant cases. A self-sufficient account of a vague or fuzzy subject matter should reflect not only our confident judgments, but also the places where confidence breaks down. Thus, I need not be burdened with the task of generating a test for disclosing, in otherwise undecidable instances, that a certain problematic case is or is not one of deviance. It serves us well enough if it can be explained why deviance prohibits perception in the general run of clearcut cases of this phenomenon, and also why rare or exotic routes in other cases are nevertheless not causally deviant and are compatible with seeing something.

I am now in a position to state the crucial covariation between a visual object and a sentient episode that, I have claimed, underlies causal nondeviance in seeing.

> (10) (a) A causal chain from A (a candidate visual object) to E (a sentient episode) is nondeviant only if
> (b) if E were not (or no longer) *of* A, (c) E would (thereby) be a different token.

Does (10) cover the sorts of cases we want to rule out? It would be tedious to canvass all those mentioned in the literature, but consider two familiar ones. In the hypnotist case, even if H commands S to conjure a certain visual image *because* that scene was then in front of S, the scene's being there has no bearing on the identity of the episode E enjoyed by S. If the woman were to have left the room, and nothing else in the chain changed, H's command would have resulted in S's enjoying the identical visual state. The chain to A, the woman, is deviant. This contrasts with Lewis's censor. Because of E's individuation through its object, the removal of the object in a censor-produced scene would have changed the identity of E, however qualitatively similar the result would have been to E. But although the original scene occurs, there is nothing in (10) to prevent us from saying that the subject saw the scene, without considering the looming monitoring device. Indeed, (10)'s alternative account at least indirectly encourages us to say just this. On the other hand, in the hypnotist case, the woman's presence is relevant to the *history* of S's having E, but not to an answer to the question, posed after the fact, about *which* experience E is.

Next, consider the case of hallucinating a brain that resembles one's own. Although one's own brain is causally relevant to having that experience, the feature of one's own brain that is its only claim to being the perceptual object—namely, its resemblance to the content of the visual experience—is indifferent to the identification of E. Had one's brain looked otherwise, once again ceteris paribus, the experience would not for that reason alone be an episode other than E. I have already noted that this may not be a proper case of deviance, for one's own brain is not a plausible candidate-object. It is perhaps for this reason that, despite the necessity of its involvement in producing E, we still believe something is wrong with this causal chain (if not its deviance). Nevertheless, it is relevant to the present discussion, because the fact that the token identity of the visual episode floats free from having that or any other object can be used to explain why no seeing has taken place.

The *centrality* of (10), beyond its necessity, is displayed in the fact that we may have unusual causal routes that we are nevertheless willing to credit as seeings because the object has not been displaced or replaced by another. Thus, prosthetic implants and external radiolike towers (to boost weak neural impulses) are very unusual visual devices, but they appear to be compatible with the subject's using them to see something. In this they no more interfere with having seen our quarry than do old-fashioned microscopes and glasses.

I have already explained how we may enlist (10) to explain why the mere presence of Lewis's censor doesn't prevent one from having seen the thing in question. But it is worth emphasis. The token experience E that I have when the censor is merely in readiness is just the token I would have had were the censor absent, and it is also different from the token E* that the censor would have produced had some other scene been before my eyes. The nondisplacement of the object renders the censor's intermediate role as insignificant as that of the band of retinal ganglion cells mentioned earlier.

VII

I now want to briefly compare (10) with the immediately preceding counterfactualist solution. Whereas Lewis relies on a match between a content of a visual experience and an object, (10) ties the nondeviance of an episode to its identity. Some may quail at any attempt to fix the token identity of a visual episode, but I find efforts to fix a qualitative match decidedly more dubious. The latter fails to get us past simple cases, and the legion of ways in which one thing might match another beggars the imagination. Of course, Lewis's apparent reading of match, in which a propositionlike content either corresponds or fails to correspond to a scene, is significantly less problematic. But, like cognitivism generally, it overlooks the fact that seeing can occur despite conveying a good bit of misinformation. (Consider again the whale example.) Thus, on my diagnosis, we must fall back on pairing pictographic elements or qualities to make match work, and, as I have just indicated, it is an ill-conceived venture. We will always be left with a flood of problem cases. This leaves us with two options. Following Peacocke, one can be provoked by counterexamples into rejecting all counterfactual solutions. If I am right about (10), such pessimism is premature. Or, following Lewis, one can choose to live with the highly counterintuitive consequences for the sake of the theory's other virtues. If my criticisms here and in chapter 5 are on the right track, that is too high a price to pay. On the other hand, I cannot see that the indeterminacies and uncertainties that infect the attribution of identity criteria to visual episodes, while no doubt pernicious to certain endeavors, count against the current solution. Thus, we can show why Peacocke's counterexamples work, why a standby censor does not prevent a seeing, but an active censor would, and why perception may be preserved through the use of unusual means and novel prostheses, without committing ourselves to the notions to which objections have been raised.

It seems worth noting that although match is the crucial ingredient in Lewis's counterfactualist solution, this isn't because he finds the business of identifying or individuating token visual experiences—my preferred substitute for match—especially troublesome. He, too, makes use of the notion of distinct, nevertheless *qualitatively* indistinguishable, tokens of visual experience to explain a decision in a test case. He even appears to invoke a reason I gave earlier for nonidentity: difference of cause. Consider, once again (see chap. 2, note 6), the wizard before my eyes creating hallucinogenic experiences, one of whose random hallucinations "happens to match the scene before my eyes" (1986a, p. 277). Lewis entertains the hypothetical objection that the probability of a matching scene would have been much better if the wizard had been ineffective in creating scenes. He replies that although true, "the probability of *this* experience would have been much lower" (1986b, p. 289n). The reply presupposes that although a hallucinatory experience might match the scene as well, indeed be qualitatively indistinguishable from a seeing, it wouldn't be the same token as *this* experience, the one taking the standard causal route from the wizard. If, as I have urged, this employment of matching experience is a quagmire, then even by his own lights Lewis allows in a notion—that of experience individuated via its cause—better prepared to do the job.

VIII

I have yet to discuss explanations of deviance that don't fall into the counterfactual family. It is time to remedy that omission, if only to assure readers that I haven't overlooked promising alternatives. Competing solutions may be collected under several headings, although, as will emerge, there is considerable overlap in the first two listed.

Reliability

We had a glimpse of this earlier, pp. 195–6, in Pears's remarks about match. A typical claim under this head might be that nondeviant chains result from reliable processes; another is that nondeviant chains are reliable consequences of processes that may or may not themselves be reliable. We might call the first the reliable-process view, the second the reliable-product view. (To appreciate the difference, consider again our lightning bolt, this time illuminating a dark sky to enable Sue to see a deer. The expectation of lightning is a very unreliable method to count on for seeing to take place, but that one is enabled to see given that it has happened is considerably more reliable.) Reliabilists might argue as follows: perception is a source of knowledge or justified belief, and its being produced reliably entitles it to that normative status. Deviance, being unreliable, defeats perception just because it cannot generate justification. Whereas some reliabilists may want to distinguish the process and product versions, I will consider views that allow mixing elments of both. This is not unfair to reliabilism since I will not be criticizing it for any conflations that may result from the corporate view, and it enables the reliabilist to defend the position with a full panoply of considerations. (Although it is not unrelated to the theory of knowledge of that title, we should distinguish that reliabilism from the one before us. The only issue of present concern is what makes visual causal chains nondeviant, and, as may be expected, this solution may differ in its implementation from the one proposed for knowledge. For example, with respect to the lightning case, it is the chain that is the product, not the justified belief that a deer is in front of one.)

(Teleo-)Function

It is maintained that we can read off the function of perception from its features or its supposed evolutionary history, namely, to supply information about the perceiver's environment. Chains that accomplish this task are nondeviant. Not surprisingly, this solution is likely to be found in conjunction with reliability. Although, on the one hand, reliability of some sort or at one stage in a lineage's history in achieving a state is an indispensable basis for claiming that such an achievement is something's function, on the other hand, the reliability, say, of an organ can be detected only relative to an end or function served by its normal,[4] hence reliable, operation. Nevertheless, it is conceivable that a reliabilist not be a functionalist. The end used to measure reliability need not be identical with the definitive end of the perceptual organ producing it. But it is difficult to see how a functionalist could get on without the distinctive tenets of reliabilism. If a natural specimen, or the species to which it belongs, or its evolutionary forbearers, never regularly (and reliably) did something, what basis could there be for maintaining that it is its function to do that thing? These minor differences may not matter. It is very likely that we will find that anyone who explicitly advocates reliabilism also readily accedes to the functional view. Thus, again, reliabilist Pears claims both that a mark of "the appropriate causal line [is to] reliably deliver matching visual experiences" (1976, p. 35) and that the concept of seeing that "put[s] restrictions on admissible causal lines . . . is a functional account" (p. 39).

Stage Explanations

The title embraces all possible views that discover nondeviance in the actual stages through which a normal perceptual transaction proceeds. In different forms, the view may describe the stages concretely or abstractly. Our concern is with a pro-posal of the latter kind. (A flowchart, typically as of a Turing machine program, is an example of an abstract description of stages.) The most refined proposal under this title is no doubt Christopher Peacocke's "Differential Explanation" (DE), which requires a certain articulated content to'preserve' the contents of pre-vious stages in the perceptual chain. This preliminary sketch reduces the view to its simplest terms: the crucial issues get raised in working out the details.

IX

First let's attend to reliabilism. Alvin Goldman, while discussing a related issue, writes, "a cognitive mechanism is reliable if it not only produces true beliefs in actual situations, but would produce true beliefs, or at least inhibit false beliefs, in relevant counterfactual situations" (1976, p. 771). Let's assume visual percep-tion is a cognitive mechanism. Although this is a sufficient condition for reliabil-ity, what we really need is one that is at least necessary. It is easy enough to amend Goldman's formula to get that: replace 'if' by either 'only if' or 'if and only if.' But more serious drawbacks await. Consider devices that produce true beliefs in actual situations only because they produce beliefs willy-nilly, perhaps even in contradictory pairs, or devices that inhibit false beliefs in counterfactual situations only because they inhibit *all* belief. Read strictly, each seems to satisfy the present requirement, but neither is reliable in any sensible way. But this char-acterization, though flawed, may give us enough of an idea about what reliabilists have in mind. Thus, I let it stand as a preliminary explanation on which to build.

Recall the passage in Pears from my discussion of match (p. 195): "E matches O perfectly if and only if E is the sort of visual experience that in normal circum-stances justifies P in making a claim about O and that claim is true of O" (1976, p. 26). Setting aside the question of *match,* the formula is fairly representative of the outlined position. (Although, in the quoted passage of note 4, Fodor is not advocating the view, notice his appeal to normalcy in elucidating *function.*) But what are "normal circumstances" in which someone is justified in claiming some-thing about O? Normal circumstances for whom? A certain species of perceiver? Being a member of a species a certain proportion of whose members possess a certain kind of information? Those with a certain ability to infer? Without the answers to a number of questions of this order, it is unclear how one would or could respond to problem cases.

An initially promising avenue might be to make the circumstances normal for all creatures having a certain sensory organ. However, consider a subject whose visual output is radically distorted by a chemical imbalance, but who infrequently enjoys 'normal' perception when her "malefactory gland" is at rest. The circum-stances in which she sees are not normal for her, and they do not justify her in making claims about the object. Nevertheless, since she sees, the causal chain must be standard. One reliabilist recourse would be to appeal to the situation of the entire species. We can then allow that she sees only because of her member-ship in a species for which this chain is normal. However, suppose virtually all of her cospecimens die out, but she breeds with the last of them before it expires and produces offspring who inherit and transmit this disability to their offspring, who now dominate the species. Do she and her offspring still see things on those rare occasions? What weight is to be given to the fact that once the species was not so afflicted? Or would a *possible* unafflicted species suffice? Is it relevant that it is *we,* the unafflicted, who are conceiving of this case? The intractability of such questions makes it all the more difficult to believe that the notion of normal circumstances can shed any light on the subject.

Pears is aware of these sorts of puzzles. He says of a case in which someone's visual mechanism deteriorates, and so becomes unreliable even in cases in which it happens to succeed, that "it is enough that the causal line should have had a fair success-rate before it deteriorated, if his defect is not congenital, and that it should have a fair success-rate in other people" (1976, p. 34). But it is difficult to avoid the conclusion that sight, if it is anything at all, cannot be other than *cum fundamento in re.* Whether we see something is not a matter of adhering to a convention. Why, then, should it matter whether this subject was the only per-ceiver who ever lived?

Teleofunctionalists have a ready answer in such cases. Applying their more sweeping view to perception, they allow that it is necessary and *almost* sufficient for S to see that S's present faculties result from S being an evolutionary descen-dant of a species for which those faculties adaptively served its members for seeing (Millikan 1984, 1989; Neander 1991). Present subjects don't need reliabil-ity so long as their distant ancestors had it. Consequently, in the foregoing case, S's current situation is irrelevant. What matters is that she be a descendant of a family having those faculties because they lent a certain edge to her ancestors. Once this is discovered, each question either is definitively resolved or admits of no clear answer. Because this is a very general theory of our basis for ascribing mental states and content, and not in the first instance a solution directed to the deviance chain problem, teleofunctionalism engages the present issue only at an oblique angle. Its potential for strengthening the reliability test at this juncture falls out merely as an implication of that larger view.

I cannot enter into a proper examination of teleofunctionalism. I take note of it (here and in chapter 5) only at those places where it can apparently be deployed to aid other views I must deal with. Nevertheless, some brief remarks are in order.

First, I argued in chapter 5, §VI, that even were we to grant that functions can be enlisted to account for the continued presence of our perceptual faculties, they are powerless to supply an account of their essence. Here is a brief account of the teleofunctionalist strategy. While they agree that sight is a natural, not an artifactual, phenomenon, they seek to overcome the strong inducement to describ-ing natural phenomena generally in terms of their current, as opposed to historical, features. This is achieved by giving the natural objects in question a further feature that makes them special, *proper functions,* thereby aligning these natural phenom-ena to artifacts in this crucial respect. For example, I can describe something as a knife even if it is too blunt to be used for the things knives are devised for, as long as it was once usable as a knife, or manufactured by the same process or on the same production line as things having that use, or so on. But there are two other features of artifacts that may be more relevant here: first, they are artifacts;

second, they have designers. It is altogether too likely that these features, rather than merely having a function, is what leads us to overlook something's current features in classifying it. Teleofunctionalists pay too little heed to the fact that with natural objects, even if we do ascribe functions to them, we were enabled to recognize them as such even before we knew they had a proper (or evolutionary) function. Their current features as well as their origins, as distinct from their former functions, seem too well entrenched simply to be subordinated to whatever functions they may have served in an ancestral population.

This may help explain what goes wrong in teleofunctionalist handling of the so-called Swamp cases of philosophical fable (see Davidson, 1987, p. 443). We may suppose that Swampman is my molecule-for-molecule duplicate, created through the cosmic coincidence of a random lightning bolt striking a tree trunk immersed in just the right combination of swampy chemicals. This is a creature with my internal complexity, which is exposed to the physical stimuli that I would be exposed to from that location. Whatever we say about Swampman's beliefs, if I can have phenomenal visual experience, it is difficult to see why it couldn't. Moreover, we can imagine its phenomenal experience produced photologically by exposure to the same stimuli. Thus, if I see a frog, why shouldn't Swampman also see a frog? Just because so much about seeing is a natural phenomenon, the pull to describe Swampman as actually seeing is very strong. It is at least symp-tomatic that when Dretske (1995) sets out to undermine this sort of judgment (in support of his teleofunctionalism), his examples are *all* artifacts: Toyota Tercels, paperweights, wedding rings, and the like. If, as Millikan has stated, "[s]uch a double has no proper function because its history is not right" (1989, p. 292), this counts not so much against Swampman's seeing as it does against requiring that sight can only be understood via proper functions.

Finally, teleofunctionalism has its own internal problems as an account of content. Because of the way it involves itself in questions of perception, and given the spectrum of views it claims as competitors, teleofunctionalism needs an ac-count of visual content. In sum, it must also provide a teleosemantics, which must in turn comprise a theory of perceptual content. It seems doomed to fail in that enterprise. How can someone's perceiving, say, *a laser printer producing a line graph* be fixed by the contents of perceptual states of one's antediluvian ancestors. It will not be enough to respond that our distant ancestors saw roughly similar types of things. The view must supply not a purported explanation of why we see things of certain sizes, configurations, and so on, but how our perceptual content is fixed. And content is too fine-grained for anything teleosemantical theories seem capable of determining. Note that this is not a variation of the familiar problem for stimulus-response theories: that is, how we can proceed from the simple case, say, of rats recognizing different colored keys to the enormous complexity of humans believing that certain plumage is a peculiar shade of blue. Although we may harbor doubts about the ability of S-R theory to bridge this galactic divide, we have some idea of the sorts of notions classical behaviorism will want to employ. On teleosemantic accounts, however, the relevant stimuli are pitched well into our prehistoric past; and *any* account that uses that past to explain perceptual contents of contemporary artifacts such as bicycles and electron microscopes will

need resources taking us from that primordial environment to contemporary perceptual objects that could have had no part in our ancestors' selective advantage.
That step, however it is fleshed out, requires resources beyond those to which this
brand of evolutionary functionalist confines itself. Indeed, this defect is just another facet of the reason why the functionalist judgment in Swampcreature cases
is so counterintuitive. Confining herself, as she does, to a sketchy history of our
faculties, she is limited by both the existence of, and the resources available to,
those speculated prelapsarian ancestors. (For further arguments on this score see
Wagner, 1996.)

This result isn't created merely by an ill-chosen example. Though it may
seem idle to speculate about how a reliability theorist would in general answer the
question 'Normal circumstances for whom?' none of the answers looks especially
hopeful. And we cannot allow a theory to escape critical scrutiny just because we
don't have instances, other than Pears's case, of its providing these further details.

Returning to standard reliabilism its solution reverses the usual order of inquiry about justification. As a rule, we would decide that a certain sort of experience under normal circumstances justifies us in believing something about O by
first determining whether we indeed perceived O. Implied in a determination that
we have perceived is a determination that the relevant cause is of the right kind.
To say the least, it is unusual to suppose that we first determine whether these
experiences under normal circumstances justify belief in order to decide whether
we have a perception. What, then, is to become of the familiar appeal to having
seen something in order to justify a belief? Moreover, justification is subject to a
variety of concerns, including the legitimacy of background assumptions, the character of the species to which the subject belongs, and so on. It is not easy to
accept the supposition that whether or not seeing takes place, because of an imagined threat of causal deviance, is contingent on considerations like these. The
circumstantial evidence leads me to conclude that reliabilism has simply read the
conditions for our valuing and being theoretically interested in visual perception
wholesale into the conditions for being a visual perception. In general, that procedure is not credible.

I have yet to mention perhaps the most fundamental shortcoming of the reliability proposal: its mislocation of the problem. This is brought out not just by the
previous counterexamples or charges of obscurity, but by the fact that reliability
clearly yields the wrong answer in modified test cases. Once again, consider the
thought experiments of the hypnotist and the neurologist used to illustrate deviance. At first, they seem to pose no threat to reliabilism. The causal chains
eventuating in their visual episodes were deviant, *and* the visual episodes were
not produced reliably. Even if the episodes could occur, consideration of how they
are produced and by whom shows that there is no prospect of their lasting long
enough to permit a subject to direct a life by them. But if, despite this, the hypnotist or neurologist were reliable, and the production of matching visual episodes
could last long enough for the subject to determine this, I would still be strongly
inclined to say that the subjects' visual episodes are not thereby seeing.[5] Inter-
jecting reliability doesn't change the outcome. For the sake of argument, let us
suppose otherwise. Then the hypnotic subject and the subject of the brain probe

would be seeing. If one accepts this result only because reliability has been added to the situation, what prevents one from persisting in the same evaluations of cases if causation (or at least object causation) is then removed? Originally, the subjects were on the same causal chains as the candidate objects, via the intentions of the hypnotist and the neurologist. If we remove this chain, we might appeal to something like the occasionalism sketched earlier (e.g., chap. 3, pp. 60–1): God is the common cause both of the object's being properly situated and of our enjoying the visual episode. I don't know that reliability can carry this conceptual weight. Here I simply reiterate what I claimed earlier. We can imagine various ways in which information even more reliable than that of vision could be produced, and that this source would not thereby count as a kind of vision. This may be true even if the information is produced via a visionlike experiential episode.

If there is to be a role left for reliability, it would appear to be in conjunction with causation (which, for our purposes, means (C)). But although some mechanisms appear suitable for working in tandem with causation to make an assault on the deviance problem, it is not easy to see how a reliability test could be subordinated to a condition like (C). We have in reliability (or, rather, its lack) the sort of condition whose force seems to derive from supplying a complete answer to why visual experience doesn't work in some cases. Incorporating it with causation into a single outlook must produce a unified, coherent account of vision, but it is yet to be made clear how that is feasible.

If anyone is still tempted to adhere to reliability and let causation fall out of the account if need be, we might recall chapter 3's problem cases and general considerations (about interaction with looks idioms and spatial restrictions). They seemed potent enough to me to eliminate occasionalism as a possible account of visual perception. And if they eliminate an account on which the reliability of perceptual evidence can be so strongly grounded, they are surely sufficient to rule out the—more realistic, but modest—naturalistic guarantees of reliability.

A similar potentiality for separation does not arise for my counterfactual solution (or, it might be mentioned, for DE, discussed in the next section). Although some counterfactuals of the right type could conceivably be true even in the absence of direct causation between natural events (e.g., with God's assistance), the role of object causation in the identity of the visual episode assures us that (10) operates only in a causal setting.[6]

X

Finally, let's turn attention to stage explanations. Once again, they come in two varieties: physical and abstract. Detailed descriptions of the physical and biological transactions taking place in normal perception are unlikely to yield definitive conclusions about standard causal chains. In effect, such proposals rely on the assumption that visual perception is a natural kind, capable of embodying a physical essence. But natural kinds, from aardvark to zinc, impose rather narrow structural limits on varieties and instances. How could such a kind cope with the multiplicity of embodiments permitted by vision? For example, something could enjoy visual perception with many sorts of imaginable prostheses, with radically different physiologies that might belong to extraterrestrials (or to our own evolutionary descendants), and with the concoctions of a future robotics. If we admit such things as distinctively visual experiences, an essential part of the understanding of which requires that one also enjoy them, then a production of such experiences that satisfies condition (C) and a content restriction should supply overwhelming evidence that something has been seen. The countercharge that the steps by which it was produced did not conform to the accustomed physiological blueprint wouldn't stand much chance of overcoming this judgment.

However, *abstract* stage explanations, as in Peacocke's (1979) Differential Explanation, stand a greater chance of success. According to DE, chains are graded on the extent to which they preserve sensitivity of content from earlier links to perceptual episode. Peacocke's general formula reads as follows: "x's being ϕ differentially explains y's being ψ if x's being ϕ is a nonredundant part of the explanation of y's being ψ and according to the principles of explanation (laws) invoked in this explanation, there are functions specified in these laws such that y's being ψ is fixed by these functions from x's being ϕ (p. 66). Where t ranges over times, n over numbers and k is a functor (numerical, for present purposes), the form Peacocke gives (p. 75) for such explanation is

(DE*) $(\forall x)(\forall t)(\forall n)(Fxt \ \& \ Gxnt \ . \ \rightarrow Hxk \ (n)(t \ + \ \delta t \ ))$.

Gxnt is the differential explanans. Quasi-colloquially, DE* reads that being G to degree n at time t (while in context F) fixes it that x is H to degree $k(n)$ at time $t + \delta t$. Peacocke concedes that in this simple case the differential explanans is part of a strongly sufficient set of conditions. But he proceeds to claim that, unlike its representation in DE*, the explanation might also operate in a nondeterministic system that lacks any sufficient conditions—although one may wonder how this is squared with his earlier claim that y's being ψ is *fixed by* the functions from x's being ϕ.

As stated earlier, Peacocke's view is intended to apply to action and perception alike; in fact, most of the discussion and examples seem directed toward action. Concerning perception in particular, Peacocke writes, "for an experience of its being ϕ to be really of its being ϕ, its being ϕ must differentially explain the occurrence of the experience event under the description 'experience as of its being ϕ' " (p. 58). This must be qualified, for—as Peacocke acknowledges elsewhere—an object's appearing as if it had a certain feature may be differentially explained by its having a different feature. I assume the view amended accordingly.

Although the final version of Peacocke's view contains additional refinements, enough of it is now before us to make the critical points that are needed. To begin, notice the following two features of DE.

First, the account is not, properly speaking, about causal *chains* but about causal *explanations*. DE* takes as arguments only the sorts of things that can figure in explanations: sentential or propositionlike entities. I return to this point presently.

Next, DE*, presumably the canonical statement of the view, seems to imply a good deal less than the author's informal explications of DE. If DE* is satisfiable at all, it is satisfiable by *any* deterministic cause (or causal explanation). (Since Peacocke loosens up the determinism, I do not take that part seriously. But not everything in the formula can be so lightly dismissed.) Any such explanans may be a function of its explanandum-effect-plus-background-conditions given as argument. But this cannot be right. All parties to our endeavor have agreed that perception involves causation: that was the point of (C). What is now needed is a way to distinguish *among* causal explanations of visual episodes—or, in the material mode, causal chains leading to them—those which are deviant from the nondeviant. If anything in Peacocke's account so much as addresses this issue, it would appear to be his subsequent Stepwise Recoverability corollary, discussed briefly in chapter 2. We can ignore that for the present, noting only how little DE* actually conveys. Instead, let us ask whether, supposing we have in front of us a completed proposal, it is on the right track.

Returning to the first point, it is important to see that using causal explanations, rather than (directly) causal chains, is not a by-product but a central attraction of the project: "it is not the properties of the events themselves but rather more complex conditions relating to the *principles* of explanation that I am claiming to be the basis of the distinction" (p. 67n). Thus, as Peacocke also notes, DE treats deviance as if an intensional idiom were relevant to its resolution. Because causal explanations are couched in an intensional idiom, true propositions of the form '*x* causally explains *y*' do not permit free substitution *salva veritate* of codesignative expressions for *x* and *y*. As a result, where 'the so-and-so = the such and such,' and each is (as described) generally visible, we may have *both*

S's experience of *y* as ϕ *is* a perception of the so-and-so,

and

S's experience of y as ϕ *is not* a perception of the such and such.

This difference can be due to the fact that the chain of explanation leading from a such and such is deviant, whereas that leading from so-and-so is standard. Evidently, what is all-important is not that the so-and-so be the cause of the experience (though it is a sine qua non), but how it is described.

Rather than a solution to the problem of causal deviance raised by counterfactualists, reliabilists, and functionalists, this seems to me the abdication of all hope for one. Remarks about perceptual idioms that don't translate more directly into conclusions about perceptions seem oddly beside the point. Thus far, test cases have not been situations in which we had perceptions *of some sort* but not of others. They have been instances—such as those of the hypnotist, David Lewis's censor, the hallucinogenic scent of an object, the intervening neural scientist, the veridical hallucination of a brain—in which potential or actual deviance threatened to prevent the episode from being a perception *sans phrase,* not just a perception of ϕ in so far as ϕ *(qua visual content) is described in a certain way.* If such cases have set the agenda for a theorist, Peacocke is not offering a direct competitor to the views he rejects—although his rejection of those accounts is a central part of the case he makes for his own. However, if those accounts were attempts to elucidate the deviance of chains, and not of their explanations, there is a clear sense in which, whatever the fate of the other accounts, he has shifted the topic.

Of course, if Peacocke has not relied on misconstruing the accounts he rejects as attempts at *explanations,* and if he can show that his own view is in some way a natural descendant of those rejected despite these differences in subject matter treated, he can be exonerated of the charge. For him to succeed along these lines, his defense must satisfy (at least) the following two conditions. First, he must be able to show that none of the other approaches works, or is likely to work, on its own turf. Second, he must be capable of producing evidence that there are single perceptual episodes (or descriptions of them) in which different descriptions of a candidate object or an episode yield different results concerning deviance, or even concerning whether an object is perceived.

As for the first condition, Peacocke does survey leading alternatives to his own solution, including counterfactual accounts (8) and (9). Some of his own counterexamples were used to reject those. This indicates that any misapprehension he may have had about what they were accounts of does not disqualify his case against them. Nevertheless, like Lewis, he employs qualitative changes in the external scene and the experience to frame the antecedents and consequents, respectively, in such views. Thus, his canvass omits any accounts along the lines of (10)—the proposal defended here. In lieu of unforeseen objections to (10), Peacocke has not met the first condition. With the aid of hindsight, we may say that it has not been shown (by Peacocke or others) that it is hopeless to attempt a solution that purports to confine itself to the original phenomena: causal chains. This itself would seem fatal to DE, since we would have an acceptable view that, unlike DE, treated the relevant phenomena directly.

What of the second condition: showing that the deviance of would-be perceptions can be relative to how they are described? Much of the defense of Peacocke's 'relativization-to-description' view rests on the fact that DE is developed for causal theories generally and not just for perception. Without commenting on its success in other areas, a striking feature of his exposition here is that when he supplies apparently telling instances of such relativization, they invariably pertain to intentional action. In fact, the argument for relativization is conducted while action, not perception, is the topic. I can't recover from the discussion a single faintly promising instance in which he would claim that the two schemata of three paragraphs ago are both instantiated; that is, in which we have the following combination: $x = y$, S sees x, S doesn't see y, S has a visual experience of x, S has a visual experience of y. The author hasn't presented a plausible instance, and none spring to mind independently. Of course, propositional seeing is highly intensional. So it may be possible to see that p without seeing that q, although 'that p' turns out, in some loose way, to be the same thing as 'that q.' In lieu of further textual evidence it would be hazardous, not to say fatuous, to suppose that Peacocke was taken in here by a failure to distinguish the propositional from the objectual construction for sight. But we can take solace in the fact that the discussion of chapter 4 has inoculated us against this possible source of confusion.

All things considered, DE seems incapable of solving the deviance problem. Some readers may be dismayed that the role of Stepwise Recoverability has been ignored in this discussion. But its employment can't resolve these difficulties. DE's most flagrant poblems are not due to its incompleteness, but to its neglect of any treatment of causal chains themselves in favor of a treatment of chains of their explanations.

XI

Earlier in this chapter, reason was given to believe that, with the proper elements of counterfactuality, CTP could resolve the problem of deviant causal chains. With the completion of this subsequent review of other leading proposals, I hope it is even clearer that the earlier solution is our best hope. This does not absolve CTP of all outstanding charges. Thinkers seem to agree that, unless more can be said about the distinctive nature of the causation claimed for o, we don't yet have a robust causal theory of perception. Let's turn our attention to that matter.

8

Object Determination

"We deal with what is," said Cadfael. "Leave what might have been to eyes that can see it plain."

ELLIS PETERS, *One Corpse Too Many*

I

When S sees a vase, among the causes of S's visual episode is the vase. But the causal factors also include the light source (say, the sun), certain photons, the transpicuous space between the vase and S's eyes, perhaps S's spectacles, S's retinas, S's optic nerve, S's lateral geniculate nucleii, projections onto V1, radiation of neurons in the peristriate cortex, the vase's potter, whatever vehicle may have transported S to the scene, and even each of S's great-grandparents. But, ex hypothesi, it is only the vase that S sees. Some of the other items might be seen via other episodes, some perhaps never. Shouldn't a *causal* theory accord pride of place to the actual perceptual object? And shouldn't it do this by way of the causal involvement of the object? If so, what is distinctive about the causation of the vase? How is it to be differentiated from the various other causal factors? (As we shall see presently, these last two questions ask for slightly different things, although their range of potential answers may overlap.) Moreover, it is not merely that we must distinguish the object's causal role from that of other causes, but we must do so without appealing to its being the object. Its objecthood is something the causal theory is called on to explain. This, in a nutshell, is the problem of object determination. Some have even regarded a causal solution to it as essential to the aspirations of CTP. Without one, so the claim goes, nothing deserves the title 'causal theory of perception.'

Let us not tarry too long over terminology. I am supposing that (C) has been established: at a minimum, accounts of perception need a causal *clause*. And it is not utterly implausible to take this as sufficient for the resulting theory's being causal. But, for the sake of clarity, I stipulate that a CTP must also solve the object determination problem. This implies that (C) may be incorporated into an account whose overall character is noncausal.

Our first task is to decide what sort of distinctive marks we must seek. The most obvious candidate would be a necessary and sufficient condition for being a perceptual object. But no one, to my knowledge, claims that this venture has much chance of success, even if we relax the demand that it be stated in strictly causal terms. A next step might be to look for a merely sufficient condition for being a perceptual object. Prima facie, this may seem clearly inadequate. It is no surety against multiply sufficient conditions, and so no assurance against an equally good noncausal alternative. However, a plausible sufficient condition, suitably causal in character and satisfied exclusively by the vase, would yield at least presumptive grounds for distinguishing the object from other causal factors. Despite the remaining possibility of a second sufficient condition, the burden is thereby shifted onto whoever would produce it. Its possibility needn't concern us in the absence of real progress in that quarter. Thus, the first question to be raised is whether we might reasonably aspire to a causally sufficient condition for objecthood.

Some have argued that there can be no such sufficient condition, consequently no adequate CTP. According to Brian McLaughlin (1984, p. 571), CTP is committed to a supervenience thesis to the effect that a causally connected (would-be) object and episode count as a perception of that object if and only if any other object and episode similarly related is also a perception of its object. He notes that perception often fails to satisfy this condition. A familiar example concerns seeing something via seeing its (proper) part. We count seeing some parts as seeing the object; others, and in relevantly similar causal circumstances, we do not. Thus, I may see someone if I have seen her head in the crowd, but perhaps not if I have seen only her legs, although her legs may be a larger share of her whole body. Even seeing what is ordinarily taken for the whole of something may not count as sufficient. For example, while in search of safety after a harrowing trek across the moors, I spot what appears as a small dot on the landscape. I have finally seen the house I was looking for. The interest here is in locating the structure. (Or I may spot it from an airplane.) But if a prospective buyer asks my opinion of the property, that mightn't pass as having seen the house. Similar examples could be multiplied. McLaughlin concludes that since "pragmatic, contextual factors" are determinants of whether or not one perceives an object, "no causal analysis of perceiving physical objects is possible" (ibid., pp. 582, 583; cf. Firth 1967, p. 382). If our search is for a distinctive mark of object causation that provides a sufficient condition for perceiving *that thing,* rather than something else, CTP fails.

But we might ask whether these options exhaust the prospects for CTP's attack on the object-determination problem. There are reasons for believing they do not. A clue is contained in the kind of inability McLaughlin discovers. He mentions two sorts of cases: those in which we at one time say only that we see a part of something and at others the thing of which it is part; and those in which we sometimes say we see a thing by seeing something else related to it, whereas sometimes we do not. In these cases the crucial discrimination is between a part and a larger part or between one sort of clearly visual something and another attached to it (supposedly, as effect to cause). A third case, just examined, is not one in which one sees only a part of something, or something else related to it, but in which viewing something very indistinctly may or may not count as seeing it. In each case, a change in judgment about what is seen can be effected with no physical alteration, including the location, of the candidate object or the perceiver.

The determinants are, as he puts it, contextual or pragmatic. Let us call all of the items that either are seen or might be seen under changes of no more than context or purpose the class of *object relatives*. The crucial point is that the sorts of nonobjectual causal factors (viz., those other than the vase) mentioned at the beginning of this chapter are not object relatives. Although many of them, such as the sun or one's ancestors, are visibilia, they are not candidates for being objects of that particular visual episode. No change in these sorts of contextual or pragmatic features could elevate any of them to the status of perceptual object. To transform any of them into an object of that perception would take something as monumental as a change in the semantics of perceptual verbs. If it were possible to isolate the causal factors falling on *a single chain*—which would exclude all object relatives that were not themselves objects—then, if we could find a mark to segregate the object from those factors, CTP will have fulfilled its duty toward object determination. In fact, this is little different from selecting not an object but a class of object relatives. What I am describing is not so much an object, but its distinctive position on the chain. (Picking out the object from its object relatives seems to be a noncausal matter, and the selected class is all that is needed to resolve the object determination problem as originally described.) Therefore, the objection does not close all avenues to CTP.

Ignoring my own sound advice to avoid terminological quagmires, I insert a word about why, if this reduced object determination task is successfully completed, the result deserves the *causal theory* mantle. For one thing, it would be at best misleading to regard as noncausal an account that achieves so substantial a causal core, including not only (C) and a solution to the deviant chain problem, but also a causally linked discrimination of the object from other nodes on the same causal chain. For another, despite the fact that causalists may have suggested, perhaps too cavalierly, that their causal conditions did or should attain sufficiency, actual efforts indicate that this hasn't really been a prime concern. (C) and related conditions have been the focus of debates between causalists and their opponents. And for the the completion of their theories, causalists have been much more exercised about the grounds for causally distinguishing the object from other nodes on a single chain. Distinctions amongst the class of object relatives, all of which occupy roughly the same or closely related nodes, has not been a preoccupation. Whether these efforts are successful strikes me as of greater interest for the view than whether they satisfy generic desiderata for a completed analysis.

Once we have taken this step, it may also be possible to loosen another restriction on successful solutions. I had said that the distinguishing mark of the object had to be causal. The causalist's task has usually been understood this way, and it may be especially apt to do so if it is regarded as the search for the causally relevant circumstances on which the perceptual object supervenes. However, I also just now characterized the mark we are looking for as 'causally linked,' and it seems to me that this should suffice for the case at hand. Let me explain.

(C) already asserts the causal involvement of the object in any seeing. Suppose that we can discover a mark that, while not inherently causal, does indicate how the object may be smoothly integrated with its role in (C). If the mark were explicable by the object's causal role and were distinctive of the object, why shouldn't that conclude our search? For example, suppose we discovered a criterion of covariation between properties of the object and features of perceptual experience. Of course, even those who subscribe to a regularity account of causation are unlikely to claim that covariation always portends a cause/effect relation between covariants. But although covariation is not itself causal, neither can a covariation pass without comment. Our range of options is limited. Something (not necessarily, but possibly, between the covariants) underlies the covariation, or it is a matter of chance. If we opt for the former, the something might just be a direct causal interaction between the covariants. Suppose then that we have uncovered just such a covariation. Rejecting chance, we might then show how (C) can be deployed to explain it. This enables us to think of the covariation criterion (the distinguishing mark of the object) as complementing, rather than competing with, a causal account.

We should also be clear that, although the subject matter is broadly epistemological, I am at present engaged in a conceptual inquiry, not a (narrowly conceived) study in epistemology. Lack of information about the facts underlying our decision thwarts the enterprise, it is not a condition of it. That is, we don't start behind a veil of ignorance about which cause on a given chain is a candidate for object and then use the mark as a *criterion* to determine which it is. Rather, we are in the position of having decided on an object in light of having all the relevant facts before us. What we want to know is whether that decision can be underwritten by a causal factor in the perceiving situation. But nothing we discover will be able to decide for us whether what S sees (in my earlier example) is a vase or, as Russell (1927, p. 146) provocatively ventures, the inside of her own brain. We may already assume, without argument, that S sees the vase, not the inside of her brain. What we want to know is, first, if this choice can be principled and, second, if it can, whether there is some way that that principle can be integrated into an account of the vase's causal role.

Finally, a minor point that may help avert some major misunderstandings. When we talk of conditions—sufficient, necessary, both, or neither—what are they conditions of? One perfectly legitimate way to view the causalist's predicament is that she is in search of a method that will take her from something of the intransitive form

(i) S sees . . . (that is, 'S sees something or other')

to something of the transitive form

(ii) S sees *o*,

in which *o* is a particular or an event, state, or feature involving a particular. Put otherwise, she can assume satisfaction of whatever other conditions, causal or noncausal, there may be for seeing taken intransitively. Her only concern is to go from the state in which those conditions are met, (i), to the transitive formula, (ii), in which what is seen is determined. Thus, we will assume seeing has taken place for the examples treated here and need be concerned only with the conditions for one rather than another node on the causal chain as being its object.

As is evident from the sequel, occasionally an account of object determination is incorporated into a broader set of conditions for seeing. When it does not appear as a separate clause, we have the task of disengaging the bit that addresses our problem from the remainder, which may be largely irrelevant to it. There is no advance guarantee that this is attainable, and we may wind up—just as with conditions for deviance in chapter 7—with a claim altogether too ambitious for the limited problem at hand. In any case, even if one is after necessary and sufficient conditions for being a perceptual object, it is well to keep in mind that they needn't provide necessary and sufficient conditions for (i), but may *assume* an unidentified set of conditions for that state of affairs in the course of providing conditions for (ii). This distinction of issues may aid us in avoiding confusions and unproductive squabbles.

II

A number of solutions to the object determination problem have been offered, and, considering the variations in the formulations mentioned earlier, they have not all aimed to perform exactly the same task. In the sequel, I propose a different, tentative, resolution of the object determination question and review the claims of other familiar efforts. I also vet Dretske's proposal, although it is explicitly noncausal. I examine it nonetheless, because no discussion of this subject can afford to ignore its major assault on our problem. Obviously, if his proposal cannot be shown to be inferior to the best causalist ones, this indicates that there is a serious question about causalists' ability to go beyond (C).

I will review various causalist solutions, indicating for each why we should continue looking for another one. My own view emerges out of the ashes of the hitherto most refined causalist proposal. This method is adopted because (what I take to be) my proposal's strengths are set off most favorably against previous attempts to capture this elusive relation. But it is useful for travelers, before embarking on a lengthy journey, to mark on their map their ultimate destination. Here is a thumbnail sketch of the view I later defend.

Keeping in mind the looseness that infects our practice of individuating visual episodes (see chap. 7), however we divide them up there would be no answer to the question 'what is the distinctive mark of the object?' if we dealt with only isolated, glimpse-sized episodes that were too brief for an object to undergo visible change. We need to be able to trace causal factors through potential changes in order to find a basis for distinguishing objects (or object relatives) from other causes. Once in possession of that capacity, we can distinguish an object relative from other causes, based on differences in the manner in which our visual episodes track each of them. Put briefly, although it is a matter of the *concept* of visual perception that a perceiver be able to track varying degrees of change in those properties of the object that she can detect on any given sight, it is at best a matter of physical law, and not of the concept of vision as such, that changes in the other causes are reflected in changes in the (qualitative features of) her visual episodes. That is, for nonobjectual factors whose changes are ordinarily reflected in changes in our experience, we can quite intelligibly imagine that, much to our amazement, massive changes in those factors are no longer reflected in our experience (or perhaps were only wrongly thought to be up to now), but that we nonetheless continue to see the same objects. This would be highly disconcerting, but it is not incoherent. At this stage, it may strike readers as being highly implausible. A short chronicle of some past failures of alternative proposals may boost its stock. I begin with a canvass of other causalist schemes of object determination.

III

In what can be regarded as a comment on a method of object determination, Grice suggests that the causalist's best hope is "to indicate the mode of causal connexion by examples": "to say that, for an object to be perceived by X, it is sufficient that it should be causally involved in the generation of some sense-impression by X in the kind of way in which, for example, when I look at my hand in a good light, my hand is causally responsible for its looking to me as if there were a hand before me, or in which . . . (and so on), whatever that kind of way may be; and to be enlightened on that question one must have recourse to the specialist."[1] As a method of object determination, this has obvious drawbacks. It assumes rather than demonstrates that there is "a kind of way," the same for all perceptual objects, in which an object causes a perceptual episode. Grice never doubts this, but only that such a kind can ever be (nontrivially) formulated. However, he is scarcely in a position to take for granted the existence of such a "way." It is one of the chief things that a successful account should establish. By alluding to it without giving us further information about it, he presupposes that a solution is in the offing, without a hint of being entitled to do so.

Strawson rejects this method on the grounds that, first of all, "we cannot be satisfied with this procedure unless we can at least state the general principles governing the selection of our examples," but, second, "it is impossible to state the general principle without revealing a circularity in the doctrine. For what qualifies the chosen example for a place in the list is nothing other than the fact that when someone is correctly described as looking at his hand in a good light, and having the impression, in part causally dependent on the presence of his hand, that he *is* seeing his hand. So the general statement of the doctrine comes to this: for an object to be perceived by X, it is sufficient that it should be causally involved in the generation of some sense-impression of X's in any one of the ways in which, when X perceives an object, that object is causally responsible for . . . X's sense-impression" (1974, pp. 72–73).

Pears sets out to rescue Grice by noting that his view 'implies' that there is a single line, or a limited disjunction of them, and this is not guaranteed. "It is a contingent fact, which evidently might have been otherwise" (1976, p. 30). Although this could show that a question has not been begged, it does rekindle the suspicion that Grice has said little more than that there is some solution or other. However, suppose we ask whether it even clears Grice of Strawson's charge.

When Pears writes of the claim implying that there is a single line, he might have in mind either of two quite different sorts of things. On the one hand, he may be fastening onto Grice's remark that we need "recourse to the specialist," in which case Pears no doubt intends that *scientifically* things might have been otherwise. The account of a "kind of way," then, would be a scientific one. On the other hand, Pears could mean that, for all we know, it might have been the case (though it is not) that no *conceptual* account of a single line, or limited disjunction of them, was in the offing. In either case, Grice is taken as claiming that one or the other of these methods indicates that there is such a single line or a manageably small collection of them, and this is not a trivial claim, because it is not guaranteed. Let us examine the attempted rescue on each interpretation.

Starting with science (the appeal to what it is reasonable to believe that science has discovered or will discover), the procedure of selecting exemplars and supposing that they can be used to point to a unified explanatory notion embodies the dubious assumption that perception is, or is sufficiently like, a natural kind. Reasons for avoiding that assumption were given in the last chapter. Peacocke has summed them up succinctly: "we wish to apply the concept of perception to conceivable creatures with different physico-chemical realizations from our own; we wish to allow prosthetic devices and re-routings in internal stages of the chain at the very least . . . [W]e cannot wholly avoid the traditional hard work of the method of imagined examples and the testing against them of the appropriate intuitions of those who have mastered the concept of perception" (1979, p. 100). Thus, unless we are prepared to exclude from the class of perceivers any creature which uses an unfamiliar means to acquire the same sort of information via roughly the same sort of experiential states, discovering the actual micromechanisms at work in ordinary cases will not reveal the basic nature of perception. For such reasons, there is little opening for Pears's defense, construed as a blank check for science to write.

Turning to the second option, if Pears's remark is meant to suggest that the examples might point to one or a few lines of causal explanation in a philosophically unified account, Strawson's objection stands. If we try to shape a general account of this sort, how can it help but end up being circular? For example, we might identify the lines through their functions. But can we collect the right cases without appealing, even implicitly, to the fact that all the relevant instances involve the perceptual object? Strawson doesn't claim this is the only possible general account. But he believes it is the only one that can be generated *solely* by enumerating clear cases. If that self-defeating method of selecting cases is not driving the general account, it is unclear what is. On the other hand, we may attempt to begin right off with a consideration of general principles for dividing cases. But doing so renders Grice's method otiose.

Ultimately, then, there is not much promise in the suggestion. Even for vision alone, many of the same causal elements will be involved for nonobjects (e.g., source of illumination, eyeglasses). The difficulty is describing the object's distinctive contribution without the content of the description essentially containing the feature *being the object*. However, I should mention that Grice's remark was rather offhand. Perhaps we are wrong to expect much from it or to fault it for failing to accomplish what it never set out to do. But, then, what serious causalist proposals are in the field? I now turn to a uniformly rejected, but well-known suggestion.

IV

H. H. Price mounted a well-known effort to work out CTP's details. For him the key to solving our problem is a distinction between standing and differential conditions. Standing conditions are those in the absence of which no seeing whatsoever would take place. Price gives as examples "a source of light, an eye, a retina, an optic nerve" (1984, p. 70). A differential condition is any causal condition that is not standing. An object of sight is the differential condition in a visual transaction.

The view has been subjected to ample critical scrutiny elsewhere, so here I briefly enumerate only a few of its more glaring deficiencies. For our purposes, we may ignore the fact that Price's conditions are designed to mark out events rather than objects, and we may overlook whatever vulnerability attaches to his adoption of a sense-datum philosophy. Still, the proposal has fatal drawbacks. For one thing, we can see sources of light (e.g., the sun, a torch), which are also standing conditions. Price's solution works for illuminated objects, but not, it appears, for luminous ones. For another, only one eye is necessary for seeing, making the other eye in bifocal vision (discounting depth) a differential condition and thus the object of every sighting. Moreover, if we count seeing in mirrors, we can see our own eyes. Finally, a bear is a differential condition of my seeing bear tracks; thus on this view when I see the tracks I also see the bear that made them. We may conclude that being a differential condition is neither necessary (e.g., seeing the sun) nor sufficient (e.g., the bear who left the tracks) for being an object or an object relative of sight.

V

More recently, causalists seem to have converged on the idea of a covariation between visual properties of the object and those of the visual episode or its content: that is, changes, say, in the experiential content are viewed as a function of those in the object (in a way that the former are not functionally dependent on any other causal condition). According to Dennis Stampe, "[t]he causal relation we have in mind is one that holds between a set of properties $F(f_1 \ldots f_n)$ of the thing represented, and a set of properties $\Phi(\phi_1 \ldots \phi_n)$ of the representation" (1979, p. 85). Similar proposals may be found in Roderick Chisholm (1957, pp. 147–48) and Frank Jackson (1977, p. 170–71); Alvin Goldman (1977) suggests at least partial agreement. I will concentrate on Jackson's version in the sequel because he exposes more functional details than are to be found in Chisholm's pioneering prototype and because, unlike Stampe's, his treatment is restricted to perception.

This seems to move in the right direction. Covariation, rather than specification of the lines of sight, seems to be what matters. But I later suggest that this is not enough. To get an adequate solution, we will need to find a basis for dividing covariants into relevant and irrelevant classes. However, I first examine the efforts just described. Before coming to grips with specifics, several preliminary remarks are in order.

First, we have seen that covariation solutions are causal only insofar as they may be linked with an independently identifiable causal element: that is, the covariation is explicable in terms of the causal condition, (C), introduced earlier. I will continue to assume this causal underpinning of such solutions.

Second, as framed, it looks as though this solution is tailored to invite back in those familiar but irksome Dopplegängers—sense-data. Strictly speaking, those items on the experiential side that are supposedly a function of the object's features might be any properties of visual episodes. But the most natural reading of this test is that the properties of visual episodes responsive to those of the object will be by and large the latter's subjective likenesses. Jackson openly embraces this interpretation, and the particular use made of *representation* in Stampe's formula suggests a similar view. Thus the question naturally arises, 'Does this method of object determination exclude direct realism?' In the broad way I am construing the proposal, the answer is negative.[2] The possibility that the fundamental relationships in question hold between the visible properties of the object and virtually any features of the perceptual episode has not strictly been ruled out. The dependent properties may be very dissimilar from those on which they depend; they may even be qualifications of the episode rather than features of its content. Ultimately, this introduces a sort of openness into the view about what can count as reflecting a certain property. But it is a sort to which it is possible to reconcile oneself. It is scarcely a reductio, but (so a proponent would aver) a mere fact of life. What is most important is that it allows advocates of the proposal to remain neutral with respect to questions of indirect versus direct realism. It is possible to sketch the view via the dependent contents of visual episodes while making no commitment to the ultimate analysis or cash value of those features.

Finally, notice some of the ways in which the foregoing sketch needs refinement. As given, the functional view fails to distinguish the object from an unseen light source or even from one's eyes. A perceiver's visual episode is functionally dependent on the state of each of these. Where the sun is the only light source, its distance, position, brightness, and so on, make systematic differences to the character of the visual experience. As for eyes, nearsightedness, floating particles, and dilation of pupils, among other things, contribute to the overall experience. Of course, *not every difference* in light source or eyes makes a difference to the features of the experience, but the same is true of a multitude of the object's intrinsic qualities, even of its so-called visual ones. Thus, enormous, much less slight, changes in the shape, color, or size of a distant star may make no difference to the content of one's experience of it. Consequently, whether the proposal under consideration succeeds hangs on as-yet-undisclosed details, and in particular on whether, given those details, the endorsed relationship still distinguishes the perceptual object from nonobjectual causal factors.

VI

Frank Jackson tackles the last requirement by confining the relationship to what
he refers to as 'functional spatial dependence'. According to him (1972, p. 170),
the features of the object on which those of the sense-datum depend are "shape,
size, distance (away), and (relative) direction." Implicit in this list are contour and
position. A conspicuously absent feature is color, the most distinctively visual of
the lot.[3] No doubt it is omitted because it is not spatial; but the omission is in
another way a genuine handicap. The proposal is alleged to capture the way our
concept of vision works in isolating one among various causal factors as the thing
seen. But color is as prominent a visual quality as the recently enumerated spatial
properties. Furthermore, changes in one's experience of color are as dependent on
changes in the properties of the object as are those of the included qualities. Ask
yourself whether you could seriously adhere to this test of object determination if
you grant that we have color experiences, but on this test your color experiences
were not as responsive to (what we ordinarily call) color changes as to changes of
spatial qualities. Such a proposal would fail a central test of reflecting visual
properties. Although Jackson's proposal implies no such oddity, neither can it
explain why it won't happen. Accordingly, something vital seems to have been
omitted. Why, then, not expand the view to include color?

Various possible answers come to mind. For example, it may be that its inclusion would result in the class of functionally relevant properties lacking any non-
circular characterization. That is, since the properties would no longer all be spatial, under what classfication would they fall? Perhaps visual! But what is a visual
property? Just a property of *what is seen*. But what is seen is the perceptual object,
and this is what the test sought to determine. Thus, our answer amounts to saying
that it is the visual properties that determine the visual object. But isn't that to
travel in a very tight circle?

In fact, this may be a good reason for Jackson, given his approach, to avoid
expanding the class of functionally relevant properties. My own solution will invoke just such an expanded class, but it avoids this sort of problem, because it
does not seek to confine the initial class of functionally relevant properties. Many
properties of nonobjects also functionally determine the character of visual episodes. On the account I offer in §VIII, the crucial difference is not discoverable
in *what* is functionally dependent but in *how* it is functionally dependent. Thus,
visual properties will be just those that are functionally dependent in the right
way. Perhaps Jackson's proposal is not developed in enough detail to know with
certainty that he is debarred from making a similar move. At any rate, such a
maneuvre would substantially change the relevant class of functional dependencies
in his account.

There are a few additional reasons why Jackson may have wanted to exclude
color.

First, he holds that colors are secondary qualities: sense-data have them; physical objects do not. When Jackson interjects this claim, originally introduced in
connection with a different subject, into the issue of object determination, the
focus seems to have shifted from functional dependence to (qualitative) similarities

between objects and sense-data. No doubt, nonrealists about color don't believe that its experiences occur or vary by way of resembling qualities inherent in the object; but neither is this required for strictly spatial qualities. Jackson himself allows that we see material surfaces despite inverting lenses and distorting media. Thus, the question of similarity between the sets of functionally independent and dependent characteristics is a distraction.[4] If we set it aside, the primary/secondary quality distinction, whatever its intrinsic merits, does not bear on the present issue. Even nonrealists about color generally hold that *something* in the physical object accounts for our particular color experiences. Thus, variations in that feature should account for many variations in those experiences. And that, once we see the irrelevance of qualitative similarity, undercuts the point of excluding color.

Next, Jackson states that even an objectivist about color would grant its irrelevancy, "because . . . material objects can (for example, by the totally colour-blind) be seen in 'black-and-white'. This means . . . that the material objects can be seen although the sense-data belonging to them differ markedly from them in colour" (p. 170). The remark once again raises the issue of qualitative similarity, which we have seen is a 'red' herring. Even so, it is not explained why something black and white is totally without color in the relevant sense. In fact, for nonluminous objects in an illuminated scene, their blackness or whiteness is accounted for in precisely the same way as any other color: by surface spectral reflectance (see Hilbert, 1987) or the absorption of light of certain wavelengths. In addition, brightness is a salient character of color, but, say, in black-and-white cinema and photographs it is just such relative brightness that accounts for the distribution of greys that allow us to discriminate shapes, contours, distances, and the like. This distribution is still a function of whatever is responsible for ordinary color perception. Once again, how is this different in principle from those wearing inverting lenses? In each case, the peculiarities themselves may not be a function of the object seen, but the character of the experiences that take on those unusual forms are.

Why such ado about color? Is it really that critical to the proposal? Indeed, it is. This is made clear by the incongruity of counting shape detection as indispensable while color is *propria non gratis*. For many, if not the overwhelmingly majority, of the shapes we detect through sight are not three-dimensional edges or contours, but patterns or designs. (For example, the letters on this page.) These are detectable only via color contrasts. We might even grant that this requires no more than a contrast between the alleged *noncolors* black and white. Nevertheless, if black and white aren't colors, neither are they spatial qualities. Thus, if this is not a case of color contrast, it has yet to be explained what sort of a contrast it is, or why its inclusion is not as inimical to the spatial-property restriction as color would have been.

VII

We might seek to rectify the situation simply by adding color to the list of functionally relevant properties. But that may be premature, because we haven't exhausted the view's shortcomings, which are worth exposing because they yield

important clues about the needed corrective. They are best brought out by per-
servering a while with the unamended version restricted to spatial properties. I
will consider a modification of Jackson's formula proposed by Michael Tye. Although it is firmly within the functional relation tradition, it has the advantage
of providing some indication of how the details of Jackson's account might be
fleshed out.

Tye's official solution is stated in terms of 'M-properties': the functionally
relevant class of an object's properties. Although at one point it is stated that these
are only those spatial properties that have "counterparts in the spatial properties
of the experienced visual sensum" (1982, p. 319), we forfeit nothing more than
problems of interpretation, while remaining in line with other things the author
holds, to regard 'M-property' merely as another title for Jackson's spatial properties. Thus understood, here in slightly simplified form (viz., omitting a clause that
doesn't bear on the present issue) is Tye's proposal:

> S sees $x =_{df}$ (i) There is a causal chain of events C which ends with S's
> having an experience of a visual sensum Q; (ii) within C some event involving
> S's eyes causally intervenes between some event involving x and S's experi-
> encing Q; (iii) x's position in C is such that it is in principle possible to vary
> each M-property of x or some surface of x and thereby produce a systematic
> variation in the corresponding spatial property of Q (p. 322).

Only (iii) bears on object determination: (i)–(iii) as a package is a more ambitious
attempt at a full analysis of 'S sees x.' We might well dissent from it taken as a
proposal for a sufficient condition of seeing. For one thing, it contains no prohibi-
tion of causal deviance; nothing in it rules out perception-defeating instances of
deviance mentioned in the last chapter. Moreover, Tye harbors doubts about (ii),
doubts I share for other reasons, leaving only the combination of (i) and (iii) as
necessary and jointly sufficient. But (ii) is the only part of the formula that even
hints at a causal role for x in generating S's experience (viz., the part played for
us by (C)).

In chapter 7 and again in this chapter (p. 215), reasons were offered for not
combining the treatment of a more specific issue, such as causal deviance or object
determination with a complete set of conditions for seeing something. Solving a
given problem of vision need not bring with it a complete analysis of seeing.
Thus, let us treat (iii) as if it were offered only as a solution to our special
problem.

The easiest way to broach the fundamental problem with this sort of answer
is to view at closer quarters the situation that could have prompted the introduction
of certain requirements in (iii)'s formulation. For this, let us begin with a very
naive functional view. Consider the flatfooted claim that, for every change in the
spatial qualities of viewed objects, a matching one will be produced in the qualities of the visual content. Not much reflection is needed to show that some
changes are too miniscule, and some objects too far away, to generate these sorts
of changes in visual states. Thus, if the sun moved a meter closer, or the pail
sank a nanometer further in the sand, these changes are unlikely to be reflected in

my sensum. All else being equal, the sun and the pail will continue to subtend their previous visual angles. Thus, it is for a very good reason that (iii) does not say that each change in an M-property will in fact produce one in the corresponding property of its sensum. It appears that the most one could claim with a semblance of plausibility is that, for every spatial property M of *x,* there is some possible change or other of M that would produce a (systematic) change in a specified subset of spatial properties of (the content of) the corresponding sensum. But this is too fragile a result once we try to say more about it, though much depends on what gets counted as an M-property (and, thus, as a change in one). For example, since it is reasonable to assume that having a definite number of sides is an M-property (shape), it is reasonable to assume that *having a million sides* is an instance of an M-property. Accordingly, changing the number of sides an object has is changing its shape. Despite this, a change to *having a million and one sides* isn't likely to produce any change in a corresponding sensum.

To avoid the unwelcome consequence, suppose we allow, consistently with (iii), that a proper subset of changes in a given range of properties constitute the relevant changes of M-property. Thus, one may hold that a very different change from this range—say, from *having a million sides* to *having ten sides*—would alter the sensum. However, if we allow that the test may be satisfied by a small subset of the changes an M-property can undergo—and *only* by such gigantic ones at that—the chances of its yielding a standard for object determination have greatly diminished. The distance and position of an unseen light source, if altered severely enough, will also alter the spatial properties of sensa. To illustrate, dimly lit objects look more distant and more bluntly edged. We might also ask how overlooking all but radical changes tallies with the systematicity of the changes in the two 'spaces.'[5] Thus, the more permissive we make (iii), the less likely it will be able to discriminate the perceptual object relative from other causal elements. Perhaps this looks more like a counsel of despair than a decisive objection. But it is at a minimum a forewarning about the very serious problems encountered when trying to implement (iii). It will continue to plague us presently, when the need for further refinements exacerbates an already desperate situation.

Moreover, some of the objects we commonly take ourselves to see apparently don't even have the sorts of spatial qualities whose variation is crucial to this criterion. Thus, the sky seems to lack size, shape, and perhaps even distance. Though it has direction, there is no clear sense to its having a change of direction. (And, as I have hinted, the view's strength rests on a subject's ability to grasp changes rather than to reflect static properties.)

It was just suggested that where an object reflects light, the source of the light might also satisfy condition (iii). Certainly, some changes in, say, the size, distance, direction, and position of the sun or a lamp would result in systematic changes in our visual experiences or the properties of the episodes. Perhaps the way to get around this is to insist that the changes be of a restricted sort. In line with the nature of the proposal, that sort would no doubt consist of changes to the strictly spatial features of sensa. (Remember, we are playing along with the omission of other visual properties, such as color.)

What is it for a sensum to have spatial properties? Were materialism true, a sensum's properties would, on analysis, be in public space. But this would hold of all properties of our experience, and thus not separate the right subclass from the foregoing undesirable ones. Perhaps the present proposal envisions a private space in which changes in experiential content take place. Let's see where that assumption leads us.

A first question is how the changes in the spatial character of the object must be reflected in it. Here I believe that, despite the admission of a few exceptions, such as inverting lenses and distortion (say, through a dense medium, such as water), the proposal is forced to lay great emphasis on resemblance. Of course, it is not the naive view, which would simply ignore such factors as distance and angle. Nevertheless, basically, as an object changes its properties, our sensum of it should reflect similar changes, ceteris paribus. Here it is difficult to know when the differences are massive enough to violate the requirement of systematicity, but I believe the facts are sufficiently mixed to require further explanation from the functionalist. For example, if the object grows smaller, can the sensum's representation grow larger? A shrinking luminous body, such as a white dwarf star, emits more intense light (up to a point), and thus looks larger, as it shrinks. Is this a systematic variation? If it is, then the sensum object needn't grow smaller in ersatz space as the ontological object does in space. And we already know that the size or shape of the sensum object can vary with the distance, angle, or location—not the size or shape—of the ontological one. A familiar example is that of a span of railroad tracks that seem to converge as we travel away from them. Thus, it is not even the same (spatial) property that need change with the object or our location. Consequently, we are in no position to rule out systematic variations in our sensa due to the positions of unseen light sources *on the grounds* that the two sorts of properties may be different. When this is added to the fact that it is only an inconsequential fraction of spatial properties with which our experience can be expected to vary, the patient's prognosis becomes grim. The functionalist has a double task. She not only must specify the right class of covariants, but must do so in a way that clearly distinguishes it from covariations with unseen things, such as light sources. And as the former is loosened, the differences between it and the unwanted covariations diminish rapidly toward insignificance.

Imagine, moreover, a case in which a subject is in a room full of pliable things, while in another room she cannot see into sits someone, O, operating a control panel. Each button pressed by O changes the shape, size, distance, or direction (from the perceiver) of the objects in the former room. *Depressing button a* seems to be a spatial property, since it expresses a spatial relation between O and the button. By depressing the button, O changes the spatial qualities of the objects, while each different button depressed manifests a different spatial property O has. (If we wished, we could even have the buttons imitate to scale the different shapes, sizes, directions, and positions of the qualities of objects they control.) According to (iii), the subject should see not only the pliable things, but also O's various relations to these buttons. Less outré, now our subject is once again tracking a bear through the snow. For many changes in the bear's position, the spatial qualities of the perceiver's sensa will change: she will see different tracks, broken twigs, torn bark. Why is it that the subject doesn't see the bear according to (iii)? (Of course, she does see the properties in question, but it is supposedly their systematic relation to the property possessor that determines what property *possessor* the subject sees.)

Tye's proposal encounters a number of stumbling blocks. Aside from the problems that, as a complete analysis of 'S sees *o'*, his original proposal makes no provision for deviance; that an object determiner that excludes color looks like a nonstarter; and that reliance on resemblance seems to consign a view to whatever faults attach to sense-datum philosophy, (iii) alone is beset by the facts that some ontological objects—for example, the sky—don't share many (or any) of the M-properties upon which the proposal operates; that in qualifying the extent of the functional relationships to avoid objections, it is difficult to see how it remains appreciably more systematic than the covariations that hold for nonobjects; and that there are straightforward counterexamples to the proposal. For all that, I believe this last view moves us closer to one we can finally accept. Its emphasis on covariation rather than the reflection of isolable properties is on the right track, and its neutrality with respect to the way in which these dependencies may be reflected in visual episodes exhibits—in its practice if not in its declarations—a way to show the restriction to spatial (M-) properties unnecessary and even gratuitous. It is the covariation of visual properties that matter, not the manner of the embodiment of the dependent values. Let us turn our attention to such a reformed proposal.

VIII

Users of the concept of vision—a proper subset of sighted subjects—expect a visual object to support changes in their experience: that is, they expect certain changes in the object to track changes in the contents of their visual experiences, *and* the object's support for such expectations is part of their understanding of vision. What I wish to emphasize here is that *this is a conceptual fact about vision.* Changes in other factors may also be expected to generate changes in the content of one's experience. But the relation of this expectation to our understanding is very different. If such things occurred in other causes but were no longer reflected in experience, that would no doubt occasion astonishment, but it would not precipitate a crisis in the very concept of vision. Of course, such changes cover a variety of factors, and not all of them are equally deeply embedded in our visual notions. But by and large our concept of vision can undergo major revision in many of the ways it works, but not in others. This is the difference I want to capture. Broadly, my claim comprises two theses:

(i) it is a fact about the concept of seeing that changes of a certain kind in the object be reflected in visual episodes,

and

ii) it is a piece of contingent information, but a nonconceptual fact about seeing, that changes in other causal factors be reflected in visual episodes.[6]

Moreover, it is the causal power of the object that supports such changes and, thereby, the conceptual expectations in (i). The proposal has been stated bluntly to ensure that its drift is not misunderstood. But it now requires elaboration, defense, and, perhaps, one or two tactical retreats.

First, there is the matter of the change from spatial to visual properties generally, including color. How are we to accomodate this without inviting the circularity scouted on p. 220? Answer: this threat is neutralized by the present approach. Remember, the signature of objecthood is not the static reflection of properties, but the capacity of some properties, once located within the visual episode (whether or not actually seen), to be tracked in certain ways. Thus, we can begin with a large list of properties—including those that do not belong to the object— and weed out items by applying this test. The individuals to which the surviving properties belong, as well as the properties themselves, are object relatives. Since whether what we see tracks or registers information about a certain subset of properties is not in question, there isn't the same urgency to specify independently and at the outset, the subclass of properties we are talking about. That comes out in the wash, as it were, by discovering what satisfies (i).

In any event, I am uncertain how serious the predicament is even if we adopt Jackson's method of designating in advance the class of relevant properties. If the spatial properties can be enumerated, we need only add color to the list to specify the entire class by enumeration. This specification can be quite independent of whether those properties occur in experience. (It is, I take it, a contingent fact that such features are apprehended at all. Our sense organs might have evolved differently.) Of course, they are of interest to us only because they are the properties of objects we see. But that alone doesn't render the enhanced procedure viciously circular. For this reason, we shouldn't regard the omission of color as a serious impediment to the success of the earlier functionalist views. Color could be added to the list of the functionally independent properties without noticeable damage. It is the constellation of other difficulties that, in my view, doom earlier functionalist efforts.

Next, the current proposal does not concern synchronically described objects as such, but only changes in them. In the preceding chapter, I emphasized the looseness that marks ordinary methods of individuating seeings and visual episodes. But it doesn't matter how many visual episodes must be considered. However we divide them, it is the potential for extended viewing of something through changes that matters for object determination. Nor need we be concerned, on the present proposal, with the accurate depiction of the relevant properties, but only with systematic changes in experience that enable us to detect changes in them. Various distortions may prevent a subject from accurately reflecting the qualities of things, but this in no way detracts from the ability to follow changes, however distortedly viewed.[7] Presently, I will note Dretske's emphasis on constancy mechanisms in object choice. These mechanisms permit us to view the features of objects as constant, despite large fluctuations in patterns of disinhibitions created in our retinas, or in firings of cells in visual pathways. Such evidence is complementary to the view under discussion. It is also relevant here, because it, too, does not rely on momentary glimpses, but on seeing over a span of time. Of course, this applies only to what we take to be the seeing of *the same thing*. If the subject believes she is hallucinating, or that she is seeing a series of different things, all bets are off. Despite this, if she is mistaken, her continued experience should register any relevant changes, though she doesn't take them as such.

It is generally accepted that, in the evolutionary and structural development of the eye, motion acuity precedes acuity for stationary features. Only higher animals can use their eyes to signal absence of motion. Indeed, the edge layers of our own retinas—those most likely to have developed first—are sensitive only to motion, not to static properties (see Gregory 1990, p. 101). Traces of these proclivities remain in our current faculties. For example, without tiny, involuntary saccades, fixation on a static location leads to a 'greying-out' effect (sometimes experienced by pilots when not moving their heads while viewing a cloudless sky). This is due to the slowness of the regeneration of the bleached chemicals in our color photoreceptors. These facts may not demonstrate that tracking the movements of a single object is built into the generally received concept of vision, much less prove the conceptual truths in question about tracking. Nevertheless, in light of the independent support for the proposal in the present section, these facts make it quite understandable why our concept should have developed along the suggested lines. (Some may even view these data as making it nearly inevitable.) Thus, they yield a secondary consideration which fits snugly into the present proposal, and which may remain unexplained or even anomalous on other proposals.

The present view does not require that a perceptual object be trackable under all circumstances. There may be impediments in either the object or the subject to tracking. In the case of objects, some may exist for only an instant. They do not last long enough, or change sufficiently in the time they do fill, to have alterations tracked. Of course, here, too, we expect their coming into, and going out of, existence to be recordable. But this is a limiting case. However, even for persisting objects, cases such as that of chapter 7's censor indicate that a subject can see something for an instant without being able to register the object's changes. (Recall that, with the censor, the same object is not seen through changes; as soon as a change occurs, the censor is directly responsible for the visual experience, and nothing is then actually seen.) This, too, is accounted for either by not activating the conceptual expectation or by doing so incorrectly. Of course, one may not be aware that a censor is responsible for one's subsequent visual episodes. Nonetheless, this is no conceptual perplexity. Since one's experiences are not tracking the object, nothing induces them to register changes in it. It is only when the object is continually seen through changes in its visual properties that the inability to register those alterations becomes problematic for the concept of sight. In other cases, the conceptual expectation is not raised, or its raising can be explained through a mistaken assumption.

Moreover, since it is not actual tracking of changes that matter, for there may be no change, but the fact that changes would be tracked, my solution introduces either a counterfactual or a typal element. (I can handle nonactual cases in either way.) That is, I can say of the token properties of the object either that they *would be tracked* under certain conditions, all things being equal, or that they belong to types such that instances of those types are in fact tracked, all things being equal, as part of our conceptual component, by continued seeing.

Moreover, many changes are due to the subject, not the object. Changes in the subject's perspective, or other changes in location, are not attributable to the object and should not properly give rise to the expectation of a change in the object.

Let's explore in a bit more detail how the present proposal differs from those preceding it. Some changes or other will often be registered in visual experience if we continue to see the same object over time. But certain of these changes, as well as many others, will be due to nonobjectual causal factors, and may have nothing to do with the identity of the object. Each sort of change constitutes a proper subset of those that actually occur. A central problem for the functional views examined in §§V–VII is to distinguish the subset in the former, objectual, case from those in the latter, nonobjectual, cases. Patrons of those views have attempted to accomplish this in terms of quantum differences in the systematicity of the two sorts of covariation. But given the great latitude of objects of sight, ranging from the astronomical to the zoological, we may be excused for suspecting that this method won't get us very far. At least, as I indicated in §VII, it leaves us with a host of examples that do not sit comfortably with the basis for the contrast. The present proposal allows me to steer clear of this messy issue. I acknowledge that both objectual and nonobjectual causal changes may be responsible for systematic alterations in our experience. Most likely, the objectual changes are moreso. But when we make adjustments for specific cases, the enormity of the difference begins to evaporate, perhaps making it impossible to give a principled accounting of their differences in systematicity. Instead, the important contrast between objectual and nonobjectual covariation occurs elsewhere: only the differences accounted for by the object's changes belong to our concept of seeing; the others may be accounted for by well-entrenched, but nonetheless intelligibly frustratable beliefs about the physical conditions attending sight. I am not obliged to say with precision *which* changes in the object exemplify each kind in order to claim the two sorts of changes, and their difference in kind, occur.

Thus far, I've been at pains to set out and elaborate the view. But other than a few comparative advantages (e.g., its ability to set aside certain difficult questions prompted by earlier views), little has been said in its defense. It is time to correct that. Of the two theses comprising the present view, (i) is easier to demonstrate; so I begin with that.

The clearest argument for (i) is a reductio: what would it be like for (i) not to be satisfied? My answer is that it would be like nothing whatsoever. That is, its nonsatisfaction describes no intelligible state of affairs. To see this, we must try to imagine not only that our continued seeing of *o* does not track changes in the size, shape, location, color, and so on, of *o,* but that all relevant factors other than those changes, which might yield alternative explanations of why this happens, are held constant. Recall that I am claiming not only that it is a characteristic of objects that they support such changes in our experience, but that this is so *because* of the causal powers of such objects. Accordingly, we cannot suppose the failure to reflect such changes is the result of anything else in the current causal chain. The laws of physics and neurophysiology must remain in force, our sense organs must operate as they do now, and we must imagine that the subject continues to see the same object. Nevertheless, on the current supposition, the subject is no longer able to track changes in *o,* however significant. This strikes me as incoherent. Imagine, for example, someone watching a balloon being inflated a few feet in front of her. We must suppose she sees the balloon before inflation and continues to see it when wholly inflated, but nothing in her experience can signify a difference in any size or shape of the balloon. This does more than beggar the imagination—it makes it difficult to conceive of there being room here for our current concept of sight.

As for (ii), it is not difficult to imagine certain other factors in a causal chain to operate on different principles, therefore for their changes to make no discernible difference to our experience, without having our current concept of sight coming unglued. Some of the causal factors in sight are relatively esoteric and not known even by most of those who currently grasp perfectly well what it is to see something. But there are other factors, such as the radiant or ambient light in which we see illuminated objects, whose changes seem to be more intimately connected in the minds of perceivers with the character of experience. However, even here, changes in gradations of lighting that did not register changes in our experience, up to the most radical kind, would be a source of amazement, but not a threat to the very notion of vision. It seems clear we would still say the subject was able *to see o,* despite the absence, mirabile dictu, of the right light. There is a borderline case about which I have less confidence: what if someone continued to see after the total disappearance of light?[8] If this plays havoc with the concept of vision, we would need to count the presence of at least some light as informing that concept. But that is perhaps an acknowledgement that the concept, like many others, admits difficult (perhaps undecidable) penumbral cases. It does not show that we track visible changes in light in the way that we do such properties as color and shape; for being able to perceive the object just as clearly so long as there is *at least some light* is not the same as tracking (what are now) visible changes in the light. In fact, for what it's worth, visual experience, unlike ordinary camera film, is not altered by certain radical changes in light (see Edwin Land 1977), and the apparent hues of objects are dependent on the relative values of the things in the visual array more than on the absolute value of the reflectance of any given surface. Some painters know this quite well, but even at the cell-firing level of our visual system, receptors respond to contrasts—say, excitatory centers and inhibitory surrounds, or vice versa—but *not* to diffuse light (Kandel 1981, pp. 238f.). This may contain a clue about why it seems as if comparable alterations of nonobjectual factors are not tracked as systematically as those of the object.

Of course, this proposal works only if it is possible to draw a distinction, however fugitive, between conceptual constituents of seeing and contingent information about sight. But what needs to be presupposed is very modest indeed: so much so that it is even compatible with moderately holistic accounts of meaning. For example, we might suppose that the range of features of visual perception form a continuum, with many borderline cases and generous latitude for indecision. Nevertheless, we can maintain that *being able to track certain changes in the visual object* is a clear case at one end of the continuum, and *being able to see despite not tracking changes in other causal factors* falls clearly on the other end. Anyone who wants to reject the current proposal because it appeals to conceptual relationships would need more than merely a holistic theory of meaning: it would take a denial sufficiently radical to prevent us from differentiating the cases of the preceding paragraphs in terms of what makes sense and what doesn't. In particular, one would have to show that it was sensible for S to continue seeing *o* despite the failure to track any of the enormous changes described. We should ask ourselves how anyone could make out such a case.

I have not considered the possibility of eliminativism: roughly, the view that the very notion of an object of perception cannot be made respectable. Depriving us of objects amounts to acknowledging that the whole business of trying to justify the selection of one among various causal factors or sources of information in perception comes to nought. Other than the present proposal for making the distinction, nothing claimed thus far strictly rules out eliminativism. Rather, I have assumed it is obvious that we can draw such a distinction, or at least that we are prima facie entitled to do so until confronted by a clearer challenge from the eliminativist. The assumption that there are perceptual objects is the sort of deeply entrenched commonsensical belief that tends to survive, without being questioned, repeated failures of various philosophical explanations of its workings. However, if the factors involved in perception are altogether fluid, and even the modest distinction I require between a conceptual and a nonconceptual component among causal elements comes to grief, then perhaps eliminativism becomes a more realistic threat.

The foregoing should not be taken as suggesting grounds for believing that things may come to this pass. The *only* point I wish to make by bringing up the subject is that the present account is largely impervious to such eliminativism. I have claimed that the extent to which we now make sense out of one thing rather than another being an object of vision depends on our equally making sense out of there being some, but not all, changes in the scene being traceable as a matter of its concept. *Conceivably* (i.e., given our current epistemic situation), both notions could fall apart. But, even if this distinction yields no scientifically important taxonomies, it is exceedingly difficult to imagine that there is no basis whatsoever for an ability to draw it. I have attempted to discern that basis. I seek to understand only what is presupposed in selecting the object-relative node in a causal chain (put otherwise, what is involved in distinguishing the object from its 'nonrelatives').

The proposal itself is fairly straightforward, although not beyond need of additional fine-tuning. Nevertheless, it may be useful to have a summary of the discussion of this section. Before I present it, bear in mind that usually an entire scene, including more than one identifiable thing, is the object of a particular seeing. Thus, I may see, at one time, a dog and a cat. These may be considered a single conjoint object or two distinct ones. Or I may see a table, its color, and its shape. Thus, we mustn't rule out, in any formula, the possibility not only of multiple objects of a single seeing, but also of seeing distinct categories of items. The condition for a property's being an object is considerably simpler than that for a property-bearing individual's being one, for in the latter case the individual is an object by virtue of its properties being seen. Thus, we seem to require two conditions: one for properties, the other for individuals. With those provisos, here is my summary:

A property P is seen *if and only if* it is a conceptual truth that continued viewing of P would track a substantial number of changes in P.

An individual O is a visual object *if and only if* O has visually detectable properties belonging to type T such that it is a conceptual truth that a continued sighting of one and the same object (be it O or any other) would track changes in tokens of T properties.

Put otherwise (and oversimply), what we see is that thing whose properties we may assume, *by the very concept of sight,* we are able to trace changes in. Thus, I see the vase rather than the lamp that illuminates it because I am conceptually entitled to hold that I can trace certain changes in the visual properties of the vase, but not that I can trace changes, even significant ones, in the visual properties of the lamp. Earlier (chap. 4, p. 110), I scouted an implicitly competing claim of Paul Churchland's that we could be said to see heat if our visual content was a function of heat; generalized, what we see is what our content is a function of. It is now clearer why this view lends itself to a revisionist, not to say eliminativist, notion of perceptual objects. Our experience may be a function of, and even yield information about, a number of things other than what we ordinarily cite as its object, and on that basis what we ordinarily cite is not likely to be distinctive. If, as I am claiming, this was a premature assumption, it illustrates how such mistakes about current practice play a pivotal role in 'legitimating' revisionary arguments.

Before concluding this review of the proposal, I want to return to an earlier objection against any causalist solution. That objection centered on the claim that objecthood does not supervene on strictly causal factors. This led me to distinguish objecthood from object relativity. Another way to look at this distinction would be to compare the following tasks:

(a) that of *determining* the (ontological) object on the basis of its causal contribution;
(b) that of *distinguishing* the contributions of the object from those of distinct items (nodes) in the present causal chain.

As before, (a) remains beyond our grasp due to noncausal factors that, in different contexts, determine what is seen. Seeing an expanse of water from the shore may count as seeing the Atlantic Ocean, although viewng a much larger fraction of a painting may not count as seeing the painting. Or, seeing a plain piece of wrapping paper used as a book cover may count as seeing the book,

although from the given vantage point it may look like nothing other than a piece
of wrapping paper. On the other hand, an otherwise indistinguishable piece of
wrapping paper may prevent me from seeing my glasses underneath it.[9] Again,
we may see a person while she is covered from head to toe in a costume, whereas
if all but her hand is occluded by a door, it may not be the case that we saw her,
despite the fact that more of her flesh is exposed to view than in the first case.
Instances can be multiplied. They show that a thing's making the causal contribution in question is not sufficient to constitute its being the thing seen. The painting
(or the owner of the hand) may be said to be a cause of the perception, though it
is not seen on some occasions. Contextual considerations—what some have
claimed to be pragmatic or conventional factors—prevent the causal element from
being the final arbiter of what is seen. Thus, we must forgo any hope of achieving (a).

But we may still aspire to (b). Given the object, none of its competitors *on
the same causal chain* make the contribution discussed: conceptually supporting
its visual changes with comparable ones in the subject's visual experience. When
an unseen object relative makes this sort of contribution, it is because a part (or
an aspect) of it or something that may be considered its extension is seen in its
stead. But this will not be a causal competitor and so does not appear on the
same causal chain.[10] Thus, for example, when a wall makes the relevant causal
contribution, it may be appropriate to say that we saw only a part (say, the facing
surface) of the wall, not the wall itself. But if in the circumstances the wall can
be said to make a causal contribution to the seeing, it will be precisely the contribution that is made by the facing surface. The wall and its facing surface are not
causal competitors because any causal chain leading to the visual experience that
contains the wall does so by way of the causal efficacy of its facing surface. They
are not separate stages in a chain that includes, say, source of illumination, ambient light, electromagnetic waves, the bleaching of chemicals in retinal cells, neuronal projections onto the optic nerve, optic radiations to the primary visual cortex, and so forth. Rather, depending on circumstance, one or the other will appear
on the chain.

It may be helpful to bear in mind the admonition of the penultimate paragraph
of §I: the answer on offer is not a criterion for picking out the object from behind
a veil of ignorance. We begin with the knowledge, say, that the vase is the object,
and the question raised is whether there is anything distinctive about this node of
the causal chain, and connected with its presence on the chain, to elucidate why
this is so. It is only with respect to that issue that I claim progress for this solution.

IX

Intoxicated with recent success, perhaps it's time to take a sobering look at a
leading noncausal competitor. I devote the rest of this chapter to just such a proposal, skillfully developed by Fred Dretske (1981).

Functional dependencies of visual episodes on visual objects not only suggest
that the relationship is causal, they also provide the best, if not only, opportunity
for one's knowledge about the object. The causal basis for the latter is *information*

in the information theorist's sense of that term, although clearly no cognizer ever takes advantage of the great majority of it. (Information is an objective quantity, whose status as such doesn't rely on its being apprehended.) Dretske proceeds on the supposition that we can gain an understanding of how objects are determined by treating the relationship of object to episode information-theoretically. This stance, since softened, was at the time militantly noncausal. The remainder of this section is devoted to outlining the view, and the next section to its assessment. (His example involves hearing; but the lessons drawn from it are perfectly general.)

Broadly, according to this view, the perceptual object is whatever the perceptual signal carries information about. To see how this works, consider the following representation of a transfer of the information that a doorbell is ringing:

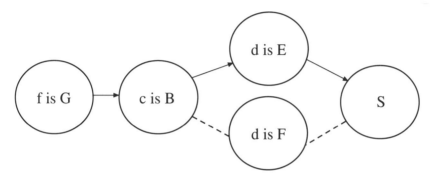

'S' is the signal reaching the perceiver. The other circles stand for actual or potential causally relevant states of affairs that might be represented by the signal. 'c is B' represents the doorbell ringing, 'd is E' and 'd is F' that the signal is transmitted through wires E and F, respectively (though, as the solid line indicates, only 'd is E' is true on the occasion), and finally 'f is G' that the door button is depressed. The subjects of these sentential schemata are to be construed *de re. A fortiori,* information contained in the sentences should not be understood as conveying that something is a doorbell, door button, and so on, but as conveying *of* the doorbell that it is ringing, *of* the door button that it is being depressed, *of* the wire that the signal is being sent through it. Finally, let S be a prolonged buzzing, and let us suppose that the alternate route for the signal (viz., wire F) is taken 40 percent of the time.

Provisionally setting aside the leftmost circle (i.e., the depression of the door button), we may ask whether the signal carries the information that the doorbell is ringing (c is B), that the sound is transmitted through the top wire (d is E), both, or neither. Dretske maintains that the signal carries the information that the doorbell is ringing, but not the information that the sound is traveling through wire E. He reasons that a signal carries information only about causal antecedents with which it is connected by law or definition, and thus connected 100 percent of the time. "Since d is E only 60 percent of the time that S occurs (carrying the information that something is B), S 'says' that c is B without 'saying' that d is E" (1981, p. 158). As he puts it, information can be carried *analytically* or *nomi-*

cally. The information that x is square analytically carries the information that x is rectangular. But it's the nomic case that concerns us, and there "if there is a natural law to the effect that whenever s is F, t is G, given s's being F . . . then no signal can bear the message that s is F without also conveying the information that t is G" (p. 71). No such relation connects the signal with the sound being transmitted through E. Indeed, one may question whether it even links the signal and the ringing of the doorbell. But rather than getting sidetracked by what is, after all, only an illustration, let us grant it: that the buzzing carries the information that the doorbell is ringing exemplifies either a natural law or a consequence of one.

The contrast between the information-carrying roles of 'c is B' and 'd is E' does double duty in the overall argument. First, it is used to indicate the superiority of the informational to the causal approach, for pure causalism "provides no way of discriminating among the variety of eligible candidates" (Dretske 1981, p. 157). Second, the foregoing contrast is the first of two mentioned for distinguishing a perceptual object from a *proximal* stimulus on the causal chain. Of course, a total solution also needs to distinguish the object from *distal* stimuli, such as the depressing of the door button, f is G. For this Dretske introduces a different sort of consideration, to which I now turn.

A perceptual object is supposedly distinguished by having *primary representation*. This is a relative notion: something has it only relative to another thing that has, in the context, secondary representation. Accordingly, "S gives primary representation to property B relative to property G" is defined as follows: "S's representation of something's being G depends on the informational relationship between B and G but not *vice versa*" (p. 160). That may arouse curiosity about what it is to have representation simpliciter. For although we have been told what it is for something that represents to do so (relatively) primarily or secondarily, we are never told explicitly what it is for something to represent. This is crucial because not everything in the communication chain does represent. I believe we can finesse this problem. Dretske's exposition makes it clear that by 'x represents' he means 'x carries information,' and he has explained the latter notion at some length. Although S does not carry the information that d is E, it does carry the information that f is G (the door button is being depressed). Because it carries information about more than one state of affairs, a distinction between primary and secondary representation is needed if we're to isolate perceptual objects.

From what has been said, it appears to follow that it is insufficient for the perceptual object merely to have primary representation: it needs primary representation *with respect to everything else that represents*. To illustrate, I add an additional leftmost member to the original example—'g is H,' or 'someone is at the door.' When compared only with 'g is H,' 'f is G' gives primary representation. Since that is not enough to show that the subject hears the doorbell being depressed, having primary representation with respect to something or other cannot be sufficient for being the object. Thus, the perceptual object must have primary representation when compared with anything else on the chain. Or, if having primary representation isn't a transitive relation, then all other represented objects must bear to the one that has absolute primary representation either secondary representation or its ancestral relation.

Before presenting the remainder of Dretske's solution, a few observations about the definition of 'representation' are in order. First, the definition contains the expression 'depends on,' which is never clarified. Is its role in the formula to convey that on the occasion in question the information that f is G depends *in fact* on having the information that c is B? Or is it included to express the more ambitious claim that one *could not get* the information f is G without first having the information that c is B? The difference is of some moment. For example, suppose that depressing the button made a squeaky noise ordinarily drowned out by the buzzing signal, so that if the doorbell did not buzz, the squeak would be heard. Then, in the case of the doorbell, the doorbell's ringing would give primary representation on the first interpretation (as a matter of contingent fact, conveying the information that f is G 'depends on' the doorbell ringing), but not on the second (the information that the door button has been depressed 'would have been conveyed' by the squeak had the ringing not occurred). Next, a significant consequence of the definition is to exclude anything grasped only inferentially from being perceptual object. Since something is an object only if it gives primary representation, and giving primary representation implies that the information is not acquired by means of any other representational information, the object as such is never inferred via anything else. (But it remains possible for the object to be inferred by another means while being perceived noninferentially.)

To complete this brief overview, I return to the distinction between an object and proximal stimuli. It may be asked why, say, a perception of a man raking leaves does not carry information about (thus having as its object) changes taking place in one's nervous system during observation. I noted earlier that Dretske claims that the object, and nothing more proximal, is analytically or nomically connected to the signal. But he also supplies another reason: object *constancy* (pp. 162–65). Briefly, our perceptual system continually changes during perceptual episodes without the perception similarly undergoing very radical changes. We perceive the color of a piece of paper as remaining the same under a variety of lightings (including a change from sunlight to a sodium vapor lamp), though the color registers very differently on ordinary camera film (see Land 1977). Dretske claims that a similar constancy of signal amidst a variety of local changes in physical stimuli holds for the perceptible properties of each sense modality. He hypothesizes "that our sensory systems are sensitive, not to localized stimuli . . . , but to more global characteristics of the entire stimulus pattern" (p. 164). However, even should this explanation be mistaken, the phenomenon itself seems beyond question: what we take as object for each sense retains a relative stability or constancy under considerable variation in perspective, orientation, lighting, and so on. Lack of constancy is, according to Dretske, a major reason why proximal links in the communication channel are not given primary representation. (Of course, this doesn't eliminate 'd is E' [the signal passing through that wire]. So, if it had not been dispatched by the earlier criterion, it would have remained a problem.)

To summarize, mining Dretske's exposition, three reasons come to light for choosing an object on the basis of its information-bearing qualities: that, unlike proximal stimuli, it is connected to the signal nomically or analytically; that it gives *absolute* primary representation; and that it is constant amidst changes in our sensory system. I next argue that the first two of these fail, while the third suits CTP as easily as information theory.

X

For starters, consider the four rightmost circles in the diagram and the first argument for favoring as object the doorbell ringing ('c is B') over an electrical impulse traveling through a certain wire ('d is E'). Now let's remove wire F. This leaves us with what I take to be the usual setup for doorbells. But this simple modification takes away the ground on which the argument stands. Now 'd is E' has as much right to claim a nomic relationship to S as 'c is B' (the original reason given by Dretske for choosing the latter). Nevertheless, in the modified case, we still want to say that only the doorbell is heard. If, as seems to be the case, Dretske's mark depends on contingencies, such as the presence of an extra wire, it isn't a good test for perceptual objects. Moreover, as we have just seen, it would be futile to attempt to supplement this criterion with the other test designed specifically to rule out proximal stimuli: constancy. This is because now the impulse traveling through wire E is as constant as the ringing.

I now turn to primary representation. The foregoing point also counts against this test. Since primary representation presupposes that we are comparing two information-bearing stimuli, it is also presupposed that we have settled the question of which nodes carry information before comparisons for primacy may be made. But if 'd is E' is made an information carrier simply by removing the other wire—'d is E' now carrying the impulse 100 percent of the time—it is difficult to see why E shouldn't be given primary representation relative to B, thereby destroying even the eligibility of c's being B from consideration as object. There may be various reasons for doubting that the relationship of 'd is E' to 'S' is nomic. But the sorts of reasons that come to mind seem to be of the same order as those that might be given for doubting that 'S' has this relation to the actual object, 'c is B.' Since we might doubt the existence of a truly nomic relationship in either case, Dretske's explanation stands in just as much or just as little need of further defense. However, I need not press this matter; there is another problem that should be of equal if not greater concern.

Earlier I mentioned that Dretske's definition prohibits the object from informing us only by inference. However, it does appear that occasionally things to which we infer are selected as perceptual object, though perhaps not exclusively so. I am not relying on well-known views in philosophy and psychology that maintain that *all* perception is mediated by an inference (often held to be unconscious) from sense-data, stimuli, or sensory cues. For my purposes, we may either dismiss such views or allow that their insights can somehow be accomodated within Dretske's interpretation. Nevertheless, there are cases in which it is more difficult to exorcise the specter that the object of perception is inferential. For example, I am listening for the oncoming train. Finally I hear it coming. But haven't I heard it only *by* hearing the noise of the vibrating tracks? Or I hear Sue in the next room; can this say more than that I hear, for example, a voice belonging to Sue? Or, to use an earlier example, I see the book, though from the angle I view it my eyes take in only the plain, brown, paper book cover. And from there it looks indistinguishable from a simple sheet of plain, brown paper. One might dismiss such cases on the grounds that they are propositional hearings and seeings—hearings and seeings *that*—and thus not (in the jargon of chap. 4) objectual. But none of the cases is intended to require that the subject realize that this is what is heard or seen (or represented). To give an example, I might mistake Sue's voice for Pam's. Nevertheless, I heard Sue in the next room. But such informational loci must always give secondary representation relative to something else. My representation of Sue being in the next room depends on my representation of Sue's voice, but not vice versa. Thus, Dretske's test for objecthood is not captured by the notion of primary representation.

The failure of these two tests is fatal to this particular information-theoretic project. One is left without any means to distinguish an object from (more) distal information carriers. Even if we can deploy the constancy mechanisms to distinguish the object from (more) proximal members of the information chain, that test is only designed to distinguish objects outside the subject's body from antecedents of experience, such as peripheral or central neuronal occurrences. It is unable, for example, to disqualify electrical impulses carried by telephone lines when these are exclusive ways of producing the signal. However, let us look more carefully at constancy mechanisms.

One can harbor various doubts about the use to which Dretske puts these. For example, if he is correct in stating that the features we heed are global, obtained through summing or averaging inputs, and not local features of certain patterns on retinas and the like, it is still not clear why we do not regard constancy as a global feature of *the nervous system*. Then in all strictness, the nervous system, rather than the perceptual object, would deliver the relevant information. Moreover, if this is feasible, it threatens to reintroduce the sort of inference in normal perception that, I have argued, is anathema to the perceptual object having absolutely primary representation. Nevertheless, the basic point stands: a relative constancy of features of the objects survives continual fluctuations in proximal signals. It is an intriguing suggestion, but one that I believe is better appreciated when viewed in light of the solution put forward in §VIII.

The explanation of constancy mechanisms is introduced with the remark, "Our visual experience . . . carries highly specific information about the properties of objects (their color, shape, size, movement) without carrying the same kind of specific information about the more proximal events (on the retina, say) on which the delivery of this information depends (causally)" (pp. 162–63). This is as true of information about *changes* as it is of constancies. In fact, constancy is just the other side of a coin already displayed in §VIII: everything else being equal, we expect constancy in our experience of a perceptual object if that object does not change its visible traits. Moreover, just as in the tracking of changes in the object's properties, this does not depend on a brief glimpse, but on a continuous sighting or a longer sequence of visual episodes. In addition, constancy of an object's features is not always a sign of the object's not changing. The *absence* of change despite certain locational or neurological changes may also signal a change in the object; as when an automobile's causing the same retinal pattern as I move away betokens that it is following me.

In §VIII, I claimed that changes in objects support changes in our experiences in a manner (i.e., conceptually) in which changes in other causal factors do not. And to say of an object that changes in neurological episodes do not mark changes in it is not to make the same claim. Nevertheless, if it is a conceptual matter that changes or constancies in features are supported only by some causes in the chain and not by others, we may quite naturally expect the conceptually supported changes to be more noticeable, whereas the others are registered in experience at most marginally or under special circumstances. This is precisely what Dretske attempts to show. Thus, there is a role for the phenomenon to which he draws our attention, if not quite the one he allotted it. This is perfectly consonant with the solution proposed in §VIII.

9

The Phenomenal Character of Seeing

Although chapter 4 addressed the question of the logical form of visual content, I have assiduously avoided, wherever possible, implicating myself in further questions about visual consciousness. But in earlier discussions, it was stressed that vision is *phenomenal,* hardly a claim to let pass without comment. Since much of what was claimed is neutral about the details, it would have been more befuddling than helpful there to go into specifics: a distraction at best, and potentially a tar baby from which we would never extricate ourselves. However, I thereby incurred a debt that could only be deferred, not canceled. Because the subject has been broached, it is time explain what is intended by 'phenomenal'. While that notion remains highly controversial on the explanation I am about to give, the extent of the commitment to it seems simpler, perhaps more harmless, than the general run of tenets defended under this title. When the whole is before us, the customary opposition may be as disappointed as it is outraged.

In claiming that experiential content is phenomenal, I need mean nothing more than that the information apprehended and the features of the world represented are apprehended and represented in a distinctively visual way. Consciousness is involved, but beyond that there is little we can say to pinpoint descriptively the manner of its involvement. For starters, we may adopt the popular expression that there is *something it is like* to see things, and agree with Thomas Nagel's (1974) attempts to elaborate this in a set of conditions are never quite satisfactory in capturing it. The 'something . . . like' in this formula alludes to a distinctive style of consciousness. Nevertheless, it is unclear that in saying this I am committing myself to the entire normal complement of claims that those who hew this line believe they are entitled to. The 'it' in my idiosyncratic employment of the phrase refers not to the felt tone of the seeing, but to a thing seen qua seen (if these are even distinguishable in the present case). I don't even require that it be *the* thing whose seeing we are attempting to account for. Thus, there are occasions on which we may say that Jones sees Daphne, though she is wearing a Mardi Gras costume that exposes none of her bodily surface. In those cases, the 'it' may be the costume qua experienced, though in the relevant instance it is Daphne, as distinct from her also glimpsed costume, that I am claiming to see. There was, however, a conscious experience in which something or other was 'something like' to me, and this (in our colloquial idiom) enabled me to see something (in this case, something else). I am not denying that the phenomenal side contains more than this, but claiming only that one cannot allow less than this for seeing.

(Although other reasons were given in chap. 5 against counting cases of blindsight as genuine seeing, even blindsight fits this profile. If I didn't have any visual experience, not even outside my blind hemifield, for that reason alone it would be questionable whether the assumed information pickup was a kind of sight.)

The point may be elaborated by reverting to a contrast appealed to earlier in this book. Let us assume that the visual content of a seeing can be wholly exhausted by a finite, if very large, list of features experienced. (Occasionally, it is said that experiential content is analog rather than digital, more like the inexhaustible punctate nature of a line than its completable division into segments. Certainly, it seems as if our experience is always more determinate and specific than any imaginable ability to report it. The colors we can see are more specific shades than we have the vocabulary to describe, the shapes more specific than our powers of geometric characterization, and so on. But whatever truth there may be in this, it is not possible to exploit that distinction to explain what is intended here by *phenomenal*. Thus, for the sake of argument, I forgo whatever advantages may attach to the vaunted analog nature of experience, and I stipulate that a finite list of features could exhaust phenomenal content.) Then, if I see a mango, I have a distinctive way of enjoying the experience of it, distinct from enjoying the reading of a complete list of that mango's features. That is, apprehending the list visually—say, a computer-generated description, rather than a digitalized image, of input to a camera—does not count as seeing the mango. Reflection on the difference between the subject's experience in the case in which the mango is seen and the one in which it isn't illustrates what I intend by the phenomenal nature of vision.

It is crucial to note what is *not* being claimed. The list's inadequacy as a fill-in for a visual mango has nothing to do with its relative reliability or accuracy (when compared with seeing the mango). For the sake of argument, we may suppose that the printout is more reliable and usually more accurate in recording features. Nor has the contrast anything to do with the use of a visual modality. One may use the same modality to read the list (as opposed, say, to reading it by braille) that one uses to see the mango. Rather, the difference concerns the distinctive way in which sighted individuals enjoy their episode of experiencing the mango. Thus, suppose my dog and I are alertly facing the mango, while my identical twin (or, if you prefer, my twin-earth duplicate) is alertly facing the list. Under normal circumstances, both my dog and I have a visual experience of a mango, despite differences in our photoreceptors, optic nerves, and brains, whereas my identical twin does not have a visual experience of a mango, despite our anatomical similarities and the fact that we are both using the same sort of visual equipment. The difference, I suggest, is not location, reliability, accuracy, or anything of that sort—it is phenomenal.

On the other hand, some may immediately assume that the 'it' in 'what it feels like' must be a felt tone, perhaps an introspectible sensation of seeing. (Talk of 'sensation' is quite natural when we are referring to the *senses*. But its association with a more colloquial use of 'sensation' to denote such things as pains, tickles, and one's limbs falling asleep is a fertile source of confusion.) Although it is not part of my purpose to confute this view, the apparent transparency of sight (discussed in chap. 2, p. 40) makes it difficult to maintain. Therefore, it is important to bear in mind that the phenomenality claimed here rests on the singular way the information is presented, and nothing more.

While the mango setup illustrates something, I realize that it demonstrates nothing. It is designed to focus attention on a specific aspect of the case, that which should both make clear what is intended by phenomenality and render plausible that such phenomena are genuine. But a diehard opponent of this element in accounts of vision needn't be swept away by the case. For example, someone could point to differences other than those I have emphasized. A functionalist, say, would note that not only is the input different, but that a description is internally processed quite differently from the (nonlinguistic) entity it describes. I do not see how anyone who maintains that the episodes compared are not only caused by or supervenient on this process, but are nothing over and above the process, could be dislodged by examples like the foregoing. (Of course, the presence of other differences does not automatically drive out the phenomenal differences with it. The differences in my example are about as striking and robust as we could expect for data; and thus far it is close to unimaginable that we might regard them as no more than differences between such functionalist relationships. Thus, the critic's case for denying a phenomenal difference of the sort intended by the example is not complete, only just begun.) Thus, I hope that the case makes my position both clear and reasonable, but beyond that I doubt that I can resolve with finality the issue over which the parties are divided.

So far, so good (or so it seems to me). But seasoned readers may expect a close alliance between this notion of phenomenality and either of two other notions familiar in the literature: *qualia* and *nonconceptual experiential content*. I have no settled antipathy toward either one, but I have resisted employing them in specifying what I mean by the phenomenal, and I continue to believe that what I intend above doesn't rest on either's viability. Should one or both notions pan out and prove useful in elucidating the phenomenal nature of perception, all to the good. But they can be auxiliary devices at best. However, if, as I believe, the above suffices to introduce a coherent notion of the phenomenal, there is no need to expose that position to vulnerabilities, including unclarities, it doesn't natively possess. Nevertheless, a brief word about qualia and nonconceptual content may be in order.

To begin with, the doctrine of qualia treats the nonrepresentational (or nonpresentational) features of visual contents. However strong the inducements for acknowledging and giving an account of them, such features are strictly a side issue for the current project. The contents of visual episodes with which we need be concerned, when the visual episodes are also instances of seeings, are the things themselves; to make my point about those, there is no need to invoke nonrepresentational features. Recall that it is the phenomenality of the mango, not its perspective, its strictly sensible size, its highlights and so on, in which I claim it differs from a written list of its features. (This is not to claim that qualia theorists suppose otherwise, but only that their theory deals with a part of experience that does not bear on the direct realism deemed here to be a significant component of the most reasonable form of CTP.) Representational features of perceptual content are as phenomenal as anything else is. If we cannot make sense of their phenomenality, qualia will not save the day.

Although qualia are unnecessary, perhaps it will be claimed that they make available a useful strategy for fleshing out the desired notion of phenomenality. But it is difficult to know how this will help if my earlier explanation doesn't already do the job. Suppose some features of perceptual content are not taken to represent anything about the scene other than our perspective on it. For argument's sake, let's assume that they count as qualia. For example, if I see the railroad tracks converging, I do not represent them as doing so. The angularly viewed obliqueness of something rectangular is ordinarily not represented even in one's perceptual belief, and perhaps never in perceptual content itself. Nor do we represent a distant human figure, thereby subtending a relatively small visual angle, as smaller than the cat in the foreground, which subtends a larger visual angle. One may quarrel with the examples, but the limited point can be made with any substitutes one may choose. However many such features we enumerate, it still seems that they are as prone as representational features to be replicated in text that supplies descriptions of the same scene. (Recall my earlier stipulation that the list of features be finite.) And, I hope I have shown, it is futile to allow the intended distinction to rest on any list of describable features. What is vital is not the number or kinds of discriminations we make, for isomorphism in this respect could conceivably be secured in a medium more like reading about a scene than viewing it. The elusive phenomenality of visual episodes cannot be captured, even in the most complicated way, by a set of descriptions. Otherwise, we just reproduce the sort of problem about a computer readout that we had with the mango to begin with. If the earlier way of picking out phenomenality succeeds, nothing more is needed. If it doesn't, it is difficult to see how importing nonrepresentational features will improve our prospects.

Those are not my only reasons for avoiding issues surrounding qualia. *At most,* and on a very broad notion of qualia, what I am claiming is that vision involves some qualia or other—not that it involves any specific qualia. To illustrate, a central dispute about qualia concerns so-called inverted spectra. Consider the question, 'Could there be one or more beings who see (what we take to be) red as (what we take to be) green, and vice versa, but nevertheless use the same words we do for *our* red objects, *our* green objects, and so on, so that the experiential differences are neither behaviorally nor functionally detectable?' Qualia theorists may defend an affirmative answer to illustrate and bolster their position. But the extent of my claim is only that certain rather different sorts of replacements (visible objects by their descriptions, by noises, and so on), which still count as gathering information about the scene, no longer count as seeing it. If that can be established, there is little to be gained for my point, and much danger of being sidetracked, by arguing that replacements anticipated by inverted spectra are possible. Officially, I need not take any position on this question. Whatever its outcome, reading that something is a mango or that it is green or feeling something (say, a certain degree of heat in the presence of red objects) will never count as the subject having seen a mango or redness (discounting, of course, the coincidence that the letters eyeballed are themselves red). There are various ways of gathering information, even gathering information by various sensory modalities. But it is not sufficient for someone to have *seen* an X that she has gathered this information about X via a sensory modality, or even via the same sensory modality (viz., the eyes and retinal pathways to the brain) used for seeing. Rather, there is a flexible, but not altogether dispensable range of experiences that a viewer of Xs must have undergone in the process of gathering this information.

'Phenomenal' is also occasionally elucidated via 'nonconceptual experiential content'. The leading idea here is that a subject can apprehend, say, a visual quality without having the concept of that quite specific quality. For example, a subject may see a mauve surface without having the concept *mauve*. Past that simple starting point—plus the various other things that advocates may want to subtract from fuller descriptions of sensory states—complications arise, both for the notion itself and for integrating it into the scheme developed here. I will approach some of those issues by way of the discussions of earlier chapters.

It would not be wholly out of line with explanations of nonconceptual content found in the literature to regard it as no more than informational content that is not, as such, a (perceptual) belief or a judgment (e.g., Evans 1982, p. 227). On this broad version, the nondoxastic, noncognitive conception of vision defended in chapters 4–6 might yield nonconceptual content. If that is what is intended (for reasons to follow, I strongly doubt that it is), it is already enshrined in my prior commitments. But then it couldn't be of any further help. The problem of phenomenality arises with just that notion in place.

Could nonconceptual content be this and no more? One reason for not thinking so is that objectual seeing is not confined to, or even designed primarily for, the sorts of things that would generally be considered purely visual characteristics: say, color, shape, and size. Prime instances of objectual seeing have been of individuals not properties, whereas as the basic examples of nonconceptual content have been such visual characteristics. Given the diversity of opinion among its expositors, I am not certain just where the boundaries of nonconceptual content are located. But it is clear that visual characteristics play a special role in the notion. A second difference emerges from the first. Even if we overlook the foregoing difference and include 'individual substances' insofar as they are detectible only via their purely visual character, nothing in objectual seeing requires that what is seen is *detected* or *noticed* as such. Of course noticing what one sees is the usual case; but that it is not invariably so is precisely the point leading to some previously underscored implicational gaps. I may not only mistake a whale for an oil spill, but I may also mistake a beached whale lying on top of an oil spill for nothing more than part of that spill. If difference of coloration or distinct outlines do not provide me with clues to the contrary, perhaps this is the result. Nevertheless, I could have seen the whale.

Beyond that, taking nonconceptual content for whatever is the object of objectual seeing blends issues best kept distinct. For example, it runs together inquiries about the logical form of perceptual objects, taken up in chapter 4, with questions concerning the state of the subject's mental condition or levels of capacity. Moreover, it threatens to throw us off the scent of the involvement of the notion *concept* in objectual seeing. The nondoxastic, noncognitive view defended in these pages does not commit me to the doctrine that the visual episode involves no concepts. That is, objectual sight may involve the seeing of discrete things accurately reportable as being seen via ordinary descriptive language. Thus, the usual case of objectual seeing not only involves concepts, but is uninfluenced qua objectual seeing by their presence. On this view, Daphne can see a chair and recognize it as one without there being any more primordial experience nested within the seeing of a chair. We might say that objectual seeing often supplies a level of conceptual content intermediate between the levels being played off by the dichotomy between the informational state and the judgmental state featured in employments of nonconceptual content.

In addition, objectual seeing—as well as Dretske's (1969) nonepistemic seeing, another notion with which nonconceptual content has been compared—normally, perhaps always, involves regarding what one sees in some way. And, subject to further argument, this seems to be a level of perception that involves fully developed concepts. The distinctive feature of nonepistemic and objectual seeing is that instances survive the possibility that the subject's primary ways of regarding her object are mistaken. This does not provide an opening for isolating the relevant kind of nonconceptual content.

Moreover, various accounts of nonconceptual content invite confusion with certain other notions that are (at best) orthogonal, perhaps even antithetical, to the point of its introduction. For example, Hamlyn (1994, p. 141) understands it in terms of an earlier distinction between sensation and perception, nonconceptual content being sensational. That distinction is itself none too clear and is subject to multiple interpretation. Nevertheless, on one common construal, sensations are not informational states, whereas for objectual seeing and nonconceptual content, according to its earliest coiners (Evans 1982, p. 227), being an informational state is part of the package.

Yet other questions arise about the fit of nonconceptual content to our issues. Does it apply only to subjects who, while lacking the concept in question, possess other relevant, perhaps more generic, concepts? Perhaps the subject doesn't possess *mauve,* but must she possess *color* or at least *visual property?* Once again, it is well to keep in mind that creatures well down the food chain see things, though their visual anatomy differs greatly from ours. Once we get past a few easy cases, attribution, and even nonattribution, of specific concepts to such a mob is a much hairier affair than ascriptions of sight. And attempts to use that *by itself* as a wedge to make their experience without our conceptualization wildly different from our own (e.g., McDowell 1994, chap. 5) are at best highly speculative. Moreover, is nonconceptual content a level of experience recoverable inside each conceptual content (see, e.g., Peacocke 1993), or is it present only when the relevant conceptual content is not? (If the latter, its extension is certainly radically different from that of objectual seeing.) Although the former option seems to be the one intended, its problems are rather different from those at the heart of my characterization of phenomenality.

This brings me back to the main point: that nonconceptual content, whatever its other virtues, does little to shed light on what is intended here by *phenomenal.* This is connected with the former's directions being largely *via negativa.* We are told that, although a nonconceptual state is informational, it does not contain belief or judgment. That is certainly true of objectual seeing and of the phenomenal status I have claimed for it. But what we want to know is more precisely what it is like to be in such a state. Some opponents will be dissatisfied with anything that falls short of a *full description* of the state, although it is highly unlikely that one is in the offing. The unavailability of a full description has to do not so much with the weakness of the position in question as it does with inherent differences between the medium of description and the phenomenality we are trying to specify with it. This does not immediately throw us into the dubious company of mysticism and the other ineffable exotica; for the sort of thing we are trying to triangulate on is not only commonplace and accessible, but it does not in any way elude the desideratum of all good controlled experimentation that it be reproducible on demand. Thus, I believe that the earlier comparison, on which I have placed great emphasis, between reading a computer printout *about* a mango and seeing one is helpful. Even if one doesn't believe it is enough, it certainly takes us a step beyond characterizing something as an informational state that contains no judgment. And that is all that I sought to show here.

We could continue with this survey indefinitely. The business of claiming that a popular notion is unhelpful or hopelessly unclear is fraught with peril. Further clarifications are always possible, and I welcome efforts that may succeed where those I have mentioned fail. The most I can do in this short space is to convey a flavor of the reasons why I have not availed myself of these popular devices for further elucidating what I intend by maintaining that sight has an indelibly phenomenal character. Thus, given the state of the art, I stand by my minimal characterization, which may strike some as too thin but seems to me sufficient to rule out a number of avidly defended alternatives. For, recall that the contrasting views that have led me to invoke the phenomenal nature of vison are undiluted informational theories. Doxasticism is one such view among others. According to its proponents, any manner of apprehending just that range of features detected by sight count as seeing, and on a doxastic scheme that seems to be the chief—perhaps only—obstacle to the phenomenal view. (Even the modest measure of phenomenality I have introduced also comes into conflict with some views motivated by the more general goal of naturalizing consciousness. But I cannot examine that issue adequately here.) Enough has been said about the distinctive nature of visual experience to pose a coherent alternative to such pure, or essentially, informational theories and to explain why I take the latter to neglect a vital aspect of seeing.

Epilogue

It is now time to try to tie together the loose threads of this exposition. The ideal situation would be to have a unified, not-very-wordy formula to encapsulate my conclusions about CTP. I have tried to devise such a summary and discovered each time that the results were forced and highly artificial: attempting to fit into a single mold a collection of theses that address issues that fly off in different directions. Of course, I don't rule out the possibility that this is due to my own shortcomings rather than to the Procrustean character of the enterprise. But evidence contained in these pages does suggest that the task can't be completed. For one thing, reasons have been presented to show why a set of purely causal necessary and sufficient conditions for visual perception isn't attainable. Sufficient conditions fail because exposure to a single part (or related element) of an object will count as seeing the object on some but not all occasions, and the determining factors are not causal (see chap. 8). And the attempt to obtain a completed set of necessary conditions leads us on a long and not-very-profitable detour. This is because various would-be noncausal requirements favored by some (e.g., that seeing involves eyes) take us well beyond issues of causalist concern. It should be indifferent to causalism whether these are conditions of seeing. For another thing, on viewing my claims regarding the ineliminability of causation, the structure of perceptual objects, principles for excluding deviant chains, and a basis for choosing objectual causal factors from among the others, it becomes clear what a miscellany of issues have been traversed. And, if you share with me a generally realistic attitude toward solutions to philosophical problems, there is simply no antecedent reason to expect that the members of such a motley collection will each contribute something to a unified and unforced formulation of a single mega-solution, one that covers each problem as a special case—at least no more reason than counting a hippogriff as a species! To borrow from J. L. Austin, truth here may be richer than diction.

Despite the foregoing, what I have set out is not merely a pale remnant of CTP. Indeed, it is robustly causal. This is not because every causal theorist is sure to be pleased with it, but because it is dificult to imagine *any* critic of CTP accepting all that has been claimed and yet remaining an anticausalist. What could possibly be left to an anticausalism that conceded all the tenets in this book? An anticausalist might try to satisfy herself with insisting that I have not supplied a set of causally necessary and sufficient conditions for vision. But she would be hard pressed to find evidence that this figures prominently in the tradition of those philosophers most closely associated with CTP. In fact, the most heated and notable controversies have centered on (C) or its variants, which purports to be only one among a selection of necessary conditions for visual perception. In any event, none of the anticausalists I've discussed would appear to admit even a fraction of these tenets. Thus, without further apologies for the messy and unsystematic nature of my conclusions, I list the various elements that compose this vigorously causalist account.

The following results have been established:

1. The principal clause of CTP is (C): for all subjects S and objects o, S sees o only if o is a cause of S's seeing of it . The case for (C) has been presented, and it has been defended against various criticisms (chap. 3). There and elsewhere (chap. 1), I set forth the reasons for its inclusion as a conceptual component. Finally, it has also been shown how (C) may figure in justificatory procedures, as well as why it is appropriate to call it a ground or foundation of perceptual knowledge (chap. 1).

2. The irrelevance of propositionality to the content of perception has been demonstrated (chap. 4). This has as corollaries that perception is not a species of belief (chaps. 5–6) and that the causation mentioned in (C) can be subsumed under familiar event (or state) causation. (Subsumption under the notion of factative causation, the smoother course for cognitivism, is not ruled out.)

3. I have established a way to distinguish a standard visual causal chain from a deviant one: a deviant chain always requires that something other than the perceptual object occupy the exact place in the chain reserved for the perceptual object of the visual episode, the would-be object being located at a different, more distant, node. This, in turn, lends itself to the irrelevance of the presence or change of would-be object to the identity of the visual episode. The standard relationship can be expressed by means of a counterfactual that presents a condition for the identity of the visual episode. Although this makes the account counterfactual, the covariants involved are different from those that have appeared in previous counterfactual solutions (chap. 7).

4. It has been determined that the causal contribution made by the occupant of the object slot on the causal chain is distinctive because of its singular conceptual status (chap. 8). Other causal factors make *merely* a causal contribution to what is seen. Their absence from a full-fledged seeing might lead to large-scale amazement, but would not threaten the coherence or intelligibility of the concept of vision. The displacement of the occupant of the object slot (which may or may not be the actual object) leads us, in concrete cases, to disqualify the perception *a priori,* and its general displacement would fundamentally alter our concept of sight.

To belabor the point, it would be pressing things to make the above results seem as if they, or any substantial part of them, could be combined into a unified principle that underlies the usual conception of vision. And a set of necessary and sufficient conditions along these lines seems out of reach. Nevertheless, these results do amount to a strong case for CTP. Not everyone agrees about what that theory is. Some have viewed (C) as the causal theory itself. Others would have its fate rest on providing a complete set of necessary and sufficient conditions for vision *in causal terms alone*. I have opted for something intermediate. That may disappoint the ultraorthodox. But, although traditional causalists, such as Descartes, Locke, and Russell, undoubtedly would be scandalized by my tilt toward direct realism, I fancy that they would not disapprove of the particular extent of causal involvement in this view.

APPENDIX: FREQUENTLY CITED PROPOSITIONS AND TENETS

(C)   For all perceivers S and objects or visual arrays *o,* S sees *o* only if *o* is a cause of S's seeing (p. 9).

Cognitivism.   The proper objects of seeing are propositional, all seeing is *seeing that* something (pp. 85).

> *Weak cognitivism.*   Whenever seeing takes place, a fully propositional report of it is available (p. 85).
>
> *Strong cognitivism.*   Weak cognitivism plus the view that an available propositional report is the correct one (viz., when compared to any objectual report of the same seeing) (p. 85).

Counterfactual accounts of deviance (chap. 7):

(8)   (a)   A causal chain from an array of objects to a visual episode is nondeviant (or standard) only if

     (b)   if the external scene were to change (in ways to be specified in the particular case), (c) the experience one has would be correspondingly different (p. 188).

(9)   (a)   A causal chain from an array of objects to a visual episode is nondeviant (or standard) only if

     (b)   if the external scene had been different and an experience had been produced under the circumstances, (c) the experience would have been correspondingly different (p. 189).

(10)   (a)   A causal chain from a candidate visual object to a sentient episode is nondeviant only if

     (b)   if the sentient episode were not (or were no longer) *of* the candidate visual object, then (c) the sentient episode would (thereby) be a different token episode (p. 198).

Doxasticism.   The content of a perception either always is a belief content, or it can only be understood via an inclination to believe that content or a potential belief of that content (p. 21): more simply, "perception is itself a distinctive form of belief" (p. 21).

Externalism (for perception).   The content of a perception has as a constituent the mind-independent objects or objects one is perceiving (pp. 21–22).

(Gr1) o looks to be F (or some way) to S $\rightarrow$ S sees o (p. 48).

(Gr2)   S sees $o \rightarrow o$ looks to be F (or some way) to S (p. 49).

(Gr3)   It looks to S as if e is F (or is something) $\rightarrow$ S sees o (p. 52).

(Gr4)   S sees $o \rightarrow$ It looks to S as if e is F (or is something) (p. 52).

(L) C_s(lizard l on rock r) (p. 159).

The Natural thesis (NT).   Perceptual content and perceptual belief content are distinct, but the former causally and regularly generates the latter by virtue of the fact that the former is reliable enough to sustain such a connection (p. 152).

Object determination.   For properties, a property P is seen if and only if it is a conceptual truth that continued viewing of the same property would track a substantial number of changes in P. For individuals, an individual O is a visual object if and only if O has visually detectable properties belonging to type T such that it is a conceptual truth that continued sighting of one and the same object (be it O or any other) would track changes in tokens of T properties (p. 231).

Objectual seeing.   Seeing described by constructions of the form 'S sees o,' in which 'o' is a nonpropositional noun clause (p. 83).

Occasionalism.   In human perception, God immediately causes both the perceptual object to be suitably placed with respect to the subject and the perceptual state the subject enjoys, no causation running from the object to the subject's perceptual state (p. 12).

Predicative seeing.   Seeing described by constructions of forms relevantly similar to 'S sees x to be F' and 'S sees of x that it is F' (p. 90).

Propositional seeing. Seeing described by constructions of the form 'S sees that p,' in which 'p' is a propositional phrase (p. 83).

Property perception.   All seeing is predicative (seeing of something that it is somehow) (p. 90).

Propositional-seeing conditions or implications (p. 88):
    Success-verb status.   'x sees that p' implies (the truth of) 'p.'
    Recognizability.   'x sees that p' implies that x both experiences and
        takes what is seen in the way expressed by the clause 'p.'
    Accuracy.   The way x takes what is seen is correct.

Three Content-restriction requirements:
    (R1)   S directly sees o only if, for any visual episode (or sensation or experience) that is a constituent of the seeing, there is an ingredient i of the episode's content such that $i = o$ (p. 36).
    (R2)   S sees o *only if*, for all constituent havings (or experiencings or sensings) of a seeing episode—including the episode itself—there is an ingredient i of its content that has a certain detailed character

just because o's character gives riseto that kind of character in i in those circumstances (p. 37).

(R2a)   S sees o *only if,* for all constituent havings (or experiencings or sensings) of a seeing episode—including the episode itself—there is an ingredient i of its content that has a certain detailed character just because o's character gives rise to that kind of character in it in those circumstances, and i's having that character is part of a suitable pattern of counterfactual dependence (p. 37).

(S)   S sees a lizard on a rock (p. 159). ((L), above, is its content.)

The Sellarsian argument.   The constellation consisting of the theses that only justified entities can themselves justify, only belieflike entities can be justified, and (therefore) there cannot be nonbelieflike vehicles (in this instance, nonpropositional perceptual contents) that could justify perceptual beliefs. In sum, perceptual beliefs can be justified by nothing but other beliefs (p. 157).

(WO)   GV sees a whale (p. 88).

(WP)   GV sees that it is a whale (p. 88).

(WP*)   GV sees that something is in front of him (p. 89).

The Whale example.   A situation in which (WO) is true and (WP) false (p. 88).

(i) o looks to be F to S (or 'looks to be some way to S') (p. 48).

(ii)   S sees o (p. 48).

(iii)   It looks to S as if e is F (or as if e is something) (p. 52).

NOTES

Chapter 1

1. Although different understandings of some crucial terms may render the use of 'mind-independence' multiply ambiguous, the term (like the qualification *external* of, e.g., the world) is not, as critics have charged, an unilluminating and uncashable metaphor. Nor need it be muddled. Each of its interpretations can be characterized with decent clarity. We might begin by taking as a basic interpretation of '*o* is mind-independent' something for which the following schematic principles hold:

> '*o* is not (/never has been/never will be) cognized (/cognizable)' *does not entail* '*o* is not';
>
> '*o* is no longer cognized (/cognizable)' *does not entail* '*o* is no longer.'

(On natural assumptions, the principles are mutually implicative.) Differences over the understanding of 'mind-independence' may ensue from different interpretations of *cognition*. For my purposes, let's say that we understand it via an enumeration of its species; *perception* and *thinking about* being two of the species enumerated. A related difference—dividing, say, rejections of idealism from those of verificationism—results from the choice of 'cognized' or 'cognizable'. Even if two thinkers should choose the latter, differences may crop up over the strength of the modality. For example, is something cognizable if it can be cognized only by creatures possessing superhuman faculties and powers? Other parts of these principles also present opportunities for disagreement; such as whether to adopt a tenseless or a tensed formula. Or entailment may be differently understood or replaced by a relation that takes into account broader conceptual affinities (e.g. 'semantically implies'). These differences lead to a variety of potential interpretations of mind-independence. The relevant point is that all of them can be seen as variations on a common basic pattern. Other than a rather ordinary problem of ambiguity arising from a host of positions in the literature, I don't see that there is anything especially vague or unseemly about philosophical employments of *mind-independence*.

2. For a detailed compendium of the flaws of holistic arguments, see Jerry Fodor and Ernest Lepore (1992). I will write interchangeably, and sloppily, about necessary connections between items (e.g., conceptual implications) and something's defining traits. But it should be kept in mind that the view about (C)'s relation to seeing is intended as a metaphysical claim, not in the first instance a linguistic one. Thus, whatever the embattled status of the analytic/synthetic distinction, it will not eo ipso bear on what I am claiming about (say) the metaphysical relation of object causation and sight; at least not without the help of further (controversial) premises.

3. What cannot be dismissed so easily would be evidence from civilizations, if there are such, that had no concept of causation whatsoever. We would do well to be suspicious

of claims that a certain group of language users have *no* concept of causation (how might they distinguish dreams from waking reality?), though it is not difficult to contemplate that they have beliefs about its operation that are very different from our own. Perhaps their views are greatly confused in ways in which ours is not, though ours may be confused in other ways. But if they had *no* concept of causation whatever, what basis might they have for behaving one way rather than any other? Even so, were such a community intelligible, I would have to say that whatever partial notion they had bore at most only some interesting similarities to the concept of perception we share with many and diverse civilizations. Their differences with us would have to be so pervasive and extensive that it would make it exceedingly difficult to calibrate any number of their concepts with those of civilizations that share some notion of causation. They would certainly be rather different from the actual historical populations vaguely alluded to when this sort of objection is raised.

4. Sellars (1956), pp. 298–99. Quoted approvingly by Rorty (1979), p. 141.

5. Some of my response to the criticism is prompted by this essay, though I take off from it in ways other than those pursued by McDowell himself (1994). I agree with him wholeheartedly in rejecting the dichotomy the objection presupposes and some forms of what has come to be known as 'nonconceptual content' (see chap. 9).

6. It is precisely the lack of a grounding in reality that leads to some of the knottiest problems concerning a priori and innate belief. If a belief is to count as knowledge, how is it regulated by its subject matter so as to assure conformity to it? If no palpable connection seems to warrant its conforming to reality, why should we regard its deliverances as *knowledge?* I am not suggesting these problems cannot be overcome. I use them here merely to illustrate the way causal concerns deeply infect those about knowledge and justification.

7. This is too large a topic to discuss properly here. I refer readers to Vision (1988), esp. chaps. 4 and 8; and Goldman (1986), on the truth-linked nature of justification.

8. Cf. Steven Pinker : "experimental studies of baby cognition have shown that infants have the concept of an object before they learn any words for objects, just as we would expect. Well before their first birthday, when first words appear, babies seem to keep track of the bits of stuff we would call objects: they show surprise if the parts of an object suddenly go their own ways, [or] if the object magically appears or disappears, passes through another solid object, or hovers in the air without visible means of support" (1994, p.156).

Chapter 2

1. If the notion of a sense-datum is taken to imply, as a number of its proponents suppose, that whenever something *looks* F, something or other *is* F, it is doubtful that any one type of thing can coherently fill this bill (see Sanford 1981).

2. Strictly, it might also be a form of indirect *idealism:* say, if the inference were to God's ideas instead of to physical reality. Berkeley (1713) comes close to this view, avoiding it only through the obscurity of the distinction between God's archetypal ideas and our ectypal translations of them. However, I will consider only versions in which the (ultimate) perceptual objects belong to the material world. This is how CTP has been universally taken.

3. These notions are crucial though far from crystal clear. Mind-independence was characterized in chapter 1. To say o is 'public' (while confining ourselves to perception) is to say that the following is true of it for some S and S*:

It is possible that S perceives o, S* perceives o^*, S $\neq$ S*, and $o = o^*$.

Or, one may perfer a dated version. To wit:

> It is possible that there is a time t such that S perceives o at t, S* perceives o* at t, S $\neq$ S*, and $o = o$*.

Some may want to add to these two conditions the further condition of (perceptual) persistence, which maintains that

> It is possible that there are times t_1 and t_2 and perceivers S and S*, such that $t_1 < t_2$, S perceives o at t_1 and S* perceives o at t_2.

Mind-independence and publicity do not imply persistence. Russell (1957, p. 146), maintains that sense-data are physical on the grounds that they possess the first two properties, but denies that they in fact persist. (He does not deny outright that they *could* persist, but it would not be inconsistent for him to do so.)

Notice that the combination of these three properties does not guarantee that o is physical or material on the usual accounts: say, that it occupies space, engages in physical interactions, or appears in an (ideal) science of physics. Each of our conditions is, broadly speaking, epistemic. Nevertheless, each is a property we believe central if our perceptions are to be of things in the material world, though the conditions might jointly hold of (perceptible) objectively existing abstracta. Since we won't have occasion to worry about distinctions between the material and the abstract, we may ignore such complications and regard objects with at least the first two features as material (as distinct from mental or subjective).

4. There are exceptions. C. A. Strong maintains that "the sense-datum is representative, but that perception by means of the sense-datum is direct" (1931, p. 217). Cf. Lovejoy (1930).

5. This isn't intended as a careful definition (whose problems are notorious here—see Dennett 1988), but merely as a handy enough explanation to make clear the reasons why qualia aren't relevant at present.

6. Lewis regards these only as considerations that are 'more or less' adequate and that can be overruled by unusual background. Thus, although he offers a similar set of conditions as sufficient for seeing, he also holds that an example of a wizard before one's eyes who casts a spell that causes one to hallucinate a wizard before one's eyes is not a seeing, though it satisfies his conditions for seeing. His reasoning is that 'secondary factors' can override the satisfaction of his conditions (see Lewis 1986a, pp. 277, 289n). This makes it unclear that his formula was intended to supply the sort of airtight condition for which I have been searching.

7. Reid may have been an exception (see De Rose 1989) and Broad may have followed Reid in this. Broad is undoubtedly a sense-datum theorist, Reid professes not to be (though his commitments are murkier; see his [1969], p. 244). But both share the view that there is a *noninferential* sign-signified relation between our experience and the material world.

8. Cf. Grice: "such experiences (if experiences they be) as seeing and feeling seem to be, as it were, diaphanous: if we were asked to pay close attention, on a given occasion, to our seeing or feeling as distinct from what was being seen or felt, we should not know how to proceed; and the attempt to describe the differences between seeing and feeling seems to dissolve into a description of what we see and what we feel" (1962, p. 144).

9. The following point is due to Brian Loar (1987), p. 100.

10. There are cases of nonperceptions that nonetheless have the 'right' cause (e.g.,

veridical hallucinations). But I take it that Jackson's point is that the sameness of the state can be determined by consideration only of the properties that would be self-evident as such to an experiencer (or introspector).

Cf. Crispin Wright's remark: "it is a completely compelling thought that experience cannot disclose its own causal provenance as part of its proper content. Knowledge of the aetiology of an experience has to be the product of inference, for which that experience can at best supply a datum" (1991, p. 91). That depends on how we construe "proper content" and what it is for experience to "disclose" something. From the start, it seems as if the question of *what we experience* is glossed as one about what we *know* or *are aware* that we experience.

11. John McDowell (1982), pp. 471–73, makes a similar point but explains it differently. I prefer to insist that the inference on which the sense-datum view is here predicated is not cogent. That is all that I need claim under the circumstances.

12. For a more extended treatment, see Vision (1993), pp. 351–55.

13. This may be the best way to construe Hyman (1992), p. 283.

14. This is a strictly question-begging way to state the situation wanted, for the point of the objection is that *o* couldn't be the cause of the visual experience under these circumstances. But an accurate formulation would be awkward and circumlocutory, and nothing I say below is compromised by this way of putting things.

15. For additional objections to the differentiation requirement, see Sanford (1976).

Chapter 3

1. John Locke produces such a case: "[T]he idea of black is no less positive to [one's] Mind, than that of White, *however the cause* of that Colour in the external Object, may *be only a privation. . . .* And thus one may truly be said to see Darkness. For supposing a hole perfectly black, from whence no light is reflected, 'tis certain one may see the Figure of it, or it may be painted" (1700, bk. 2, ch. 8, §§ 3, 6). Locke suggests that a privation can still be a cause: thus the darkness isn't prohibited from being seen, on a causal view. Others have maintained that when a patch is uniformly or perfectly dark, or a uniformly illuminated hue, one does not see it. (See, e.g., Avant 1965, pp. 252–53. Cf. Hall 1979, p. 132.) Thus, if we see a black hole, it is only by contrast with its surroundings, so that, in Lockean terms, we "may see the Figure of it." But then what is someone to say if she first sees a perfectly dark scene against contrasting surroundings—say, a doorway—but continues moving closer until the surroundings disappear altogether from her peripheral vision? Does she cease to see the darkness at the moment the lighter surroundings are no longer perceived? This strikes me as untenable. The view that one sees a black hole because of the surrounding lit objects confuses, or so it seems to me, what one sees with what one can make of it. For more on this distinction, see chapter 4 in this book.

2. I am not suggesting that there is a distinctive kind of dependence called 'counterfactual.' This is merely a cover term for an idiom that is useful for displaying a variety of more specific dependencies, one of which is causal.

3. In all strictness, Mackie's acroynym stands for "an insufficient but nonredundant part of an unnecessary but sufficient condition," but its import in the context is the same. Mackie credits D. C. Stove with suggesting the term.

4. By some accounts (e.g., Goodman 1955, pp. 5–6), this is a semifactual, since its consequent may be, in the presumed circumstances, true.

5. Indeed he states just the opposite in another essay: " 'If the match had not been struck, it would not have ignited.' " This counterfactual expresses a relationship of depen-

dency between two events: the ignition of the match was dependent on the match's being struck. Here, the dependency is a causal one: *the striking of the match caused it to light"* (1974, p. 41, emphasis added).

Chapter 4

1. These formulations are intended to be neutral on whether such object clauses should be reconstrued adverbially. They also avoid any commitment about the so-called demonstrative character of perceptual content.

2. As usually held, the more precise doctrine is that seeing is *the acquisition of belief.* Although I use the phrase 'a form of belief' for simplicity, it doesn't matter whether the 'acquisition' interpretation is always kept in mind. The conclusions reached about doxasticism make no capital out of the common observation that much of what we see we already believe, and thus could not be the acquisition of (new) belief. Doxasticists have proposed a number of ways to handle this. In any event, if the view harbors no deeper problems, that difficulty would at most be a superficial flaw, a problem of proper formulation and not a crisis for it.

3. "The content of our perceptions . . . is simply the content of the beliefs involved" (Armstrong 1968, p. 226). See also, e. g., Armstrong (1961), esp. pt. 3; Goldman (1977); Dennett (1991), p. 364; Pitcher ("A person's seeing something . . . is nothing but his causally-receiving via (or by using) his eyes, certain true beliefs" [1971], p. 74. Later amended.); Sibley (1971).

4. Searle (1983), p. 40. Cf. Roxbee Cox: "For a man to perceive a thing, a *y,* is for him to perceive that some thing, a *z,* which is in fact the *y,* is at a certain place" (1971, p. 24). Irvin Rock may be giving utterance to essentially the same credo when he writes, "the goal of [perceptual] processing is to arrive at a description of the outer object or event . . . This *description* of the object or event is cognitive in the sense that its 'language' is conceptual and it has the formal status of a proposition" (1983, p. 16).

5. Even if allowable substitution extended only to the class of what was (independently determined to be) visually detectable replacements, this wouldn't matter. The crucial point is that there are many more allowable substitutions than things S could notice on the occasion. See also Sanford (1976), pp. 206–8.

6. G.E.M. Anscombe (1963), pp.169–70 and John Mackie (1976), pp. 47–48 claim that some occurrences of objectual constructions substitutions, such as the one made in the whale example, are blocked. Each uses this to show that sight (or sensation) has intentional objects. But both agree—to what is, in any case, evident—that similar substitutions are allowed for some occurrences of this construction. Nothing more is needed to generate the difficulty for cognitivism.

7. Shoemaker (1975), p. 300. He displays the analysis without explicitly endorsing it. But the nature of its discussion and Shoemaker's subsequent remarks (e.g., pp. 305–6) indicate that he accepts at least this much of it.

8. Searle (1983) pp. 48–49. A brief list to illustrate the prevalence of this bias: G.E.M. Anscombe (1963), p. 176; A. J. Ayer (1940), pp. 4–5; D. M. Armstrong (1961), p. 101; Gilbert Harman (1968), p. 172; Don Locke (1967), pp. 92–93; Anthony Quinton (1973), pp. 178–79.

9. Searle suggests 'mislead,' 'distort,' 'deceive,' and 'illusion' as contrasts of 'veridical.' In common parlance, a misleading, disorted, deceptive, and occasionally even an illusory view might still be of something that is seen.

10. In chapters 7 and 8 we shall see how much is packed into this qualification.

11. Searle says that speech acts have 'derived Intentionality' (1983, p. 175). But since this is meant to follow from their having conditions of satisfaction, the issue is not thereby interestingly resolved. The better question is whether their having conditions of satisfaction is due to their being in any further respect mental or Intentional.

12. Cf. Pitcher (1971), pp. 82–83, where he supplies the case of a weary desert traveler who sees an oasis but justifiably believes it is a mirage.

13. At least as much as is possible given the fact that an extension via metaphorical appropriation is nearly inevitable for any well-entrenched usage, and there are no semantic police to arrest it.

14. As I hinted earlier (p. 89), there may be limits here too. But so long as I confine myself to descriptions that belong, in the broadest sense, to the ordinary class of the visible, no problems ensue. The point is not that there may be some things we can't say, but that, on just about any account, the enormous number of things we can say far outstrips what the (ideally naive) perceiver is in a position to claim.

15. In true-to-life scientific contexts, all sorts of things count as observations (relative to the theory under discussion). For ease of exposition, I plead philosopher's license and mean by it reporting that goes on roughly at the level of objectual and propositional vision. That seems to be typical of what philosophers and psychologists have in mind when they take up the issue of observation as such.

16. I assume that in its first occurrence 'perceive' is tacitly qualified by 'visually.' Otherwise the clause has no tendency to show that the creatures *see* heat.

Chapter 5

1. McDowell (1994) and Putnam (1994) also develop responses that reject the assumed dichotomy. Although there are significant differences between even the sketchy proposal of chap. 1, §V, and those more thoroughly developed (though equally divergent) ones, McDowell does a masterful job of showing (what we all agree on) just how problematic is the coherentist-doxasticist restriction of the alternatives.

2. It has been proposed that our first inclination is to treat her as having faulty vision, but with a defect the reverse of colorblind patients. However, we are considerably more deferential toward those who make more discriminations than we do than we are toward those who make fewer. We regularly defer, say, to artists and paint salespersons, who are competent at discriminating shades that seem the same to us on close inspection.

No doubt, science fiction aside, the hypothesized result is improbable. Although very few mammals have more than three types of cones, there are rare tetrachromatics (e.g., certain birds). However, the evidence suggests that chromancy beyond three yields diminishing returns rather than enhanced chromatic perspicuity (see Gouras 1981, p. 251). Additional cones are more likely to make the current system redundant than to add new powers of discrimination.

3. Talk of 'intuition' comes with the weighty baggage of philosophical tradition and, as such, it is likely to jar some sensibilities. See Bealer (1989) for a sobering view of what may be called intuitions in inquiries of this sort, as well as for a view of what intuitions *are not*. Intuitions of some sort appear unavoidable if we are even to demarcate our subject matter.

4. If an alternative account of vision, leaving no (indispensable) place for the phenomenal, were to succeed, I believe it would have to be by slow erosion, a graceful degradation of the concept. For example, discoveries might gradually insinuate further features—say, f, g, and h—into our concept of vision. Subsequently, it would be found that f, g, and h are separable in experience from our modes of detecting color and shape. Next, f, g, and

h displace color/shape detection from the center of the visual concept, and perhaps eventually even off of its periphery. But in lieu of a solid reason to suppose this is on the horizon—by a *solid* reason, I mean something more concrete than a sweeping allusion to what has occurred in scattered cases in the history of science—my intuition about what is vital for seeing remains firm.

5. This part, at least, has an explanation at hand. There is much parallel processing in vision, and some neural impulses that leave the retina project directly to the superior colliculus, bypassing the geniculo-lateral pathway. Superior collicular projections have been shown to be significant for our perception of motion. Other, less-well-understood parallel processing may account for the remainder of blindsight functioning.

6. Perhaps such quite basic appeals to simplicity rest on a deeply rooted antirealism about explanation and theory, such that, in otherwise thoroughly mixed evidential situations, it is rational to *choose* one on the basis of such formal virtues as overall simplicity. I must confess that I don't see much in this extreme antirealism. Theories and explanations, in philosophy at any rate, are things to be 'believed', and I fail to see any merit in volitional views of belief. Thus, I couldn't choose, say, my theory in any event. Those issues cannot be properly aired here. But I can try to bring home the hidden costs of such bedrock appeals to simplicity. (Of course, many philosophers think simplicity is a virtue because it is one among other indicators of correctness, correctness being an independent feature. I have no argument with that. But as I have outlined the case (fairly, I hope), it is apparent that the above appeal to simplicity is not intended to support such a hunch about doxasticism's independently constituted veracity.)

7. Richard Sorabji (1964, p. 290) maintains that 'design' is too strong a description to cover many members of the category for which an inference of this general sort seems right (roughly, things of human devising). I use the term only as a well-marked convenience that readers will easily recognize. But Sorabji's point is well taken, and I do not intend to suggest that all human devices—such as nations and moral codes—are literally designed by people.

8. Searle supplies powerful reasons for holding that functions are "never intrinsic, . . . always observer relative" (1995), p. 14. (Consequently, in a terminology encountered in the chap. 4, they have "derived" rather than "intrinsic" Intentionality.) This would appear to be a serious blow to a functionalist characterization of sensory modalities. I do not rely on it here because, even if true, since it doesn't impair attempts to define clear examples of artifacts (say, chairs or forks) functionally, it also doesn't close off all avenue for functional definition.

9. I am not taking sides in the lively debate over the unit of selection. My claims apply equally to whichever unit is chosen.

10. No doubt it is neither true nor false if the objectual idiom is employed. I have been forced into this clumsy phrasing to avoid assuming a robust cognitivism. Stating the point straightforwardly is complicated by this discovery of hidden complexity inside doxasticism.

11. 'Event' is Armstrong's term (1968, p. 214). Visual episodes, as I prefer to call them, are events in this sense as well.

Chapter 6

1. A backtracking counterfactual is one in which, assuming A precedes and is responsible for B, we reason that if B hadn't occurred, then (its cause) A wouldn't have occurred.

2. Evidence for acknowledged perceptual beliefs is seldom demanded, or even appropriate in the circumstances. But it is never absurd, though it may be conversationally pecu-

liar, for me to defend a claim about what is observable by saying that I have seen it (or even that someone else has).

3. Of course, any belief *can be* inferred from other beliefs. For example, for any candidate for basic belief, q, I might come to believe that q only because a (known) reliable authority says that q. Thus, putting the point more precisely, what we should say is not that basic beliefs lack all justification by inference from other beliefs, but that they are sufficiently justified independently of their inferrability from other beliefs.

4. BonJour (1985) would add that S must also *know* (or justifiably believe) that her perception has been reliable; but it is unnecessary to decide that issue here. It harks back to differences in epistemology between internalists and externalists. Very roughly, externalists hold that it is sufficient for S's knowledge that S be in circumstances that would adequately support her true proposition. Internalists add that an awareness that one is in these circumstances and of their potency are also necessary. I mention the difference here only because the Sellarsian view occasionally gets conflated with internalist polemics; for internalism is another weapon against foundationalism. (To illustrate the differences, we only need notice how the Davidsonian challenge to the NTist gets framed internalistically two sentences hence. It is not put in terms of the reliability of perception, but in terms of our reasons for believing that it is reliable.) I can proceed with either formulation here. I usually employ the externalist one for its simplicity.

5. But not universally. Sometimes a conclusion will lead one instead to doubt the premises.

6. We must distinguish two interpretations to which Davidson's claim lends itself. It may be the view that because experience is not concept-involving, it cannot fit in belief's "space of concepts." This is the way McDowell (1994, p. 14) takes it; I have dealt with this interpretation in chap. 1, §V. Or, as taken here (as it seems Rorty's claim demands), it may mean that whether or not experience is conceptual, it is impossible to see how something is available *to me* to justify a belief if I don't already in some sense countenance it. That is the objection now under consideration. Both interpretations should be distinguished from yet another possible claim about belief/experience misfit: nonpropositional content lacks the proper form of a justifier.

7. Berkeley (1710) has famously held that "an idea can be like nothing but an idea. . . . If we look but ever so little into our thoughts, we shall find it impossible for us to conceive a likeness except only between ideas" (1710, pt. 1, §8). Sense-datum theorists have followed him in holding that if in its qualitative character an appearance cannot be distinguished from what we take to be a mind-independent object, then both must be appearances. But if we eliminate a confusion between what we see and what we can know that we see, there remains little support for such ontological theses.

8. See also McDowell (1994, chap. 4).

Chapter 7

1. I only need say 'might.' Perhaps the different kind of light makes a difference in the tone of what is seen, and someone may hold that this makes it a distinct visual episode. I have no quarrel with those who hold that such qualitative differences can change the identity of the episode. I claim only that the change of cause of illumination, by itself and ceteris paribus, has no bearing on the deviance of the chain.

2. I preface each of the three separate clauses in counterfactual proposals, (8)–(10), for later cross-reference. Of course, to test case we must concoct examples of would-be defeaters in which the antecedent of the conditional in (b) is assumed true. In those cases,

they will not be strictly *counterfactuals,* so one shouldn't take the title of this group of solutions too seriously.

3. I write as if identity isn't subject to further analysis as, say, in counterpart theory. (See Lewis 1968.) The view here isn't adversely effected by reductionism, but it would require a cumbersome reexpression of the point. Thus, instead of distinguishing one token visual episode from another, we would dstinguish an entire class of counterpart tokens from other such classes. No doubt, this implies a new debatable assumption: that classes of counterparts that fall short of absolute identity are distinguishable from various other sorts of similarity classes. (Though possible in some cases, is it possible in all?) But vagueness in counterpart classes and in identity are comparable, if not "identical," problems (see Lewis 1993). Thus, no novel difficulty is posed by this switch of vocabulary.

4. Cf. Fodor: "nothing is the proper function of Xs except what Xs Normally help to cause; and . . . if Xs Normally help to cause Ys, then presumably *when the situation is Normal Ys can be relied upon to happen when(ever) it's the case that X*" (1990, p. 67).

5. This is evident not primarily because the episodes' contents *were not* produced reliably, but because we know too much about the way they *were* produced. For example, the method of utilizing stored memory content defeats a claim in the hypnotist case, even if it can be shown that some stored content is utilized in a more indirect way in actual seeing.

6. That this is not so for Pears is indicated by the discussion of a case he takes to establish (C). He says of what would be called a "veridical hallucination" of an oasis that "P cannot be seeing O, because, though the match is perfect, it is entirely coincidental" (1976, p. 26). But as described, a different evaluation of the case might result from making it noncoincidental ('reliable' on Pears's understanding) without introducing the requisite causation running from O to P's visual episode. Thus, if the coincidence is the only fault in the case described (it is the only one Pears mentions), it would appear that P could have seen O without the requisite causation.

Chapter 8

1. Grice (1961), pp. 143–44. In Grice's words, his goal is "to formulate the required restriction in terms of the way in which a perceived object contributes towards the occurrence of the sense-impression" (p. 143). It is possible to take this as addressing the problem of deviant chains rather than—or in addition to—that of object determination. We can imagine a single solution that would work for both problems: say, one in which (a) a certain distinguishable causal chain always terminated in the object, and (b) that type of chain was the only sort that turned out to be nondeviant. Despite this, deviance and object determination are distinct problems. Where previous discussions of CTP have not clearly distinguished them, a sufficiently ambiguous single line of reasoning may be taken as an assault on either or both.

2. But of course when evaluating Jackson's view (1977), his commitment to sense-data is part of what he thinks makes it work. Thus, the commitment is fair game in any assessment of Jackson's version of this view.

3. Cf. Aristotle: "For the visible is color, and it is this which covers what is in itself visible" (*De Anima,* 418a29).

4. Some philosophers (e.g., Russell 1912) hold that emerging doctrines of modern physics may wean us from believing that objects even resemble the conception of them obtained through perceptual apprehension of the so-called spatial qualities. I do not know whether Jackson (1977) would want to allow his view to rest on the supposition of such a similarity. But he doesn't require it to set up a functional relationship, and further justifica-

tion would at least be in order before allowing a view of object determination to be held accountable for a quite independent theory about the nature of physical reality. Of course, another reason for eschewing this notion of similarity is that some adherents of this sort of solution (see §VII below) are not sense-datum theorists. Thus, ultimately the sort of similarity tokened by subjective likenesses must be eliminable, replaced by something else more fundamental, in their versions.

5. And what are we to make of the vague qualification that it is "in principle possible" to produce the relevant variations in the sensa by producing them in the object's M-properties? It, too, can be a way of letting in too little or too much. Taken seriously, it detracts from, rather than enhancing, the appeal of the clause.

6. Earlier, this was put in terms of conceptual *expectations,* here in terms of what belongs to the concept itself. It is the latter that is crucial. The concept itself explains why the conceptual expectations occur. But it will assist the exposition if I occasionally adopt the expectation jargon. For those instances, I assume, unless explicitly stated otherwise, an idealized subject who makes no mistakes about whether and what she is seeing.

7. One kind of change in particular, that of location, is something for which a creature may have good acuity without having a high acuity for static forms. See Gibson (1966), p. 160. More on this shortly.

8. Cf. Wittgenstein: "Two pictures of a rose in the dark. One is quite black; for the rose is invisible. In the other, it is painted in full detail and surrounded by black. Is one of them right, the other wrong?" (1953, pt. I, §515, p. 141e). Although Wittgenstein evidently had in mind a painting or a mental image, the second scenario brings out in a lively way the intelligibility of each actual scene appearing before one's eyes.

9. For similar examples, see Warnock, (1965); Firth (1967); Sanford (1976); and McLaughlin (1984).

10. McLaughlin (1984, pp. 583–84) affirms that in cases like those of the covered book and the woman in costume, we are seeing something by seeing its effect. That may be so, but we are seeing it not as an effect, but as an extension of the thing in question. Had the cover been independently molded first, then put on the book, so that it fit perfectly without any alteration of the paper, one would still be seeing the book. Thus, the book's causing the cover to have that shape is incidental to our being able to say that we see the book. The same could be said for the shape of clothes worn by the costumed woman. Whether these are indeed effects of the objects we claim to see is indifferent to the reason we say of such things that we see the objects they cover. Similarly for seeing the lighthouse (or car) by seeing the beam of light. The case may be different for other sensory modalities, but it doesn't thereby translate to sight. Accordingly, it appears that whenever there is more than one candidate between which context chooses the object, the candidates are things that stand in part/whole (aspect/whole) relations, or we decide to say we see the thing by seeing what is taken (in the context) for *an extension* of it.

WORKS CITED

Alston, William P. (1990). "Externalist Theories of Perception," *Philosophy and Phenomenological Research* 50 (supp.):73–97.

Anscombe, G.E.M. (1963). "The Intentionality of Sensation: A Grammatical Feature," in *Analytical Philosophy,* second series, ed. by R. J. Butler (Barnes & Noble):158–80.

Aquinas, Thomas [1265–72] (1945). *Summa Theologica,* in *Basic Writings of Saint Thomas Aquinas,* vol. 1, ed. by Anton C. Pegis (Random House).

Aristotle (1968). *De Anima,* trans. by D. W. Hamlyn (Oxford University Press).

Armstrong, D. M. (1961). *Perception and the Physical World* (Routledge & Kegan Paul).

——— (1968). *A Materialist Theory of Mind* (Routledge & Kegan Paul).

Armstrong, Sharon Lee, Lila R. Gleitman, and Henry Gleitman (1983). "What Some Concepts Might Not Be," *Cognition* 13:263–308.

Austin, J. L. (1962). *Sense and Sensibilia,* reconstructed from notes by G. J. Warnock (Oxford University Press).

Avant, Lloyd L. (1965). "Vision in the Ganzfield," *Psychological Bulletin* 64:246–58.

Ayer, A. J. (1940). *The Foundations of Empirical Knowledge* (Macmillan).

——— (1956). *The Problem of Knowledge* (Macmillan).

——— (1973). *The Central Questions of Philosophy* (Weidenfeld & Nicolson).

Bach-y-Rita, Paul (1972). *Brain Mechanisms in Sensory Substitution* (Academic Press).

Baylor, Denis A., and Julie L. Schnapf (1987). "How Photoreceptor Cells Respond to Light," *Scientific American.* 256 (April):40–47.

Bealer, George (1989). "What's Wrong with Empiricism," *Proceedings of the Aristotelian Society.* 66 (supp.):99–138.

Berkeley, George [1710] (1970). *A Treatise concerning the Principles of Human Knowledge,* ed. by Colin Murray Turbayne (Bobbs-Merrill).

——— [1713] (1979). *Three Dialogues between Hylas and Philonous,* ed. by Robert Merrihew Adams (Hackett).

Block, Ned (1993). "Review: Consciousness Explained," *Journal of Philosophy* 90, no. 4:181–93.

BonJour, Laurence (1985). *The Structure of Empirical Knowledge* (Harvard University Press).

Broad, C. D. (1923). *Scientific Thought* (Routledge & Kegan Paul).

Burge, Tyler (1979). "Individualism and the Mental," *Midwest Studies in Philosophy,* vol. 4, ed. by Peter A. French, Theodore E. Uehling, Jr., and Howard K. Wettstein (University of Minnesota Press):73–121.

Buss, Leo (1987). *The Evolution of Individuality* (Princeton University Press).

Campion, J., R. Latto, and Y. M. Smith (1983). "Is Blindsight an Effect of Scattered Light, Spared Cortex, and Near-Threshold Vision?" *Behavioral and Brain Sciences* 6:423–86.

Child, William (1992). "Vision and Experience: The Causal Theory and the Disjunctive Conception," *Philosophical Quarterly* 42:297–316.

Chisholm, Roderick (1957). *Perceiving: A Philosophical Study* (Cornell University Press).

Churchland, Paul (1979). *Scientific Realism and the Plasticity of Mind* (Cambridge University Press).

Cummins, Robert (1975). "Functional Analysis," in Sober (1994):49–69. Originally published in *Journal of Philosophy* 72:741–64.

Darwin, Charles [1859, 1871]. *The Origin of Species* (5th ed.) and *The Descent of Man* (Random House: The Modern Library).

Davidson, Donald (1967). "Causal Relations," *Journal of Philosophy* 64:691–703.

——— (1986). "A Coherence Theory of Truth and Knowledge," in *Truth and Interpretation*, ed. by Ernest LePore (Blackwell):307–19.

——— (1987). "Knowing One's Own Mind," *Proceedings and Addresses of the American Philosophical Association* 60, no. 3 (American Philosophical Association): 441–58.

Davies, Martin (1983). "Function in Perception," *Australasian Journal of Philosophy* 61:409–26.

Dennett, Daniel (1988). "Quining Qualia." in *Consciousness in Contemporary Science,* ed. by A. Marcel and E. Bisiach (Oxford University Press):42–77.

——— (1991). *Consciousness Explained* (Little, Brown).

De Rose, Keith (1989). "Reid's Anti-Sensationalism and His Realism," *Philosophical Review* 98:313–48.

Descartes, Rene [1641] (1984). *Meditations on First Philosophy, in The Philosophical Writings of Descartes,* vol. II, trans. by John Cottingham, Robert Stoothoff, and Dugald Murdoch (Cambridge University Press).

Dretske, Fred (1969). *Seeing and Knowing* (University of Chicago Press).

——— (1977). "Causal Theories of Reference," *Journal of Philosophy* 84:621–25.

——— (1979). "Simple Seeing." in *Body, Mind and Method,* ed. by Donald Gustafson and Bangs Tapscott (Reidel):1–15.

——— (1981). *Knowledge and the Flow of Information* (MIT Press).

——— (1988). *Explaining Behavior: Reasons in a World of Causes* (MIT Press).

——— (1993). "Mental Events as Structuring Causes of Behaviour," in *Mental Causation,* ed. by John Heil & Alfred Mele (Oxford University Press):121–36.

——— (1995). *Naturalizing the Mind* (MIT Press).

Evans, Gareth (1982). *The Varieties of Reference,* ed. by John McDowell (Oxford University Press).

Firth, Roderick (1967). "The Men Themselves; Or the Role of Seeing in Our Concept of Perception," in *Intentionality, Mind and Perception,* ed. by Hector Castañeda (Wayne State University Press):357–82.

Fodor, Jerry (1990). *A Theory of Content and Other Essays* (MIT Press).

Fodor, Jerry, and Ernest Lepore (1992). *Holism: A Shopper's Guide* (Blackwell).

Geach, Peter (1957). *Mental Acts* (Routledge & Kegan Paul).

Gibson, James J. (1966). *The Senses Considered as Perceptual Systems* (Houghton Mifflin).

Goldman, Alvin (1976). "Discrimination and Perceptual Knowledge," *Journal of Philosophy* 73:771–91.

——— (1977). "Perceptual Objects," *Synthese* 35:257–83.

——— (1986). *Epistemology and Cognition* (Harvard University Press).

Goodman, Nelson (1955). *Fact, Fiction, and Forecast* (Bobbs-Merrill).

Gould, Stephen Jay (1983). "Kingdoms without Wheels," in *Hen's Teeth and Horse's Toes* (Penguin Books):158–65.

Gould, Stephen Jay, and R. C. Lewontin (1979). "The Spandrels of San Marco and the Panglossian Paradigm: A Critique of the Adaptationist Programme," *Proceedings of the Royal Society of London* series B, no. 205:581–98.

Gould, Stephen Jay, and Elizabeth S. Vrba (1982). "Exaptation—A Missing Term in the Science of Form," *Paleobiology* 8, no. 1:4–15.

Gouras, Peter (1981). "Color Vision," in Kandel & Schwartz (1981):249–57.

Gregory, Richard L. (1990). *Eye and Brain: the Psychology of Seeing.* 4th ed. (Princeton University Press).

Grice, H. P. (1961). "The Causal Theory of Perception," *Proceedings of the Aristotelian Society,* (suppl) 35:121–68.

——— (1962). "Some Remarks about the Senses," in *Analytical Philosophy,* first series, ed. by R. J. Butler (Oxford University Press):133–53.

Hall, Richard J. (1979). "Seeing Perfectly Dark Things and the Casual Conditions of Seeing," *Theoria* 45:127–34.

Hamlyn, D. W. (1994). "Perception, Sensation and Non-conceptual Content," *Philosophical Quarterly* vol. 44 no. 175:139–53.

Harman, Gilbert (1968). "Knowledge, Inference and Explanation," *American Philosophical Quarterly* 5:164–73.

Heil, John (1983). *Perception and Cognition* (University of California Press).

Hempel, Carl G. (1934–35). "Some Remarks on 'Facts' and Propositions," *Analysis* 2:93–96.

——— (1965). "The Logic of Functional Analysis," *Aspects of Scientific Explanation* (Free Press):297–330. Originally published in *Symposium on Sociological Theory,* ed. by Llewellyn Gross (Harper & Row, 1959).

Hilbert, David R. (1987). *Color and Color Perception: A Study in Anthropocentric Realism* (Center for the Study of Language and Information).

Hinton, J. M. (1967). "Visual Experiences," *Mind* 76:217–27.

Hume, David [1723] (1888). *A Treatise of Human Nature,* ed. by L. A. Selby-Bigge (Oxford University Press).

Hyman, John (1992). "The Causal Theory of Perception," *Philosophical Quarterly* 42:277–96.

——— (1993). "Vision, Causation and Occlusion," *Philosophical Quarterly* 43:72–76.

Jackson, Frank (1977). *Perception: A Representative Theory* (Cambridge University Press).

——— (1982). "Epiphenomenal Qualia," *Philosophical Quarterly* 32:127–36.

Kandel, Eric R. (1981). "Physiology of the Central Visual Pathways," in Kandel and Schwartz (1981): 236–48.

Kandel, Eric R., James H. Schwartz (eds.) (1981). *Principles of Neural Science* (Elsevier).

Kant, Immanuel [1764] (1958). *Critique of Pure Reason,* trans. by Norman Kemp Smith (Macmillan).

Keil, Frank C. (1989). *Concepts, Kinds, and Cognitive Development* (MIT Press).

Kim, Jaegwon (1974). "Noncausal Connections," *Noûs* 8:41–52.

——— (1977). "Perception and Reference without Causality," *Journal of Philosophy* 84:606–20.

——— (1993). *Supervenience and Mind: Selected Philosophical Essays* (Cambridge University Press).

Kneale, William (1971). "An Analysis of Perceiving in Terms of the Causation of Beliefs II," in *Perception: A Philosophical Symposium,* ed. by F. N. Sibley (Methuen):65–80.

Land, Edwin (1977). "The Retinex Theory of Color Vision," *Scientific American* 237: 108–29.

Le Catt, Bruce (1982). "Censored Vision," *Australasian Journal of Philosophy* 60:158–62.

Leibniz, Gottfried Wilhelm [1686, 1714] (1989). *Discourse on Metaphysics* and *The Monadology*, reprinted in *Philosophical Essays*, ed. by Roger Ariew and Daniel Garber (Hackett).

Levine, David, Joshua Warach, and Martha Farah (1985). "Two Visual Systems in Mental Imagery: Dissociation of 'What' and 'Where' in Imagery Disorders due to Bilateral Posterior Cerebral Lesions," *Neurology* 35:1010–18.

Lewis, David (1968). "Counterpart Theory and Quantified Modal Logic," *Journal of Philosophy* 65:113–26.

——— (1983). "Attitudes *De Dicto* and *De Se* (with postscript)," reprinted in *Philosophical Papers*. Vol. 1 (Oxford University Press):133–59.

——— (1986a). "Veridical Hallucination and Prosthetic Vision," *Philosophical Papers*. Vol. 2 (Oxford University Press):273–86. Originally published in *Australasian Journal of Philosophy* 58 (1980):239–49.

——— (1986b). "Postscript to 'Veridical Hallucination and Prosthetic Vision,' " *Philosophical Papers*. Vol. 2 (Oxford University Press):287–90.

——— (1993). "Many, but Almost One," in *Ontology, Causality and Mind: Essays in Honour of D. M. Armstrong*, ed. by Keith Campbell and John Bacon (Cambridge University Press).

Loar, Brian (1987). "Subjective Intentionality," *Philosophical Topics* 15:89–124.

Locke, Don (1967). *Perception and Our Knowledge of the External World* (George Allen & Unwin).

Locke, John [1700] (1975). *An Essay concerning Human Understanding*, 4th ed., ed. by Peter H. Nidditch (Oxford University Press).

Lovejoy, Arthur O. (1930). *The Revolt against Dualism* (Open Court).

Lucretius (1940). *On the Nature of Things*, trans. by H.A.J. Munro (Random House).

Mackie, John (1974). *The Cement of the Universe* (Oxford University Press).

——— (1976). *Problems from Locke* (Oxford University Press).

——— (1985). "Mind, Brain and Causation," in *Logic and Knowledge*, ed. by Joan Mackie and Penelope Mackie (Oxford University Press):131–44.

Malebranche, Nicholas [1675] (1992). *The Search after Truth*, reprinted in *Philosophical Selections*, ed. by Steven Nadler (Hackett).

Marr, David (1982). *Vision* (W. H. Freeman).

Martin, C. B. (1959). *Religious Belief* (Cornell University Press).

Matilal, Bimal Krishna (1986). *Perception: An Essay on Classical Indian Theory of Knowledge* (Oxford University Press).

McDowell, John (1982). "Criteria, Defeasibility, and Knowledge," *Proceedings of the British Academy* 68:455–79.

——— (1990). "Scheme-Content Dualism, Experience, and Subjectivity," unpublished manuscript.

——— (1994). *Mind and World* (Harvard University Press).

McLaughlin, Brian (1984). "Perception, Causation and Supervenience," *Midwest Studies in Philosophy*, vol. 9 (University of Minnesota Press):569–91.

——— (1996). "Lewis on What Distinguishes Perception from Hallucination," in *Perception*, ed. by Kathleen Akins (Oxford University Press).

Millikan, Ruth (1984). *Language, Thought and Other Biological Categories* (MIT Press).

——— (1989). "In Defense of Proper Functions," *Philosophy of Science* 56:288–302.

Mohanty, Jitendra N. (1988). "A Fragment of the Indian Philosophical Tradition—Theory of Pramāna," *Philosophy East and West* 31:251–60.

Montaigne, Michel (1987). *An Apology for Raymond Sebond,* trans. by M. A. Screech (Penguin).

Moore, G. E. (1922). *Philosophical Studies* (Routledge & Kegan Paul).

Nagel, Ernest (1961). *The Structure of Science* (Harcourt, Brace & World).

Nagel, Thomas (1974). "What Is It Like to Be a Bat?" *Philosophical Review* 83:435–50.

Neander, Karen (1991). "Functions as Selected Effects: The Conceptual Analyst's Defense," *Philosophy of Science.* 58:168–84.

Ockham, William (1957). *Quodlibeta,* in *Philosophical Writings,* trans. by Philotheus Boehner (Thomas Nelson and Sons).

Peacocke, Christopher (1979). *Holistic Explanation* (Oxford University Press).

——— (1993). *A Study of Concepts* (MIT Press).

Pears, David (1976). "The Causal Conditions of Perception," *Synthese* 33:25–40.

Perenin, M. T., and M. Jeannerod (1975). "Residual Vision in Cortically Blind Hemifields," *Neuropsychologia* 13:1–7.

Pinker, Steven (1994). *The Language Instinct* (Monroe).

Pitcher, George (1971). *A Theory of Perception* (Princeton University Press).

Plato (1961), *Meno,* trans. by W.K.C. Guthrie, *The Collected Dialogues of Plato,* ed. by Edith Hamilton and Huntington Cairns (Pantheon).

Price, H. H. (1950). *Perception,* rev. 2nd ed. (Methuen).

Putnam, Hilary (1975). "The Meaning of 'Meaning'," *Minnesota Studies in the Philosophy of Science,* vol. 7, ed. by Keith Gunderson (University of Minnesota Press):131–93.

——— (1994). "Sense, Nonsense, and the Senses: an Inquiry into the Powers of the Human Mind," *Journal of Philosophy* 91:445–517.

Quinton, Antony (1973). *The Nature of Things* (Routledge & Kegan Paul).

Reid, Thomas [1814–15] (1969). *Essays on the Intellectual Powers of Man* (MIT Press).

Rock, Irvin (1983). *The Logic of Perception* (MIT Press).

Rorty, Richard (1979). *Philosophy and the Mirror of Nature* (Princeton University Press).

Roxbee Cox, J. W. (1971). "An Analysis of Perceiving in Terms of the Causation of Beliefs I," in *Perception: A Philosophical Symposium,* ed. by F. N. Sibley (Methuen):23–64.

Runzo, Joseph (1977). "The Propositional Structure of Perception," *American Philosophical Quarterly* 14, no. 3:211–20.

Russell, Bertrand (1912). *Problems of Philosophy* (Oxford University Press).

——— (1927). *An Outline of Philosophy* (George Allen & Unwin).

——— (1957). "The Relation of Sense-data to Physics," in *Mysticism and Logic* (Doubleday):140–73.

Ryle, Gilbert (1960). "Perception," in *Dilemmas* (Cambridge University Press):93–110.

Sanford, David (1976). "The Primary Objects of Perception," *Mind* 85:189–208.

——— (1981). "Illusions and Sense-Data," *Midwest Studies in Philosophy,* vol. 6, ed. by Peter C. French, Theodore E. Uehling, and Howard K. Wettstein (University of Minnesota Press):371–85.

——— (1984). "The Direction of Causation and the Direction of Time," *Midwest Studies in Philosophy,* vol. 9, ed. by Peter C. French, Theordore E. Uehling, and Howard K. Wettstein (University of Minnesota Press):53–75.

Schlick, Moritz (1934–35). "Facts and Propositions," *Analysis* 2:65–70.

Searle, John (1983). *Intentionality: An Essay in the Philosophy of Mind* (Cambridge University Press).

——— (1991). "Response: Perception and the Satisfactions of Intentionality," in *John Searle and His Critics,* ed. by Ernest Lepore and Robert Van Gulick (Blackwell):181–92, 227–41.

———— (1995). *The Construction of Social Reality* (Free Press).

Sellars, Wilfrid (1956). "Empiricism and the Philosophy of Mind," in *Minnesota Studies in the Philosophy of Science,* vol. 1, ed. by H. Fiegl and M. Scriven (University of Minnesota Press):253–329.

———— (1973). "Givenness and Explanatory Coherence," *Journal of Philosophy* 70:612–24.

———— (1979). "More on Givenness and Explanatory Coherence," in *Justification and Knowledge,* ed. by G. Pappas (Reidel):169–82.

Shoemaker, Sidney (1970). "Persons and Their Pasts," *American Philosophical Quarterly* 7:269–85.

———— (1975). "Functionalism and Qualia," *Philosophical Studies* 27:291–315.

Sibley, Frank (1971). "Analysing Seeing," in *Perception: A Philosophical Symposium* (Methuen):81—132.

Snowdon, Paul (1981). "Perception, Vision and Causation," *Proceedings of the Aristotelian Society* 81:175–92.

Sober, Eliot (ed.) (1994). *Conceptual Issues in Evolutionary Biology,* 2nd ed. (MIT Press).

Sorabji, Richard (1964). "Function," *Philosophical Quarterly* 14:289–302.

Spinoza, Benedict de [1677] (1949). *Ethics,* ed. by James Guttman, based on a translation by William Hale White (Hafner).

Stalnaker, Robert C. (1987). *Inquiry* (MIT Press).

Stampe, Dennis (1979). "Toward a Causal Theory of Linguistic Representation," in *Contemporary Perspectives in the Philosophy of Language,* ed. by Peter A. French, Theodore E. Uehling, and Howard K. Wettstein (University of Minnesota Press):81–102.

Stoerig, P., and A. Cowey (1990). "Wavelength Sensitivity in Blindsight," *Nature* 342:916–18.

Strawson, P. F. (1974). "Causation in Perception," in *Freedom and Resentment* (Methuen):66–84.

———— (1979). "Percpetion and Its Objects," in *Perception and Identity,* ed. by G. F. Macdonald (Cornell University Press):41–60.

Strong, C. A. (1931). "Is Perception Direct, or Representative?" *Mind* 40:217–20.

Stryer, Lubert (1987). "The Molecules of Visual Excitation," *Scientific American* 257 (July):42–50.

Tye, Michael (1982). "A Causal Analysis of Seeing," *Philosophy and Phenomenological Research* 42:311–25.

Vesey, G.N.A. (1965). "Seeing and Seeing As," reprinted in *Perceiving, Sensing, and Knowing,* ed. by Robert J. Swartz (Doubleday):68–83.

Vision, Gerald (1988). *Modern Anti-Realism and Manufactured Truth* (Routledge & Chapman Hall).

———— (1993). "Animadversions on the Causal Theory of Perception," *Philosophical Quarterly* 43:344–57.

Wagner, Steven J. (1996). "Teleosemantics and the Troubles of Naturalism," *Philosophical Studies* 82:81–110.

Warnock, G. J. (1965). "Seeing," in *Perceiving, Sensing, and Knowing,* ed. by Robert J. Swartz (Doubleday):49–67.

Weiskrantz, Lawrence (1990). "Outlooks for Blindsight: Explicit Methodologies for Implicit Processes," *Proceedings of the Royal Academy* 239F:247–78.

Whorf, Benjiman Lee (1956). *Language, Thought, and Reality,* ed. by John B. Carroll (MIT Press).

Wittgenstein, Ludwig (1953). *Philosophical Investigations,* trans. by G.E.M. Anscombe (Macmillan).

Wright, Crispin (1991). "Scepticism and Dreaming: Imploding the Demon," *Mind* 100:87–115.

Wright, Larry (1974). "Functions," *Philosophical Review* 82:139–68.

Young, J. Z. (1987). *Philosophy and the Brain* (Oxford University Press).

INDEX